STRATEGIC MARKETING DECISIONS IN GLOBAL MARKETS

STRATEGIC MARKETING DECISIONS IN GLOBAL MARKETS

ISOBEL DOOLE AND ROBIN LOWE

THOMSON

Australia • Canada • Mexico • Singapore • Spain • United Kingdom • United States

Strategic Marketing Decisions in Global Markets

Copyright © 2005 Thomson Learning

The Thomson logo is a registered trademark used herein under licence.

For more information, contact Thomson Learning, High Holborn House, 50–51 Bedford Row, London, WC1R 4LR or visit us on the World Wide Web at:
http://www.thomsonlearning.co.uk

British Library Cataloguing-in-Publication Data
A catalogue record for this book is available from the British Library

ISBN 1-84480-142-X

First edition published 2005 by Thomson Learning

Typeset by Photoprint, Torquay

Printed in Italy by G. Canale and Co.

We give especial thanks to our families;
Sylvia, Catherine and Jonathan;
and to Will, Libby and Rob for their
unstinting support and their patient belief
that one day soon they will get
our undivided attention.

Contents

List of figures, tables, challenges and spotlights

Spotlights

Preface

Introduction

Decision making is at the heart of the marketing strategy process. Decisions are taken by managers at all levels that serve to reinforce, adjust or completely change the direction of the organisation's marketing strategy.

Whilst there is much more written about planning and the concepts that influence strategy development, there is insufficient focus on making quality decisions within the overall planning process, identifying the really critical 'life changing' decisions that need to be taken at any point in the marketing strategy process (analysis, development or implementation). The aim of this book is to give the reader an opportunity to reflect on the issues faced at each stage of the strategic process and to consider how better and more effective decisions can be taken. Critical decisions are taken at any time, not necessarily within the formal planning or budgeting cycle, because marketing strategy development is a continuous process requiring a constant stream of strategic decisions to be made that are individually sound and collectively add value for all stakeholders.

All organisations now operate in a competitive environment, which is dynamic and complex. This complexity may have arisen from the need for companies to compete internationally or perhaps through the challenges of fast moving technological changes in their markets. Whatever the reason, marketing managers are constantly facing new marketing challenges requiring new sets of strategic decisions to be made. Senior marketing managers need not only the ability to develop problem solving strategies, but also the mindset that enables them to reinvent periodically the basis on which an organisation can compete in response to changes in their markets.

Creativity and innovation are therefore needed at every point in the marketing process if an organisation is to sustain its competitive advantage. Organisations must continuously reassess their successful strategy to see whether it will be sustainable in the future. Businesses that are under-performing or in crisis must reinvent themselves.

Markets and marketing are becoming ever more global in their nature and managers around the world ignore this fact at their peril. To achieve sustainable growth in markets that are becoming increasingly global or merely to survive in domestic markets that are increasingly attacked by international players, it is essential for organisations to understand the complexity and diversity of global markets and for their managers to develop the skills, aptitudes and knowledge that are necessary in order to compete effectively. This is why in this book we focus on strategic marketing decision making in a global context.

Recently the marketing practitioner has been inundated by many new and varied marketing concepts to take on board, relationship marketing, customer relationship management, value based marketing, hard edged marketing, to name but a few. Sometimes there is an implicit assumption that the new concept replaces existing marketing thinking, and disappointment sets in at the realisation that it does not. In this book we try to show how the new and evolved thinking in marketing has to be used in the right context and that it should complement and contribute to our greater understanding of marketing and so form part of the building blocks of a company's marketing capability. Taken on board in this manner the marketing strategy development process in an organisation can be strengthened and the quality of its strategic marketing decisions enhanced.

This book aims to meet the needs of marketing students and practitioners in an up-to-date and innovative manner. It recognises the increasing time pressures on both students and managers and so strives to maintain readability and clarity through a straightforward and logical structure that will enable them to apply their learning to the tasks ahead.

Learning objectives

On completion the reader should be able to:

- Analyse and evaluate an organisation's competitive market position in relation to investment decisions made concerning the organisation's marketing based assets

- Identify the changing bases of competitive advantage and how these might be leveraged across geographically diverse markets

- Identify strategic options and critically evaluate the implications of strategic marketing decisions in relation to *shareholder value*

- Evaluate the role of brands, innovation, integrated marketing communications, alliances, the value chain, customer relationships and service in contributing added value to the customer

- Demonstrate the ability to develop innovative and creative solutions to enhance an organisation's global competitive position

- Assess how product, market, brand and customer life cycles might be managed strategically across a variety of markets

- Demonstrate the ability to reorient the formulation and control of cost effective competitive strategies, appropriate for the objectives and context of an organisation operating in a dynamic global environment

Structure of the book

Quality marketing decisions are made by analysing a situation, developing a strategy to deal with the situation from the options available and implementing the solution. In this book it is assumed that the reader is familiar with the marketing planning process and understands the steps involved in the development of a marketing plan. The aim is not to provide another book telling the reader how to construct a marketing plan, rather at each stage of the process we examine the critical strategic marketing decisions that need to be made and the issues and complexities involved in ensuring effective and appropriate decisions are taken. The book is structured in two parts. In Part 1 we focus on the capabilities that need to be built in an organisation to build a sustainable competitive advantage that offers value to the customer and to the shareholders/owners. In Part 2 we focus on the decisions themselves. An outline of the book is given on pages xv and xvi.

Structure of the book

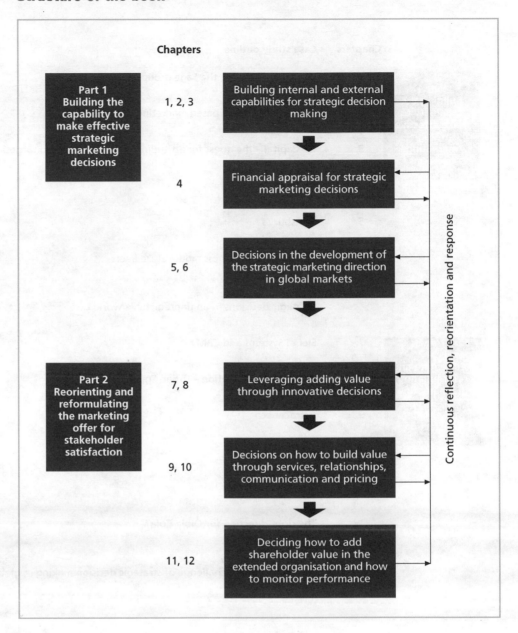

Case studies at the end of each chapter

Chapters	Case study outline
Part 1 **Building the capability to make effective strategic marketing decisions**	
1	Wise guys – buying the Sage group
2	Diageo – the value based marketing company
3	GE Capital – the quest for attitudinal segmentation and targeting
4	Fastparts
5	Sainsbury's
6	Changing the business model at De Beers

Integrative Learning Activity
Strategic decisions in an unpredictable world

Chapters	Case study outline
Part 2 **Reorienting and reformulating the marketing offer for stakeholder satisfaction**	
7	Siebel Systems and CRM
8	Inner city regeneration – Urban Splash
9	AstraZeneca
10	MyTravel
11	Star Alliance – ever closer
12	The right direction for Qibla-Cola?

Integrative Learning Activity
The management challenge of strategic decision making in global markets

How to study using this book

The aim of the book is to give readers an accessible and readable resource for use both as a course book and for revision. The text also incorporates the syllabus of the Strategic Marketing Decisions module of the Chartered Institute of Marketing Professional Postgraduate Diploma and so is essential reading for students of the CIM qualifications.

It has a clear structure which is easy to use and easy for the reader to follow. Its geocentric view of marketing with examples of good practice of firms competing on global markets makes it ideal for use on courses with multi-cultural students.

The two parts focus on the topics of building strategic capability and redefining the marketing portfolio to achieve a sustainable competitive advantage. Each part contains an introduction to the six chapters.

- In Part 1 we focus on the development of the capabilities within an organisation to make effective strategic marketing decisions
- In Part 2 we focus on the development of innovative marketing solutions that enhance an organisation's competitive position in its chosen markets whilst delivering superior value to the customers and to the shareholders of the company.

Part 1 Building capability to make effective strategic marketing decisions

Part 1 is concerned with assessing the capabilities required by organisations to make effective strategic marketing decisions that deliver value to the customer and add economic value to the shareholders/owners. We examine the dynamic global marketing environment, the changing nature of competitive advantage and the type of capabilities organisations need to compete globally. Effective learning is critical for strategic marketing decision making and is essential in making effective investment decisions. As such this part focuses on building a knowledge management with the capability to assess the global marketing environment, organisational learning and the development of the ability to formulate cost effective competitive strategies in the context of an organisation competing in a dynamic global environment. If a marketing manager is to show how the strategic marketing decisions taken can add value to the organisation then he/she needs to be competent in the financial tools to do this. In Chapter 4 we focus on the financial techniques required in appraising long term and short term decisions and examine the tools available for evaluating the performance outcome of those decisions.

The focus is on the capabilities a company needs to make decisions that will lead to a strategic reorientation of the organisation in order to secure a sustainable future. In Chapters 5 and 6 we look at organisations, whether they are small or large, and how they must respond to the increasing globalisation of markets by developing approaches to business that are underpinned by robust generic strategies and a clearly defined scope of operations.

Part 2 Reorienting and reformulating the marketing offer for stakeholder satisfaction

Increasing competition is leading to greater commoditisation of products and services and the need to find new ways of differentiation. The application of new technology is leading to ever faster change and this places increasing demands on organisations for their strategic marketing decision making to be more innovative and technology-enabled across all their activities. They must add greater value to the customer offer through incremental growth and, additionally, by leveraging to the maximum their tangible and intangible assets.

The focus of Part 2 is on the need to maximise the marketing and business performance of the organisation by leveraging the organisation's capability to create a competitive advantage across markets. Specifically we address the strategic marketing decisions required for the development of a marketing offer that customers value and also the consequences of the strategic marketing decisions for the organisation's other stakeholders. In these chapters we examine the decisions that are needed to maximise the marketing performance of the organisation. First, we focus on the creation of a profitable, flexible portfolio of products and services that will provide enduring customer satisfaction. Second, we explore the communications at the customer interface that can be used to deliver immediate satisfaction and build enduring, valuable relationships. Third, we explore how the organisation's delivery and overall value chain capability can be further increased, in the form of an effective extended organisation, through partnerships and alliances. Finally we examine the consequences of strategic marketing decision making for the organisation's wide range of stakeholders including the particular challenge of meeting their differing expectations, such as social responsibility and increasing shareholder value.

Chapters

The chapters each focus on particular areas of the strategic marketing decision process which need to be considered by managers when developing a more innovative approach to the strategic development of an organisation and trying to build competitive advantage by creating added value for customers and other stakeholders. An important theme running through the chapters therefore is the development of the capability to develop innovative solutions that enhance an organisation's competitive position in its chosen markets and add value to the organisation.

After the introduction in each chapter the learning objectives for the chapter are set out and these should provide the focus for study. To help to reinforce the learning and encourage the reader to explore the issues more fully, the chapters contain a number of additional aids to learning.

Challenges

The challenges in each chapter are intended to reinforce a key issue or learning point that has been discussed within the chapter. Each challenge contains further questions intended to enable the reader to reflect upon the deeper and broader implications of the scenario and thus provide a further opportunity for discussion. The aim has been for the settings for the challenges to be as diverse as possible, geographically, culturally, by business sector, size and type of organisation, in order to try to help the reader consider the situations described from alternative perspectives.

Spotlights

The spotlights in each chapter focus on decisions made at a critical time which proved to be crucial for successful marketing managers. We have not attempted to tell the life stories of successful marketers but rather identify decisions that offer lessons for students and other practitioners.

Case studies

At the end of each chapter a case study provides an opportunity for the reader to carry out more comprehensive analysis on key chapter topics before deciding what strategic decisions and plans should be made. These short cases provide only limited information and, where possible, readers should obtain more information on the case study subject from appropriate websites in order to complete the tasks. The reader should start with the questions that have been supplied in order to help guide the analysis or discussion. After this, however, the reader should think more broadly around the issues raised and decide whether these are indeed the right questions to ask and answer. Global markets change continuously and new factors that have recently emerged may completely alter the situation.

Integrative learning activities

At the end of each of the two parts of the book, we have included an *Integrative Learning Activity*. The purpose of the integrated learning activities is to integrate the six chapters that make up each of the parts. More important, however, is that the activities provide a framework for planning a marketing strategy and give the opportunity for readers to consider the strategic marketing decisions involved in developing, planning and implementing a marketing strategy in a global context.

The aims of the integrated learning activities (ILAs) are therefore much wider in scope than the short case studies found at the end of each chapter. The objective is to provide a vehicle through which the reader is able to develop practical decision making skills in analysis, evaluation and strategy development. In completing these activities you will need to synthesise the various strands and themes explored throughout the book and apply them to a practical situation. To complete each of the activities the reader must move well beyond the boundaries of the textbook, researching new material and exploring the interplay of the concepts discussed in the text and possible solutions to the practical problems identified in each activity.

Web support

The textbook is fully supported by an accompanying website that can be found at www.thomsonlearning.co.uk. This enables students and lecturers to access a number of resources in order to explore the subject further. Lecturers can use the site to access valuable on-line teaching resources including a full set of PowerPoint slides to accompany the text and hints and tips on how to use the cases studies, challenges, etc. in a classroom situation. Students are able to access learning resources to accompany the textbook and hot links to other websites which may be useful in exploring the cases and challenges in the text.

ACCOMPANYING WEBSITE

Visit the *Strategic Marketing Decisions in Global Markets* accompanying website at www.thomsonlearning.co.uk/marketing/doolesmd to find further teaching and learning material including:

For Students

- Internet Projects
- Multiple Choice Questions for each chapter
- Additional Cases with accompanying questions
- Related weblinks

For Lecturers

- Instructors Manual – including teaching notes, how to use the text and answers to the questions within the text
- Downloadable PowerPoint™ slides
- Case Study Teaching Notes to accompany cases within the text

Acknowledgements

Inevitably in the task of writing this textbook we have had help, support and valuable contributions from many people. We would especially like to thank our colleagues from Sheffield Hallam University and other universities who have contributed to the chapters, case studies, management challenges and the integrated learning activities.

We are indebted to our students from many countries who have shared their learning experiences with us and whose insights have informed the development of the pedagogical features of this book. We would also like to express our gratitude to the managers of the numerous businesses across the globe, who have freely given their time to share their expert knowledge of strategic marketing decision making with us and enabled us to present to the reader such a rich array of examples and illustrations. Our contacts are too numerous to mention individually but they have all been tremendously important to us in helping to shape and influence our views as to how global marketing strategic decisions are made in practice.

We would like to acknowledge the encouragement of the Chartered Institute of Marketing and the support of the team at Thomson Learning, we are grateful for their professionalism in turning our manuscripts into such a professional finished form.

Every effort has been made to obtain permission from the copyright holders for material reproduced in this book. Any rights not acknowledged here will be acknowledged in subsequent printings if due notice is given to the publisher.

Isobel Doole, Robin Lowe
September 2004

The publisher would also like to thank the following reviewers:

Henrik Agndal, Jönköping International Business School
John Goodfellow, London Metropolitan University
Chris Hackley, Royal Holloway College
Steve Hogan, University of Brighton
Poul Houman Andersen, Aarhus University
Robert E. Morgan, Cardiff University
Caroline Tynan, The University of Nottingham
Björn Walliser, University of Nancy II

Walk-through tour

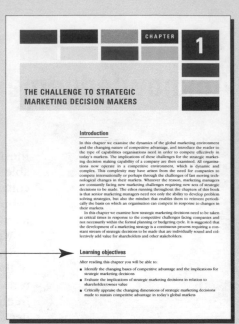

Learning objectives
Listed at the start of each chapter, highlighting the core coverage that you should acquire after studying each chapter.

Challenges
Reinforce key issues discussed within the chapter, accompanied by questions.

Summary

Bulleted list at the end of each chapter reviewing briefly the main concepts and key points covered in each chapter.

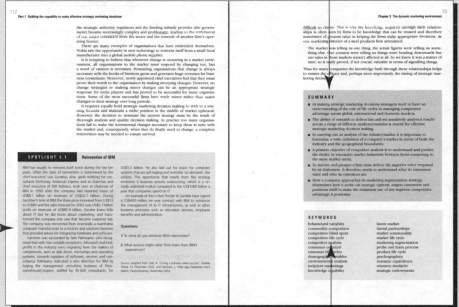

Spotlights

Focus on decisions which have proved to be crucial for successful marketing managers.

Key words

Highlighted throughout the text where they first appear alerting the student to the core concepts and techniques. Listed at the end of each chapter and emboldened within the index as well.

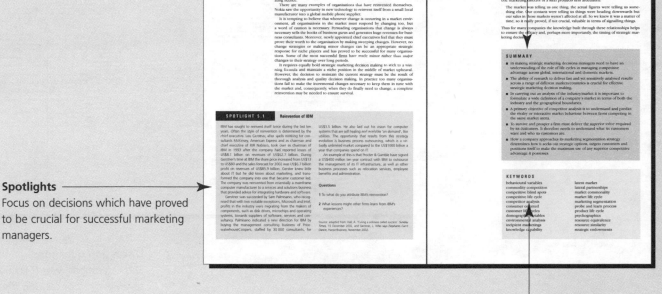

End of chapter case

Cases are provided at the end of each chapter which draw upon real-world companies and help to demonstrate the theory in practice. Each case is accompanied by questions to test the understanding.

Discussion questions

Short questions, which encourage you to review and/or critically discuss your understanding of the main topics and issues.

Integrative learning activities

A series of learning activities presented at the end of each part, integrating the chapters and taken together as a whole they integrate both parts.

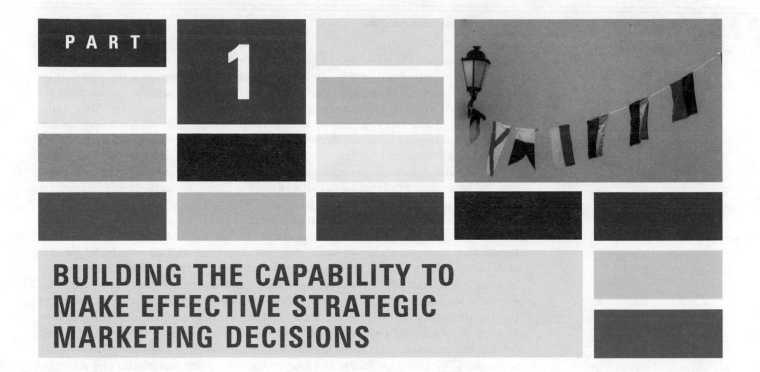

PART 1

BUILDING THE CAPABILITY TO MAKE EFFECTIVE STRATEGIC MARKETING DECISIONS

Introduction

Throughout this book the development of a sustainable competitive advantage is viewed as a continual process requiring a constant stream of strategic marketing decisions to be made that are individually sound and collectively contribute to the marketing planning process and add value for shareholders as well as other stakeholders. Strategic marketing decisions need to be made throughout the marketing planning process as well as at critical times in response to the competitive challenges facing the company. In Part 1 we examine the changing global competitive landscape and consider what capabilities companies need to make effective strategic marketing decisions that respond to the competitive challenges in today's global markets.

Part 1 is specifically concerned with assessing the capabilities required by organisations to make effective strategic marketing decisions that deliver value to the customer and add economic value to the shareholders/owners. In Chapter 1 we examine the changing nature of competitive advantage and the type of capabilities organisations need to compete globally. The development of strategies that build upon and leverage an organisation's competitive position globally is fundamental to the achievement of a sustainable competitive advantage. The challenges of doing this across a spectrum of fast moving, geographically and culturally varied markets in an effective manner, represent a significant intellectual challenge and require the development and refinement of decision making skills.

A strong marketing orientation and effective learning in an organisation are critical for strategic marketing decision making. As such in Chapter 2 we focus on the signal learning and 3R learning and consider the skills a company needs in order to build a knowledge management capability. In this chapter it is argued that by having a high level of orientation towards its markets, combined with a clear core purpose and effective learning, firms are able to achieve clarity of thinking with regard to their strategic direction and the subsequent decisions needed for effective strategy development. Firms that have a high marketing orientation have the ability to work with customers, build a knowledge capability and use the information appropriately. In Chapter 3 this is further developed by examining the dynamics of the global marketing environment and the implications for strategic marketing decision making. In this chapter we focus on the building of a knowledge capability of the external environment. In the first section we examine the importance of understanding the various life cycles driving markets and then turn our attention to the type of knowledge that needs to be built. We focus on analysis at four levels, the macro-environmental analysis, analysis of the market/industry, competitor analysis and customer analysis. In the final sections we examine some of the research methods used specifically in signal learning and 3R learning.

If a marketing manager is to show how the strategic marketing decisions taken can add value to the organisation then he/she needs to be competent in the financial tools to do this. In Chapter 4 we focus on the financial techniques required in appraising long term and short term decisions, and examine the tools available for evaluating the performance outcome of those decisions.

As said previously the focus of Part 1 is on the capabilities a company needs to make decisions that will lead to a strategic reorientation of the organisation in order to secure a sustainable future. In Chapters 5 and 6 we look at organisations, whether they are small or large, and how they respond to the increasing globalisation of markets by developing approaches to business that are underpinned by robust generic strategies and a clearly defined scope of operations. Finally in this part, in Chapter 6 we consider strategies for the global market and look at the competitive strategies pursued by companies on the global markets.

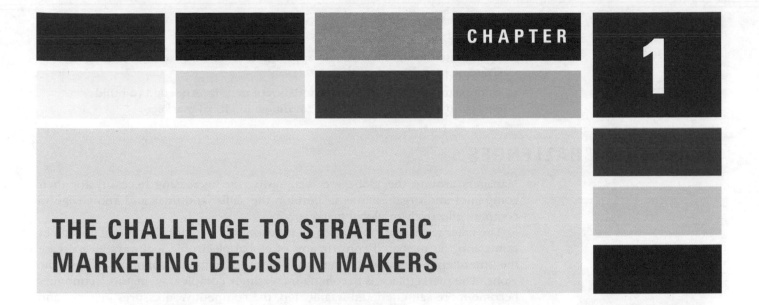

CHAPTER

1

THE CHALLENGE TO STRATEGIC MARKETING DECISION MAKERS

Introduction

In this chapter we examine the dynamics of the global marketing environment and the changing nature of competitive advantage, and introduce the reader to the type of capabilities organisations need in order to compete effectively in today's markets. The implications of these challenges for the strategic marketing decision making capability of a company are then examined. All organisations now operate in a competitive environment, which is dynamic and complex. This complexity may have arisen from the need for companies to compete internationally or perhaps through the challenges of fast moving technological changes in their markets. Whatever the reason, marketing managers are constantly facing new marketing challenges requiring new sets of strategic decisions to be made. The ethos running throughout the chapters of this book is that senior marketing managers need not only the ability to develop problem solving strategies, but also the mindset that enables them to reinvent periodically the basis on which an organisation can compete in response to changes in their markets.

In this chapter we examine how strategic marketing decisions need to be taken at critical times in response to the competitive challenges facing companies and not necessarily within the formal planning or budgeting cycle. It is suggested that the development of a marketing strategy is a continuous process requiring a constant stream of strategic decisions to be made that are individually sound and collectively add value for shareholders and other stakeholders.

Learning objectives

After reading this chapter you will be able to:

■ Identify the changing bases of competitive advantage and the implications for strategic marketing decisions

■ Evaluate the implications of strategic marketing decisions in relation to shareholder/owner value

■ Critically appraise the changing dimensions of strategic marketing decisions made to sustain competitive advantage in today's global markets

■ Appreciate the significance and application of new marketing thinking to strategic marketing decisions

■ Understand the required characteristics of decisions needed to build competitive capability to create advantage in global markets

MARKETING CHALLENGES

Managers around the globe are recognising the increasing necessity for their companies and organisations to develop the skills, aptitudes and knowledge to compete effectively in global markets.

The emergence of a more open world economy, the globalisation of consumer tastes and the unabated construction of global electronic highways all increase the inter-dependency and inter-connections of nation economies across the globe. The marketplace is becoming increasingly complex. As mature economies become more saturated and fragmented, the competitive pressures increase and survival and growth become more difficult to sustain. The need for managers to develop the skills to respond to these pressures affects companies of all sizes.

The global marketplace consists of a population of 6 billion people which is expected to reach 10 billion by 2050 according to the latest projections by the United Nations. Last year's global trade in merchandise exceeded US$7 trillion and world trade in services is estimated at around US$1.5 trillion. Whilst most of us cannot visualise such huge amounts, it does serve to give some indication of the scale of expenditure across global markets today.

Global wealth overall is increasing, and this is again reflected in higher demand across markets. Increasing affluence and demand means that consumers are now actively seeking choice across the globe with the result that competition is emerging as companies compete to win the battle for disposable income. Commercial dynamism has seen nations across Asia, South America and Eastern Europe emerge as high growth economies, and as their companies increasingly seek new markets globally, so they themselves are emerging as powerful competitors in today's global markets.

Population growth and increased affluence have together helped create a 'global youth culture'. In many countries, more than half the population is pre-adult, creating one of the world's biggest single markets, the youth market. Everywhere adolescents project worldwide cultural icons, Nike, Coke, Benetton and the Sony Walkman, as well as Sega, Nintendo and the Sony Playstation. When 'virtual reality' is commonplace, the one-world youth culture market will exceed all others as a general category for marketers. Parochial, local and ethnic growth products may face difficult times. This means paying particular attention to the youth market as suggested in Challenge 1.1.

Older consumers are also increasingly non-national in their identity, not from their personal identity but from the perspective of the consumable fabric of their lives. They drive cars produced from around the world, watch programmes on television sourced from many different countries, use computer hardware and software no longer the primary domain of the USA but designed and produced in India, China and Asia. Older consumers themselves are the new target consumer in the beauty market whereas a decade ago such companies primarily targeted the youth market, as Challenge 1.2 shows.

Schwartz, in his book, *Inevitable Surprises*, identifies what he sees as the environmental challenges facing marketing decision makers today. The lengthening of the human life-span, where 60 becomes the equivalent of 40; the changing patterns of migration; the dominance of American economic and military might; and the existence of 'a set of disorderly nations with the capacity to unleash terror, disease and disruption' on the rest of the world.

CHALLENGE 1.1   The youth market

The youth market controls in excess of $3.00 trillion of expenditure a year. Eight to twelve year olds alone control $1.88 trillion. These children, known as 'tweens', access the world through their computer screens. They do not differentiate between offline and online, to them the world is truly wired up to their computers. In a family they can be the primary decision makers in 80 per cent of purchases, dictate their own purchase of brands and influence family purchases in diverse areas such as cars, clothes and leisure activities. The group are sceptical and media and technology savvy, and have little patience with established marketing techniques, so to create a position in this group of consumers a company would need to be innovative and use a multimedia approach.

The US Jones Soda Company established their new brand as one of the fastest growing soda brands in the USA by focusing entirely on 12–24 year olds. They knew that to reach this market would require innovative marketing techniques to get their attention. The company designed a marketing strategy that would make the soda cool by association, by backing alternative and extreme sports, stocking the brand in non-traditional outlets and even showing customer photos on the labels, all to try to develop an emotional connection with their young consumers.

Source: Jones Soda Co.

Question How far do the trends in the youth market require a new approach to strategic marketing decision making?

Sources: adapted from *Financial Times,* 18 March 2004 and *Marketing Business,* December 2003

CHALLENGE 1.2   The beautification of the ageing baby boomers

Analysts at Goldman Sachs estimate that the global beauty industry is worth about US$100 billion a year and is growing at up to 7 per cent a year, more than twice the rate of the developed world's GDP. This growth is being driven by richer, ageing baby-boomers and increased discretionary income in the West, and by the growing middle classes in developing countries. China, Russia and South Korea are turning into huge markets. In India, sales of anti-ageing creams are growing by 40 per cent a year. Avon is expanding rapidly in Eastern Europe and Russia as well as in South America. Brazil now has more than 900 000 Avon Ladies.

Global competition in the market is becoming increasingly intense. Unilever and Procter & Gamble, facing maturity in many of their traditional businesses, are devoting more resources to developing global beauty brands. Luxury product manufacturers such as Dior, Chanel and Yves St Laurent are moving into mainstream beauty products and

many of the global giants are growing by buying up smaller brands. Japan's Kao have gone into the hair dye market by buying John Frieda while Estée Lauder has acquired Stila, MAC and Bobbi Brown, all of which are innovative and growing make-up brands.

The traditional global beauty brands established by companies such as L'Oreal, Arden and Rubenstein now have to fight hard in a global market where traditionally they have earned huge margins and enjoyed continuous growth for many years.

Question What are the key strategic marketing decisions facing the major players in this highly competitive global market?

Source: adapted from *The Economist,* 22 May 2003

On the supply side, there is a trend towards global nationalisation, seeking world standards for efficiency and productivity. Glaxo Wellcome formed a global alliance in the pharmaceutical market with SmithKline Beecham creating the world's largest research-based pharmaceutical company, and are looking to further extend their global alliances. General Electric formed a strategic alliance with the French aircraft company Snecma. In the software market Oracle are merging with Peoplesoft and in the aluminium industry Alcan are joining with Pechiney, a move which could trigger consolidation in that industry. Such trends can also be seen in the service sector. In the USA, Morgan Stanley and Dean Witter merged to offer global investment as well as global private banking and credit card services.

There is also a rationalisation and consolidation of **global competitors** in many industries. Multi-national and global corporations are increasing in size and embracing more global power. The top 500 companies in the world now account for 70 per cent of global spend and 80 per cent of global investment. To deal with the size and inter-relatedness of the global economy, companies are consolidating through mergers, acquisitions and alliances to reach the scale considered necessary to compete in the global arena. McKinsey examined a sample of 1000 listed companies in America from 15 different industries over the period from 1969 to 1999, when companies experienced more wrenching changes in their environment than ever seen before in peacetime. They measured the market value added (MVA) by companies, the change in their outstanding debt and their stock market capitalisation. They found that 80 per cent or more of all 15 industries' MVA over the period was accounted for by the top 20 per cent of companies. Moreover, this 80/20 split remained remarkably steady over the whole 30-year period. The implication of course being that in any market the companies that adapt their strategies to environmental challenges and succeed do exceedingly well, whereas the ones that do not may well disappear altogether or survive making relatively low returns for their shareholders. Survival then does not necessarily mean long standing companies have achieved the highest market value added.

Foster and Kaplan (2002), in their book *Creative Destruction* suggest that too many managers assume the future will be much like the past, what worked before will work again, an attitude they suggest that can all too often destroy company value. Many managers, they argue, appear to make the mistake of focusing upon what competitors have done in the past rather than what they are most likely to do in the future. Although, quite obviously, behaviour in the future is often influenced by what has been done previously, even small changes on the part of a competitor or in the environment can invalidate the assumptions being made.

The two authors compared the original 1917 Forbes magazine list of the top 100 American companies with a comparable list that the magazine published in 1987. By then, 61 of the original group had ceased to exist; of the remainder, only 18 had managed to stay in the top 100. They included such firms as Kodak, DuPont, General Electric, Ford, General Motors and Procter & Gamble.

These all survived depression, world war, the oil price shocks and unprecedented technological change. But survival did not mean that they were more profitable than their peers. Of the 18, only General Electric and Kodak outperformed the stock market. The group as a whole had returns that were 20 per cent below the market's compound annual growth rate of 7.5 per cent over those 70 years.

The global marketplace is simultaneously becoming inter-dependent, economically, culturally and technically through the consistent thrust in technological innovation. Newbold *et al.* (2002) suggest:

> The new economy is being shaped not only by the development and diffusion of computer hardware and software but also by much cheaper and rapidly

increasing electronic connectivity. The internet in particular is helping to level the playing field among large and small firms in B2B e-commerce.

Newbold et al. 2002

Information moves anywhere in the world at the speed of light and what is becoming known as the global civilisation is being facilitated by the convergence of long distance telecommunications, cuts in the cost of electronic processing and the growth of internet business.

The implications for marketing decision makers

Markets today have become increasingly complex and dynamic, the proliferation of customers' needs has led to shifts in the balance of channel and competitor power as companies have realigned their strategies to respond to changing consumer needs. The globalisation of markets and competition has in turn led to a consolidation of competition as industries rationalise and markets become dominated by fewer but larger and more powerful players. The combination of all these forces has meant that companies need to develop a marketing orientation which is global and have managers who are able to analyse, plan and implement strategies across a global market that is dynamic, challenging and turbulent.

The problem is that as companies grow, decision making itself can slow down as the bureaucracy of the organisation builds and managers have to adhere to the rules and regulations from head office as to the management processes they must go through in order to make any marketing decision. Thus **innovation** ceases, managers fail to respond to signals in the marketplace, and the organisation no longer has the capability or flexibility to respond appropriately to market challenges. Peters (2003) suggests that as companies grow in size 'gigantism' becomes an unbearable burden, and managers spend too much time looking inwards to their corporate headquarters and not enough time making innovative decisions.

In this new world order Gilligan and Wilson (2003) identify the priorities for **strategic marketing decision** makers as being:

- Pace of change and the need for marketing managers to rapidly respond with innovative solutions with regard to products, services and marketing processes.
- Fragmented markets and the increasing need for customisation to smaller targeted niches.
- The delivery of superior customer value as a basic ingredient of competitiveness.
- Information, market knowledge and the ability to learn as the premier source of competitive advantage.
- The strategic significance of new types of partnerships and new networks of relationships in the supply chain. The pressure for speed and efficiency means marketers have to consider more innovative and effective ways of building routes to their markets; this means new forms of partnerships and relationships are being sought.

The challenges outlined mean it is now vital that marketing within companies takes on a much more strategic role and has a more prominent influence in the corporate strategic direction the company takes. The boundary lines between marketing and other function areas such as operations, finance and human resources are much more blurred as marketing takes this more strategic role within an organisation. Anthony Brown of IBM suggests there are two types of corporations: those with marketing departments and those with marketing souls. Piercy (2002) argues quite strongly that companies should aim to have a marketing soul rather than be hamstrung by traditional demarcation of marketing as a functional discipline primarily responsible for the formation of marketing plans and procedures with little input at a corporate level. This means that companies should be more concerned with the process of how a company goes to market rather than focusing on marketing mix planning. This process, he argues, needs to be owned by everyone in the company, not just the marketing department, and should be concerned with bringing together all the business processes that:

Define **customer value**: for example, marketing research, marketing information systems and the analysis of the company's **core competences**.

Develop customer value: for example, new product development, pricing and value positioning, design of distribution channels and the selection of alliances and partners.

Deliver customer value: for example, the logistics and sales functions, after sales service, transaction/credit processing and partner and customer support.

However all these processes have implications for the management within the company with regard to:

■ How they will manage the technological/analytical dimensions in order to ensure the information systems and operations deliver customer value.

■ How they will motivate staff and build a culture within the company in which employees are committed to the development and delivery of customer value.

■ How they will develop the learning capabilities to define customer value and develop the ability to respond to the changing nature of value and reinvent strategies to sustain customer value over time.

To do this managers need to develop the capability to understand customers as well as to develop and deliver superior customer value. The marketing decisions need to foster a marketing strategy process that focuses on how to choose target markets and how to build a strong competitive position based on a sustainable value proposition which is differentiated from its competitors. They also need to know how to drive things that matter through the company and so ensure the effective implementation of customer value in the marketplace.

As Wilson and Gilligan (2004) articulate, competition between organisations can be seen in much the same way as a game, in that the outcome in terms of an organisation's performance is determined not only by its own actions but also by the actions and reactions of the other players, such as competitors, customers, governments and other stakeholders. However, as the pace of environmental change increases and the nature, sources and bases of competition alter, markets become more complex and the competitive game consequently becomes more difficult to win. The difficulties in achieving this have been illustrated in a number of markets, including the dot.com bubble, telecommunications, mobile phones, airline travel, financial services, the automobile market and many others. Nohria and Joyce (2003) studied 160 companies over a ten-year period to ascertain which competitive capabilities were key to companies who consistently outperformed competitors. They found that such companies had a company culture based on aiming high, a structure that was flexible and responsive, and a strategy that was clear and focused; and that they flawlessly executed the implementation of the strategic decisions made.

If companies are to compete on such a basis they need to rethink their approach to strategic marketing decision making. Senior marketing managers need the ability not only to develop **problem solving strategies**, but also, the mindset that enables them to reinvent periodically the basis on which organisations can compete in response to changes in their markets. The challenges in the environment outlined above therefore cannot be met if marketing decision makers follow the same linear rational planning procedures that have been propagated in the last decades. The challenges in today's marketing environment require transformational thinking if marketers are to build a sustainable competitive advantage. In static markets the simplification of reality suggested by the mental models used in many rational linear planning models may be adequate in thinking through the implications of competitive and customer intelligence. However such simplification may well prove inadequate in markets in which there is any real degree of competitive intensity and **turbulent change**. Because of this, competitively successful organisations need to put a great deal of effort into learning not only about their customers and competitors, but also into developing a detailed understanding of environmental factors, which may impact on their markets, and the perceptions and expectations of partners in their supply chain and other stakeholders. Firms therefore need to devote significant resources to building their learning on all these aspects to ensure future strategies can then be built upon genuine understanding.

Furthermore if marketing decision makers are to take on a more strategic role then they need more than ever to show how the marketing decisions taken can deliver better revenue growth, more profit and increased customer satisfaction. In today's highly competitive marketplace marketing managers are required to be much more accountable for their actions, to be able to show the cost effectiveness of marketing tactics and to show how marketing strategies add to the shareholder/owner value of an organisation. It is this concept we will now explore in the following section.

SHAREHOLDER/OWNER VALUE MARKETING

PA Consulting found in their research that 97 per cent of chief executives believe long term shareholder/owner value creation is their primary objective, whereas it is fifth on the list for marketers, below driving short term sales and developing strategy and innovation. The research identifies that companies which returned a higher than average shareholder value were ones in which marketing accountability was prioritised and where the chief executive was versed in marketing, and yet these successful marketing driven companies remain very much the exception. This issue has become very prevalent in marketing circles as the desire for marketing to have a more prominent influence in company board rooms grows. Much of the literature linking marketing to the creation of added value for a company presupposes a company owned by shareholders and makes constant reference to shareholder value. In this book we recognise the limitations of this approach and the fact that for many privately or family owned companies such a principle may seem irrelevant. Therefore, in the following sections we refer to shareholder/owner value.

According to Doyle (2000), by delivering shareholder/owner value, marketing is more able to influence strategic decisions in the board room at a corporate level. **Shareholder/owner value marketing** offers a way for managers to show how marketing strategies increase the value of the firm as well as providing a framework and language for integrating marketing more effectively with other functions of the business. The traditional marketing objectives of increasing market share and building customer loyalty, he argues, are not enough in themselves, unless they can be linked to an increase in economic added value and higher **financial performance**. The techniques and tools for assessing the viability of strategic marketing decisions and measuring economic added value are examined more thoroughly in Chapter 4; in this chapter we are simply concerned with introducing the concept of the shareholder/owner value principle and discussing its implications for strategic marketing decision makers.

The shareholder value principle

The purpose of strategic marketing decisions is to help the company to create value for the shareholders/owners. Fundamentally, companies operate in the interest of their owners by seeking to maximise profits over the longer term. The underlying interest of all stakeholders is the survival of the firm. In a highly competitive global market firms have to follow goals that will contribute to the maximisation of profit in the firm. Few firms have the luxury of doing otherwise. Managers that do not serve the interests of shareholders/owners will be replaced by those thought to do so, as we have seen in many cases over the last few years. Firms have a number of different **stakeholders**, such as employees, suppliers and the community in which they operate. The demands and expectations of these stakeholders need to be met; however, meeting the wider stakeholder expectations may well conflict with the requirements of the shareholders/owners. Thus, companies have to create value for shareholders/owners whilst at the same time satisfying stakeholder expectations. The management issues that such a conflict can raise will be examined in some depth in Chapter 12. As stated previously in this chapter, we are primarily concerned with introducing the concept of shareholder/owner value and its implications for strategic marketing decision makers.

The shareholder/owner value principle asserts that marketing strategies should be judged by the economic returns they generate for the company, the returns being measured by dividends and increases in the economic value added to the company. This is based on two principles:

- the primary obligation of managers is to maximise returns for shareholders/owners;
- the value of a company is based on the investors expectations of the cash generating abilities of the company.

This of course means that the role of marketing managers is to deliver marketing strategies that maximise the cash flow of a company over time and so create value. The essence of the shareholder/owner value principle is that managers create value which in turn generates greater returns than their cost of capital.

According to Doyle (2000) there are a number of environmental changes which have led to the rise of value based marketing:

- The growth of equity markets around the world and the decline of government participation in business.
- The globalisation of trade and industry has meant companies are not only competing globally for customers but also for capital. If companies are to attract capital they need to be able to convince potential investors that their strategies will deliver positive future economic returns.
- More powerful data processing capabilities and software availability mean it is much easier to run tests to assess the financial implications of marketing decisions.

■ There has been an explosion of the quantity and quality of data available to investors.

■ The globalisation of telecommunications has meant that information can be very easily transferred around the world, so actions of marketing managers have to be more transparent and are under increasing scrutiny. They have to be prepared to be held accountable for the decisions they make, as companies are more vulnerable to acquisition than before, especially when there is a *value gap*, that is when there is a difference between the value of the company if it were operated to maximise value and its current value on the stock market.

Value based marketing

Strategic marketing decisions made by marketing managers therefore have to clearly show how they contribute to economic added value. According to Piercy (2002) this means companies have to develop customer focused strategies based on offering value to customers which in turn enhances company performance and so increases shareholder/owner value. This means strategic marketing decisions need to be concerned with :

How to create value: Piercy views this as the key issue in achieving and sustaining competitive success, particularly in relation to branding and customer relationship management given the increasing demands made by customers.

How to harness the power and impact of the internet: Particularly in relation to the need to develop an integrated and multi channel route to a company's markets.

*How to achieve a **totally integrated marketing effort***: The need to ensure the strategic decisions made exploit all the company's resources and capabilities to deliver value to the customer.

How to engender creativity in the strategy of a company: Piercy argues the focus of strategic decision making should be on *strategising and creativity*, not on the bureaucracy and structures of formal planning.

The concept of **value based marketing** suggests the need for decision makers to focus on the marketing processes that can deliver such value rather than the marketing transaction itself or simply getting the product to market. Marketing over the past decades has evolved through several stages from the early days of transaction marketing through to the concept of value based marketing. According to Doyle (2000), in doing this, marketing thinking has travelled through four stages:

Transactional marketing: where the focus was on the actual exchange and building of short term profits for the company. The main performance indicator was sales volume and so marketing decisions were primarily concerned with enhancing the efficiency and effectiveness of that sale.

Brand marketing: in this stage the focus was on building the augmented product where value was built through the brand image and related product benefits. In brand marketing customer loyalty is built by building an emotional relationship between the customer's lifestyle and the lifestyle built around the brand. In the past few years we have seen customers questioning the price differential sought by major brands, especially when customers, through the price transparency achieved through internet sources, can clearly see the price differential charged by some brands across international markets. This has led to the growth of grey marketing where brands sold for a lower price in one market have been bought directly from that market for other geographical sectors where a higher price is charged. Levi's jeans and Tesco stores have recently been in a court battle due to Tesco sourcing cheaper Levi's jeans outside the EU to sell in the UK at prices lower than the authorised Levi's distributors. Whilst brand leadership is still the basis on which companies build competitive leverage, it has become increasingly recognised that the key differentiator in the marketplace is how, and the extent to which, an organisation is able to add value and deliver greater value to the brand.

Relationship marketing: in relationship marketing customer retention is the key strategic objective. It is based on the notion that profitability is sustained by building customer loyalty and so achieving customer retention. The focus is on getting existing customers to buy more and to keep them in the habit of buying the company's products through loyalty schemes such as store cards and rewards for loyal customers. Customer relationship management has been seen by some as an expensive exercise which has shown little return on the necessary investment made. Other companies have built a successful competitive leverage by building an intimacy with their customers which has proved to be a barrier to other competitors. This close relationship with customers is not an end point in itself; it is the management of those relationships to deliver value to customers at a cost which also delivers value to the company that is the important strategic objective.

Value based marketing (VBM): this recognises the need for a totally integrated marketing effort that manages the whole of the marketing process to deliver customer value and so build value for the shareholders/ owners of the company. Proponents of value based marketing argue that to compete effectively a company needs to do more than build a brand or build relationships, it has to build value. Thus whilst relationships and brands are important, markets are changing the basis for competition and new types of competition are emerging which mean to achieve a **sustainable competitive advantage** companies need to offer a total value proposition to their customers. As Doyle (2000) says, it is 'By delivering superior value to customers that management can in turn deliver superior value to shareholders.'

According to Doyle (2000) delivering value based marketing requires four major steps:

1 The development of a deep understanding of customer needs, operating procedures and decision making processes.
2 The formulation of **value propositions** that meet the needs of customers and create a differential advantage.
3 The building of long term relationships with customers so a level of loyalty and trust is built based on satisfaction and confidence in the supplier.
4 An understanding that the delivery of superior value to customers requires superior knowledge, skills, systems and marketing assets.

Incorporating this concept redefines marketing as being 'the management process that seeks to maximise returns to shareholders by developing and implementing strategies to build relationships of trust with high value customers and create a sustainable differential advantage' (Doyle 2000, p. 70). According to Wilson & Gilligan (2004), value based marketing requires:

*A **market orientation*** that gives the highest priority to the profitable creation and maintenance of superior customer value and the use of market information to achieve continuous learning within the organisation to enable the company to respond to changing consumer demands. The development of these capabilities will be further explored in the discussion in Chapters 2 and 3.

*A **commitment to innovation*** that is customer value focused in order to sustain competitive advantage. This innovation may involve the creation of new businesses within the existing framework or the rejuvenation of existing businesses that have stagnated. It may involve new products or reformulating existing ones, developing new approaches to manufacturing or distribution, or discovering new approaches to management or competitive strategy. This is something that Samsung is working hard to do as illustrated in Challenge 1.3.

Irrespective of which or whether all of these steps are pursued, it is essential that the organisation develops and reflects a market oriented culture and reinforces this with entrepreneurial values. There is therefore a need to take risks and learn from mistakes. The need for **creativity and innovation** is a central theme of this book which will be returned to throughout. Because of its centrality to strategic marketing decision making we specifically focus on how to create an innovative decision making culture in Chapter 7.

*A **customer value process focused organisation.*** The major organisational challenge in value based marketing involves maximising the effectiveness of the firm's customer value creating activities. These activities are best seen as processes that are not just limited to marketing but cut across the entire organisation. A process perspective therefore involves starting with customers and what they want and then working backwards from there. The processes involved in the delivery of value are the focus of Part Two of this book.

CHALLENGE 1.3	Samsung go for totally integrated marketing

Samsung, according to speakers at the UK Marketing Forum in 2003, provides the financial, empirical and analytical evidence marketers need to state their case and make senior management take notice. The electronics giant recently became the world's fastest growing brand for the second year running, according to Interbrand's survey of global brands. Last year they achieved £72 billion in sales and 10 per cent of the global mobile phone market, up from 2.7 per cent in 1999.

Samsung's phenomenal success – and reinvention from cheap volume supplier – is seen to be due to the introduction of a fully holistic and empowered approach to marketing.

The company's chairman, Kun-Hee Lee, has led a marketing charge that has created competitive value by building a premium brand out of seemingly very little. The start of the process was the setting of increased brand value as a key corporate target.

Received wisdom has it that Samsung is succeeding because of its speed at technological innovation, but this is an effect of the corporate strategy rather than the cause itself. Quite simply, there are few organisations that put marketing first across new product development, channels to market and communications with customers and staff.

Samsung believe their totally integrated marketing effort has resulted in added value to the brand and to the company to the extent that Nokia, the market leader (see Challenge 1.4), are now closely monitoring their progress as are a host of other rivals.

Question What can be learnt from Samsung's marketing focus? How far do you think they have achieved a sustainable competitive advantage?

Source: adapted from UK Marketing Forum, 2003

It is perhaps obvious to the reader that if a company is to achieve all that is required by value based marketing as outlined above there needs to be a recognition that no company can succeed by trying to do everything. Instead, it must identify the unique value which it alone can deliver to its chosen markets. In doing this, according to Treacy and Wiersema (1995), managers need to come to terms with making three key strategic marketing decisions:

What is its value proposition? The implicit promise the company is going to make to customers to deliver its particular combination of values.

What is its value-driven operating model? The combination of operating processes, management systems, structure and culture that the company feels it needs to have if it is to have the ability to deliver on its value proposition.

What are its value disciplines? In other words what is the way the company is going to combine its operating models and value propositions to achieve a differential competitive advantage in its market.

The four value disciplines which Treacy and Wiersema consider to be important are operational excellence, product leadership, customer intimacy and brand leadership.

Operational excellence: companies which pursue this value and discipline are not product or service innovators, nor are they necessarily concerned with developing deep and long-lasting relationships with their customers. Rather, they offer middle market products at the best price with the least inconvenience; it is this no frills approach which characterises many retailers such as Wal-Mart, Matalan and Gap. It is a position that is also pursued by companies who identify that their customers are willing to pay a premium to receive a high level of service and so they develop a value proposition based on the services they offer. Harrods, British Airways, luxury hotels; all try to compete on the level of service they offer. In highly competitive and largely mature markets, for example, an ever greater number of organisations are having to compete directly against competitors who offer almost identical products across 70–80 per cent of the range. Because of this, the focus of competitive advantage is increasingly shifting away from major product and technological breakthroughs to an emphasis upon a series of process improvements and the achievement of **operational excellence**, thus the focus of their operations is on speed and dependability to offer a fast and timely service at a cost that delivers value to the shareholder/owner as well as to the customer. This is what Oracle has been trying to achieve by shifting all their business processes to the web.

Product leadership involves focusing upon developing and offering products which consistently push at the boundaries of innovation; both Intel and Nike are examples of this. Offering innovative solutions with the latest product developments requires a high investment in research and development and a strong innovation capability. This means employing the leading researchers in the field and building an organisational culture where creativity can flourish. Examples of such companies are Microsoft, GlaxoSmithKline, Procter & Gamble and 3M.

Customer intimacy is based on the idea that the organisation concentrates upon building relationships and, in many cases, satisfying specialised or unique needs. In a time when technology has allowed marketers to move from mass marketing to customised one-to-one marketing, companies now have the technical capability to target on an individual basis and so create customer value through the illusion of having an individual personal relationship with their customers. Lastminute.com, Amazon.com and a number of other internet suppliers are able to offer individual buying solutions through the information built from purchasing profiles. However, customer intimacy is much more prevalent in B2B marketing when customers often require high value bespoke solutions to technical problems. A relationship based on long term commitment and knowledge of the customer's business is a necessary prerequisite to building greater value than competitors.

Brand leadership: building an emotional connection between the consumer and the product through strong branding can mean increased customer loyalty and the ability to charge a price differential and so achieve greater cash returns. The global brands of Nike, Sony and McDonald's have become worldwide phenomena by pursuing such a policy. Customers will, therefore, actively seek out a particular brand of clothes, watches, computers or cars not necessarily because it is better in absolute terms than a competing product, but because of the image and the individual's perception of this. However, as said earlier **brand leadership** is only sustainable if it offers superior value to the customer. Companies basing their strategic positioning on brand leadership need to work actively to deliver an **extra value proposition** which is valued by the customer in order to sustain brand leadership over a period of time. Nokia believe they have achieved this by focusing their efforts on designing and manufacturing a user interface which is more customer friendly than its main competitors, as discussed in Challenge 1.4. The proposition which will deliver a differential advantage and create value must deliver real benefits as perceived by the customer. The differential needs to be grounded in the dimensions sought by the customer. It must also be a unique proposition and differentiated from competitors, and the company needs to have the ability to produce and deliver the proposition with a price/cost/volume structure that makes it profitable and sustainable over time. This will make it difficult for competitors to copy and create sufficient barriers to entry to avoid competitors eroding the competitive differential.

CHALLENGE 1.4	Nokia's differential advantage

In a highly competitive market where innovations move at great speed, Nokia claim they have managed to build a long term competitive advantage by ensuring the usability of their mobile phone handsets. The result is that the company now has a world market share of nearly 40 per cent and every day over 400 million people use their products.

Nokia have achieved this by focusing their efforts on designing and manufacturing a user interface which is more customer friendly than those of its main competitors; this has meant the company has been able to build a strong loyalty of users to their brand. Even when upgrading their mobile phones, their users are reluctant to switch to other brands.

Jorma Ollila, chairman and chief executive, says usability is 'at the heart' of the company's approach. He adds that they were one of the first to realise that ease of use had to become 'the main goal in design'. They view mobile phones not as a technological device but as 'a reflection of the owner's personality and mood'.

The company describes design as 'a fundamental building block of the brand', adding that it is 'central to our product creation and is a core competence integrated into the entire company'. A core competence that is difficult to replicate and hard for some of its competitors to keep pace with. Yet as we saw in Challenge 1.3 Samsung believe they are not too far behind.

Question What are the major threats Nokia face in sustaining their competitive advantage through brand leadership in the next few years?

Source: adapted from McCartney, N. (2003) 'Squaring up to usability at Nokia' *Financial Times*, 13 October

The choice of which value discipline to pursue cannot be decided upon in an arbitrary way but must be based on a detailed understanding of both the company and its markets. Equally, Treacy and Wiersema (1995) suggest the value discipline chosen requires the company to then make that discipline a central core value in the strategic thinking of the company, and so shape the subsequent marketing decisions a company makes. The choice of value discipline, in effect, therefore shapes the core purpose of the company. However, as said previously, if companies are to build a sustainable competitive advantage that delivers value to customers and to the company, innovative and creative thinking is required. Companies will need to do more of the same but better, and occasionally break the mould and reinvent the basis on which they compete in the marketplace. Breaking free of the strictures of the industry and the rules on which a company has previously competed may be the key to their deliverance of customer value over the longer term as will be discussed in the following section.

BREAKING THE MOULD

Innovative organisations do not necessarily focus their efforts on matching or beating the competition. Instead, they concentrate on making competition irrelevant by offering buyers a quantum leap in value. They do this by rethinking market boundaries and by basing their market definition in terms of the customers they serve rather than the product market they are in. Sometimes this means breaking free of the notion that they have a localised customer base and seeking new customers globally, or they may break free in terms of the product/service boundaries that prevail within the market and so create innovative strategies that change the basis on which they compete.

According to Hamel and Prahalad (1994) innovative and creative strategies are about breaking free:

■ *Breaking free from the latest with management tools*. CRM, TQM, supply chain management, etc. These are important in helping to achieve operational effectiveness and delivering customer value but they are not about strategy and not what strategic marketing decisions should be primarily concerned with.

■ *Breaking free of industry dogma*. Supermarkets were effective in defining themselves in terms of customers not their industry, and so were able to move into new unrelated product areas such as financial services and banking; all of which were important needs of their consumers but unrelated to the food industry.

■ *Breaking free of industry rules*. Hamel and Prahalad argue there are three types of companies: rule makers who build a market, rule takers who follow and imitate and rule breakers who implement a revolution in an industry by breaking the rules. Virgin, Dell Computers and easyJet all broke the rules of standard common practice in their industries.

■ *Breaking free of a limited mindset*. Companies need to question why they follow the same strategy and tactics year after year and break free of a company culture that is hostile to change. Toyota are a good example of a company who have achieved this, as discussed in Spotlight 1.1 below.

According to Wilson and Gilligan (2004), the emergence of the need for a company to break free from existing patterns of behaviour is sometimes stimulated by the anticipation, or precipitation, of a major structural change in the environment. Sometimes referred to as *industry breakpoints*, the consequences of major change are seen in a variety of ways but most obviously in terms of how a previously successful strategy is made obsolete. An understanding of how breakpoints work and how they might best be managed is therefore an essential part of strategic marketing decision making.

In discussing **industry breakpoints,** Strebel (1996) defines them as:

> a new offering to the market that is so superior in terms of customer value and delivered cost that it disrupts the rules of the competitive game: a new business system is required to deliver it. The new offering typically causes a sharp shift in the industry's growth rate while the competitive response to the new business system results in a dramatic realignment of market shares.

(Strebel 1996, p. 13)

SPOTLIGHT 1.1   Toyota breaks free

In the early 1990s Toyota was seen as a company in the doldrums. It suffered low growth, was seen to have uninspiring cars and the brand had little appeal, being generally viewed by all as the humdrum motor brand. A decade later the scenario has completely changed. Since 1992 Toyota has tripled its annual sales in the UK. In Europe it has gone from ninth in the market to sixth and over the next four years its European production is expected to increase by at least 200 per cent. In the USA Toyota now has a greater market share than Chrysler and is mounting a serious challenge to Ford for market leadership. Its sales growth in the USA has made it the second largest global car manufacturer after General Motors.

In ten years it has shifted its brand's perceptions from being boring and nondescript to one which exudes engineering quality and emotional appeal. Paul Philpott the commercial director reflects: 'Until 1999 we were seen as reliable, rational and dull. We wanted to take that rational brand strength and give it emotional appeal; to do that we had to be braver in our marketing.' Using Volkswagen as a benchmark, as the prestige volume brand, they set about injecting an emotional appeal and pride of ownership into the Toyota brand. To achieve this Toyota needed to break free from the mindset in which they had been operating and change the company culture itself.

Source: Saatchi and Saatchi

In order to become braver in their marketing, Toyota transformed themselves from a sales led to a marketing led company. In 1998 they were merged into a single commercial division, ensuring both departments fully co-operated and worked closely together. At the same time Toyota also greatly increased its marketing investment worldwide.

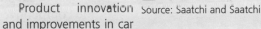

Source: Saatchi and Saatchi

Product innovation and improvements in car design, which have enabled Toyota to add value to their product portfolio, have also been critical. The *Yaris,* launched in 2000, sold 30 000 units in its first year. The *Yaris,* the *Avensis* and the new *Corolla* launched in 2002, were designed specifically for the European market from Toyota's studios in France. The success of these cars is seen by Toyota as being proof of the wisdom of their regionalised strategy.

The view in the market is that Toyota is now definitely *the car in front.*

Question Fully evaluate whether you think the strategic marketing decisions made by Toyota have helped them break free from their previous position. What do they need to do to ensure they continue to leverage a competitive advantage?

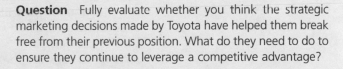

Source: adapted from Curtis, J. (2003) 'Toyota turnaround', *Marketing*, 16 October

Given the changes in the marketing environment discussed above and the changes wrought by the growth of e-business, the greater pace of competition, shorter product, market and brand life cycles, and the consequent more intensive search for competitive advantage, it is almost inevitable that at some stage a majority of marketing managers will be faced with the problems that breakpoints create.

According to Wilson and Gilligan (2004), breakpoints can be created by a variety of factors, including:

- Technological breakthroughs which provide the innovative organisation with a major competitive advantage but which, in turn, put competitors at a disadvantage.
- The economic cycle which, in a downturn, forces a radical rethink of the product and how it is to be marketed.
- A new source of supply which offers scope for major reductions in cost;
- Changes in government policy.
- Shifts in customer values and/or expectations.
- The identification by one company of new business opportunities, with the result that there is a divergence in competitors' responses and behaviour as they try to work out how best to exploit these opportunities.
- Shifts within the distribution network which lead to changes in the balance of power between manufacturers and retailers and very different sets of expectations.
- New entrants to the market who bring with them different sets of skills and expectations, as well as a different perspective.
- Declining returns which force a radical rethink of how the company is operating and how it should develop in the future.

All of the above factors could lead to breakpoints occurring, which according to Strebel (1996) could be one of two types:

Divergent breakpoints, which are associated with sharply increasing variety in the competitive offerings and consequently higher value for the customer.

Convergent breakpoints, which are the result of improvements in the systems and processes used to deliver the offerings, with these then being reflected in lower delivered costs.

The capability to identify potential breakpoints is one of the reasons why the organisational learning ability of a company is so vital if a company is to have the ability to sustain its company value over time. Successful companies recognise the strategic significance of market breakpoints and, where possible, create them in order to gain competitive advantage. Dell Computers created a breakpoint in the computer industry by revolutionising the design-build processes as did Southwestern Airlines in the USA and easyJet and Ryanair in Europe by the introduction of no frills airlines. It is a company's learning capability that will ensure the signals for such breakpoints are identified and evaluated and the culture of the company is open to the possible strategic changes such learning may require. In organisations with a closed culture which is not oriented to the marketplace, such signals may be viewed as largely irrelevant to their market domain. The defining of market boundaries and the identity of the market domain in which a company operates is something we will look at more closely in Chapter 3. In the following section we will discuss the importance of a company's core purpose in breaking free and in shaping the decisions that are made.

CORE VALUES AND CORE PURPOSE

Collins and Porras (1998; see also Collins 2000), in their six year longitudinal study of high performing companies in the USA, found that businesses with long standing reputations for business excellence had a strong **core ideology**. The ideology, they suggest, consists of three components: core values, core purpose and an envisioned future.

Core values are defined as being 'a small set of guiding principles that require no external justification, they have intrinsic value and importance to those inside the organisation' (Collins and Porras 1998, p. 223). These core values could relate to the expertise the company has, its commitment to innovation, reliability, customer focus or perhaps product leadership. Collins and Porras propose that the values and principles held by the firm are critical in creating the climate in which business strategies can develop, and it is these values that underpin the *core purpose* developed by the firm.

The *core purpose* is seen to be the fundamental reason for being a company, the reason the firm exists. Collins and Porras view an effective purpose as reflecting the importance people attach to the company's work, 'the purpose gets to the deeper reasons for an organisation's existence beyond just making money . . . like a guiding star on the horizon, forever pursued but never reached' (1997, p.224).The core purpose of the firm plays an important role in defining the direction of a firm's strategy and therefore guides the strategic decisions made by a company.

The envisioned future is viewed as the defining direction of the firm's strategy, a view of the future that comprises of BHAGs (big hairy audacious goals). These are not measurable or even perhaps achievable marketing objectives but they are important in establishing the ambitions of the company and its vision of the future. To be meaningful of course, such BHAGs need to be shared by all the employees of an organisation.

The role of the core ideology of an organisation not only establishes the strategic base for any future marketing decisions but also acts to unify and motivate the members of the organisation. The core ideology therefore has implications for how strategic marketing decisions should be led by the executive and it will also determine the orientation of the company to its strategic decision making processes.

Leadership

The formulation of a core ideology for a company has implications for the role of the executive team responsible for making strategic marketing decisions, in terms of the leadership it offers. If a strong core ideology is to be developed which unifies and motivates the members of the organisation then according to Grant (2002) the key responsibilities of the executive are to:

- Clarify the shared vision and core values of the organisation.
- Enrich the culture of the organisation.
- Develop alignment between the different business functions.
- Promote the understanding and interpretation of information within the context of the shared vision.

Grant then goes on to suggest that in today's organisations executives need *emotional intelligence* if they are to have the skills that such a role requires. These skills comprise of:

> *Self awareness*: a positive self-worth and an ability to assess one's own strengths and weaknesses.

Self-management: in terms of integrity, conscientiousness, initiative and achievement orientation.

Social awareness: an ability to empathise, read the organisation and recognise customer needs.

Social skills: in relation to inspiring and influencing others. The ability to build relationships, manage change and manage conflict.

Proactive/reactive orientation to decision making

The strategic orientation of a firm is manifested in terms of how an organisation adapts its marketing strategy to achieve a more favourable alignment with changes and trends within its environment. Wood and Robertson (1997) differentiate between firms along a continuum of *proactive* and *reactive* assertiveness. A proactive orientation they suggest reflects a highly assertive firm and a reactive orientation reflects a short term perspective with relatively little value placed on a long term strategy. There is an assumption by Wood and Robertson that a highly proactive company is better able to compete over the longer term and that a firm is either proactive or reactive and so does not exhibit characteristics of both traits. To meet the challenges of today's markets, firms need to make strategic decisions as to how they proactively develop new markets and new strategies, whilst at the same time being equally vigorous in making decisions as to how they should react to changes and developments in the marketplace. This is much akin to the strategy development process proposed by Mintzberg (1973). He distinguishes between deliberate strategy (rigid plans set from above) and emergent strategy (that changes as new market insights arise). Mintzberg sees strategy development as something that emerges through the creative and iterative process of crafting a strategy of proactively seeking new opportunities whilst reacting to the challenges faced in the marketplace, stating that strategy 'is developed through long experience and commitment. Formulation and implementation merge into the fluid process of learning through which creative strategies emerge'. Strategic decision making in this view is therefore a multi-dimensional process. There has to be thorough systematic analysis, but it also requires intuition and experience, innovation and creativity.

In the decisions that are required in value based marketing, managers can be neither exclusively proactive nor exclusively reactive, and in fact at different times, depending on the decisions in which they are primarily involved, exhibit a variety of orientations. Thus marketing managers need to be both proactive and reactive. In having this orientation decision makers can ensure they have the capability to evaluate and re-evaluate opportunities and the flexibility to react to strategic challenges, in order to maintain their competitive positions in global markets. A critical factor in the development of this capability is the knowledge base a firm builds over a period of time. First, in terms of monitoring the external market environment, and second, in the tight management and financial controls employed by the firm. It is these issues the following chapters in the first part of this book are primarily concerned with.

Implications for strategy development

Peters and Waterman (1995) suggest strategic decisions that have characteristics which lead to above average performance and excellence in complex and turbulent environments are:

1 *A bias for action*. Successful organisations show an ability and desire to try things – to respond to situations rather than to sit back and hope for

environments to change in favour of the organisation. Peters (2003) in his new book *Reimagine* sees the absence of a bias for action as the biggest problem facing large corporations in their decision making. He argues that in the world of the internet, speed is of the essence as obsolescence is just around the corner. Companies that plan too much accomplish too little and adjust too slowly.

2 *Closeness to the customer*. Success for these firms is founded on understanding customers and serving them well.

3 *Autonomy and entrepreneurship*. Many successful firms push responsibility and the authority (autonomy) for decision making 'down the line' to product managers and venture teams. In addition they encourage staff to be entrepreneurial. Peters (2003) suggests companies need to be quick and daring and even a little weird and mad in their innovative thinking.

4 *Productivity through people*. Above average companies treat their workers as mature people who respond better to high expectations and peer group assessment rather than heavy handed 'boss' control.

5 *Hands-on value-driven*. This characteristic refers to the way that leaders, through personal example and involvement, indoctrinate their organisations to accept and adhere to those core values that are essential to the organisation's identity and success. They believe it is the responsibility of the leadership to retain the entrepreneurial spirit throughout the organisation.

Doyle (2000) argues that the greater focus on economic value added and the pressure on a firm to achieve long term profitability can be summarised in five principles:

Strategy must fit the environment: if companies are to offer products and services that offer customers superior value, they must be in line with the changes in the marketing environment in which companies and customers operate.

Successful strategies erode: as the environment changes so do the requirements of customers, making once successful products and services obsolete.

Effectiveness is more important than efficiency: success is about renewal of company strategies, not necessarily about the eternal quest for cost cutting, especially if the offerings by a company are no longer delivering superior value in the market.

Speed and decisiveness: the flexibility to make strategic marketing decisions that allow companies to shift resources to exploit new opportunities and so maintain competitive advantage.

Organisational adaptation: the creation of a customer oriented business with appropriate leadership that is able to deliver transformational marketing.

Thus strategy decision making needs to foster an environment where the strategy making is an evolutionary development that is responsive to market challenges, through a proactive/reactive strategic orientation and a core purpose that is balanced with a high level of market orientation. The strategy is then operationalised through constant evaluation and re-evaluation and customer focused strategies are developed which are highly differentiated from those of competitors through innovation and added value. The development of the capabilities to formulate and deliver such strategies is the focus of the following chapters.

SUMMARY

■ The global marketing environment is often dynamic, unstable and competitive, and holds many ambiguities. This is why the emphasis needs to be placed on competitive advantage, goal achievement and strategic focus, in making the strategic marketing decisions at critical times.

■ If firms are to compete effectively in today's global markets they need to exhibit a positive marketing orientation and have a strong core purpose on which is generated a clearly based strategic direction.

■ Over a period of time, through an iterative strategy development process, firms build a sustainable competitive advantage in their markets by designing and delivering superior customer value with a totally integrated marketing effort which delivers value to their company.

■ It is through the dynamic process of organisational learning that firms develop innovative and creative capabilities and so enhance their ability to make strategic marketing decisions which ensure the company sustains a competitive advantage over a period of time.

KEYWORDS

brand leadership	operational excellence
core competences	problem solving strategies
core ideology	shareholder/owner value marketing
creativity and innovation	stakeholders
customer value	strategic marketing decisions
extra value proposition	sustainable competitive advantage
financial performance	totally integrated marketing effort
global competitors	turbulent change
industry breakpoints	value based marketing
innovation	value propositions
market orientation	

CASE STUDY

Wise guys – building the Sage group
by Ann Norton, Sheffield Hallam University

From student inspiration to a global company

The creation of Sage started when a university student, Graham Wylie, had the idea of developing an accounting computer program.

Graham started selling the program to the printing industry, using a government grant to modify the software. It was here that fortuitously he met David Goldman, a local entrepreneur and the owner of a print company in the North East of England. David recognised a business opportunity and joined forces with Graham to market the software by travelling round the UK demonstrating the -

products and selling software directly to customers in the print industry. Eventually these customers became the first Sage resellers, providing the company with an important distribution channel.

The company was formally established in 1981 in Newcastle upon Tyne; since that time it has grown from a small business concern to a multi-national company with over 3 million customers worldwide, and over 5500 employees. The company was floated on the London Stock Exchange in 1989, and in 1999 entered the FTSE 100. In 2003 it had a turnover of £560 million and profits exceeding £155 million.

The rapid growth of the company was helped by the market explosion of affordable computer systems in the early 1980s. Sage exploited this market opportunity and adapted its accounting software to be compatible with PCs in both Windows and DOS environments. The result was that sales grew from 30 copies a month to 300 copies.

Today the Sage group is a global concern and the market leader in both Europe and North America in the supply of business management software. Sage's strategy is based on creating brand leading accounting software and related services for small and medium sized enterprises (SMEs). The strength of the company now lies in the breadth of the product range, the reseller distribution channels and the size of the customer base. This is reflected in Sage's mission, which is 'to be the leading supplier of business management software solutions and related products and services to the small and medium sized business community worldwide'.

Growth through innovation and product development

Sage's current product range is based on over 21 years of continuous development and product enhancement, exploiting technological advancements. Its business model is built on developing its product portfolio, adding value through high quality customer service, and effective relationship management. More recent product strategies have been in web based applications to access e-commerce opportunities, and the launch of Sage.com.

Whilst product development is driven by customer needs, the nature of the customer base presents inherent challenges to Sage, since SMEs are often cautious in their spending on IT. One implication of this is that customers are increasingly focusing on extracting greater value from existing software, investing in upgrades and complementary products. In 2003 product enhancements and new features accounted for 37 per cent of the business compared with 12 per cent for replacements and new software.

Sage has recognised that it is expedient to segment the SME market, with larger SMEs having different needs to those of newly formed businesses. At the same time research has shown that businesses in different industries have different information needs and manage business processes in different ways with growing demand for customised solutions. Sage has met this by tailoring products for specific industries including manufacturing, construction and not-for-profit organisations.

Sage has also diversified its product range to increase the breadth of its portfolio. It has found that as SMEs automate their businesses they have needs for other business solutions. Responding to this Sage has diversified into new product areas introducing non-accounting products, for example, CRM and HR software solutions.

Around 95 per cent of Sage's customers are SMEs employing less than 100 people and very few have dedicated IT staff. This is seen as a further business development opportunity for Sage to add value through support for firms that do not have their own in-house IT expertise. The support service is seen as a way of developing relationships with customers, providing the company with an understanding of their changing needs which will, in turn, shape future product development.

The provision of high quality support service is critical to developing strong customer relationships, is integral to the company's business model and is also an important revenue stream in terms of support contracts.

Growth through acquisition

The company's growth strategy encompasses a number of different strands: attracting new customers; encouraging existing customers to subscribe and retain contracts; and selling additional products to existing customers.

One way of achieving all of these aims is via acquisition. This method of development has been used by Sage not only to enter new markets, but also to expand in territories where the company already has a presence, acquiring businesses with well established brands and customer bases.

In the late 1980s, having established its market leader position in the UK, Sage continued its growth strategy by acquiring a number of software houses in the UK, the USA, France and Germany. The aim was to generate more revenue from the customer bases of the acquired companies, to open up new markets and to make the most of further growth opportunities.

Target companies for acquisition are those with a strong customer base and a strong possibility for cross selling. Growth from new businesses has been achieved by selling support contracts and cross-selling complementary products. The acquired companies gain marketing and business development expertise from Sage, whilst Sage benefits from gaining new customer bases and additional products to sell to its existing customers.

Sage's growth through acquisition strategy is based on combining the scale and synergies of the global organisation with the knowledge and expertise of local markets. The Sage brand is one of the company's most valuable assets in entering new markets The approach the company adopts to managing the group is an example of a global company that recognises the need to be responsive to local markets.

In 2003 Sage extended its global reach with the acquisition of businesses in South Africa, Australia and Spain.

Growth through building relationships

Fundamental to the business are the relationships Sage develops, not only with its existing customers, but also with other business partners including acquired companies, accountants and other resellers of its products and services.

The distribution strategy for Sage products is an example of their business model, based on building strong relationships and partnerships. It developed from the early days of using printing companies as resellers. This reseller network is now formalised and provides installation, training and support for Sage software. Resellers receive product training and technical support from Sage and benefit from additional revenue and cross-selling opportunities along with the incentives that Sage offer.

A substantial proportion of revenue comes from existing customers. SMEs are constantly developing their business to exploit new opportunities and to manage the challenges they face from the business environment, such as economic, social and competitive forces. These changes in business often lead to the need for software upgrades with new features and enhancements. This creates high cost barriers to entry and Sage would say gives them a strong competitive position. The company also benefits from its support and customer contact function by systematically collecting information on customer needs which in turn feeds into continuous product development.

New customers come from the large number of business start-ups. The importance of attracting customers at an early stage of development is not just based on initial spend, which is often only a modest amount, but on the development of a longer term customer relationship. The expansion of small businesses often means that their needs become more complex, for example if they move into the export business, at which time they may purchase more products and services from Sage. To gain access to this business Sage has built relationships with accountants and other business partners who recommend and resell Sage products to new businesses, in addition to the retail channel of distribution.

Encouraging entrepreneurship and innovation

The nature of Sage's technology based business means that perpetual innovation is critical to its success, and the company views people as the core to delivering this strategy. Given the origins of the company, founded on entrepreneurship and innovation, there is the danger that as the company grows creativity and innovation could be stifled by management controls that often come with global expansion.

To encourage innovation, the company operates in a decentralised manner, in which the global network of businesses is based on nurturing the entrepreneurship and creativity of employees. Regional businesses maintain a high degree of autonomy, and local management make decisions about product development and marketing. The company has formed virtual teams with key management from its major businesses who meet regularly to discuss and exchange ideas and best practice.

Sage's approach to global management recognises that changes in the operating environment are often country specific. For example fiscal and legislative accounting conventions vary in different countries, hence the need for local responsiveness. The understanding of local customers is vital to ensure the company continues to develop products and services appropriate for the diverse marketplace in which Sage now operates.

So, Sage has come a long way since start-up in 1981. Graham Wylie, the founder, retired in 2003, a multi-millionaire at the age of 43.

Questions

1 Discuss the basis on which Sage has built competitive advantage.

2 How does Sage create 'added value'?

3 What are the likely challenges that Sage will face in the future?

4 Describe the nature of the different relationship on which Sage's business model is based.

Source: adapted from The Sage Group 2003 Annual Report and Accounts; www.sage.com; www.sage.co.uk

DISCUSSION QUESTIONS

1 Taking the two themes of competitive advantage and value based marketing, identify five ways in which an organisation might improve its performance by a more rigorous application of these ideas.

2 In the telecommunications market what breakpoints have been evident over the past three years? Have these been created by organisations or by environmental change? What have been the implications of these breakpoints for strategic marketing decisions made by the companies operating in that market?

3 The shareholder/owner value principle asserts that marketing strategies should be judged by the economic returns they generate. Fully evaluate this statement. Use examples to illustrate your answer.

4 What do you consider the important elements in the making of quality strategic marketing decisions within the overall marketing planning process?

5 What are the main components of value based marketing? For a company of your choice evaluate the extent to which these components are evident in the strategic marketing decisions they make.

REFERENCES

Collins, J. (2000) *Good to Great: Why Some Companies Make the Leap . . . and Others Don't*, New York: Century.

Collins, J.C. & Porras, J.I. (1998) *Built to Last: Successful Habits of Visionary Companies*, New York: Century.

Doyle, P. (2000) *Value Based Marketing: Marketing Strategies for Corporate Growth and Shareholder Value*, Chicester: Wiley.

Foster, R. and Kaplan, S. (2002) *Creative Destruction: Why Companies That Are Built to Last Underperform the Market – and How to Successfully Transform Them*, New York: Doubleday.

Gilligan, C.T. and Wilson, R.M.S (2003) *Strategic Marketing Planning*, Oxford: Butterworth-Heinemann.

Grant, R.M. (2002) *Contemporary Strategy Analysis: Concepts, Techniques, Applications* 4th edn, Oxford: Blackwell.

Hamel, G. and Prahalad, C.K. (1994) *Competing For The Future*, Boston: Harvard Business School Press.

Mintzberg, H. (1973) *The Nature of Managerial Work*, New York: Harper & Row.

Newbold, C., Boyd-Barrett, O. and Van der Bulck, H. (2002) *The Media Book*, London: Arnold.

Nohria, N. and Joyce, W. (2003) 'What Really Works', *Harvard Business Review*, July.

Peters, T. (2003) *Re-imagine*, London: Dorling Kindersley.

Peters. T, and Waterman, R.H. (1995) *In Search of Excellence: Lessons from America's Best-run Companies*, Profile Business.

Piercy, N.F. (2002) *Market Led Strategic Change*, 3rd edn, Oxford: Butterworth-Heinemann.

Strebel, P. (1996) 'Breakpoint, how to stay in the game', *Financial Times*, Mastering Management Part 17, 13–14.

Treacy, M. and Wiersema, F. (1995) *The Discipline of Market Leaders*, London: HarperCollins.

Wilson, R.M.S and Gilligan, C.T. (2004), *Strategic Marketing Management: Planning, Implementation and Control*, 3rd edn, Oxford: Butterworth-Heinemann.

Wood, V. R. and Robertson, K.R. (1997) 'Strategic orientation and export success – an empirical study', *International Marketing Review*, 14(6): 424–444.

BUILDING A LEARNING CAPABILITY FOR EFFECTIVE STRATEGIC DECISION MAKING

Introduction

In this chapter we examine the role of organisational learning in helping companies build the capability to make effective strategic decisions to enable them to sustain their competitiveness in global markets. In order to build superior performance over time, a firm must be able to deliver superior customer value that is unique and difficult to imitate. To do this, firms need to develop the capability to adapt and develop competencies in a changing environment. Thus, the strategy should be one of building internal capabilities, not necessarily one of chasing every sales opportunity.

The starting point of many strategic marketing decisions is the perceptions of the senior management of their competitive situation. Understanding how those perceptions influence the strategic decisions made is critical to understanding effective strategy implementation. The process that links the two is the company's orientation towards the market and towards learning. It is the skills developed by the learning in an organisation that drive the strategic decisions which develop the strategy and the tactics, which in turn generate competitive advantage.

Learning objectives

After reading this chapter you should be able to:

- Appreciate the process of developing competitive marketing strategy as an emergent/learning process
- Evaluate the need for a strong marketing orientation as a pre-requisite to learning
- Identify the characteristics and components of an effective learning organisation
- Understand the role of knowledge management in creating and sustaining competitive advantage
- Evaluate an organisation's learning capability to leverage individual and corporate learning for competitive advantage

MARKETING ORIENTATION

Successful companies maintain their competitive position in a global marketing environment that is constantly changing and developing, by maintaining a strong marketing oriented perspective towards the markets in which they operate. This positive **marketing orientation** has a significant influence on the ability of companies to compete effectively on global markets. It is from this orientation that companies develop a customer focused strategy and build distinctive advantages to their products through a process of adding value, either through product innovation or the incorporation of key services into their offering. This allows them to target specific customers and differentiate themselves from competitors in global markets.

As we saw in Chapter 1, value based marketing suggests that superior performance is the result of a customer value based organisational culture, characterised by managers who are, 'skilled at learning about customers and their changing needs and at managing the innovation process', (Slater 1997, p. 164). Thus attitudes and mindsets are important starting points for the strategic marketing decision process. It is these attitudes and mind sets that articulate the marketing orientation of a company.

According to Gilligan and Wilson (2003), the three key elements of a customer value-based philosophy are:

A market orientation that gives the highest priority to the profitable creation and maintenance of superior customer value and the use of market information.

Continuous learning about customers through the development of formal and informal dialogue.

A **commitment to innovation** that is customer value focused in order to sustain competitive advantage. This innovation may involve the creation of new businesses within the existing framework or the rejuvenation of existing businesses that have stagnated.

Irrespective of whether any or all of these is pursued, it is essential that the organisation develops and reflects a market oriented culture and reinforces this with a commitment to learning.

The concept of marketing orientation can be viewed from two different perspectives, the cultural or the information processing perspective.

The cultural perspective (Narver and Slater 1991; Slater and Narver 1996; Hult *et. al.* 2002) prioritises the behavioural components within a firm and views marketing oriented firms as having:

■ a strong customer orientation

■ a strong competitor orientation

■ a high level of inter-functional co-operation within the firm.

In taking a cultural perspective in defining market orientation, Slater and Narver (1996), articulate marketing orientation as: 'the **organisational culture** that most effectively and efficiently creates the necessary behaviour to the creation of superior value for buyers and thus continuous superior performance for the business'. Such firms focus on customer and competitor based activities and emphasise the acquisition, sharing and acting on the marketing intelligence acquired. It is a firm's marketing orientation that steers the management of its market information gathering activities. Such firms endeavour to have highly refined market sensing capabilities, and so are well placed to anticipate changes and trends in the market and thus respond to them by the development of new customer valued capabilities and innovative products and services (Hult *et. al.* 2002).

The information processing perspective – Jaworski and Kohli, (1996) view marketing orientation as being the 'Organisation wide generation of market intelligence pertaining to current and future customer need, dissemination of intelligence across departments, and organisation wide responsiveness to it'. In their view, therefore, marketing oriented firms prioritise:

- The organisation wide generation of market intelligence pertaining to current and future customer needs.
- Dissemination of the intelligence across departments (R&D, design, manufacturing, finance).
- Organization wide responsiveness to it (selecting target markets, offering products that cater for current and anticipated customer needs).

Jaworski and Kohli therefore focus on the activities that underpin the generation and dissemination of market intelligence. They also maintain that marketing orientation appears to be facilitated by the amount of emphasis top managers place on it, through continual reminders to employees that it is critical for them to be sensitive to market developments. Morgan *et. al.* (1998) likewise take an information systems view of marketing orientation. They suggest marketing orientation is the mechanism for the information processing activities of the firm. This is similar to the view of Day (1994, p. 38), who defines marketing orientation as the 'complex bundles of skills and collective learning exercised through organisational processes, that ensure superior co-ordination of functional activities'.

Like Morgan *et. al.* (1998), Day argued that market orientation was an outcome of learning, and proposed that organisations became more market oriented 'by identifying and building the special capabilities that set market-driven organisations apart' (Day 1994, p. 39).

In their view, therefore, the scope of market orientation goes beyond customers and incorporates competitors. It involves the understanding of customer needs in a manner that allows superior value to be provided; and integrating the effort of the organisation's resources towards creating superior value for customers, as illustrated in the survival of Creative Technology (Challenge 2.1).

Firms with positive marketing orientated values have the capacity to understand the needs of the customer in a manner that allows superior value to be provided; because the firm is geared towards the market it is aware of both existing and potential competitor activities and so is able to identify potential opportunities and threats. As they are organised with the emphasis on achieving competitive advantage, they are able to marshal the firm's resources towards creating superior value for customers. Thus marketing oriented firms are seen to be innovative, to have a strong customer focus, to make decisions with reference to competitor activities, to have an integrated marketing approach and most of all to be able to deliver a high level of shareholder/owner value. According to Lambin (2000) marketing oriented firms are able to build the following internal capabilities:

- Top management that have customer oriented values and beliefs.
- Inter-departmental dynamics and connectedness.
- Well organised structures and processes for the gathering and dissemination of information.
- Departmentalisation or specialisation as well as cross-functional communication.

ORGANISATIONAL LEARNING AND BUILDING THE CAPABILITY TO COMPETE ON GLOBAL MARKETS

As discussed in Chapter 1, firms compete by building superior value in markets either through clearly differentiating their products from competitors, or by focusing on one particular market segment and competing by adding value to the product through customer support. A pre-requisite to this is strong marketing oriented values within the firm. A strong marketing orientation means that firms show a willingness to evaluate and re-evaluate opportunities and challenges in the global markets. They build the capability to maintain their competitive advantage over a period of time, by reacting positively to the strategic challenges faced. Such firms have a clear marketing orientation and the development of their global marketing strategy is a process of reflection and examination which enables the strategy to be developed and clarified over a period of time based on the learning developed. It is the building of that learning capability to which we will now turn our attention.

The achievement of competitive advantage

In Chapter 5 we will discuss in some detail the two principal views as to how competitive advantage is achieved, the **resource based view** and the **competitive forces view.** Firms following the competitive forces view believe the success of a company's competitive strategy depends on the positioning of the organisation

---

CHALLENGE 2.1   Creativity turns Creative around

Creative Technology, a company based in Singapore, was highly successful in the dotcom boom, making huge profits simply from selling soundcards and PC speakers via the web. In the heady days of the early millennium, Creative Technology's star burned brightly with all the other stars, but like many, by the end of 2001 it had all but faded away. However, unlike many of its competitors, Creative Technology is shining brightly again.

The turnaround happened because Creative were wise enough to reflect on their salutary experience and learn. This enabled them to reorient their thinking and go on to reinvent themselves through an innovative and highly customer focused strategy.

They no longer consider themselves an IT company, but a personal digital entertainment (PDE) provider. They have expanded their product portfolio and created a range of new product offerings including MP3 players, LCD monitors, web cameras, digital piano keyboards, optical mice, audio control pods, wireless keyboards and digital handheld cameras.

Creative have focused their research on identifying high growth niche markets where they think they have a high competitive capability. Digital camera sales, for instance, are growing 40 per cent a year in Singapore. The market for MP3 players is soaring at over 300 per cent annual growth.

But what of the future? How do Creative build on their present success? In considering many options to secure further growth, they see strengthening the distribution operations as a priority. The question is how this should be done. Should they build links with retail outlets in order to push retail sales? Should they try and expand their on-line operations or should they look at bundling their products with other fast-selling high-end items? Or perhaps they could go in a completely different direction. One suggestion by the chairman was to open different types of retail outlets, such as fast food outlets, which evidently he is seriously considering in China!

Question   Identify what you consider to be Creative Technologies core competences. What do they need to do to build future growth?

Source: adapted from: Chellam, R. (2003) *The Business Times*, Singapore, 29 October

within its environment, particularly its industry and its ability to defend itself against competitive forces, or influence them in its favour. Firms following the resource based view believe that their firm will perform well if it is able to develop a *distinctive competence* which allows it to outperform its competitors. The emphasis therefore is more on the capabilities of the firm to succeed in what it chooses to do, rather than on the environment in which the firm operates.

The competitive forces approach (Porter 1985) places emphasis on the intensity of competition (differentiation) and the identification of market segments that attract profit potential (market focus). The capabilities approach, by contrast, locates the source of a defensible competitive position in the distinctive, hard-to-duplicate resources the firm develops (Hamel and Prahalad 1994).

However, for a firm to maintain a defensible competitive position over a period of time in an ever changing global marketing environment, there must be a dynamic learning process, within the firm, through which it decides how best to maintain its competitive advantage. Thus, whilst both these approaches give insights as to how firms compete on global markets, they only partially explain sustained success by a firm over time.

With regard to the Porter view of competitive strategy, a firm would need to develop competent skills in scanning global markets to understand the industry forces driving market change, and from that, develop the ability gradually to build a strategy in response to the knowledge acquired. This may involve reshaping the firm in order to build the capability to implement its strategy over a period of time.

With regard to the Hamel and Prahalad view, a firm, over a period of time, would need to develop core competencies, both technical and managerial, to maintain competitive advantage in the marketplace. Hamel and Prahalad viewed the core competencies as being 'the collective learning of the organisation'.

They view technical competencies as necessary to maintain a competitive position in terms of the product offering, and managerial competencies as necessary to help the firm change and reshape itself over a period of time. Thus, learning is the basis for achieving competitive success over a period of time. Learning at a slower rate than the pace of change in a market indicates therefore a **learning deficiency** which is likely to lead to an eroding position in the market and strategic drift. Thus as De Geus (1988) of Shell Petroleum has stated, 'the ability to learn faster than competitors may be the only source of sustainable competitive advantage'.

Over time, whatever the industry and whatever the market a firm may compete in, all industries at some point will go through a period of substantial change, whether driven by customers, competitors or technology suppliers. There is a continuous pressure therefore on businesses to reshape themselves as well as to augment their products and services to maintain or increase their value to customers. It can be argued that firms are only able to sustain their competitiveness by understanding customer needs in a manner that allows superior value to be provided, and it is only by being aware of both existing and potential competitor activities that firms are in a position to take appropriate action to respond to identified opportunities and threats. It is the firms that develop the **learning capability** to achieve this that are able to reshape themselves and so sustain their competitiveness.

Morgan *et al.* (1998) suggest that organisational learning capabilities help firms sustain a competitive advantage over the long term in two ways:

■ By minimising the incidence and potential impact of serious environmental disturbances, through advance acquisition of knowledge.

■ By the flexibility, built through organisational learning, which enables the firm to develop rapid company responses in order to exploit emerging opportunities or extinguish threats.

ORGANISATIONAL LEARNING VALUES

Four organisational values are necessary for firms if they are to be effective learning organisations: a commitment to learning, open mindedness, a shared vision and organisational knowledge sharing.

Commitment to learning: central to a firm's ability to learn is the degree to which an organisation values and promotes learning. It is this that determines the value placed on the outcomes of learning. The more an organisation values learning the more likely it is to make the necessary investment that allows it to occur. It is learning-efficient companies that are reflective, encourage the development of knowledge amongst their employees and see the need to understand the causes and effects of their actions as crucial to their survival.

Open mindedness: open mindedness is the degree to which an organisation is willing to critically evaluate its practices and processes and is open to new ideas and knowledge. Firms need to proactively question long held routines, assumptions and beliefs, to engage in the first phase of learning, which is at the heart of ensuring the company is aligned to a changing market environment. In turbulent fast changing markets the rate of knowledge obsolescence is high; in such sectors the need to unlearn old ways is high, as is the need to create new areas of knowledge. The markets in which companies such as Siemens operate have fundamentally changed over the past decade as have the needs of their customers. To stay in business its transport division has had to accept that it needs to do more than just make electrical systems for trains. Its customers want complete delivery of locomotives and carriages. Siemens has had to unlearn old ways and broaden its operations to reshape its business to satisfy the emergent customer needs.

Shared vision: this refers to the organisational focus on learning. If members of an organisation are to be motivated to learn they need to share in the common direction the organisation is taking. The concept of a shared vision has been viewed by commentators as being the foundation for proactive learning. It provides direction and a focus for learning that fosters energy, commitment and purpose among organisational members.

Slater and Narver (1996, p. 70) view the **motivating vision** as 'grounded in a sound understanding of the market, guid[ing] the business' competitive advantage efforts and [being] communicated continuously throughout the organisation' (p. 70). Collins and Porras (1998), as seen in Chapter 1, use the term *core purpose*. Hamel and Prahalad (1994, p. 73) prefer the term *foresight*, which they consider to be 'based on deep insights into the trends in technology, demographics, regulations and lifestyles that can be harnessed to rewrite industry rules and create new competitive space'.

The importance of a clear foresight (or core purpose, or motivating vision), shared by the staff and management of the firm, is considered to be a fundamental basis for effective strategic decision making. Such foresight gives firms the strategic direction to build a superior competitive position in global markets which moves beyond the short term view of the firms' current markets and is an outcome of the marketing oriented values of the firm.

To generate such a foresight requires not only **marketing intelligence**, but an analysis of how the market will be affected by such factors as government regulation, technology, competitors and other environmental forces, and so requires a knowledge acquisition strategy for the external environment. This is something we will look at in some detail in Chapter 3. Likewise the clear strategic direction gives evidence to employees of the commitment from senior management to growth and development. It therefore gives focus to the efforts to build a **knowledge capability** within the firm.

The creation of a conducive learning environment cannot be achieved without commitment from the top. The executive of a company needs to communicate a well crafted vision for the organisation and personally motivate and instil a learning orientation. Without a shared vision employees may be motivated to learn but they do not know what to learn. A shared vision co-ordinates the focus of the various departments and encourages employees to overcome cross functional communication barriers and ensure the free flow of information between them, thus encouraging intra-organisational knowledge sharing.

> **Intra-organisational knowledge sharing**: This refers to the sharing of collective knowledge and routines related to the spread of learning amongst the different departments in the organisation and their extended partners. Organisational learning cannot really occur unless the company has an effective and efficient system for sharing and re-examining information. The German company Knorr-Bremse decided to focus on the brake business, but soon learnt from their customers that to focus simply on brakes was not enough. It had to develop complete systems that offered its customers more value. This meant customers needed to be involved in the design process and, even more challenging for Knorr-Bremse, it meant they had to share much more information with their customers and external partners than they had previously done. Intra-organisational knowledge sharing is not simply the ability of an organisation to obtain its information from various departments and partners but its ability to share experience and lessons across departments and partners, so enabling the learning to be stored in the organisational memory of the entire organisation. This is important when one considers how much knowledge and learning is lost in organisations by the movement and turnover of employees, as emphasised by the professionals who focus on creating learning organisations such as the ones in Spotlight 2.1.

ORGANISATIONAL LEARNING AND THE STRATEGY DEVELOPMENT PROCESS

The learning capability required to overcome barriers and develop solutions to deal with the ambiguities and challenges encountered, is an important part of the strategy development process itself. As we discussed in Chapter 1, firms need to be proactive in the building of knowledge of the marketplace so they are better able to react to environmental changes and defend their competitive positions in their markets. The focus of the strategy then is proactive in developing the knowledge base and building the resources to react and respond to the learning derived from the knowledge gained. According to Hamel and Prahalad (1994), it is the companies that are not able to transfer their learning to the strategy development process that fail to maintain their competitiveness, as depicted in Figure 2.1.

In strategic marketing decision making therefore, there needs to be a process of reflection and examination, developed and clarified over a period of time. The strategy development process itself is an iterative learning process from which the resultant strategy gradually emerges. A firm's long term strategy tends to be incrementally built as a firm undergoes the process of reflecting on its experiences and responding to the challenges faced. If firms are to build this capability two types of learning activity are important, the learning necessary to *signal* critical developments and trends, and the learning necessary to *reflect*, *re-evaluate* and *respond*. Various labels have been used to denote different types of learning activities, such as adaptive and generative learning (Senge 1992), single loop and double loop (Argyris and Schon 1996), and lower and higher learning. The authors of this book suggest the terms **signal learning** and **3R learning** more adequately reflect the type of learning needed if effective strategic marketing decisions are to be made. These types of learning are explored in the following section.

Signal learning

Signal learning is concerned with monitoring and maintaining a position in global markets. It is the ability to undertake such learning activities that enable firms to generate the knowledge to signal the likely challenges and ambiguities in their markets and so ensure the firm is able to adapt and ensure the appropriateness of

---

SPOTLIGHT 2.1   **Creating a learning organisation**

In creating a learning organisation, a company needs to develop a comprehensive learning strategy which integrates knowledge management (KM) and learning. Integrating learning activities with an effective knowledge management system is not easy. William Ives, a Boston based Accenture associate partner who leads a knowledge management practice, quotes Plato, who famously said that to get good knowledge or understanding, you need a dialogue, 'and that's still the essence of knowledge management', says Ives. He believes that a knowledge management system that foregoes that dialogue simply becomes a massive repository of information that nobody uses. Showing how KM can help meet specific business goals and be of benefit to the user makes it much easier to deploy knowledge management across the enterprise.

Another consideration, he suggests, is deciding where knowledge management should be located. 'Knowledge management should always be part of learning, but if it should be part of a learning organisation is another issue', says Ives.

KM often originates in IT or even as a stand-alone department. It could also be housed in learning, human resources, marketing and communications, research or business strategy. 'There is no wrong or right answer', says Ives, 'as long as you define what services KM is going to provide and what its relationship is to the governing organisation'. Combining it with learning offers risks and advantages. 'If knowledge management is just a small piece of the learning organisation, learning can just swamp it, and it becomes just training support. It doesn't grow into the robust mode that it would if it were a stand-alone organisation', says Ives. 'The advantage of housing it in learning is that there is a similarity of goals and approaches'.

A few years ago, Accenture combined its learning and KM organisations into one organisation called 'people enablement'. The integration process was relatively painless, says Ives, because the two organizations came into the integration as peers.

Collaboration amongst functional departments is also important. The IT department may be responsible for building the architecture but it is important in the marketing context that the decision of what constitutes meaningful information and the management of that information is the responsibility of the marketing executives who will be using the information. Another point of collaboration is how best to make use of existing systems. Often, learning organisations aren't aware of the KM capabilities that already exist in their companies and spend time reinventing the wheel. Admittedly, turf issues can be a barrier here. The business units might prefer to build their own KM system to get it done quickly, while corporate IT might want to control it to get standardisation across the company. Such issues need to be resolved if the learning strategy is to have the capability to link with the relevant existing KM capabilities. Although many organisations are already benefiting by integrating learning and KM, building those bridges and working out how KM and learning interact is still in its infancy.

Question   What do you see as the major barriers to the integration of knowledge management and learning activities? How can these be overcome?

Source: adapted From Kristine Ellis (2003) training.edit@trainingmag.com

the strategic decisions they make. This type of learning is concerned with the traditional activities of the operations of a company. However, it also means companies need to have an understanding of the indicators they need to monitor in their markets so the right signals are picked up. Hendrix (2003) uses the term **limited visibility** to describe when companies cannot see their market clearly because they are using the wrong type of indicators. He argues that companies should use real-time indicators rather than the traditional lag indicators to see through the fog. This is especially important for companies working in complex or turbulent markets.

Signal learning is also a central component to the firms' ability to control the delivery of their strategies. An important function of signal learning is to establish the control mechanisms to ensure objectives are achieved and any deviations or potential problems signalled, enabling advance knowledge to be built. By doing this the marketing capabilities of the firm are enhanced and hopefully they learn how to further add value in the marketplace as Cathay Pacific did in Challenge 2.2.

FIGURE 2.1 **Past barriers and future obstacles**

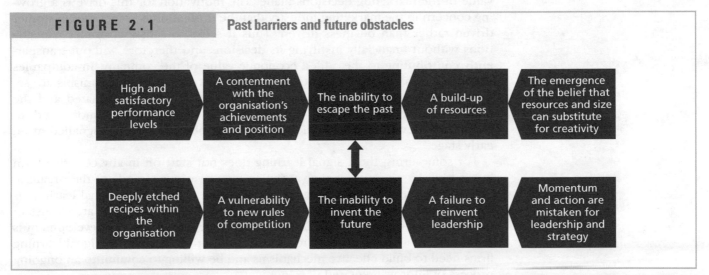

Source: adapted from Hamel and Prahalad (1994)

CHALLENGE 2.2 **Data warehousing at Cathay Pacific**

To answer the question which customers are the most profitable, companies need to have efficient and effective data mining and decision support capabilities so they are able to analyse huge amounts of information quickly. Cathay Pacific have built this capability by implementing an enterprise-wide customer-centric data warehouse. Through this they examine key performance indicators such as booking patterns, travel agency performance, customer satisfaction and customer service levels.

A central aim of every customer focused organisation is to get closer to its customers. Cathay Pacific has the capability to identify its varying sectors of customers and target its more profitable customers. The data warehouse provides informed decision support, more personalised customer service and improved target marketing. They claim it has generated a 300 per cent return on its investment in two years. The data warehouse also provides the basis for their campaign management system. Better targeting has led to a 50 per cent increase in campaign generated revenue.

Question   Is the learning capability the data mining warehouse provides good for signal and 3R learning?

Source: adapted from: 'Meeting Demand' *Marketing Business*, January 2004

Another important function of signal learning is to help marketing managers develop the mechanisms through which they can justify the marketing investments made and so show how they contribute to shareholder/owner value. If marketing managers are to deliver marketing strategies that are accountable, and where the marketing investments made can be shown to add value to the organisation, then signal learning is a necessary activity, as we will examine further in Chapter 4. It is through efficient monitoring and control procedures that companies can not only gain advance knowledge of potential problems in the market but also provide visibility in the performance rates achieved in the implementation of the strategies developed.

However, it would be wrong to give the impression that this type of learning activity is something that comes easily to firms, or something in which all successful firms have a high capability. There is much current talk, as we have discussed in Chapter 1, of the need for marketing managers to follow a much more disciplined process in making strategic marketing decisions. The CIM itself in its push for *hard edged marketing* calls for the use of robust business metrics to marketing activities, which demonstrate to the company and its stakeholders the value of the marketing decisions made. The motivation for this drive is a growing concern in the marketing industry that the profession is sometimes customer driven rather than business driven. Thus it seeks to satisfy customer expectations without financially justifying its decisions and therefore without transparently contributing to the added economic value of the company. In companies which follow a systematic approach to signal learning, such mechanisms are set up and rigorously monitored, investment decisions can be evaluated and the implementation of marketing programmes is controlled and monitored to enable any deviation from achieving expected objectives to be signalled at an early stage.

For some firms, then, signal learning does not start off in any cohesive form but is built by piecing together activities across various strands of the organisation. The process of developing the mechanisms necessary for signal learning is itself a learning process which many firms need to undergo if they are to sustain their competitiveness over the longer term. Thus, just as strategy development is seen to be an iterative process, to ensure an effective capability in signal learning firms need to build effective mechanisms and be willing to commit to an ongoing process of improvement and development.

Organisational knowledge

There are two types of organisational knowledge to be gained through the learning process: *explicit* and *tacit knowledge*.

- *Explicit knowledge* is knowledge that can be displayed as numbers and words and can be shared easily. This type of knowledge is developed through *signal learning* processes. It is through this type of learning that firms build information against which they can monitor performance and ensure that strategies are effectively implemented and controlled. Thus, firms need a clear sense of the key indicators required to gain the understanding to improve and adjust strategies within the scope of the firm's activities.

- *Tacit knowledge* is slightly more ambiguous than explicit knowledge. It can perhaps best be described as unarticulated knowledge, hard to formalise and difficult to express. Tacit knowledge is developed by an individual's or an organisation's insights, beliefs, values and perspectives developed over time and therefore is more akin to the type of knowledge developed through what we have termed *3R learning*.

At the heart of Hamel and Prahalad's (1994) thinking on strategy is the idea that, in order to cope with the demands of the future, managers need to make a series of fundamental changes to the way they think. The starting point in this process, they suggest, involves getting off the treadmill of day-to-day activities and moving away from existing patterns of thought. A fundamental part of this involves managers 'learning to forget'. In other words, managers need to recognise that, by adhering to the old but possibly successful formulae and to the existing cultural paradigms, failure is almost certain. There needs to be an emphasis upon a series of steps including:

- Competing for industry foresight by identifying how the market will or can be encouraged to develop.
- Developing the skills and structures within the firm that will be needed in order to compete in the new environment.
- Ensuring the organisation's resources are focused, developed and exploited to the full.
- Developing a clear understanding of the core competencies the firm has now and will need in the future.

To achieve this a firm needs the capabilities inherent in 3R learning.

3R learning

3R learning (reflect, re-evaluate and respond) occurs in anticipation of, or in response to, critical events occurring in a firm's markets. It is this type of learning that firms who successfully reinvent themselves undergo in reflecting on the demise of traditional markets. Dell Computers, Ryanair and Skoda (see Challenge 2.3) are good examples of companies who have undergone such a process. They were able to question long held assumptions about themselves, their customer base and their strategic focus, and so developed a new way of looking at the world. Thus, it is not merely about adaptation, but challenging traditional assumptions, reflecting, evaluating the new learning and responding with newly developed strategic thinking.

Costa Markides, in *Marketing Business* (January 2004), argues that the role of marketing is to guide an organisation towards strategic innovation. He raises concerns that too many companies focus simply on incremental innovation, which is no defence against the newcomers that move in and win by breaking all the established rules. Many firms operate in dynamic global environments which can undergo periods of rapid change. In recent years we have seen this in the airline market, electronics and the high tech industries. Firms in these markets experience intensive phases of learning where in order to survive they have to find new ways of competing to maintain their differentiated competitive advantage in the market. In such cases firms have only been able to maintain their competitive advantage through speedy and effective learning through which they have developed new marketing strategies to maintain their competitiveness. Siemens completely reshaped its ailing medical equipment business to maintain its market leadership. In reshaping its business, the entire organisation changed from being focused on functions to being focused on customers. Response times to customers as well as the effectiveness of collaboration among staff are now key determinants of performance.

Important to this learning process is the ability to acquire knowledge, reflect and then generalise those experiences in the new competitive situation. 3R learning, it is suggested, is the type of learning required by the firm to help it move forward and reduce the magnitude of the impact of events in a turbulent environment. This type of capability enables firms to develop *advance knowledge* of key events in markets and build the *flexibility* to quickly reconfigure operations and reallocate resources to focus on an emergent opportunity or threat identified and so achieve a *rapid response* to it. Stephan Haeckel (*Marketing Business*, January 2004) suggests that in today's markets, companies have to transform themselves from a make and sell model to one that can sense and respond. To achieve this they need to replace the focus on ensuring the steps of the strategic plan of action have logically been gone through, with one where the ethos of decision making is adaptability and accountability. An adaptive business design makes the most of the knowledge built through learning and makes it plain what roles everybody should play in delivering customer value.

Critical to this learning capability is the ability to acquire knowledg*e, reflect* and share that reflection within the firm itself, *re-evaluate strategic thinking* and then *respond* by *transferring* that knowledge to new situations and challenges. It is therefore through the organisational learning processes that knowledge is acquired and the capability built within the firm to respond to strategic challenges faced in an innovative and creative manner. Innovation and creativity are critical components of strategic decision making in any dynamic marketing environment and will be examined in some depth in Chapter 7. As Ghosal *et al.* (1999) articulate, 'Competitive advantage is anchored in the company's ability to innovate its way temporarily out of relentless market pressures'.

3R learning is a central component of building a culture of innovation and creativity in an organisation. 3R learning occurs largely through a firm's interaction with, and its observation of, the environment. Customer demand uncertainty, technological turbulence and competitive uncertainty are crucial environmental

CHALLENGE 2.3   Skoda has the last laugh

The Czech word *skoda* means pity or shame. Thus, on spying a passing Skoda car, Czechs used to say 'there goes a shame', and nobody would argue. However, Skoda Auto (of the Czech Republic), once the butt of jokes, has now completely overhauled its image and its profitability with the help of its German partner Volkswagen (VW) who have the controlling share in Skoda. The company employs some 4 per cent of the Czech workforce, or 150 000 people, directly or indirectly. An impressive 14 per cent of Czech exports is attributable to Skoda and its suppliers. These other firms now account for US$3 billion in combined revenues.

The production line near Prague now makes one of a growing number of world class mass market manufactured products developed in Eastern Europe and being marketed across the pan-European market. Productivity is higher than Western levels and labour costs are much lower than at other VW plants in Europe. Analysts reckon that Skoda is the most successful former Communist company anywhere. Production has trebled since 1991. In 1997, Skoda overtook Fiat's Polish affiliate as Central Europe's largest car manufacturer. Despite a three year recession in the Czech Republic, Skoda has doubled its sales to US$3.2 billion, and last year it made a respectable profit of US$75 million. In 2003 VW bought the remaining 30 per cent stake owned by the Czech government for a further US$320 million.

The growth has been driven by exports. In 1991 around 30 per cent of Skodas were sold abroad; now around 80 per cent are exported. Skoda has plants in Poland and Bosnia, and one on the way in India. Its controlled expansion into Western Europe has continued apace, especially into Germany, the firm's biggest Western market.

Volkswagen's presence in Central Europe has had three advantages. First, it increased Volkswagen's leadership in Europe through the conquest of local Central European markets. Second, it increased competitiveness through local manufacturing and purchases. Third, it has allowed them the possibility of using Skoda to penetrate other emerging markets in Europe, Russia and Asia.

Question   Why do you think Skoda has successfully reoriented its strategy in a competitive environment where others have failed to do so?

Source: adapted from *The Economist,* 2001

factors which demand an innovative capability from a company if it is to survive in such environments. A company that is committed to 3R learning can enhance its innovative capability in a number of ways:

■ It is more likely to have developed the internal competence to build and market a technological breakthrough.

■ It has the knowledge and the ability to understand and anticipate latent needs in potential customers and so has the ability to spot opportunities created by emerging market demand.

■ An organisation committed to 3R learning is likely to have a greater innovation capability than its competitors and to be much more prepared to learn from its failures as well as its successes.

Thus 3R learning is important for the development of new knowledge, building a firm's innovative capability and ensuring they have the capacity to compete in a turbulent market environment. This is something the French winegrowers could perhaps consider in the challenges facing them in their global competitive market. (See Challenge 2.4)

Wang and Ahmed (2003) suggest companies need to develop this type of learning activity by:

■ Questioning existing products, services, processes and systems and examining how they contribute strategically to the future marketplace.

■ Learning how to discard things they have done previously in order to create the capacity to make step changes or even quantum leaps. This is what is referred to as *organisational un-learning*.

■ Creating new knowledge through radical changes. An innovative capacity is developed through a continuous process of knowledge creation and not necessarily the simple accumulation and retention of existing knowledge.

■ Thinking creatively, rather than following predictable traditional paths. Breakthrough innovations sometimes need unexpected leaps of creativity and insight.

■ Building competencies both within the organisation and in the marketplace to undermine the innovations of competitors.

■ Developing creative quality processes to help the company deliver value innovations in the marketplace.

LEARNING ACTIVITIES

Market information processing is a necessary condition for the acquisition of knowledge; organisational learning, essentially, is the process by which information is transformed into knowledge and understanding. Effective learning organisations, according to Huber (1991), are skilled in five main activities: congenital learning; experiential learning; vicarious learning; grafting; and searching.

■ *Congenital learning* is the combination of knowledge inherited by the firm and the additional knowledge acquired from previous experience. The learning that senior managers bring to a firm determines what the firm searches for, and how it interprets what it encounters.

■ *Experiential learning* can be unintentional and unsystematic. For instance, the strategic challenges facing firms can in themselves be critical learning experiences, where solutions have to be sought to specific problems and the learning then transferred to other situations.

■ *Vicarious learning* is the acquisition of knowledge through second hand experience. This can be an important source of knowledge for firms in competitive situations where they have no previous experience. Networking and relationships and other partnerships can be a source of vicarious learning, particularly suppliers and businesses in different industries operating in similar situations.

■ *Grafting.* Firms acquire knowledge by grafting knowledge from the relationships they have established in their markets. This type of learning is particularly relevant to the firms who have close contact with supply chain partners. Information generation can often be a result of interplay between the firm and the partners it has established. The extent of knowledge acquisition through the process of grafting is determined by the closeness of the working practices of the two partners and the level of trust between them. Thus, to learn effectively, the partners need to have reached agreement that joint learning can take place, to have a consensus of views as to what constitutes acceptable territory for learning and to hold similar views as to how the issues being studied affect the individual partners.

■ *Searching.* This involves both internally and externally focused scanning. Searching is the basis for the knowledge acquisition for signal learning and can be acquired through formal research processes. It can also be acquired through the relationships a firm forms with both its customers and other external partners, as well as through internal company partners who operate close to the markets in which they compete. In externally scanning for opportunities and threats, and internally assessing how well the firms are

---

CHALLENGE 2.4   French winegrowers resist market learning?

A major barrier to learning is the refusal to accept the signals the market is giving. Open mindedness was not a value in evidence in the recent statement by Maurice Large, president of the Beaujolais winegrowers' association, who accused modern wine buyers of being 'philistines'. On a recent trip to Australia he explained that 'many new wine-drinkers are attracted to Australian or Argentine labels because they know no better than to treat wine like Coca-Cola'.

France has met increasing competition from high quality wines from Australia, Argentina, Chile, South Africa and the USA. Recently they destroyed 10 million litres of unsold Beaujolais wine, around 13 million bottles.

However, rather than examining the reasons for their loss of competitive advantage in the global market, the French winegrowers seem to prefer to insult consumers and blame their government. Earlier this year their association sued the government over its campaign against drink driving. The growers claim that it is illegal under French law for safety campaigns to discriminate between products; the government, they said, could not advertise against products in advertising campaigns that led to people becoming drunk! The French winegrowers have also failed to notice that the days of the traditional long French lunch where

several bottles of wine are consumed are long gone. It is mineral water, not wine, that seems to adorn the lunch tables these days.

The reality for the French winegrowers is that their product superiority on world wine markets has now been challenged by the growth of high quality new world wines which have the production capacity, the climate and the technical expertise to deliver consistent high quality wines in large quantities at a reasonable price. Australia's wine exports rose in volume by 21 per cent last year and by 350 per cent over the past decade. The French winegrowers, in recent angry demonstrations, refused to acknowledge that international competitors were able to make wine of superior quality to their own, and are angry that such competitors are marketing products at much lower prices, so eroding the French winegrowers profit margins.

Question Evaluate the barriers to learning evident amongst French winegrowers. What recommendations would you make to them?

Sources: adapted from: *The Economist*, 3 October 2002; Doole and Hall, 'Cross cultural segmentation, a case study of the wine market', Association of Consumer Research, Asia-Pacific Conference, Singapore, June 1994

meeting both their own standards and expectations of the external stakeholders, firms identify possible threats and opportunities.

In Chapters 10 and 11 we examine the role of external relationships in strategic marketing decision making. As we can see from the preceding section, relationships are significant in the learning process, especially in experiential, grafting and vicarious learning. The way firms learn and share the results of that learning is part of an ongoing dialogue and an integral part of the strategic decision making process. Effective learning organisations enjoy good relationships with suppliers, customers and other relevant organisations that can contribute to the decision making process. The learning process itself can be an ongoing dialogue with the partnerships established, and firms use this information as a basis for learning.

The learning spiral

Garvin (1993, p. 80) considers that effective learning takes place in organisations that become skilled at 'creating, acquiring and transferring knowledge, and at modifying behaviour to reflect new knowledge and insights'. Senge (1992, p. 1), more poetically, describes such organisations as: 'organisations where people continually expand their capacity to create the results they truly desire, where new and expansive patterns of thinking are nurtured, where collective aspiration is set free, and where people are continually learning how to learn together'.

Thus the effectiveness of the learning process is couched in terms of the learning activity itself and not intrinsically linked to performance improvements within a firm. This seems to suggest a narrow view of the concept of organisational learning and is obviously at odds with the notion that strategic marketing decisions need to be seen to add value to the organisation, and that organisational learning is a central component to this capability. Whilst it is recognised that there may be many outcomes of effective learning which may not have any direct link to performance improvements, there needs to be some examination as to whether the learning activity is a valid one. An organisation might effectively learn, but the learning outcome may itself be misguided. As Huber (1991) points out 'entities can incorrectly learn and they can learn correctly that which is incorrect'. The link, perhaps, between effective learning and performance improvements, therefore, is the use of an organisation's memory of its learning.

Organisational memory is the fundamental result of organisational learning. Without an effective organisational memory, firms can be caught in a trap where ongoing learning efforts breed long term dynamism in their marketing programmes but fail to produce long term market performance improvements. As can be seen in the case study at the end of this chapter, Diageo is seen by the CIM as an effective *hard edged marketing company*. However, its **organisational memory** is obviously very short, given it went through exactly the same exercise and came up with the same conclusion ten years ago, as is discussed in the case study on page 45. So how does the process of **effective organisational learning** work? We propose it can be depicted as a learning spiral as shown in Figure 2.2.

The first stage is the acquisition of explicit knowledge through the process of signal learning, either in anticipation of an event or in response to it. The indicators used by firms as part of the signal learning process inform a company as to whether strategic and performance objectives are being achieved and help generate advance knowledge of emergent opportunities and threats which are input into the strategic decision process. However if the company fails to transfer that knowledge and use it to re-evaluate their strategic decision making, the firm will simply go around on the same track and never progress forward. The linkage between effective 3R learning and sustained and effective strategic decision making would be more akin therefore to an open ended **learning spiral**.

The starting point of the learning spiral could be an occurrence in the marketplace to which a firm has to respond, or perhaps, the acquisition of knowledge prior to an event through signal learning. That knowledge would then be reflected upon and the enhanced understanding would lead to strategic marketing decisions being made which would realign the firm with the changes in the environment. The lessons learnt from that would then be fed back into the decision making process. The learning response would incorporate a re-evaluation of the company's strategic thinking as to how it can respond as it strategically realigns itself to further build its competitive advantage. The learning generated from this success would enhance further strategy development and lead to a step change in the level of aspirations. A more creative and innovative strategy and a more complex network of relationships could then be developed, and so the sustained ability of global competitiveness is achieved. This, in turn, would lead to a new level in the learning spiral and so the process continues. Thus, the outcome of learning becomes the sustainability of competitive success, a dynamic entity which shifts and grows as the firm generates its capacity to learn.

Effective strategic marketing decision making

At the beginning of this chapter we suggested that the nature of effective strategic marketing decision making is rooted in the dynamic processes by which firms develop their learning capability to acquire knowledge of their markets, reflect on that knowledge and develop the organisational capabilities to respond to the strategic challenges faced. Having investigated the learning processes within a firm in this chapter it is perhaps now necessary to pull together the concepts we have discussed in Chapters 1 and 2 and show how, taken together, the concepts studied lay the groundwork for a strategic marketing decision process through which a company can develop the capabilities to sustain its competitiveness over time. As we have previously stated the process of strategic marketing decision making is an iterative ongoing process within an organisation. We therefore see it

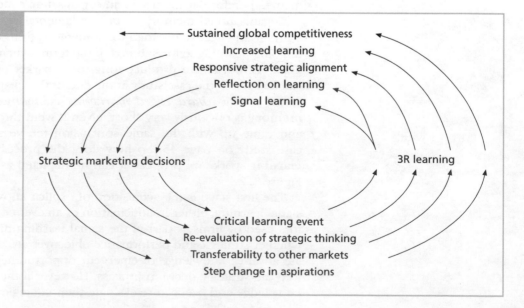

FIGURE 2.2

The learning spiral

Source: Doole (2004)

- Sustained global competitiveness
- Increased learning
- Responsive strategic alignment
- Reflection on learning
- Signal learning
- Strategic marketing decisions
- 3R learning
- Critical learning event
- Re-evaluation of strategic thinking
- Transferability to other markets
- Step change in aspirations

best depicted as a wheel, where all the components have to work in harness together to ensure its smooth and effective running. Thus we see the strategic marketing decision process as shown in Figure 2.3.

At the heart of the strategic marketing decision process are the marketing oriented values of the company that foster a culture of open mindedness, shared vision and a shared commitment to learning. The strategic marketing decisions are made in concert with the iterative strategy development process and as an outcome of the learning process, where the company proactively builds knowledge and develops creative and innovative responses based on a process of reflecting on its learning, re-evaluating its strategic positions and reorienting itself to respond effectively to the challenges identified. The outcome is effective strategic marketing decisions which offer superior value to customers and give

FIGURE 2.3 The strategic marketing decision wheel

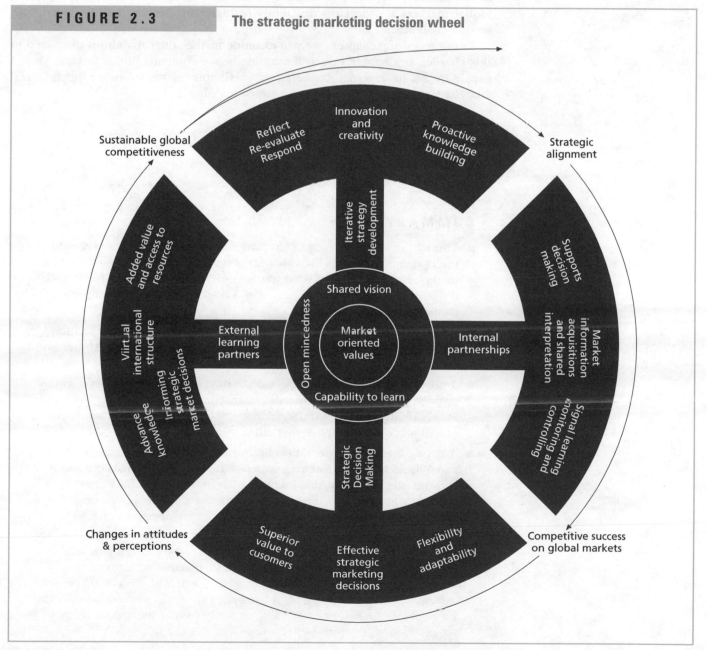

Source: Doole (2004)

them the flexibility and adaptability to respond to challenges over time. Such a capability is built from a supporting structure of internal and external partnerships which build and share the knowledge management gained through signal and 3R learning. It is the organisational learning processes that provide the dynamics within firms to manage effectively the interplay between the strategies of the firm and the global marketing environment. The external partners in the environment are important in that they provide a vehicle through which a company can build a virtual structure to the market, through which a company can gain access to resources which both inform the decision making process and add value by validating the decisions made. As the wheel of the strategic marketing decision process then progresses, strategies are re-aligned, attitudes and perceptions in the market change and develop to reflect this, and a sustainable competitive advantage is developed. Over a period of time, through an iterative strategy development process, firms build a sustainable competitive advantage in their global markets and develop the ability to maintain this, even when faced with hostile challenges.

In the following chapters we will examine further the capabilities discussed in this chapter. In Chapter 3 we will examine how a company builds the knowledge capability on its external markets and in Chapter 4 we examine the financial analysis techniques a firm needs for signal learning.

SUMMARY

- The nature of effective strategic marketing decision making is rooted in the dynamic processes by which firms develop their learning capability to acquire knowledge of their markets, reflect on that knowledge and develop the organisational capabilities to respond to the strategic challenges faced.

- It is the organisational learning processes that provide the dynamics within firms to manage effectively the interplay between the strategies of the firm and the global marketing environment.

- Whilst organisational learning is not a new idea, it has not been widely applied in the context of strategic marketing decision making and yet it is this ability which often differentiates those companies that succeed in global markets from those that fail.

- A strong marketing orientation helps build the organisational capabilities in firms to deliver superior value in global markets and it is through the organisational learning process that firms build the capability to make the step change in their aspirations, their operations and in their attitudes to make effective strategic decisions and so sustain competitive success over a period of time.

- Sustained competitiveness on global markets, is in itself a part of the learning process. As the firm achieves a sustainable advantage, the aspirations of the firm in terms of development and growth also makes a step change. As they use their learning experiences, perceptions to barriers change and firms are able to further build the capability to sustain their competitive effectiveness.

KEYWORDS

commitment to innovation
commitment to learning
competitive forces view
continuous learning
effective organisational learning
intra-organisational knowledge
  sharing
knowledge capability
learning capability
learning deficiency
learning spiral

limited visibility
marketing intelligence
marketing orientation
motivating vision
open mindedness
organisational culture
organisational memory
resource based view
3R learning
shared vision
signal learning

CASE STUDY   Diageo – the value based marketing company

Diageo is one of the world's foremost alcoholic drinks businesses, formed in 1997 through the merger of Grand Metropolitan and Guinness. As a result of the merger, Grand Metropolitan Plc became a wholly owned subsidiary of Guinness Plc, and Guinness Plc was renamed Diageo Plc.

Diageo Plc is an alcoholic beverage business with a portfolio of international brands. Today the group is one of the world leaders in the alcoholic drinks distribution sector with a large number of leading brands, such as Guinness stout, Johnny Walker, Cardhu and J&B whiskies, Smirnoff vodka, Tanqueray gin, Malibu rum and Bailey's liquor. Through its partnership with LVMH it distributes Moët & Chandon.

The CIM Hard Edged Marketing Agenda highlights Diageo as an example of a company practicing value based marketing. Since 2000 it has transformed its business through a programme of brand rationalisation and refocusing its business on premium drinks brands. It sold off low value creation food operations, Pillsbury and Burger King in 2001 and 2002, while also adding high value creating brands from the Seagram portfolio that had recently been acquired. The driver behind the rationalisation was the need for value creation. Each brand was evaluated in terms of the value it created. This involved not only analysing market performance but also analysing the real cost of holding a long term inventory of products. Thus the costs of maturing Scotch whisky, sherry and port tied up capital long term and in some cases meant the return on capital was, at the very least, inadequate or, worse, that the actual production process destroyed value, even though Scotch, premium priced, tends to generate good returns. By contrast, drinks such as vodka and liqueurs that could be sold within weeks of distillation created real value for the company.

The consequence of the analysis was a restructuring of the brand portfolio. Diageo identified eight global priority brands, which accounted for 80 per cent of the group's operating profits and invested heavily in these brands. It also re-examined its investment in advertising. *Advertising Age* estimate a 2002 global measured media spend of US$479 million, making Diageo the world's 51st biggest advertiser. As a result of the value creation analysis exercise Diageo diverted advertising funds from the lower value added brands to the higher ones to maximize returns on advertising investment.

Diageo is also causing rumbles in the way it is changing operations to meet market demand. Malt whiskies have to be kept in casks for 10–15 years, sometimes longer. A couple of years ago, Diageo realised that it was going to run short of Cardhu which had seen high growth in the Spanish market. In response it developed a blended whisky which was much the same as the Cardhu single malt whisky. Rivals say this is not malt at all, but a vatted whisky. Diageo is selling it under the Cardhu brand name but as a 'pure' rather than a 'single' malt.

Other Scottish brewers are enraged; usually when supply runs short the prices go up. It is in these instances that the price of the 30 year old Glenfiddich can reach £110. Innovations such as these, they argue, will destroy value in the market. However others believe Diageo's new pure whisky could be the way forward in regularising supply of whisky to the benefit of the consumer, and that the new pure Cardhu could be highly successful.

There is no doubting Diageo's success. According to the CIM (2003), dividends are up 8 per cent, operating profits are up 14 per cent and last year the company returned an economic profit of US$880 million. However, whilst this success is to be lauded, haven't we heard a similar story before? In the early 1990s in one of Diageo's previous incarnations, United Distillers, there was a recognition that many of their brands were not creating value and so the company carried out a huge research study to ascertain the reasons why. In the whisky market as a result of the exercise they segmented the global market along two axes, the degree of sociability required from the brand (traditional, social or extrovert) and its desired level of quality (standard, premium and deluxe). Segmenting the market on these criteria showed why some brands were not creating value. United Distillers ascertained that their brands were targeting similar segments and so cannibalising each others' sales. As a result of this exercise United Distillers then went through a radical brand rationalisation and repositioning exercise.

Questions

1 What different types of learning can be identified in Diageo from the case study information?

2 Evaluate how far you think Diageo meets the criteria of a hard edged marketing company.

3 How can the company build on its previous learning so that previous experience can be used to maximum value?

Sources: adapted from; www.adbrands.net/uk/diageo; www.euromonitor.com/diageo, CIM Hard Edged Marketing, September 2003, *The Economist*, 27 November 2003; *Sunday Times*, September 1993

DISCUSSION QUESTIONS

1 Identify six characteristics of an effective learning organisation and then rank these in order of importance. Fully justify your choices and the reasons for the order in which they have been put.

2 De Geus (1988) claims that 'the ability to learn faster than competitors may be the only source of sustainable competitive advantage'. Fully evaluate how far you agree with this statement.

3 Is marketing orientation necessary for success? Identify three companies you think have a strong marketing orientation and fully justify the reasons for your choice.

4 How might a knowledge of organisational learning be helpful in seeking to ensure that a company makes effective strategic marketing decisions?

5 What do you understand by the term knowledge management? Critically evaluate its role in building a sustainable competitive advantage in a global market.

REFERENCES

Argyris, C. and Schon, D.A. (1996) *Organizational Learning II: Theory, Method and Practice*, Reading, MA: Addison-Wesley.

Collins, J.C. and Porras, J.I. (1998) *Built to Last: Successful Habits of Visionary Companies*, New York: Century.

Day, G.S. (1994) 'The capabilities of market-driven organizations', *Journal of Marketing*, October–December.

De Geus, A.P. (1988) 'Planning as learning', *Harvard Business Review*, 66 (March–April): 70–74.

Garvin, D.A. (1993) 'Building a learning organization', *Harvard Business Review*, July–August: 78–90.

Ghosal, S., Bartlett, C.A. and Moran, P. (1999) 'A new manifesto for management', *Sloan Management Review*, Spring: 9–20.

Gilligan, C.T., and Wilson, R.M.S. (2003) *Strategic Marketing Planning*, Oxford: Butterworth-Heinemann.

Haeckel, S. (2004) *Marketing Business*, December 2003/January 2004.

Hamel, G. and Prahalad, C.K. (1994) *Competing For The Future*, Boston: Harvard Business School Press.

Hendrix, P.E. (2003) 'Limited visibility', *Marketing Management*, pp. 41–47.

Huber, G.B. (1991) 'Organizational learning: the contributing processes and the literatures', *Organisational Science*, 2(February): 88–115.

Hult, G.T.M., Ketchen, D.J. and Slater, S.F. (2002) 'A longitudinal study of the learning climate and cycle time in supply chains', *Journal of Business and Industrial Marketing*, 17(4).

Jaworski, B.J. and Kohli, A.K. (1996) 'Market orientation: review, refinement and road map', *Journal of Market Focused Management*, 1(2): 119–135.

Lambin, J.J. (2000) *Market Drive Managment*, London: Palgrave.

Morgan, R.E., Katsikeas, C.S. and Appiah-Adu, Kwaku (1998) 'Market orientation and organizational learning capabilities' *Journal of Marketing Management*, 14: 353–381.

Narver, J.C. and Slater, S.F. (1991) 'Becoming more market oriented: an exploratory study of programmatic and market back approaches', *Marketing Science Institute Working Paper Series*, Report No. 91–128.

Porter, M.E. (1985) *Competitive Advantage: Creating and Sustaining Superior Performance*, New York: The Free Press.

Senge, P.M. (1992) *The Fifth Discipline: The Art and Practice of The Learning Organisation*, New York: Century.

Slater S.F. (1997) 'Developing a customer value based theory of the firm', *Journal of The Academy of Marketing Science*, 25(2): 162–167.

Slater, S.F. and Narver, J.C. (1996) 'Competitive strategy in the market focused business', *Journal of Market Focused Management*, 1(2): 159–174.

Smith, B. (2003) 'Success and failure in marketing strategy making: results of an empirical study across medical markets'. *Journal of Medical Marketing* 3(4): 287–315.

Wang, C.L. and Ahmed, P.K. (2003) 'Organisational learning: a critical review', *The Learning Organisation*. 10(1): 8–17.

CHAPTER

3

THE DYNAMIC MARKETING ENVIRONMENT

Introduction

It was suggested in previous chapters that in a global marketing environment that is often dynamic, unstable and ambiguous, the firm that emphasises marketing oriented values is able to develop the capabilities necessary to compete and make effective strategic marketing decisions. It is by having a high level of orientation towards the markets, combined with a clear core purpose, that firms are able to achieve the clarity of thinking with regard to their strategic direction and the subsequent decisions needed for effective strategy development. Firms that have a high marketing orientation have the ability to work with customers, build a knowledge capability and use the information appropriately. This yields a knowledge management capability that enables them to identify new market opportunities, offer superior value to customers and so contribute to shareholder/owner value. In this chapter we examine the building of this knowledge capability of the external environment. In the first section we examine the importance of understanding the various life cycles driving markets, we then turn our attention to the type of knowledge that needs to be built and in the final sections examine how companies obtain such knowledge.

Learning objectives

After reading this chapter you should be able to:

■ Understand the role of life cycles in strategic decisions to manage competitive advantage across global, international and domestic markets

■ Assess how product/market/brand/customer life cycles can be managed strategically across markets

■ Critically evaluate the marketing environment in which a company operates

■ Make strategic decisions with regard to the development of a trans-national segmentation strategy for a company competing in a global market

THE ROLE OF LIFE CYCLES

In making strategic marketing decisions managers need to have an understanding of the role of life cycles in managing competitive advantage across global, international and domestic markets.

Market/product life cycles

Whilst most readers of this book will be well aware of what the **product life cycle** is and what it looks like, it is still true to say that many companies do not have the necessary knowledge to enable them to judge the shape of the product life cycle or pinpoint their position on it. Furthermore it is important in making strategic decisions with regard to a company's marketing strategy not just to understand the product life cycle but also how all life cycles, be they the **market life cycle**, the **competitive life cycle** or the brand and **customer life cycles**, affect the company's strategic position in the marketplace. Thus an understanding of these concepts is important in building the knowledge capability of a company on its external markets.

According to Kroeger *et.al.* (2003) an individual company's strategy is determined by the stage of life that its industry/market has reached. They suggest there are four distinct stages. In the first, there is little or no market concentration. Newly deregulated firms, start-ups and industries spun off from others are all present at this stage. Concentration, measured by the combined market share of the three biggest companies, is usually less than 20 per cent.

In the second stage, leading companies start to emerge, and concentration increases to around 30–45 per cent. In the third phase, companies extend their core businesses and eliminate secondary operations or swap them with other companies for assets closer to their core activity. By this point, industry leaders have come to account for nearly 70 per cent of their market. Finally, there are a few companies that enjoy about 90 per cent of their industry's worldwide market. The corporate titans of this fourth stage, in such industries as pharmaceuticals, tobacco and automobiles, tend to form alliances in order to boost growth, which by now has become hard to find. Thus General Motors has 25 per cent of the global car market, but only through its strategy of forming alliances with other car makers such as Fiat, Fuji, Daewoo and Suzuki.

Companies and especially senior marketing executives of companies therefore need a detailed understanding of the nature of their life cycle at three levels: the overall market life cycle, the product life cycle and the customer life cycle.

Wilson and Gilligan (2004) suggest that in markets where there is change or turbulence, the real focus of effort needs to be placed on the market or customer life cycle and not necessarily the product life cycle, as one of the primary determinants of growth/development is the nature of the market itself and so the product life cycle is a function of both product and market evolution. In practice, however, emphasis tends to be placed on the product's life cycle rather than that of the market, with the result that many strategic decision makers work to a product oriented picture rather than to a market oriented picture. In their work on fast growth firms Wilson and Gilligan suggest a market oriented view of life-cycles should predominate. In fast changing markets firms need to adapt to changes quickly, so there should not only be a focus upon those markets and sectors that are growing rapidly currently, or are likely to grow rapidly in the future, but there should also be a willingness and an ability to move out of the market when growth rates slow.

Thus Wilson and Gilligan suggest that decision makers sometimes need to focus periodically upon the market overall in order to identify how it is likely to evolve and how it will be affected by changing needs, new technology, developments in the channels of distribution, and so on. This, in turn, points to the need for strategic decision makers to recognise the nature of the interrelationships between the demand life cycle and the technology life cycle, and how an understanding of the shape and movement in these impacts on the management of products and brands.

In doing this, the starting point involves focusing upon the demand life cycle, since it is the demand life cycle which is concerned with the underlying need. The technology life cycle, by contrast, is concerned with the particular ways in which this need is satisfied. To illustrate this one can look at the need for a data processing capability. The demand life cycle for this has been there for many long years and is still growing. Whilst the actual growth rate itself has slackened in recent years the overall demand for faster data processing capability still continues on its upward trend. However the way that need has been satisfied over the years and the technology used to process data has changed substantially and itself gone through several life cycles, from paper based technology to mechanical aids, to large computers and then to smaller and smaller but faster and faster computers. Each of these phases had a technology life cycle in itself within the overall framework of the demand life cycle. The demand life cycle therefore is concerned with the evolution of the need itself, the technology life cycle is concerned with the detail of how the need is met. There is a need to understand how the technology/demand life cycles interact for a company to identify clearly what type of demand technology to invest in and when to shift emphasis to a new technology. This is not an easy decision to get right. Years ago Xerox decided that the office of the future was a fully integrated office, phones, computers and copiers all in one. For them to stay competitive they therefore had to keep ahead as the technology life cycle moved quickly on. They bought into computers and non-copier equipment in order to gain a competitive advantage. Unfortunately, having spent several billion dollars Xerox realised that the demand life cycle for the office of the future was still well in the future and that what their customers wanted was a Xerox machine that made good efficient copies.

For many firms understanding such life cycles when they are involved in many markets which incorporate many different technologies, all of which are changing at differing rates, is something that is very difficult to accomplish. A decision therefore needs to be made about where the firm's emphasis should be placed.

The competitive life cycle

As well as market life cycles the firm also needs an understanding of the competitive life cycle. At the beginning of this life cycle the company which is the pioneer in the market may have achieved a first mover advantage and so may be, if only for a short time, the sole supplier and thus have no direct competitors. As the market progresses, competitors move in and the market share of the first mover may be affected. As more competition penetrates, the market price competition tends to increase, with the result that the scope for premium pricing on the part of the pioneer declines. As the market develops still further and more firms enter the market, the perceived value of the product tends to decline, with the result that there is a gradual shift towards what Wilson and Gilligan (2004) refer to as **commodity competition.** It is at this stage that price competition tends to be more intense, impacting on the profit margins of companies which may result in some competitors withdrawing from the market. The company that achieved the first mover advantage may have managed to build up a large market share and so have the best cost structure in the market, in which case they may still dominate the market and as other companies withdraw they may take the opportunity to increase their share further. On the other hand, if it is the followers that have managed to build a stronger competitive advantage, the first company into the market may find it hard to compete against them and so may withdraw from the market altogether. This cycle is illustrated in Figure 3.1.

Managing life cycles across the globe

Companies competing globally will have a plethora of such life cycles to manage simultaneously as life cycles across the globe may well be at differing stages. Having said that, the cycles will be working within a framework of an overall global life cycle. Writing from an American perspective, Vernon and Wells suggest that on an international level, the competitive/product life cycles move through four distinct phases:

- US firms manufacture for the home market and have a strong competitive position, so begin exporting and competing in international markets.

- The USA then starts producing overseas and becomes a strong international competitor.

- Foreign producers become increasingly competitive in world markets.

- Foreign competitors move into the USA and begin providing significant competition.

This cycle begins with companies primarily competing in their home markets. Products developed and manufactured in the home market are subsequently introduced into other markets in the form of exports. The second phase begins to emerge as the technology is developed further and becomes more easily transferable. Companies in other countries then begin manufacturing and, because of lower transportation and labour costs, are able to compete effectively against the foreign companies in their own markets. The third phase is characterised by foreign companies competing on world markets which leads to a further decline

---

FIGURE 3.1

The competitive life cycle

Source: adapted from Wilson and Gilligan (2004)

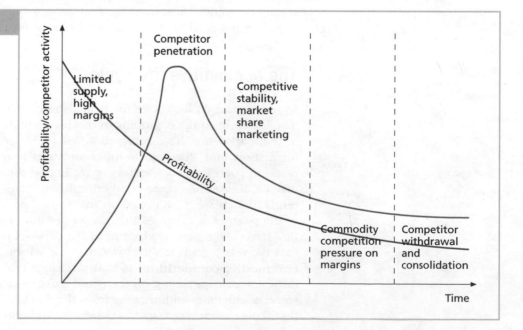

in the market of the original producer. Typically, it is at this stage that the original companies either begin to withdraw from selected markets or, in an attempt to compete more effectively, begin investing in manufacturing capacity overseas to regain sales.

The fourth and final stage begins when foreign companies, having established a strong presence in their home and export markets, themselves start producing globally and so competing against the products produced domestically in the original lead market. It is these four stages, Vernon suggests, which illustrate graphically how American firms eventually find themselves being squeezed out of their domestic markets having enjoyed a world monopoly just a few years earlier.

However in managing life cycles across the globe managers need to recognise that life cycles do not always follow such a set pattern. Competition today in many markets is global rather than domestic for many products and services. Consequently, there is a reduced time lag between product research, development and production, leading to the simultaneous appearance of standardised products in major world markets. It is not production in the highly labour intensive industries which is moving to the low labour cost countries but the capital intensive industries such as electronics, and now services such as data processing and customer call centres, creating the anomalous situation of basing high value services and the production of high technology goods in the countries where customers are least able to afford them. Nor does the model go very far in explaining the rapid development of trans-national companies networking production and marketing facilities across many countries. Having said that, firms operating globally still need to develop an understanding of how to manage such life cycles across their markets. The knowledge capabilities they need to build in their efforts to achieve this will be discussed in the following sections.

THE ROLE OF MARKETING INFORMATION AND OPPORTUNITY ANALYSIS

Marketing research can be defined as the systematic gathering, recording, analysis and interpretation of data on problems relating to the marketing of goods and services. The role of research is primarily to act as an aid to the decision maker. It is a tool that can help to reduce the risk in decision making caused by environmental uncertainties and lack of knowledge of markets. It ensures that the manager bases a decision on the solid foundation of knowledge. By focusing strategic thinking on the needs of the marketplace a strong marketing orientation is achieved.

The ability of research to deliver fast and yet sensitively analysed results across a range of different markets/countries is crucial for effective strategic marketing decision making. In the past decade, we have seen the development of improved techniques, web based data availability and research supplier networks in countries where research was in its infancy, especially in such places as India and South East Asia. There has been an increase in the usage of continent-wide or even worldwide surveys which transcend national boundaries, the development of global niche marketing with differing research requirements, and a rapid increase in the rate of change in the life cycles discussed in the previous section, all of which research must keep abreast with.

There has also been an information explosion. The availability of on-line databases, CD ROMS and the World Wide Web has transformed the nature of marketing research and the role knowledge management plays in making marketing decisions.

The task involved in developing a knowledge management system sufficient to provide the market intelligence necessary to make sound global marketing decisions is enormous. Such a system would not only have to identify and analyse potential markets, but would also need to have the capacity to generate an understanding of the many environmental variables. As such, marketing decision makers need to be provided with an assessment of market demand globally, an evaluation of potential markets and of the risks and costs involved in operating in different markets, as well as detailed information on which to base effective marketing strategies.

In this chapter we will focus upon the areas of priority for a company concerned with building their knowledge capability on the external marketing environment. Such knowledge capability will incorporate three levels of analysis:

■ analysis of the macro-environment

■ analysis at an industry/market level

■ analysis of customers and competitors.

In the following sections we examine each of these levels of analysis in some detail.

Macro-environmental analysis

There are many **environmental analysis** models which the reader may have come across. For the purposes of this textbook, we will use the SLEPT (social, legal, economic, political and technological) approach and examine the various aspects where managers need to develop a knowledge. Such a knowledge building is necessary if managers are to understand the trends and changes in the marketing environment which may impact on life cycles discussed above and the consequent strategic marketing decisions that need to be made. In examining the macro-environment a manager needs to evaluate which variables will be the key market drivers in the future. In other words, which factors are likely to exert the greatest influence on the market over the next one to two years as well as in the longer term. Once these variables have been identified it will be necessary to assess the impact of those factors on the marketing process. The company will need to make an evaluation of what difference the drivers will make (favourable/unfavourable) to their market/product/brand/customer life cycles over the next few years and what strategic marketing decisions need to be made if the company is to maintain its ability to sustain a competitive advantage. In the following section we will look briefly at some of the key drivers in the global marketing environment that may need to be considered by companies in their analysis.

Social/cultural environment

Social conditions, religion and material culture all affect consumers' perceptions and patterns of buying behaviour.

Cultural factors have a significant impact on the way a product may be used in a market, its brand name and the advertising campaign. Johnson's floor wax was doomed to failure in Japan as it made the wooden floors very slippery and Johnson's failed to take into account the custom of not wearing shoes inside the home. Initially, Coca-Cola had enormous problems in China as Coca-Cola sounded like 'Kooke Koula' which translates into 'a thirsty mouthful of candle wax'. They managed to find a new pronunciation 'Kee Kou Keele' which means 'joyful tastes and happiness'. Disney is a global brand but their efforts to make a success of the theme park Disneyland Paris are still beset with difficulties, a decade after its inauguration. As can be seen in Challenge 3.1 some commentators suggest this is due to Disney's failure to understand the social/cultural nuances of the European market.

To operate effectively across the globe requires recognition that there may be considerable differences between the various regions, although there are visible trends that show social and cultural differences are becoming less of a barrier. This has led to the emergence of a number of world brands such as Microsoft, Intel, Coca-Cola, McDonald's, Nike, etc., all competing in global markets that transcend national and political boundaries.

However, there are a number of cultural paradoxes which exist. For example, in Asia, the Middle East, Africa and Latin America there is evidence of both the Westernisation of tastes and the assertion of ethnic, religious and cultural differences. These differences do not necessarily constitute unbridgeable cultural chasms in all sectors of a society. Instead there are trends towards similarities both in cultures and outlooks of consumers. There are more than 600 000 Avon ladies now in China and a growing number of them in Eastern Europe, Brazil and the Amazon.

Social factors such as growth and movement in populations around the world are important factors heralding social changes. Whilst the world population is growing dramatically, the growth patterns are not consistent around the world.

CHALLENGE 3.1   What must Disneyland Paris do to be a success?

Much has been written on the traumas of Disneyland Paris over the last decade, but even after many changes to financial structures and their marketing strategy, the theme park is still struggling. Its losses have doubled in the past year and its visitor numbers are down by 700 000; even so it is still the number one tourist attraction in Europe. In 2002 Disney opened a second park in Paris, Walt Disney Studios, but even this has failed to attract the projected number of visitors.

The company blame their poor performance on the downturn in the European travel market, strikes in France and poor economic conditions in Europe. But are these the real reasons? Is it simply that the Disney magic does not have the same appeal in Europe or is it that Disney have failed even after ten years to understand the market in which they are operating and have failed to put in the necessary investment to serve the needs and requirements of the European consumer.

Source: Disneyland Paris

David Muir, writing for *Marketing*, suggests Disneyland Paris faces a number of challenges, the main ones being that the birth rate in Western Europe is declining and that young children in Europe are getting older sooner. He suggests that this is where Disney need to prioritise their marketing research resources. Before they make any further changes to their strategy they need to immerse themselves in the lives of four to seven year olds. Children between the ages of four and seven, he argues, are they key drivers to sales at Disney, therefore Disney need to spend more time trying to understand this consumer and what motivates him/her.

Source: Disneyland Paris

Question How should Disney go about better understanding the four to seven year old European consumer?

Source: adapted from: 'Disney magic has yet to take hold of Europe', *Marketing*, 27 November 2003

Eighty per cent of the world's population live in developing countries; by 2005 this is likely to reach 85 per cent. Over the next half century, Africa's population will almost treble. In 1995 700 million people lived in Africa; by 2050 there will be just over 2 billion. China's population will rise much more slowly, from 1.2 billion to 1.5 billion. With a population of 1.53 billion people, India will have more inhabitants than China in 50 years time. Europe is the only region where the population is expected to decline.

There are also visible moves in the population within many countries leading to the formation of huge urban areas where consumers have a growing similarity of needs across the globe. The world is moving into gigantic conurbations. The population of Greater Tokyo is soon to be close to 30 million and Mexico 20 million. Cities such as Lagos, Buenos Aires and Djakarta will soon outstrip cities such as Paris, London and Rome. In the year 2015, no European city will be in the top 30 and 17 of the world's mega-cities of 10 million plus will be in emerging and lesser developed economies. This has powerful implications for companies making strategic decisions with regard to global markets. These cities will be markets in themselves. Urban dwellers require similar products (packaged conveniently and easy to carry). Similarly, they demand services, telephones and transportation of all kinds and modern visual communications. It also means that customers are accessible. They are identifiable and firms can communicate with them efficiently via supermarkets, advertising and other marketing communication tools.

Legal environment

Legal systems around the globe vary both in content and interpretation. A company is bound not only by the laws of its home country but also by those of the countries in which it is operating and by the growing body of international law. Firms operating in the European Union are facing ever increasing directives which affect their markets across Europe. These can influence many aspects of a marketing strategy – for instance advertising – in the form of media restrictions and the acceptability of particular creative appeals. Product acceptability in a country can be affected by minor regulations on such things as packaging and by more major changes in legislation. It is important, therefore, for the firm to know the legal environment of its markets. These laws constitute the 'rules of the game' for business activity. The global legal environment has three dimensions:

Local domestic laws. The only way to find a route through the legal maze across markets is to use experts on the separate legal systems and laws pertaining in each market targeted.

International law. There are a number of 'international laws' that can affect the organisation's activity. Some are international laws covering piracy and hijacking; others are more international conventions and agreements and cover items such as IMF and World Trade Organization (WTO) treaties, patents and trademarks legislation and harmonisation of legal systems within regional economic groupings, e.g. the European Union.

Domestic laws in the home country. A firm will have to abide by its own national laws in all its activities whether domestic or global. It will be readily understandable how domestic, international and local legal systems can have a major impact upon the organisation's ability to compete on the global market. Laws will affect the marketing mix in terms of products, price, distribution and promotional activities quite dramatically.

For many firms, the legal challenges they face across global markets is almost a double edged sword. Often firms operating globally face ethical challenges in deciding how to deal with differing cultural perceptions of business practices that are illegal in one country and perfectly acceptable in another. In some countries the practice of gift giving is a normal part of business; in others it is construed as bribery. We will explore this issue further in Chapter 12. In many mature markets firms face quite specific and, sometimes, burdensome regulations. In Germany for instance, environmental laws mean a firm is responsible for the retrieval and disposal of the packaging waste it creates and must produce packaging which is recyclable, whereas in many emerging markets there may be limited patent and trademark protection, still evolving judicial systems, non-tariff barriers and instability through an ever evolving reform programme. Piracy in markets with limited trademark and patent protection is another challenge. Bootlegged software constitutes 87 per cent of all personal computer software in use in India, 92 per cent in Thailand and 98 per cent in China, resulting in a loss of US$8 billion for software makers a year.

Economic environment

One of the key challenges facing companies trying to develop a globally integrated strategy is the divergent levels of economic development they have to deal with, making it often very difficult to have a cohesive strategy, certainly in pricing. Whilst it is a simplification, it is useful to think of the economies of markets as being either developed, emerging or less developed.

The developed triad economies

The triad economies of NAFTA countries, the European Union and Japan account for 80 per cent of world trade. For many firms this constitutes much of what is termed the global market. It is from this triangle that the global consumer with similar lifestyles, needs and desires emanates. However, emerging markets are now becoming more economically powerful and moving up the ranks so that by the year 2020 it is projected that China, South Korea and Taiwan will be amongst the top tier of national economies.

The emerging economies

In countries such as China, Brazil, Vietnam and India there is a huge and growing demand for everything from automobiles to cellular phones. Many of the countries which were seen only a few years ago as lesser developed countries (LDCs) have shown considerable economic advancement. Countries such as China, Mexico, Chile, Hungary, Poland, Turkey, the Czech Republic and South Africa are all viewed as key growth markets.

In these emerging markets, there is an evolving pattern of government directed economic reforms, lowering of restrictions on foreign investment and increasing privatisation of state owned monopolies. All these herald significant opportunities.

Less developed countries (LDCs)

This group includes under-developed countries and developing countries. The main features are a low GDP per capita, a limited amount of manufacturing activity and a very poor and fragmented infrastructure. Typical infrastructure weaknesses are in transport, communications, education and healthcare. In addition, the public sector is often slow moving and bureaucratic.

Political environment

The political environment includes any national or international political factor that can affect the organisation's operations or its decision making. Politics has come to be recognised as the major factor in many global marketing decisions, especially in terms of whether to invest in and how to develop markets.

Politics is intrinsically linked to a government's attitude to business and the freedom within which it allows firms to operate. Unstable political regimes expose foreign businesses to a variety of risks that they would generally not face in the home market. This often means that the political arena is the most volatile area of global marketing. The tendencies of governments to change regulations can seriously affect a marketing strategy providing both opportunities and threats. One only has to consider the impact of the events of September 11, 2001 and the volatility of the politics in such key potential global markets as Russia, China and in the Middle East to appreciate the need for firms to monitor the political risk factors.

Technological environment

Technology is a major driving force in the global marketplace. The importance of understanding how the technology life cycle impacts on a company was discussed earlier. This is a vitally important area as the impact of technological advances can be seen in all aspects of the marketing process and the speed of change continues unabated. The ability to gather data on markets, management control capabilities and the practicalities of carrying out the business function globally have been revolutionised over the past few years with the advancement of electronic communications.

Satellite communications, the internet and the World Wide Web, client server technologies, ISDN and cable as well as e-mail, faxes and advanced telephone networks have all led to dramatic shrinkages in worldwide communications.

Shrinking communications mean, increasingly, that in the global marketplace information is power. At the touch of a button we can access information on the key factors that determine our business. News is a 24 hour a day service (BBC24 offers global transmission and communication of events throughout the world). Manufacturers wanting to know the price of components around the globe or the relative positions of competitors in terms of their share price or in terms of new product activity have the information at their immediate disposal.

As satellite technology renders land cables and telephone lines redundant, developing countries are abandoning plans to invest in land based communication. They are bypassing terrestrial communication systems, enabling them to catch up with and, in some cases, overtake developed countries in the marketplace. In emerging economies consumers are jumping from no telephone to a cellular telephone. China currently has 85 million mobile telephone users, ranking second in the world. Wireless application protocol (WAP) technology allows on-line shopping services to be available to mobile phone users whilst they are on the move, wherever they happen to be in the world. The use of global system for mobile communications (GSM) technology enables mobile phone operators to determine the location of a customer globally to send them relevant and timely advertising messages.

British Airways operates its worldwide 'exceptional request' facility, such as wheelchair assistance needed for a passenger, from a centre in Bombay. The ease of hiring computer-literate graduates by the hundred, who are intelligent, capable, keen and inexpensive to hire, as is local property to rent, make India an attractive location. The cost of transmitting data processing from London to Mumbai, a distance of some 7000 miles, is no more than sending the same information 7 miles. British Airways now plans to run its worldwide ticketing operation from Mumbai. The technological innovations in retailing have led to a number of interesting developments as we can see in Challenge 3.2.

The internet and access gained to the World Wide Web are revolutionising international marketing practices. EasyJet estimate 90 per cent of its ticket reservations are made on-line. E-Toys, a virtual company based in the US has no retail outlets but a higher market capitalisation than Toys'R'Us. A projected 500 million people now have access to the internet, which will grow to 765 million by the end of 2005. The United Nations estimates that global e-Business is now worth US$200 billion and could grow to as much as US$10 trillion by 2005. Most of this is B2B marketing as opposed to B2C marketing. By 2005, 80 million households across Europe will have digital television and the interactive shopping services it offers. All this has changed the way many of us operate as consumers and the way we structure our working lives, as seen in Spotlight 3.1.

The implications of the World Wide Web to global marketing have been far reaching. It has led to increased standardisation of prices across borders and the narrowing of price differentials as consumers become more aware of

---

CHALLENGE 3.2   The shopper's dream?

Retailers are turning their attention more and more to the opportunities offered in the international marketing environment and are also quick to adopt new technology that can increase store efficiency and reduce overheads. In a radical approach to future development potential, the METRO Group Future Store Initiative is one such innovation.

A cooperation project between METRO Group, SAP, Intel and IBM, amongst others, its objective is to promote innovations in retailing on a national and international level. This is aimed at allowing technologies and technical systems to be tested and developed in practice, with a long term focus on setting standards for retailing that can be implemented on an international scale.

Technologies, it is claimed, will render retailing processes faster, more transparent and effective. Ordering, delivery and warehousing of the merchandise will be simplified. It will also be possible to track the transport and whereabouts of the merchandise throughout the whole supply chain. New technologies also hold options for reacting to the consumers' needs with target group oriented offers, providing dual benefits for retailers: cost savings and improved customer satisfaction.

On their website at http://www.future-store.org is a computer generated video of the total concept in practice. It starts with a consumer entering the store and swiping a card across a reader attached to a shopping trolley. This identifies the customer, brings up a screen with their last shopping list and asks if it needs amending. By entering your shopping list into the reader it then calculates the most efficient way round the store and brings up a map to guide you to the produce.

Along the way, the store tracks your progress and messages are transmitted to the trolley as you pass offers that the database suggests you would be interested in. All produce is scanned into the trolley and a simple card swipe is enough to leave the store.

Question If a decision comes to launch the complete future-store concept, what research would be required in order to identify a suitable market in which it could be introduced?

Source: Andy Cropper, Sheffield Hallam University

prices in different countries. It has reduced the importance of traditional intermediaries as producers and customers find it increasingly easy to be in direct contact. The internet has developed as an efficient medium for conducting worldwide market research and gaining feedback from customers around the globe.

Thus the internet offers the opportunity for companies to rethink their strategic approach and reorient their companies to maximise potential benefits in all areas of the marketing process. Table 3.1 gives a brief overview of the

---

SPOTLIGHT 3.1   eBay: Meg Whitman's baby grows up

Meg Whitman has been chief executive of eBay since 1998 and in that time has nurtured its development to become the world's on-line marketplace for the sale of goods and services of a globally diverse community of individuals and businesses. Today, the eBay community includes tens of millions of registered members from around the world. People spend more time on eBay than any other on-line site, making it the most popular shopping destination on the internet. Some US$20 billion worth of goods was traded on the site last year. In its latest quarter, the company reported that net profits had reached US$103 million, up 69 per cent from the same period a year earlier. By 2005, its net revenue is expected to reach U$3 billion and Meg Whitman sees no limit to what the eBay baby could become now it has fully grown up. The company is now expanding across Europe and Asia. Growth is through buying what Ms Whitman calls 'baby eBay's', local imitators who help pioneer the concept. She is currently looking at India, which potentially could be a huge new market to enter. She is viewed as the queen of

the on-line flea market and has set as eBay's mission to provide a global trading platform where practically anyone can trade practically anything.

Many individuals and companies now depend on eBay to reach their customers. Several million part time businesses are run on eBay, and it is reckoned that tens of thousands of people have given up their jobs to make a full time living selling on the site. They often see eBay as a way of profiting from a hobby or other interest. A unique peer assessment system enables buyers and sellers to evaluate each other and help keep the fraudsters at bay. For many it has changed the face of retailing and it has also changed their working lives.

Question   Why do you think eBay has been so successful?

Sources: adapted from *The Economist*, 30 December 2003; http://pages.ebay.com/community/aboutebay/overview

---

TABLE 3.1   The macro environment

Political-legal environment	Economic environment	Socio-economic environment	Technological environment
Legislation regulating business	Income distribution	Population growth	Pace of technological change
Environmental legislation	Disposable income	Age mix	Government incentives and investment in technology
Employment law	Money supply	Population mobility	
Monopolies legislation etc.	Taxation	Income distribution	R&D budgets/management
Foreign trade regulations	Interest rates, debt, and credit availability	Ethnic markets	Technology-related legislation
Growth of special interest groups	Inflation	Social mobility	Changing telecommunications
Government functions		Life style changes	WWW/e-business
	Unemployment	Levels of education	Satellite communications
	Energy availability and cost	Household patterns	Electronic data transfer
	Business cycles	Reference groups	

variables that should be considered when making an analysis of the macro-environment.

INDUSTRY/MARKET ANALYSIS

The second stage of external analysis is that of the industry/market. When carrying out such an analysis the starting point is to formulate a wide definition of a company's market in terms of both the industry and the geographical boundaries. In defining markets by geography a firm needs to determine whether it is competing in a single global market or a series of separate, national or regional markets and, if the latter, how wide a geographical area can be defined as its market.

In defining market boundaries by geographical criteria, the ease with which customers can switch from buying in one geographical market to another as well as the ease with which a company can offer its products and services to another geographical unit, will determine market boundaries. With the emergence of e-business and speedy global communications customers are increasingly sourcing products from outside their traditional national markets in the search for cheap prices. As said previously, many markets are global in nature and certainly most markets now cross national boundaries in terms of competitive activity. Even if the firm itself is only competing within one national boundary, it may be facing competitors from other countries and perhaps sourcing itself from around the globe. Many marketing managers in perhaps the health service or local government view themselves as being in a national market. However, with the privatisation of many of the functions in their supply chain and in the services they offer, international competitors have moved into these markets. Strategic marketing decisions have to be made in the light of trends and changes in the international environment.

Industry market boundaries likewise have to be defined broadly. Industry market boundaries are defined by the potential of substitute products and services. An industry is a group of firms that supplies any given market. Thus, in defining its market a firm needs to consider also the boundaries of its industry. On the demand side a market will be defined by the ability of customers to substitute a firm's product or service for another. Mobile phones can now do many wondrous things including taking pictures, thus redefining the traditional boundaries of the camera market.

On the supply side the industry boundaries are defined by the ease with which a firm can transfer products and services to new market segments. On the supply side of the automobile industry it has been relatively easy for firms such as Toyota and Honda to shift their efforts from the mass car market to the luxury car segment, as well as vans and trucks. They use the same manufacturing plants and distribution channels and often even use the same engines and parts, so the different sectors are classified as being of the same market.

M.E. Porter (1985) suggests that in carrying out a competitor analysis within an industry there are five competitive forces, the power of which needs to be assessed and evaluated.

New entrants to an industry: the likelihood and ease with which new entrants may increase the competitive pressure on existing companies.

Substitute products/services: the possibilities of alternative products or services substituting for existing offerings in the marketplace.

Bargaining power of buyers: the structure and concentration of buyers in the market, particularly in B2B marketing where business or government organisations may wield considerable buying power.

Bargaining power of suppliers: The size of suppliers in the market and their potential to dictate the terms and supply of goods and services to the market.

Rivalry between existing industry competitors: this can be affected by the size and number of competitors, the level of differences between the products and services and the level of barriers to entry into a market.

In order to carry out such an analysis firms need to ask a number of questions to form a coherent view of key opportunities and threats in the industry/market which can then inform the necessary strategic marketing decisions. Questions would include:

- What is the size and value of the sector/industry?
- Who are the major players (market leader, market followers), and what are the market shares of the major players?
- What factors taken for granted within the company and industry could be changed or eliminated?
- What factors that the industry competes in could be made more efficient?
- What are the levels of concentration or fragmentation in the sector/industry?
- Is the industry growing or declining and what are the growth/decline rates?
- What are the product characteristics and nature and pace of technological change within the industry?
- What is the availability of product/industry substitutes?
- What is the power balance among suppliers, buyers and competitors in the sector/industry?
- What are the entry and exit barriers?
- What products/services could be created that the industry has never offered?
- What economies of scale are present in the sector?
- What are the future trends in the sector/industry?
- What is the industry profitability?

Other important questions to obtain a comprehensive view of the industry/market relate to the basis of competitive activity in the market and an understanding of the customer base. These factors will be examined in the following sections.

COMPETITOR IDENTIFICATION AND ANALYSIS

A primary objective of **competitor analysis** is to understand and predict the rivalry or interactive market behaviour between firms competing in the same market arena.

There is a danger of allowing competitive analysis to receive less than adequate attention when a customer driven focus is driving the market analysis. As important as customers clearly are, they should not dominate the external marketing analysis to the exclusion of other influential groups, one of these being competitors.

The identification and analysis of competitor threats, whilst universally acclaimed as important, is for many companies difficult to carry out in practice. In order to assess the relative strengths and weaknesses of rivals or to track their moves, a firm must be able to identify who their competitors are and from which direction their future competitors are likely to emerge. Managers who simply focus their competitor analysis on their current product/market arena may fail to notice threats that are developing due to the resources and latent capabilities of indirect and potential competitors. How a firm decides to define its market boundaries is therefore a critical decision in the way the company then chooses to identify and analyse the competition.

An important objective in identifying competitors is to increase a company's awareness of opportunities and threats. According to Bergen and P'eteraf (2002), to maximise awareness of these it is essential that the competitive landscape is broadly defined and broadly scanned in the initial stages of the analysis. This will reduce the incidence of **competitive blind spots**. It is also important at this early stage to simultaneously consider demand side and supply side factors which may influence the emergence of new competitors. Thus the analysis has to include potential suppliers of products/services that consumers view as substitutes, as well as those suppliers of related products and services in the arena the company has defined as its potential market. Competitor identification should include an analysis of the degree to which products and services fulfil similar functions and address similar needs in the eyes of the consumer as well as an analysis of the degree to which firms have similar capabilities and benefits.

Having identified competitors it is of course necessary to evaluate their relative capabilities and compare their relative strengths and weaknesses. In order to predict which in the future is likely to be the stronger competitor, it is necessary to assess how their capabilities differ and which competitor has the capabilities best suited to the market needs being served. The Bergen and P'eteraf (2002) model depicted in Figure 3.2 provides a framework for such an analysis.

Bergen *et. al.* suggest that competitors should be mapped against two criteria:

Market commonality: the degree to which competitors are competing in common markets, that is, the degree to which the market arenas of rival companies overlap in terms of customer needs served. This measure indicates to what extent the company being assessed is a direct or indirect competitor. By defining markets in terms of customer needs as opposed to a product/service definition, a much broader area of potential competitors can be scanned by the firm.

Resource similarity: This is a measure of the commonality in strategic strengths of the firms being assessed. Bergen *et.al.* define **resource similarity** as the degree to which a competitor has the capabilities to serve the needs of the defined market, currently and potentially in the future.

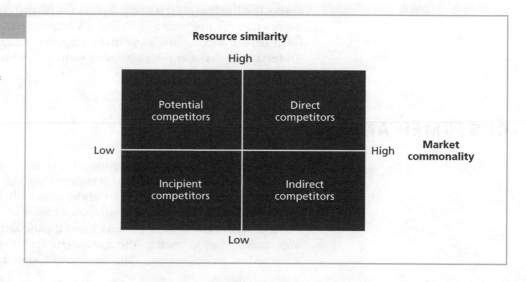

FIGURE 3.2

Identification of competitors

Source: adapted from Bergen and P'eteraf (2002)

Thus it is an assessment of the **strategic endowments** of a competitor relative to the market being served.

A firm that scores high on both axes will be identified as a direct competitor, whilst a firm with similar strategic capabilities not operating in the same market arena will be identified as a potential competitor. Firms scoring low on both axis may be deemed to be on the periphery of the competitive landscape at present but changes and developments in these firms perhaps need to be monitored to spot any changes in resource capability or market activity. Of greatest interest are companies who score high on **market commonality** but low on resource similarity. These are indirect competitors. Indirect competitors are important simply because they are difficult to identify, but with knowledge of a market sector a significant environmental shift, such as a technological advance, could make them a powerful direct competitor; this is what happened when, as discussed above, the mobile phone makers moved into the camera market.

Identification of competitors on its own has a limited usage, it is also necessary to evaluate and rank the competitive threats and opportunities. Bergen *et. al.* suggest that competitors be ranked by **resource equivalence**, that is, the extent to which a given competitor is capable of satisfying the same customer needs as another. Thus if two companies score high on resource equivalence then they are equally capable of satisfying the same customer needs.

By carrying out this analysis the company will form a view as to how intense the competition is and what the key dimensions are. Grant (2002) suggests the following questions need to be addressed in analysing competitors:

- How is the firm competing?
- What assumptions does the competitor hold about itself and the industry?
- What are the competitor's current goals and are these likely to change?
- What drives competition?
- What are the main dimensions of competition?
- How intense is competition?
- What are the competitor's key strengths and weaknesses ?
- How can we obtain a superior competitive position?

A function of competitor analysis is to try to predict the strategic marketing decision a competitor will initiate and how the competitor may respond to the marketing decisions made by the firm carrying out the analysis and other competitors in the market. A company who can make this evaluation is then in a position to assess the likely critical success factors for its own company and so make the optimum strategic marketing decisions to achieve the superior competitive position. Of course if a company is to make effective strategic decisions it also needs to understand what it is the customers want and who they are.

CUSTOMER ANALYSIS

To survive and prosper a firm must survive the competition, but primarily it has to supply products and services which deliver the superior value required by its customers. It therefore needs to understand what its customers want and who its customers are. An energy company based in the UK decided it needed to build closer relationships with its most loyal customers and so sent them greetings cards. Unfortunately the campaign failed and many of the cards were returned as undeliverable. The company found to its surprise that many of its most valuable customers were, in fact, streetlights – with addresses at the local sub-stations.

Central to the success of any commercial enterprise is the organisation's relationship with its customers. If an organisation is to be truly **consumer oriented** then the analysis and understanding of its customers is of paramount importance. Without customers, businesses cannot operate. Meeting the needs of customers more effectively than competitors is central to a business if it is to achieve any advantages over its competitors and so survive in the marketplace. It is for this reason that *Playboy* magazine use a Mantrack study to monitor trends in their customer base (see Challenge 3.3).

In order to meet the needs of the customer a company needs to know who their existing and potential customers are and understand their current and emergent needs.

In principle there are two main types of customers, the individual/family customers, often referred to as business to consumer (B2C) and organisational customers. However there are several different types of organisational customers, principally business to business (B2B), business to government (B2G), not-for-profit organisations and internal customers. Internal customers are those who buy products and services supplied by another department within the organisation or perhaps another subsidiary in a larger company. A customer operating in an organisational environment can differ from the individual customer in a number of ways:

CHALLENGE 3.3 *Playboy* uses qualitative research to identify customer trends

Playboy, one of the world's leading men's magazines, monitors men's attitudes and behaviour through the Mantrack study, which is carried out twice a year to identify emerging consumer trends. The study uses focus groups to encourage dynamic and interactive thinking in the group discussions. The groups are organised on the basis of age (18–24, 25–34 and 35–49). This gives a clearer picture of generational differences and it was thought men together in the same age group would more readily be active in group discussions. A separate focus group called 'trendsetters', for men aged 18–29 was also held. The trendsetters were viewed as being ahead of mainstream consumers in creating and adopting new ideas, behaviours and products. To find the trendsetters, respondents were screened as to how readily they tried new things and took on board new ideas in several different areas. They all went out frequently and generally viewed themselves as being 'ahead on trends'. All the focus groups mixed singles and married men, men with and without children, in different occupations.

Each group was asked a number of general questions to start, then a number of specific probes about the areas of interest for the study. Projective techniques were also used, these included a photo sort on role models, a self-pie (respondents drew a pie chart assigning percentages to the satisfaction they get from the various aspects of their lives) and materials for a collage on men's lives. Interestingly *Playboy* found that all the focus groups worked well except for the trendsetter group. In this group the men never connected with one another and, as a result, gave relatively little information.

From the research *Playboy* was able to elicit insights into the men's views on relationships, attitudes towards women and their level of satisfaction with life, as well as an understanding of their aspirations with regard to careers, family life and personal goals. Such qualitative research is seen as a valuable tool by the company to help them better understand their consumer and so help them to market more effectively to men as well as using the research to identify new opportunities. An added bonus is the buzz carrying out the research causes in the media and in the advertising community twice a year.

Question How valuable do you think such research is? Why do you think the trendsetter focus group did not work as well as the groups split on the basis of age?

Source: adapted from Langer, J. (2001) *The Mirrored Window: Focus Groups from a Moderator's Point of View*, Ithaca, NY: Paramount Publishing

- They generally go through a more complex buying process.
- The purchases they make may be infrequent or one-offs.
- The decision to buy can be postponed indefinitely.
- The demand for products and services is derived from their clients and the end users.
- Traditionally they have been highly concentrated either geographically or by industrial sector.
- Lead and delivery times are of paramount importance.

B2B customers are usually concerned with obtaining inputs to create an added value in either goods or services that flow down the supply chain. In the purchasing of products this means B2B customers are usually either manufacturers or intermediaries in the supply chain who will either add value to the product or sell it on to the next link in the supply chain. This means, in buying products and services, added value for them would incorporate such factors as: delivery time, ordering convenience, reliability and frequency of supply, product quality and after-sales support as well as the depth of relationship with the supplier.

Whatever the type of B2B customer, we can discern from the above that B2B customers have a number of special characteristics. First, both B2B buyers and sellers are usually active participants in the buying process. The process is one of active negotiation on both sides. This can differ from the individual customer, where impulse purchases or purchases made in response to aggressive advertising are much more common. Second, B2B customers are much more likely to form a long term relationship with their suppliers which can in some cases be sustained over a long period of time. However, the nature and the strength of this relationship may well depend of the characteristics of the buying problem itself. If the purchase is perceived as highly important to the buyer and they are reliant on the seller's capabilities to help them solve the buying problem, the relationship will be stronger and closer than more routine purchases, which are not seen as problematic and where the buyer feels they have the capability of making the correct purchase decision.

However non-business organisations are also customers. In many countries in the European Union, the government is the biggest buyer of products and services, far larger than any individual consumer or business buyer. Governments (B2G customers) buy a wide range of goods and services: roads, education, military, health and welfare.

It has been estimated that 20 per cent of the gross domestic product of the European Union is controlled through purchases and contracts awarded by the government/public sector. In the USA approximately 30 per cent of the gross national product is accounted for by the purchases of US governmental units. For some companies the main or even the only customer may be a buyer in either local or national government. The requirements of public accountability and the need to be seen as equitable and fair has led to procedures in government buying that many companies see as being cumbersome and bureaucratic. It is sometimes only the stout hearted companies, therefore, that persevere through the sometimes arduous processes. As with B2B customers, close relationships are important with potential B2G buyers, if only to ascertain when contracts may be going out to tender so that advance preparations can be made.

Putting the customer at the centre of the organisation's efforts, irrespective of who that customer is, assumes some knowledge of the customer and the environment in which they operate. So, for any business aiming to be customer oriented, the acquisition of knowledge of its customers and how they behave is a necessary pre-requisite of any effective strategic decision making. Part of that knowledge building for a consumer oriented company is their evaluation of how the market is segmented and how as a result of that can they most appropriately position themselves in the segments they decide to target.

MARKETING SEGMENTATION

Having built up a picture of the market environment and the customers within it, the manager must now consider how that market is structured in terms of potential market opportunity. In assessing how the market is structured the company is deciding its **marketing segmentation** strategy. How a company approaches this task is important in enabling it to seek out strategic options, to decide how best to target customers and how to position themselves as offering superior value to customers, and to make the maximum use of any superior competitive advantage they possess.

Market segmentation is the strategy by which a firm partitions a market into sub-markets or segments likely to manifest similar responses to marketing inputs. Most readers will have come across the term before; marketing segmentation is a well known marketing concept, but strangely one of the least well understood of all marketing terms. Yet, when used correctly, a company's segmentation strategy can be the source of significant competitive advantage and provide the basis on which marketing activities can be adapted, focused or differentiated in order to address the needs of each segment identified. The aim is to identify the markets on which a company can concentrate its resources and efforts so that it can achieve maximum penetration of that market, rather than perhaps going for a market spreading strategy where it aims to achieve a presence, however small, in as many markets as possible. The first stage of segmentation analysis is to make a decision as to the basis on which the segmentation strategy would be developed. The various variables that can be used as a basis for a segmentation analysis are as follows.

Geographical variables

In global marketing the traditional practice is to use a country based classification system as a basis for classifying markets. The business portfolio matrix is indicative of the approach taken by many companies. In this, markets are classified in three categories, primary, secondary and tertiary markets, as a consequence of evaluating the level of attractiveness of the markets and the strength of the company's competitive capability in them.

Primary markets. These markets indicate the best opportunities for long term strategic development and would score high on both criteria. Companies may want to establish a thorough knowledge capability of these markets.

Secondary markets. These are the markets where opportunities are identified but competitor/economic risk is perceived as being too high to make long term irrevocable commitments. These markets would be handled in a more pragmatic way due to the potential risks identified.

Tertiary markets. These are the catch-what-you-can markets. These markets will be perceived as high risk and so the allocation of resources will be minimal. Objectives in such markets would be short term and opportunistic, companies would give no real commitment.

This is a particularly useful segmentation basis for companies operating in a portfolio of markets to help them prioritise market opportunity.

Level of market development

Another segmentation basis by which marketing opportunities can be identified and prioritised to divides the market by level of maturity on the market life cycle. This could give rise to three types of market opportunities:

Existing markets. Here customer's needs are already serviced by existing suppliers. The competitive activity is intense but there is a well developed infrastructure supporting the market. It may be difficult for new entrants to make an impact on the market unless they are able to offer a clear superiority of value or have a totally new innovative concept to offer the market.

Latent markets. In **latent markets** there are recognised potential customers but no company has yet offered a product to fulfil the latent need. As there is no direct competition, a market entrant would find it easier than trying to compete in existing markets as long as the company could convey the benefits of its product/service to the market.

Incipient markets. **Incipient markets** are ones that do not exist at present but conditions and trends can be identified that indicate the future emergence of needs that, under present circumstances, would be unfulfilled. It may be, of course, that existing companies in the market are positioning themselves to take advantage of emerging markets, but at present there is no direct competition. Such markets of course may take a long time to develop, if indeed they do, and could require considerable investment to build the awareness amongst customers of their existence. Obviously the greatest opportunities, together with the greatest risk and potential for profit, are in the identification of incipient markets. The recognition of incipient markets enables companies to develop strategies by which to be first into the market.

A major drawback using either a market or country based approach is the difficulty in applying the segmentation strategy consistently across markets. However, perhaps more important is that it is not countries or markets that buy products and services but consumers. It can therefore be argued that segmentation of the market should use consumer based criteria and it should be the decision making unit that is used as a basis for marketing segmentation.

Consumer based variables

In analysing the individual decision maker, the key bases for segmentation would include **demographic** and **behavioural variables** and **psychographics**

Demographic variables have obvious potential segmentation criteria. Retailers such as ASDA, Oasis, Next and H&M can all be seen to use demographic segmentation criteria. The most commonly used variables include sex, age, income level, social class and educational achievement. Frequently, use is made of a battery of demographic variables when delineating market segments to achieve a more sophisticated method of segmenting the market.

Psychographic segmentation involves using 'lifestyle' factors in the segmentation process. Companies such as Harrods, Armani, Versace, Ikea and Harley Davidson all use such variables to segment their markets. Appropriate criteria are usually of an inferred nature and concern consumer interests and perceptions of 'way of living' with regard to work and leisure habits. Critical dimensions of lifestyle thus include activities, interests and opinions. Objective criteria, normally of a demographic or a geographic nature, may also be helpful when defining life segments. Research International, when researching the global segments of young adults, globally divided them into four broad categories. 'Enthusiastic materialists' are optimistic and aspirational and to be found in developing countries and emerging markets such as India and Latin America. 'Swimmers against the tide' on the other hand demonstrate a degree of underlying pessimism, and tend to live for the moment, and are likely to be found in southern Europe. In northern Europe, the USA and Australasia are the 'new realists', looking for a balance between work and leisure with some underlying pessimism in outlook and, finally, the 'complacent materialists' defined as passively optimistic and located in Japan.

Behavioural variables are often used as a basis for market segmentation. Factors incorporate such things as attitudes and knowledge of the consumer and benefits they seek. The status of the consumer – are they non-users, potential users, first time users, regulars? In particular, attention to patterns of consumption and loyalty in respect of product category and brand can be useful, along with a focus on the context for usage. Perhaps segmenting by the degree of consumer loyalty, hardcore loyal, softcore loyal, shifting loyal or switchers.

Goodyear have effectively used behavioural characteristics to develop a global segmentation strategy and GE Capital have also attempted this type of segmentation strategy as seen in the case study at the end of the chapter.

Geo-demographic variables: one of the trends enabling segmentation, using individualistic characteristics to become a feasible strategy for many companies, is the development of geo-demographic databases. One such database is the CCN Euro-Mosaic. This is claimed to be the first pan-European segmentation system allowing the classification of 380 million consumers across the European Union on the basis of the types of neighbourhood in which they live. Ten Euro-Mosaic types have been identified, elite suburbs, average areas, luxury flats, low-income inner city, high rise social housing, industrial communities, dynamic families, low income families, rural agricultural and vacation retirement. The distribution of these typologies can be mapped by country and across Europe. Given the addresses of a company's customers, the system gives the manager the ability to identify the type of people using certain products and services and to identify at a local level where the similar geo-demographic types are, thus acting as an aid to the segmentation of markets and the identification of primary and secondary markets.

Once the segmentation variables have been selected, the next stage is to map individual segments perhaps using either a two or three dimensional matrix based on the variables used for the segmentation basis. Each of the potential segments would then be evaluated in terms of ease of access, potential level of profitability and size of segment. In deciding which segments to then target, a company would need to evaluate the differences in competitive structure and consumer preferences between segments to determine which have the best possibilities for building a profitable and sustainable competitive advantage and thus form the basis for marketing strategy development.

KNOWLEDGE BUILDING ACTIVITIES

To understand the life cycles discussed, identify the drivers in the turbulent marketing environment and carry out the necessary competitor and customer analysis to understand and evaluate markets, as well as decide how they should be segmented, a company has to carry out knowledge building activities. To generate this level of understanding a company has to systematically manage the knowledge gained in all its analysis. A planned and rigorous approach to the research undertaken is of paramount importance if the knowledge built is to be trustworthy, credible and verifiable. The research process (Malhotra *et al.* 1997) consists of six key stages. These steps are the logical process for any research study to go through in its implementation.

Defining the problem. It is important to decide what information is needed and set the objectives of the research, ensuring it is both commercially worthwhile and that the objective is feasible and achievable.

Developing the approach to be taken. The planning phase will concern itself with timescales, resources to carry out the work and the expertise required to meet the objectives. Also, the decision as to whether a qualitative or quantitative approach is to be taken.

Designing the research. In designing the research strategy consideration will be given to the different action steps that need to be taken. Ensuring full use of secondary data sources will be important as will the use of a pilot study to ensure the development of an effective and meaningful questionnaire.

Carrying out the field work. Decisions as to how the questionnaires will be administered (telephone, mail, personal interviews or focus groups) will be made as well as decisions as to who will do the work and what resources are required.

Analysing the data. The data analysis stage will need to take full account of the objectives of the research and the client's needs. Many researchers will argue that the methodology to be used should be decided in the first stages of the research planning, as it will impact on the questionnaire design and how the interviews are administered.

Preparing the report and presentation. The report and presentation are the researcher's outputs and vital in establishing the credibility of the research methods used and the validity of the findings of the research.

It is not in the scope of this chapter to give any in-depth attention to the tools and techniques of marketing research. However, it is perhaps useful to spend some time reflecting on the learning capabilities outlined in Chapter 2 and examining the type of data gathering techniques used in the external marketing environment that are useful in building these capabilities.

Activities leading to signal learning

The knowledge gathering activities used in signal learning are intended to help the company build the capability to be responsive to external changes in the environment. Such changes and developments could require an incremental strategic response, perhaps a decision to amend or adapt part of the marketing offering or make small changes to the services offered. Ford Motors use their customer viewpoint study to help them build the knowledge capability to spot changes in the market (see Challenge 3.4).

According to Slater (1997), the type of information gathering tools that could help develop the capability to recognise the signals of potential problems and opportunities and be responsive are such tools as:

■ Use of focus groups and customer surveys to understand customer wants and perceptions of current products and services.

■ Concept testing, conjoint analysis to guide the development of new products and services.

■ Relationships with customers to gain insights into customer desires.

■ Customer information files to improve segmentation and targeting efforts.

■ Customer satisfaction surveys to improve ways of keeping and maintaining customers.

However, this knowledge building focuses on the existing customers and their existing needs, and is limited in that it does not help the firm to identify new unarticulated needs or perhaps the latent or incipient markets identified above. In order to develop the knowledge capability that can lead to the development of products and services targeting unarticulated needs and breakthrough innovations, building the knowledge capability for 3R learning will require a new set of systems and techniques.

Activities leading to 3R learning

To be truly marketing oriented companies need to acquire and evaluate market information in a systematic and anticipatory manner so they are able to understand the unexpressed needs of customers and the capabilities and plans of their competitors. To do these firms need to:

■ Scan the market broadly.

■ Have a long term focus to their information gathering activities.

■ Share knowledge throughout the organisation in a co-ordinated and focused manner.

■ Combine traditional marketing research techniques with other techniques to uncover customers' unarticulated needs.

Information gathering activities which lead to 3R learning could include:

■ Observing customers using and consuming products in their daily routines. Procter & Gamble set up a global research study which involved videoing participants in their homes as they went about their daily activities, to help them understand how consumers actually used their products and to generate ideas for new products and improve existing products to better suit actual behaviour patterns.

CHALLENGE 3.4   **Ford's European customer viewpoint programme**

Each year Ford, through a company called Lorien Customer Focus, mails more than 3 million questionnaires in 26 languages to Ford customers in 22 European markets. What they wish to find out is how these customers rate not only the car they have recently purchased but how they view their total buying experience with Ford. Customers receive their first questionnaire a few weeks after their initial purchase, and then annually for at least four years. This enables the company to build a highly detailed picture of the actual purchase, the ownership experience and how well customers feel they have been looked after in the years following their purchase.

The responses when analysed are fed back to Ford management and their dealers all over Europe. The research provides Ford with a rich information bank that can be analysed at regional, dealership and individual employee levels. The detail of this insight enables Ford, together with

its dealers, to implement actions that further improve service quality which in turn they hope will lead to increased brand loyalty. They certainly believe this has been the result. The research they say enables them to signal problem areas and so helps them to take early action to rectify problems. Over the years they believe it is this type of research that has enabled them to take timely decisions which have contributed to constantly increasing satisfaction ratings. As a result, the number of customers who rate the Ford ownership experience highly continues to grow, year on year.

Question   Evaluate how effective you think such research is in building a signal learning capability within a company.

Source: adapted from: Little, B. (2003) 'The twenty-first century business frontier', *Industrial and Commercial Training*, 35(6)

- Working closely with lead users. Lead users are customers who have needs that are advanced compared to other market members and who expect to benefit significantly from the satisfaction of those needs. This is especially relevant in B2B marketing and in markets which are in the early stages of development.

- Conducting market experiments and then probing to learn how products and services can improve or change to serve emergent needs. Motorola and General Electric carry out market experiments as part of their **probe and learn process** in order to refine products and services and to try to anticipate the needs to satisfy in the next generation of new product development.

- Searching for unserved markets which may have either latent or incipient demand.

Creating knowledge through relationships

As can be seen from the above section, partnerships are an important source of knowledge. Companies form partnerships with customers and members of the supply chain, as well as with a range of other partners such as consultants, universities, government agencies, financial institutions and other organisations that possess knowledge perceived as valuable to business.

Customer relationships are an important vehicle for the acquisition of much of the knowledge identified above. In the age of e-business companies work to align their information systems not only with offering customer service but also with capturing as much information as possible about the customer and their exchange with the company. However, the replacement of sales representatives by on-line purchasing systems has meant that some companies have lost the everyday connection with the marketplace. The challenge for such companies is to try and build real connections in what is now the virtual marketplace.

Supply chain partnerships are an important source of market knowledge and are used by companies to gather information on new markets and as vehicles through which companies can identify and analyse potential opportunities. In smaller firms a large proportion of their information can emerge from such contacts. In these companies decision making often takes place in situations that are sometimes confusing and beset by tight deadlines. Managers therefore need to cut short the analytical process as they do not have the time or the resources for more formal analysis. In such cases supply chain relationships are important, not only because they give the company access to information but also because that information is often timely, relevant and up to date, and so trusted by the firm in receipt of it.

Lateral partnerships are used in varying ways during the process of knowledge acquisition by firms. In the development of a knowledge base firms develop a wide network of **lateral partnerships** (Hunt and Morgan 1995) from a range of contacts in the governments of the different international markets in which they operate, financial circles, producers of complimentary products and trade associations. The objective of the relationship is to gain access to specialist knowledge, either to understand better the most efficient route to market or to obtain advance signals of imminent occurrences in the market.

These relationships are often used either to enhance the quality of decision making or perhaps to seek assurances that the decisions made are valid and appropriate. They enable firms to draw up a picture of what is really happening in the marketplace, which is sometimes not easy to ascertain from formal sources, so the knowledge gained from lateral relationships can be important for allaying fears and building confidence that the decisions being made are appropriate for the situation. This is particularly true in global markets where reliable information from the formal sources of market research data may be more difficult to obtain. This is why the knowledge acquired through such relationships is often seen by firms to be knowledge that can be trusted and therefore sometimes of greatest value in helping the firms make appropriate decisions. As one marketing director of a steel products firm articulated:

> The market was telling us one thing; the actual figures were telling us something else. Our contacts were telling us things were heading downwards but our sales in those markets weren't affected at all. So we knew it was a matter of time, so it really proved, if not crucial, valuable in terms of signalling things.

Thus for many companies the knowledge built through these relationships helps to ensure the efficacy and, perhaps more importantly, the timing of strategic marketing decisions.

SUMMARY

- In making strategic marketing decisions managers need to have an understanding of the role of life cycles in managing competitive advantage across global, international and domestic markets.

- The ability of research to deliver fast and yet sensitively analysed results across a range of different markets/countries is crucial for effective strategic marketing decision making.

- In carrying out an analysis of the industry/market it is important to formulate a wide definition of a company's market in terms of both the industry and the geographical boundaries.

- A primary objective of competitor analysis is to understand and predict the rivalry or interactive market behaviour between firms competing in the same market arena.

- To survive and prosper a firm must deliver the superior value required by its customers. It therefore needs to understand what its customers want and who its customers are.

- How a company approaches its marketing segmentation strategy determines how it seeks out strategic options, targets customers and positions itself to make the maximum use of any superior competitive advantage it possesses.

KEYWORDS

behavioural variables
commodity competition
competitive blind spots
competitive life cycle
competitor analysis
consumer oriented
customer life cycles
demographic variables
environmental analysis
incipient markets
knowledge capability

latent markets
lateral partnerships
market commonality
market life cycle
marketing segmentation
probe and learn process
product life cycle
psychographics
resource equivalence
resource similarity
strategic endowments

CASE STUDY   GE Capital – the quest for attitudinal segmentation and targeting

In 1998, Andy Baxter, then Customer Insight Manager for Boots the Chemist Plc, made the following observation:

> As understanding grows in the future, and technology becomes more accessible, really customer-focused 'segments of one' will be developed. The real prize lies in using attitudinal data, together with purchasing behaviour, in order to gain a total picture of the customer.

Boots the Chemist is an international leader in health, beauty and general fitness products, with more than 1500 stores throughout the UK and a growing portfolio in other countries. It has a turnover of more than US$4 billion. Each year the company develops over 1300 products and manufactures 400 million units. It is a major player in a highly competitive consumer market in which segmentation and targeting hold the key to performance.

Indeed, the same could be said of just about every maturing consumer marketplace around the world. Increasingly, success in the battle for share of these complex and cluttered markets has become focused on how well managers have dealt with the challenges of segmentation and targeting. Effective, efficient and meaningful methods of segmentation have become a major source of competitive advantage.

However, in recent years at least, few markets can be seen to have simultaneously grown and fragmented at the same breakneck speed as those for financial services. Since deregulation in the late 1980s, long term trends, such as technological advancement, consumerism and the removal of competitive restrictions, have led to a vast proliferation in the number, diversity and complexity of products, providers and customers.

The doors have been thrown open to companies as diverse as Virgin, Marks & Spencer and General Electric (GE) to shake the foundations of the traditional banking monoliths that once dominated this arena.

Of all of these, GE Capital Bank has become one of Europe's biggest non-bank financial players. With a presence in some 20 fields of business and 21 European countries, it is already a market leader in fleet and aircraft leasing, and in consumer finance.

GE Capital is hugely profitable, consistently accounting for around 40 per cent of GE's total annual revenue in recent years. In Europe it has grown through acquisitions, buying up more than 100 European companies with more than US$30 billion in assets between the early and late 1990s, and this has been a major driver of its phenomenal growth. In 2002, the burgeoning organisation was subdivided into four distinct businesses – one of which was to focus on the highly complex, competitive and lucrative consumer finance market.

At the beginning of the 1990s, GE had only a very small presence on the UK high street. Now, it is hard to miss. If you hold a Harrods, Debenhams, House of Fraser, Burtons, B&Q, Comet or one of many other storecards, your account will be owned and managed by GE Consumer Finance.

One of the major drivers of GE's success in consumer finance has been its devotion to the collection and use of information to maximise revenue opportunities from every individual customer.

Whilst financial service providers have traditionally made great use of geographic, demographic, socio-economic and lifestyle characteristics to segment their markets, GE recognised very early on that these are rarely efficient predictors of future buying behaviour. Although it is relatively easy to identify these characteristics, they are at best only rough indicators of the needs, wants, desires and reaction patterns of consumers.

At GE Consumer Finance, the business is driven by customer information. Data is continuously collected, analysed and stored in a way that enables the company to segment customers according to their card use and consumption behaviour. It is these databases that power the vast and frequent direct mail campaigns that, in the absence of other forms of advertising, underpin the organisation's marketing and communications strategy.

In turn, it is this reliance on direct marketing that elevates the importance of effective segmentation and targeting to its exceptionally lofty heights. After all, direct mail is junk mail if you have no need or interest in the product. At best it ends up in the bin, at worst it can seriously damage the relationship between customer and organisation.

However, direct mail can be a great source of information and influence for those customers who are in the market for those particular products and benefits at that particular time.

Instead of seeking to identify segments with a view to then inferring behaviour in that segment, the databases that GE have developed allow them to identify a certain kind of behaviour and then find out what kind of people are in this segment. New products, benefits and, in particular, direct mail campaigns are then developed according to when, where, how often and for what purchases the customer's card is used. In this way, GE has developed a detailed behavioural aspect to its segmentation. This enables it to tailor its marketing strategy in a way that is much more meaningful to its customers.

However, with such a focus on segmentation as the heart of its marketing strategy, the marketing team at GE Consumer Finance are well aware of a key question that has in some ways been missing from their detailed customer picture – 'Why?'

Just as Boots the Chemist have their eye on the prize of understanding the attitudes, values and beliefs that underpin behaviour in their markets, so too have the team at GE.

They understand that a young, professional woman, for example, might use her storecard to purchase the same amount of goods, in the same store at the same time of year, but for very different reasons. It may be that she loathes the shopping experience, but needs the goods and finds it quick and easy to buy them in this way. It may be that she loves the store, its range, its staff and shops as much for pleasure and fun as for value and convenience. At the extreme, it might be that she is a shopping addict and painfully suffers the after-purchase guilt for the thrill of the hunt and the capture.

Only by understanding the critical, attitudinal drivers behind the behaviour, it would seem, can the organisation develop a truly meaningful method of segmentation through which to deliver its tailored marketing offerings.

A research agency was commissioned to design and deliver a programme of research that would identify and profile the key attitudinal characteristics across the customer base. This research incorporated a raft of exploratory studies, culminating in two major quantitative surveys of nearly 3000 cardholders. The result was the identification of five attitudinal segments, complete with a description of the typical attitudinal characteristics a customer in each group would be likely to exhibit.

This alone was a major development, and provided a useful basis on which to develop new product concepts, but the process was far from over. The next big question was how to operationalise these segments so that they could be used to target marketing communications. After all, it's OK knowing that your customers are likely to fall into one of five attitudinal segments, but how do you know which segment each customer is in?

This was to prove a difficult issue. Beyond surveying every one of the company's millions of cardholders, it was difficult to see how these new segments could be used to target them with the appropriate communications.

One possibility was to profile each customer using a small number of key questions at various points of customer contact, e.g. by post with the statement, response to direct mail, during customer service telephone calls, etc. Discriminant analysis on the survey results revealed that just 12 specific questions could be effective in placing customers into these segments. However, in order to monitor changes over time, this would need to be done continuously.

Alternative work began to explore the possibility that behavioural indicators in the GE database might relate specifically to the new attitudinal segments that had been created, thus enabling all customers to be regrouped. This, however, would be an enormously complex undertaking with no guarantee of success.

Inspiration from outside the organisation was in short supply. Barclaycard had been early pioneers of database marketing and the drive to provide each individual customer with communications tailored to their needs. However, from the outside it seemed that this was still largely based on demographic and lifestyle factors, not specific attitudes, values and beliefs.

Boots the Chemist, a company similarly driven by data and the quest for a truly meaningful method of segmentation and targeting, seemed to be in a similar position. Through the Boots Advantage loyalty card they had established a system of collecting and analysing both behavioural and attitudinal data on their customers. However, it appeared that this data was then used to target marketing communications in a much broader way. By developing characters in TV adverts that embodied the attitudes, values and beliefs of the target segments, they created what might be seen as 'fictional friends' and thus opinion leaders for consumers who recognised themselves, as it were.

Without a major overhaul of marketing strategy, and a shift away from its focus on targeting individual customers with direct messages and offers at particular points in time, GE did not have such an option.

And so the quest goes on. The development of Andy Baxter's 'segment of one' remains elusive. But with the world's fourth largest company on the case, who would bet against it becoming a reality in financial services marketing very soon.

Questions

1 Critically evaluate the methods used by GE to segment its markets.

2 How can the building of consumer profiles aid GE capital in its decision making?

3 What are the five main critical learning issues in the case of GE Capital?

Source: Tony Grimes, University of Hull

DISCUSSION QUESTIONS

1 Strategic marketing decisions are about what to do in the future; how can managers ensure their analysis reflects a future oriented view of the marketing environment rather than reflecting historical patterns?

2 How can an understanding of the market and competitive life cycles contribute to the strategic decisions with regard to brand management?

3 For a company of your choice propose and justify a segmentation strategy that could form the basis of a global marketing strategy.

4 For a company marketing high technology products, what are the major environmental trends impacting on the development of the market life cycle?

5 What are the problems and difficulties in carrying out a competitive analysis? Suggest ways in which the issues you identify can be overcome.

REFERENCES

Bergen, M. and P'eteraf, M.A. (2002) 'Competitor identification and competitor analysis: a broad based managerial approach', *Managerial and Decision Economics*, 23: 157–169.

Grant, R.M. (2002) *Contemporary Strategy Analysis: Concepts, Techniques and Applications*, Oxford: Blackwell Publishing.

Hunt, S.D. and Morgan, R.M. (1995) 'The comparative advantage theory of competition', *Journal of Marketing*, 59(April–June): 1–23.

Kroeger, F., Deans, S. and Zeisal, S. (2003) *Winning the End Game*, McGraw-Hill.

Malhotra, N.K., Agrawal, J. and Peterson, M. (1997) 'Methodological issues in cross cultural marketing research', *International Marketing Review*, 13(6): 7–43.

Porter, M.E. (1985) *Competitive Advantage: Creating and Sustaining Superior Performance*, New York: The Free Press.

Slater, S. F. (1997) 'Developing a customer value based theory of the firm', *Journal of the Academy of Marketing Science*, 25(2): 162–67.

Wilson, R.M.S. and Gilligan, C.T. (2004) *Strategic Marketing Management: Planning, Implementation and Control,* 3rd edn, Oxford: Butterworth-Heinemann.

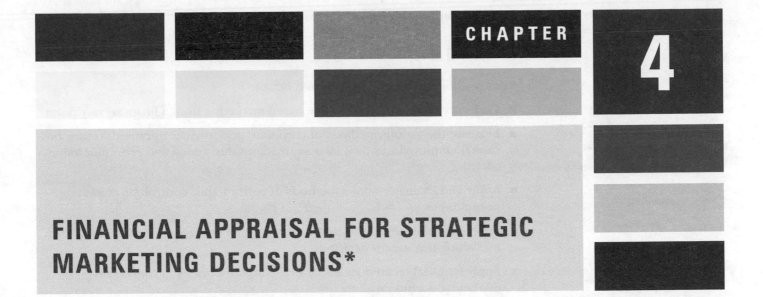

FINANCIAL APPRAISAL FOR STRATEGIC MARKETING DECISIONS*

Introduction

Much has been said in previous chapters of the importance of value based marketing and the need for marketing managers to be able to quantify the economic benefits to the company of the strategic marketing decisions taken. Value based marketing requires that the marketing manager is able to employ effectively a range of financial techniques for the evaluation of company performance and in the evaluation of strategic options in the marketing decision making process.

The main objective of any business is to maximise its shareholders'/owners' wealth. If marketing managers are to operate at a strategic level within a company, they need to develop the financial skills to demonstrate the contribution marketing strategies make to the business. They also need to justify financially the budgets needed in their strategic marketing decisions and to be able to evaluate financially potential investment decisions in order to focus on those marketing activities that offer the best returns.

Finance is the common language of business, enabling the costs and benefits of the different strategic options being considered to be quantified, evaluated and compared. Thus in studying this chapter you will develop the skills to understand the impact of the decisions made on the financial health of the company and be able to use financial techniques to assess the viability of potential decisions.

In this chapter we primarily examine two issues:

- the problems of measuring performance
- the use of financial tools in the long term and short term decision making processes.

We start the chapter by examining what is meant by value based marketing from the financial viewpoint and introducing the reader to a number of techniques for evaluating the performance of marketing activities, including those of a company at a corporate level. In the latter half of the chapter we investigate the financial techniques that can be used by the marketing manager in appraising investment decisions required in long term strategic marketing decision making and the financial techniques for evaluating the viability of short term strategic marketing decisions.

* The authors would like to acknowledge the major contribution to this chapter made by Nick Payne of Sheffield Hallam University.

Learning objectives

After reading this chapter you should be able to:

- Understand the concept of value based marketing from a financial viewpoint

- Evaluate the various methods of corporate performance appraisal: return on capital employed, residual income, market value added and economic value added

- Apply and evaluate various methods of performance control for marketing programmes

- Apply financial techniques to the evaluation of strategic options in long term marketing investment decisions

- Apply financial techniques in the evaluation of options in short term marketing decision making

VALUE BASED MARKETING AND FINANCIAL MEASURES OF PERFORMANCE

Value based marketing is concerned with enhancing long term shareholder value. According to Doyle (2000) the marketing manager needs to able to demonstrate how marketing contributes 'to the economic returns generated for shareholders as measured by dividends and increase in the company's share price'. (p. 21) However, whilst this requirement appears on the surface straightforward, it does in fact pose several problems for the marketing manager in its application.

What is meant by enhancing long term value? The definition of the long term in some industries may be as little as two years, whereas in others two years is viewed as the short term and the long term is viewed as ten or more years. What is viewed as long term varies enormously from industry to industry. Selecting a planning time horizon will always be a fairly arbitrary process for a marketing manager. One of two approaches is generally taken in the assessment of long term shareholder value.

- Life of the firm's fixed assets. This approach is favoured by accountants.

- Time period over which investors hold shares in a company. Sixty per cent of the UK equity market is held by pension funds that have an investment horizon of 20 years or more. A recent survey by the UK's National Association of Pension funds found that members held stocks on average for 8 years.

What do we mean by shareholder value? Doyle (2000) talks about enhancing dividends and share price. However, improvements in dividends are only possible if the firm makes profits. This is why some commentators suggest enhanced profitability is a much more appropriate measure of added value. The problem with profit as a measure of performance in the short term is that it can be distorted by accounting procedures. The solution for many companies is to use the measure of net free cash flow, as a measure of added value, that is, the cash flow after all debts have been paid.

Is the share price an appropriate indicator of improvements in shareholder value? The stock market is a second hand market that determines a price for a company's shares; this is not a value. In the short term the market price of shares is determined by supply and demand and market sentiment. The stock market has been known to make mistakes in its assessment of the value of stocks as we saw in the dotcom boom and bust scenario. Also the share price is of little relevance to many small and medium size enterprises who do not raise capital on the equity markets and so do not have a quoted share price.

Thus, whilst the authors accept the prevalence of the concept of enhanced shareholder value in today's markets, its application can be ambiguous and requires the resolution of the questions outlined above by the company employing the concept. Measuring the performance of the firm reflects to some degree the concept of added value. However, a further problem for marketing managers is that many of these can only be applied at a corporate level. This means they are not appropriate to the marketing manager assessing added value related to decisions that are taken within a division or a strategic business unit of a company. For such managers there is no divisional share price to monitor. Thus in examining the financial measures of performance it is important that we use techniques that are appropriate to a manager operating within a small and medium sized company or perhaps at a divisional level of a larger company and do not simply focus on the value of shares on the stock market.

In evaluating the performance of a division or strategic business unit a number of financial measures are available to the marketing manager. There are two types of measures.

Feedback control indicators: these signal the results of decisions that have already been taken and include such measures as:

- **return on capital employed**
- **residual income**
- Value based approaches
  - market value added
  - economic value added

Feed forward indicators: these signal the possible impact of decisions we are about to take and include such measures as payback and net present value.

In the following sections we will examine the benefits and problems associated with feedback measures before going on to consider feed forward indicators.

Feed control indicators

Return on capital employed (ROCE)

ROCE is calculated by the following formula.

ROCE = Earnings before interest and tax (EBIT) / capital employed $\times$ 100

This financial ratio has been used by firms and analysts to assess the overall performance of companies for many years. This all embracing ratio suffers from two major problems that the marketing manager needs to be aware of:

- How do you calculate earnings when profit can be distorted by accounting policies?
- How do you value capital employed? Is it the historic book value of the assets or the replacement costs? Let us consider the following scenario.

Scenario: Should historic or replacement cost be used to assess the value of capital?

For example

EBIT =	£35 000
Historic cost of assets =	£175 000
Replacement cost of assets =	£350 000

$$\text{Historic ROCE} = \frac{£35\,000}{£175\,000} = 20\%$$

$$\text{Replacement ROCE} = \frac{£35\,000}{£350\,000} = 10\%$$

From the above figures it can be seen that most marketing managers will want to use the historic cost ROCE, especially if their annual bonus is based on return on capital employed!

If the historic cost is used, however, it may discourage future investment in the company. Due to depreciation, the capital employed will reduce each year, which will result, if profits remain the same, in an improvement in ROCE! For example,

EBIT each year =	£ 30 000
Assets employed =	£150 000
Depreciation =	£20 000

Year 1	Year 2	Year 3
$\text{ROCE} = \frac{£30\,000}{£150\,000} = 20\%$	$\text{ROCE} = \frac{£30\,000}{£130\,000} = 23\%$	$\text{ROCE} = \frac{£30\,000}{£110\,000} = 27\%$

This is an important point for the marketing manager to take note of. The use of ROCE in assessing performance could result in dysfunctional decision making. When considering investment in new projects, a marketing manager of a strategic business unit (SBU) may be motivated to only think favourably of the projects that will maintain or improve the return on capital of the SBU. If the SBU's ROCE is 25 per cent then the manager will accept only those *capital expenditure* projects which show a projected return of 25 per cent or above in the coming year. If the holding company's ROCE is 15 per cent then the manager who rejects projects with a return of between 15 and 25 per cent is not making the best decision for the company as a whole.

ROCE is a performance measurement technique. The firm's current ROCE can also be used as the **cost of capital** in feedforward investment decisions. A firm's cost of capital and investment decisions will be considered later in the chapter.

ROCE may also discourage marketing investment because marketing is treated as *revenue expenditure*, in such cases the costs are charged to the profits in the current year. If the benefits of a marketing campaign are not seen until two or three years later then there is no incentive in the current year to incur the increased marketing expenditure.

Residual income (RI)

With this method of performance measurement the holding company is operating like a bank, charging SBUs/departments for the capital they are using. The formula for this ratio is:

Earnings before interest and tax − (invested capital × cost of capital).

For example:

	Div X	Div Y
Proposed investment	£100 000	£100 000
Profit on investment	£16 000	£11 000
Less interest on capital at 13%	−£13 000	−£13 000
Residual income (RI)	£3 000	−£2000

Using RI as a performance measurement has a number of problems. As it is an absolute measure of performance it is difficult to make inter-SBU comparisons and it does not take account of the fact that profits may result from the expenditure in different years. RI therefore discourages investment in projects with negative returns in early years. It can also be problematic to establish an appropriate cost of capital. The firm's average cost of capital does not take into account the risks incurred in each of the SBUs. We will return to this issue of the cost of capital later in the chapter.

ROCE and RI are both profit based measures of performance and suffer from similar problems.

■ Profit figures can be distorted by the accounting conventions surrounding financial reporting. For example differing methods of asset valuation and depreciation influence the profits reported in an accounting period.

■ Accounting treatment of items of expenditure impacts on reported profits. For example whether advertising is viewed as a capital or revenue expenditure. It is normally classified as a revenue expenditure that reduces profits and therefore reduces ROCE/RI.

■ Managers are encouraged by these methods to deplete capital assets so as to reduce the capital invested figure and so improve ROCE/RI in the short term. This can be achieved by scrapping assets that are temporarily not required.

■ Contracting out capital intensive investment so as to reduce the capital employed figure can in the long run reduce the firm's ability to compete.

■ Delaying or avoiding replacing worn out fixed assets again reduces the capital employed figure.

Using ROCE/RI to compare SBUs that occupy different parts of the supply chain or are in different geographical locations can also result in dysfunctional decision making. For example the retail SBU may have a higher ROCE than the manufacturing division, but if the manufacturing division is closed it may be that the firm is unable to source supplies at a competitive price. The performance of UK retail/service outlets in the north of the country may be higher than those in the south simply because factor costs are lower in the north. This is illustrated in Challenge 4.1.

Other problems ROCE/RI suffer from are:

■ The age of a division in which performance is being evaluated will also influence its ROCE/RI. Older SBUs will have a higher ROCE simply because the process of depreciation will have reduced the value of the capital employed.

■ Profit measures are not appropriate for products in the early stage of the product life cycle and can lead to a failure to invest in new products because they reduce current earnings. ROCE encourages investment in old products that give a short term improvement in performance. The measures are backward looking, they focus on what the SBUs have done and not future earnings.

ROCE and RI are profit based measures of performance that as we have seen have many problems. Alternatives to the profit approaches are the value based approaches which we will now consider.

Value based approaches

Two value based approaches will be considered:

- market value added
- economic value added.

Market value added This approach looks at changes in invested capital against changes in stock market capitalisation and attempts to indicate how much better off shareholders are as a consequence of management performance. This is an external feedback measure of performance.

For example, if a firm invests an additional £50 million in new products and capital equipment, and the market capitalisation (the value placed on the company by the stock market) increases by £100 million, it then follows that shareholder value has increased by £50 million. But is this as a consequence of effective management performance or due to changes in stock market conditions? As said previously, this measure is also of little use to firms that are not listed on a stock market, or to marketing managers of SBUs.

Economic value added This measure is very similar to residual income. Basically, if a company achieves a positive EVA then the investment will have generated a surplus greater than the firm's weighted average cost of capital and will therefore have created value for the shareholders.

Economic value added (EVA) = adjusted profits after tax
− (adjusted invested capital
× weighted average cost of capital).

To employ EVA requires up to 170+ adjustments to standard financial accounts. (CIMA 2002, p. 429). The adjustments are an attempt to get back to a cash flow based measure of profit. In making the adjustments EVA views certain items of expenditure as investments, adds them back to profit for the period, and treats them as asset investments; for example, advertising, R&D and training. EVA also adds back to the asset value of the firm all capital expenditure write-offs such as depreciation and goodwill. In calculating EVA the firm's debt is treated as an asset so that the effect of gearing is minimised. (Gearing is the relationship between equity finance and debt finance.)

CHALLENGE 4.1   Budget hotels

The majority of budget hotels in the UK as part of their marketing strategy employ a standard pricing policy, except in the capital city of London. A customer will pay the same price for a room in Gateshead in the north of England as they will in Portsmouth which is in the south of the country. The cost of land and buildings in Portsmouth is probably higher which means, given similar occupancy rates, the ROCE/RI will be higher in Gateshead.

A possible solution is to charge differential prices throughout the country, but this will damage the strategic

objective of achieving a consistency in brand value across the country – a consumer being able to obtain the same quality of room, service and price throughout the UK.

Question If the budget hotels operated as independent SBUs, how would you assess their performance when operating in differing cost structures?

Source: Nick Payne, Sheffield Hallam University

The method of calculating EVA is currently open to debate especially as regards the treatment of debt. McLaren (2003, p. 18) defines capital as being debt plus equity capital, whereas CIMA (2002, p. 429) suggest that debt be added to net assets as part of capital employed. However, despite the difficulties in applying the measure it is increasingly being used to differentiate between companies in assessing their performance, as can be seen in Challenge 4.2.

To illustrate the impact of the different methods of evaluation discussed above, i.e. ROCE, RI and economic value added, let us consider the following example of Bobron Ltd.

The firm has the following financial results for the first year of trading. The firm's cost of equity is 20 per cent.

Income statement	£	£
Income		110 000
Less depreciation	20 000	
Net profit before interest and tax		90 000
Less interest (10%)	5000	
		85 000
Less tax (20%)	17 000	
Net profit after tax and interest		68 000

Balance sheet	£	£
Assets		500 000
Less depreciation	20 000	
		480 000

CHALLENGE 4.2 **The economic value added league table**

The economic value added measure of financial performance shows which companies have created the highest value for their shareholders. The consultants Stern Stewart believe this measure comes closer than any other to capturing the true economic profit of a business. Their league table is being used by many analysts to identify the companies that return the highest EVA for their shareholders. For a comprehensive review of EVA see the Stern Stewart website (http://www.sternstewart.com/).

When it comes to creating value for airline investors Ryanair beats all of its competitors. In the supermarket sector Wm Morrison heads the pack. At the other end of the table, firms such as Vodafone, Shell, Sainsbury's and Scottish & Newcastle have been relative destroyers of shareholder wealth.

What is surprising with these findings is the scale of the difference in performance of firms at the top and bottom of the inter-firm performance tables. The results are based on the Stern Stewart research technique that for the first time tries to create league tables for each stock market sector. Its designers, the management consultants Stern Stewart, hope they will be scrutinised in the same spirit as the Premiership football league table – as a transparent measure of performance.

Question Using the Stern Stewart league table found on their web site identify the most successful company in a sector of your choice and suggest possible reasons for this success.

Source: adapted from 'The true creators of wealth', *Sunday Times*, 26 January 2003

Cash	20 000
Net asset value	500 000
Less debt	−50 000
Capital employed	450 000
Equity finance	**450 000**

Return on capital employed

ROCE = earnings before interest and tax/capital employed × 100

= (90 000/450 000+50 000) × 100

= 18%

Residual income

RI = earnings before interest and tax
   − (invested capital
   × weighted average cost of capital)

= 90 000 − (500 000 × ((20% × 0.9) + (10% × 0.1))

= 90 000 − (500 000 × 19%)

= −5000

A negative RI indicates that we have destroyed value!

Economic value added

For this example the method suggested by CIMA for calculating economic value added has been used.

EVA = Adjusted profits after tax − (adjusted invested capital × cost of capital)

Adjusted profits	
Net profit before tax =	85 000
Add back	
Depreciation =	20 000
Interest =	5000
	110 000
Less tax	−17 000
	93 000
Adjusted capital	
Equity =	45 000
Debt	5000
	500 000

EVA =   93 000 − (50 000 × 0.20)

EVA =   −7000

Using the three measures of performance for Bobron we get the following results:

$$ROCE = +18\%$$
$$RI = -5000$$
$$EVA = -7000$$

The three measures of corporate performance give different messages. ROCE is positive but is less than the firm's cost of capital which means the managers are destroying value. Residual income and EVA both give negative figures due to the cost of capital being higher than ROCE. EVA gives a higher negative figure because the influence of gearing has been removed.

So far in this chapter we have considered four feedback methods of performance measurement. These are aggregate measures for calculating overall company performance. The marketing manager also needs more detailed measures of performance that will assist in the day to day operational management of the marketing function. We will now look at these operational measures of performance.

ENSURING ADDED VALUE IN MARKETING PERFORMANCE

Adding value requires that the marketing manager makes effective and efficient use of the marketing resources. A marketing manager needs to be able to evaluate the performance of the marketing programmes and the performance of individual products, customers and customer segments.

Financial performance indicators: design and benchmarking

In Chapter 12 we will examine in some detail the issues involved in establishing a management process for monitoring and controlling the performance of marketing operations. In this section we focus on discussing the financial indicators used to assess marketing performance. Financial indicators are lag indicators, in that they indicate the results of a decision that has already been taken. Performance indicators need to be carefully designed to ensure that they provide useful information and do not create dysfunctional management behaviour. To illustrate the design issue let us consider the market share ratio. Table 4.1 illustrates the problems.

Meaningful performance indicators need to be benchmarked either internally, for example, what did the department achieve this year compared to last year, or externally, for example the firm's ROCE compared to the industry average or to competitors.

Performance indicators are covered by a range of terms, critical success factors, key performance indicators and ratios to name but a few. Financial indicators are generally referred to as **ratios** or **variances**, the design and use of these ratios and variances will now be considered.

Marketing ratios

The value of ratio analysis is based on the relative measures of performance that they provide to an organisation. Good ratio design is based on relating an input factor to an output factor. For example, the marketing sales ratio looks at the relationship between a firm's expenditure on marketing, an input factor, and the sales revenue that is generated, an output factor.

Marketing sales ratio = sales revenue/marketing spend

$$£100\ 000/£20\ 000 = 5:1$$

This ratio indicates that each £1 of marketing spend generates £5 of sales revenue.

To be meaningful ratios must be based on related input and output factors. For example, a ratio of marketing expenditure to staff turnover is not meaningful.

In the first part of this chapter we considered the return on capital employed ratio. This ratio is at such a high level of aggregation that it is of little help to the marketing manager. However ROCE, a primary ratio, can be broken into secondary and tertiary ratios to provide more detailed and useful information on the firm's performance.

Primary ratio: ROCE = net profit/capital employed

Secondary ratios: net profit/sales revenue × sales revenue/capital employed.

This use of primary and secondary ratios leads to what is referred to by Wilson (1999) as the marketing ratio pyramid.

Ratios can be used to assess two elements of the marketing function. The efficiency and effectiveness of the use of marketing resources and the performance of individual products and customers/market segments within the firm's portfolio.

The following ratios are useful in assessing the efficiency and effectiveness of the marketing function, but there are many more!

- marketing expenditure to sales revenue
- marketing staff to sales revenue
- market research costs to sales revenue
- marketing expenditure to new customers
- bad debt to sales ratio.

TABLE 4.1	**Problems in the design of performance indicators**			
Market share	*Ratio*	*Variance*	*Comment*	
£30 000 January			This tells us almost nothing	
30%			More informative, but still not that useful.	
Sales £30 000 January Total market £100 000	30%		The indicator is providing useful informative data. We are benchmarking our performance.	
Sales £30 000 January Total market £100 000	30%	−5%	The indicator is providing detailed management information. Benchmarked both internally and externally.	
Sales £35 000 December Total market £100 000	35%			

Source: Nick Payne, Sheffield Hallam University

Ratios for assessing the performance of products/customers/market segments include:

- profit margin
- contribution sales ratio
- Break even volume
- margin of safety
- stock turnover.

Whether you apply ratios to products or customers or use a combination of both depends on the company's view as to what creates profits – products or customers!

The ratios that are used to assess the performance of the marketing function should be kcpt to a manageable number and applied consistently over time. In this age of the computer the danger is that a company reports large numbers of ratios each period which the marketing manager does not have the time to assess and evaluate, this practice does not add value!

Marketing variances

Variance analysis is the process of comparing actual performance with the budgeted performance of the organisation. The important point to remember when using ratios to assess the performance of a manager, is that the manager must have the authority and responsibility for managing the element of performance that is being assessed.

For the marketing/sales function the primary variance is the total sales variance and the two secondary variances are sales price variance and sales volume variance, as shown in the following example:

Budget		Actual	
Volume	100 units	Volume	110 units
Standard price	£2 per unit	Actual price	£1.90 per unit
Standard cost	£1 per unit	Actual costs	£0.80 per unit

Primary variance – total sales variance

Budgeted profit

Budgeted volume × (standard price – standard cost)

100	(£2 – £1)	= £100

Actual profit

Actual volume × (actual price – standard costs*)

110	× (£1.90 – £1)	= £99

Sales variance		£1 adverse

Secondary variance - sales price variance

Actual volume × (actual price – standard price)

110	× (£1.90 – £2.00)	
110	× – 0.10	= £11 adverse

Secondary variance – sales volume variance

Actual volume – standard volume × standard price – standard cost

| 110 | – 100 | £2.00 | £1.00* – 10 favourable |

The use of budgets and variances as a management tool has come under a great deal of criticism over the years. Whether they are an appropriate management tool for all companies is open to question. The value of variance analysis is to a large extent determined by the quality of the standards that are established at the start of the budget period. If the standards do not reflect current market conditions then the whole variance analysis process will largely be a waste of management resources and will fail to create value!

For the marketing manager the challenge is to design a performance measurement system that enables them to effectively manage the marketing process and create value for the firm's shareholders. So far in this chapter we have considered the issues relating to the measurement of performance at the corporate level and at the level of the marketing function. We now turn our attention to assessing the financial implications of strategic marketing decision making and the modelling techniques that the marketing manager needs to apply to the process of managing marketing resources and creating shareholder value.

FINANCIAL IMPLICATIONS OF STRATEGIC MARKETING DECISION MAKING

We now need to turn our attention to assessing the financial implications of strategic marketing decision making and the financial techniques that marketing managers can use to help them ensure the decisions made create value for the company. But before doing so we need to consider some general issues regarding assessing the financial implications of the decision making process.

Decision making

Decision making is at the heart of the management process and involves the use of a number of different financial tools. The starting point in the decision making process is the identification of the type of decision you are dealing with, short or long term.

From a financial perspective short term decisions are those decisions that do not involve any major change in the **fixed assets/costs** of the enterprise. Long term decision making is concerned with the problems of evaluating strategic options in making decisions involving investment in long term fixed assets both tangible and intangible. With this type of decision the main problem is the uncertainty of data. Examples of possible long term decisions for the marketing manager are new product development, major advertising campaigns where the impact on consumer demand is expected to last for a number of years or perhaps the redesign of the corporate image. For example what was the value added by British Airways corporate re-branding in the late 1900s? (see Challenge 4.3).

---

* When calculating the sales variance you must always use the standard cost of production. If the actual cost was used the resulting variance would not be the sole responsibility of the marketing manager!

Before an investment project is undertaken the enterprise must attempt to establish the financial viability of the strategic options under consideration. This means carrying out an appraisal of the potential investments to estimate the probable return from the investment, gained from either an increase in profits or a reduction in costs. Thus the marketing manager needs to assess if the potential investments will create value. The purpose of the **investment appraisal** process is to:

■ create profitable investment opportunities

■ forecast results of potential projects

■ evaluate potential projects

■ financially control development/acquisitions

■ carry out a post-decision audit, to assess the accuracy of the estimates made.

A structured approach to investment appraisal encourages managers to consider the problems in a logical manner. The post-decision audit, in particular, examines the project estimates against actual performance and so discourages managers from making unrealistic estimates simply to gain approval for investment projects.

FINANCIAL TOOLS FOR LONG TERM DECISION MAKING/FEED FORWARD INDICATORS

Earlier in the chapter we introduced the reader to the concept of feedback indicators at both the corporate and operational levels. In this section we will be going on to examine the feed forward indicators for long and short term decision making. The long term feed forward indicators used for investment appraisal are in keeping with EVA because they use a cash flow approach. Two methods will be considered:

■ **payback**

■ **discounted cash flow**

CHALLENGE 4.3   British Airways rebrand

In 1997 British Airways undertook the biggest corporate makeover in the UK. The Union Jack logo on the tailfins was replaced with art from around the world. Sources for this art included a council flat in Poland and a village in the Kalahari Desert.

BA's chief executive at the time, Bob Ayling, explained the changes saying, 'Some people abroad saw the airline as staid, conservative and a little cold, to continue to be the world leader we have to put clear blue sky between us and our rivals.'

The new corporate identity, which included a softer colour scheme, a new 'speedmarque' design on the fuselage and the ethnic art on the tailfins cost British Airways in the region of £60 million.

Question What problems did BA face in attempting to evaluate this investment in terms of creating value for the shareholders?

Source: adapted from 'BA takes ethnic route in £60 million bid to stay in front around the globe', *The Times*, 11 June 1997

Payback

Payback simply measures the number of years it will take to recover the original investment from the net cash flows resulting from a project. The method is based on being able to estimate a future flow of funds.

For example, an enterprise has budgeted £1000k for the launch strategy of a new product. Two strategic options are being considered. The estimated net cash flows for each option are as follows:

Option	A		B	
Investment	£1000k		£1000k	
Cash flow		Cum		Cum
Year 1	200	200	–	–
Year 2	250	450	100	100
Year 3	150	600	150	250
Year 4	150	750	150	400
Year 5	150	900	150	550
Year 6	100	1000	200	750
Year 7	100		150	900
Year 8	–		100	1000
Year 9	–		100	
Year 10	–		100	
Payback		6 years		8 years

Using payback the firm would choose option A as it takes the least time to restore the company's liquidity position.

Advantages:

■ The calculations are simple.
■ The company's cash flow is at risk for the shortest possible time. The strategic option selected will lead to the quickest expected restoration of the company's liquidity position.
■ The technique acknowledges that uncertainty increases with time.

Disadvantages:

■ The method ignores receipts expected after the end of the payback period. Projects which offer substantial returns, but only in the long term, may be rejected.
■ No account is taken of the time value of money.
■ Expected overall profitability is not considered.

This method on its own provides only a limited guide as to which option should be selected. It would normally be used in conjunction with another method of appraisal.

Net present value and discounted cash flow

This technique appears complex but in essence rests upon one simple principle, that ignoring inflation, money received today is worth more than money received next year because of the opportunity to invest and consequently earn a return. It can be explained through the following example:

Money received now	year 0 = £100
If invested at 10% value at the end of	year 1 = £110
value at the end of	year 2 = £121

(compound interest)

So if the investment rate is 10 per cent:

£121 received at end of year 2 is worth £100 at year 0.

£110 received at end of year 1 is worth £100 at year 0.

To convert the cash flow at the end of year 2 into today's value we calculate a **discount rate**.

$$\frac{£100}{£121} = 0.826$$

The discount rate for year 1 at a 10 per cent interest rate:

$$\frac{£100}{£110} = 0.909$$

Discount tables are available for all interest rates and are published in most good accounting textbooks.

In evaluating strategic options in strategic marketing decision making **net present value** (NPV) and discounted cash flow can be applied in the following way:

Capital investment appraisal using NPV

An enterprise has a choice of two strategic options, A or B. The firm's cost of capital is 10 per cent. Both options involve an investment of £800k and have the following profits and cash flows.

Projects		A	B
		£K	£K
Initial sum invested	year 0	£800	£800
Cash flow generated			
by each option	year 1	£100	£900
	year 2	£900	£100

Discounted cash flows (using a 10 per cent discount rate):

	A			B		
	CF	DR	DCF	CF	DR	DCF
	£		£	£		£
Year 1	100 × 0.909 =		90	900 × 0.909 =		818
Year 2	900 × 0.826 =		743	100 × 0.826 =		83
			834			901
Initial investment			(800)			(800)
Net present value			34			101

Using the NPV of the cash flows the enterprise would select option B. Option B NPV is greater because the bulk of the cash flow occurs in year 1. NPV has three investment rules that are as follows:

NPV = 0	You would be indifferent to the investment.
NPV = negative	The strategic option fails to generate sufficient funds to cover the cost of capital and so destroys shareholder value.
NPV = positive	The strategic option generates a return greater than the cost of capital and should be considered as it increases shareholder value.

The practical problems

The two methods of investment appraisal reviewed are relatively simple techniques. The application of these techniques is however more problematical. The main problems are as follows:

- The NPV method requires the identification of the cost of capital for the project. If this cannot be identified firms tend to use cost of equity. Following the EVA approach would seem to suggest that the equity cost of capital should be used.

- In marketing investment decisions it is sometimes difficult to identify the cash flow that will result from the investment. For example, it is difficult to isolate what additional income results from a specific advertising campaign.

- Specifying the life of the investment. In marketing investments it is difficult to ascertain, for example, over what time period a major advertising campaign will influence demand for a product. By extending the life of the investment a negative NPV can turn into a positive NPV! One solution to this problem is to set a standard time period for the assessment of all capital investment projects.

- A danger exists that the estimated figures of costs and cash flows will be distorted to ensure that a project is accepted. A rigorous post-decision audit can do much to discourage this practice.

- How does the company assess the risk associated with each strategic option being evaluated? The greater the risk then the greater should be the return! Any strategic option requiring new product development will carry a higher cost of capital than a market extension strategy, as the risk involved is much higher.

- The uncertainty surrounding the estimates of costs and cash flows from an investment. Using a single estimate of costs and revenues does not reflect the uncertainty surrounding this type of decision. Several estimates of costs and revenues should be used in conjunction with their associated probabilities.

- How should qualitative factors enter into the decision? For example, the importance to the company's mission statement, etc.

Long term decision making is a complex process that requires managers to look outside the organisation for investment opportunities that will create value for the business. No one method of financial appraisal will provide the perfect solution. Firms and marketing managers need to adopt a structured approach based on NPV to the appraisal of investment decisions. This may mean setting guide lines such as:

- The maximum time period over which any strategic options should be assessed, e.g. five years.

- A cost of capital hurdle rate which should possibly be higher than the current cost of equity.

- A requirement to provide a number of estimates of revenue and costs with associated probabilities.

In this section we have briefly looked at methods of long term decision making, payback and net present value, and the role they can play in helping to create value. The next section will consider financial approaches to short term tactical decision making.

SHORT TERM TACTICAL DECISION MAKING

In financial terms short term decision making is concerned with how alternative potential courses of action influence the firm's cash flow. Short term decision making is concerned with variable costing and the use of a marginal approach to costing. Fixed overhead costs are not taken into account when evaluating the options in making short term decisions.

The alternative to **marginal costing** is **absorption costing**. This approach attempts to allocate all costs, both fixed and variable, to individual units of production. The problem with absorption costing is that it makes use of arbitrary allocations of overhead costs to products. This method of costing is often referred to as peanut butter costing. It simply spreads the overhead costs across all products at the same rate, irrespective of the actual overhead costs created by an individual product. Absorption costing is the appropriate method of costing for long term pricing decisions. In the long term a product must recover all of its costs, both variable and fixed. In absorption costing the issue for marketing managers and accountants is what methods should be used to allocate fixed costs to products. Over the last 20 years much work has been done to develop alternative methods for allocating fixed costs to products. According to Drury (2000), many firms are now using activity based costing, which attempts to allocate fixed costs to products on a usage basis.

Relevant costs for short term tactical decision making

The relevant costs for short term decision making purposes are the potential cash flows resulting from various alternatives being considered in the short term decision in question. The relevant costs for short term decision making are the variable costs associated with the decision; fixed costs are generally irrelevant. This is really all we need to know for any particular short term decision. However, it may be useful to the reader to briefly explain the various cost concepts to understand why such costs are not considered in short term decision making.

The main cost concepts are:

- *Sunk costs,* are costs that have already been incurred or committed as a result of a previous decision and cannot now be changed. For example, the cost of a promotional campaign for a product which has already taken place. Sunk costs are generally excluded from evaluating short term options.

- *Differential/incremental costs* are costs that are changed by a decision. They are not just variable costs. They can also be costs that are normally classified as fixed but which change as a result of a decision, and as such have to be considered when taking a decision. For example, the decision to open a retail outlet on a Sunday would create additional overhead costs such as heating and lighting.

- *Opportunity costs* are costs that measure the opportunity that is lost when the choice of one course of action requires that an alternative course of action be given up. For example a firm produces two products as follows:

Cost/product	A	B
Selling price £	100	200
Variable cost £	50	75
Contribution £	50	125

The firm has limited production capacity and is currently producing product A. An order is received for product B, but to fulfil this order production of product A will have to stop. The £50 contribution from product A is an opportunity cost. The firm's position will improve by £125 – £50 opportunity cost = £75.

The example introduces the concept of **contribution**. Contribution (selling price – variable cost) is an important concept for short term decision making. The term contribution means the contribution a product makes to cover fixed costs and provide some profit. Up to the break even point (BEP) the product's contribution is used to cover the fixed cost, but after BEP it's all profit.

Based on this concept of contribution and marginal costing we will now go on to consider its use in short term decision making and cost/volume/price modelling. The final part of the chapter will look at the use of costs in the general pricing decision.

Using marginal costing for short term decisions

Managers encounter many types of short term decisions that require the use of a marginal cost approach.

To highlight the marginal cost approach that should be employed in short term decision making, an example of a decision to use promotional pricing to increase market share will be used. The qualitative aspects of this type of decision will be reviewed as they can be just as important as the financial considerations. The promotional pricing decision involves deciding whether or not to reduce the price of a product in order to increase sales. For example, a company produces a single product and has budgeted for the production of 100 units during the next quarter. Estimated costs for the quarter are as follows:

Direct labour	£600
Direct material	£200
Variable overheads	£200
Fixed overheads	£400
	£1400
Cost per unit	£14 per unit
Selling price	£18 per unit
Profit	£4 per unit
Total profit	£400

At the start of the quarter the firm receives orders for 80 units at £18 each. A customer will take the remaining 20 units but only at a promotional price of £12 per unit.

What should the firm do?

If we compare the price the customer is willing to pay with the full cost of the product, the decision would be not to sell at the lower price.

Selling price £12; full cost £14 = loss of £2 per unit

However in the short term this would be the wrong decision because we have not considered the firm's cash flow, and it is cash flow which is the short term objective. We need to consider the relevant costs for the decision! Those costs that vary with output, in this case direct labour, direct materials and variable overheads.

The decision using the relevant costs only:

Selling price	£12
Less costs	
Direct labour	£6
Direct materials	£2
Variable overheads	£2
Total	(£10)
Contribution	£2 per unit

The two profit statements for the decision

	Reject £	Accepted £
Sales 80 × 18	1440	1440
20 × 12	–	240
	1440	1680
Less costs		
Direct labour	480	600
Direct material	160	200
Variable overheads	160	200
	(800)	(1000)
Contribution	640	680
Less fixed overheads	(400)	(400)
Profit	240	280

Using the marginal cost approach you would accept the order.

The decision so far has been based simply on the quantitative factors; there are, however, several qualitative factors that also need to be considered:

- Selling at a lower price may result in a general downward movement in prices.

- Customers that have paid the full price may feel they are being discriminated against and move to other suppliers.

- The decision to accept the order prevents the firm from accepting other orders that may arise during the period at a higher price.

- Using a marginal approach may create problems with customers in the future when the firm attempts to return to prices based on the full cost of the product.

During difficult trading conditions there is a danger that all orders are taken on at less than full cost which means the firm fails to recover its overheads and makes a loss. Price cutting to sell off capacity in the short term can create long term pricing and profit problems for the firm. Pricing decisions cause many headaches for marketing managers as in the case of Hamleys in Challenge 4.4.

UNDERSTANDING COST BEHAVIOURS FOR SHORT TERM TACTICAL DECISION MAKING: COST VOLUME PROFIT ANALYSIS

Managers must understand the cost structure and behaviour of costs if they are to effectively make short term marketing decisions. **Cost volume profit** (CVP) analysis provides the marketing manager with a model of the behaviour of the firm's costs and revenues. The model is a decision support system for managers. It allows management to test out the implications of their plans without committing the enterprise to expensive experiments. CVP is also known as **break even analysis**; the reason for this is that one of the main functions of the model is to predict the volume of sales that must be achieved for the enterprise to make neither a profit nor a loss (break even). Understanding the relationship between volume, costs and profits is essential for any marketing manager. In high fixed costs businesses volume is the key to success as can be seen in Spotlight 4.1.

If managers are to use this model then they must be aware of the assumptions upon which the model is based. The assumptions underlying the CVP model are:

- Costs can be accurately divided into their fixed and variable elements.
- Profits are calculated on a variable cost basis, this means they will reflect the firm's cash flow.
- Total cost and total revenue are linear functions of output.
- A single product or constant sales mix.
- All other variables remain constant.
- The analysis applies to the relevant range only.

CHALLENGE 4.4   Hamleys pricing dilemma

Hamleys, the famous London toy store, was in trouble last year with profits down to just £27 000. Simon Burke the new chief executive identified a number of reasons for the store's problems, one of them being pricing. He felt that Hamleys had acquired a reputation for being a rip off, particularly due to pricing scarce items at an exploitative level. Hamleys had come to realise that such strategies work in the short term, but in the long term they had damaged the reputation of the store.

Hamleys have now abolished such practices and aim to offer fair prices for all their products irrespective of the supply situation. However, fair does not mean cheap. They differentiate themselves from other cheaper sources of supply, such as Argos, and believe they can achieve their premium but fair prices in the unparalleled services they offer, the diversity in their product range and because they are a big flagship store in the West End of London.

Question What issues, both financial and marketing, should Hamleys consider when pricing products?

Source: adapted from 'Twenty questions: Simon Burke, chief executive of Hamleys – I abolished our former high-prices policy', The Independent, 26 September 2001

Building a CVP model

Having considered the assumptions upon which the CVP model is based let us now construct a model. The model will be developed by looking at:

- the impact of volume on costs
- the impact of volume on profit
- the calculation of the break even volume for an enterprise
- the calculation of the volume of sales required to achieve a target profit.

Dash the box maker: a CVP model

Dash Ltd manufactures and sells boxes. The costs for sales of 10 000 boxes per year are as follows:

	£
Materials	5000
Variable expenses	5000
Total variable cost	10 000
Fixed costs	
Occupancy costs	2000
Employee costs	4000
Administration costs	3000
Total fixed costs	9000
Total costs	19 000

SPOTLIGHT 4.1 **Mr Fernandes, the Branson of low cost airlines in South East Asia**

The drive to build low cost airlines has now taken off in South East Asia. Mr Fernandes, dubbed as Asia's Richard Branson, has successfully built a low cost airline called Air Asia following the no frills model of Dublin based Ryanair. This is South East Asia's first regional budget airline. He started in Malaysia in 2001 and is now preparing to expand to the rest of South East Asia. If he succeeds, Mr Fernandes may serve as a catalyst for the growth of discount carriers in the region. The carrier uses 18 Boeing 737s, the workhorse of budget airlines, to serve destinations within three hours' flight time from its hub in Kuala Lumpur, as well as seven jets used to serve 13 cities in Malaysia.

Controlling costs and understanding the revenue management system is seen by Mr Fernandes as critical to the company's success. It costs only 2.8 US cents for Air Asia to fly one passenger one kilometre, against 4.8 US cents for Ryanair in Europe and 5.8 US cents for Southwest Airlines in the USA, according to the Sydney based Centre for Asia Pacific Aviation. 'Cost is our enemy,' says Mr Fernandes. Like its European counterparts Air Asia does not offer any free in-flight snacks and it sells all its tickets via the internet to cut the administration cost of ticketing and to avoid the hefty commissions charges from agents. They also claim to be the first airline to sell tickets by mobile phone texting. Mr Fernandes also has a very conservative view as to how growth should be financed, insisting on financing his growth from the cash flow, and claims any growth will only come if they are able to fully fund it.

Another key element in controlling costs is the flat management structure and the desire to avoid a bureaucratic hierarchy. Mr Fernandes himself has been known to roll up his sleeves and help the baggage handlers and the check-in counters. Such flexibility, he argues, is important if they are to maintain their low cost advantage.

Question What do you consider to be the major factors Mr Fernandes must consider in his efforts to maintain his status as the world's lowest cost airline?

Source: adapted from Burton, J. (2003) *Financial Times*, 14 October, p. 15

Analysis of these costs has led to the identification of the following fixed and variable costs:

Variable costs associated with producing 10 000 boxes

	Total £	£ Per box
Materials	5000	0.50
Variable expenses	5000	0.50
	10 000	1.00

Therefore, the variable cost per box = £1.00

Fixed costs

		£
Fixed costs:	Occupancy costs	2000
	Employee costs	4000
	Administration costs	3000
		9000 per year

Fixed costs are associated with a particular time period and not each individual box produced. These costs will be incurred irrespective of the number of boxes sold.

THE IMPACT OF VOLUME ON UNIT COSTS

Because some of the costs are fixed, not changing as volume changes, the total average cost per unit will fall as volume increases, as the following example shows:

Production (units)	5000	10 000	15 000
	£	£	£
Variable cost £1 per unit	5000	10 000	15 000
Fixed costs	9000	9000	9000
Total costs	14 000	19 000	24 000
Cost per unit	£14 000/5000	£19 000/10 000	£24 000/15 000
	= £2.80	= £1.90	= £1.60

The average cost per unit falls from £2.80 to £1.60. This is due to the fact that the fixed costs are being shared amongst a larger number of units. The impact of volume on fixed costs must also lead us to question the whole concept of profit per unit. Profit per unit is based on the assumption that a certain volume of sales will be achieved during the year. If we fail to achieve that volume, profit per unit will be less.

Having looked at the impact of volume on the cost per unit, the model will now be developed further to include revenue and profit. The selling price per box is £2.00. Given this additional information it is now possible to calculate the profit or loss achieved at any given level of sales.

Sales/production in units	5000	10 000	15 000
	£	£	£
Revenue £2.00 per unit	10 000	20 000	30 000
Less			
Variable cost £1 per unit	(5000)	(10 000)	(15 000)
Fixed costs	(9000)	(9000)	(9000)
Profit/loss	(4000)	1000	6000

From the above calculations we can see that as volume increases so profit increases.

The break even point

From the above analysis we can see that the break-even level of activity lies somewhere between 5000 and 10 000 boxes. CVP enables the manager to calculate the break-even level of activity for the enterprise using the following formula:

$$\text{Break even volume} = \frac{\text{total fixed costs}}{\text{contribution per unit}}$$

$$\text{Contribution} = \text{selling price} - \text{variable cost}$$

$$\text{For Dash the break even volume is} = \frac{£9000}{£2 - £1}$$

$$= 9000 \text{ boxes}$$

The volume of sales at which Dash will make neither a profit nor a loss is 9000 units.

Break even point plus a required level of profit

Suppose Dash wished to make a profit of £6000, how many boxes must it sell? This problem can be solved by simply treating the target profit as an additional fixed cost.

$$\text{Required sales units} = \frac{\text{fixed costs + profit}}{\text{contribution per unit}}$$

$$= \frac{£9000 + £6000}{£1}$$

$$= 15\ 000 \text{ boxes}$$

Alternatively an enterprise may specify a percentage profit margin target per unit.
   Suppose Dash requires a profit margin of 20 per cent of the selling price. How many units must Dash sell? The profit margin target is in this case treated as a variable cost!

Selling price	£2.00
Target profit margin 20%	£0.40

$$\text{BEP} + \text{target} = \frac{\text{fixed cost}}{\text{selling price} - (\text{variable cost} + \text{profit target})}$$

$$= \frac{£9000}{£2.00 - (£1.00 + £0.40)}$$

$$= \frac{£9000}{£0.60}$$

$$= 15\ 000 \text{ boxes}$$

CVP ratios

CVP analysis also provides a number of ratios for the analysis of the performance of a product.

The margin of safety (MOS) ratio indicates by how much sales may fall before an enterprise will suffer a loss.

$$\% \text{ margin of safety} = \frac{\text{expected sales} - \text{break-even sales} \times 100}{\text{expected sales}}$$

For the Dash example the margin of safety if the firm expects to sell 15 000 units would be:

$$\% \text{ margin of safety} = \frac{15\ 000 - 9000 \times 100}{15\ 000}$$

$$= 40\%$$

The margin of safety is an indicator of the risk profile of a product, the smaller the margin of safety the greater is the risk that the enterprise's level of activity may fall below the break even point.

$$\text{Contribution sales ratio CSR} = \frac{\text{selling price} - \text{variable cost}}{\text{selling price}}$$

Using Dash as an example with the enterprise selling 15 000 units at a price of £2.00 per unit and a variable cost of £1.00:

$$= \frac{£2.00 - £1.00}{£2.00}$$

$$= 0.50 \text{ or } 50\%$$

$$\text{Profit volume ratio PVR} = \frac{\text{sales revenue} - \text{total variable cost}}{\text{sales revenue}}$$

$$= \frac{(15\ 000 \times £2.00) - (15\ 000 \times £1.00)}{15\ 000 \times £2.00}$$

$$= \frac{£15\ 000}{£30\ 000}$$

$$= 0.50 \text{ or } 50\%$$

CSR and PVR are simply different ways of calculating the same ratio. The ratios tell us what percentage from an additional £1 of sales will go towards covering the fixed costs and providing for profit. In the case of Dash an additional £1 of sales will give 50 pence towards covering fixed costs and profit.

The CSR/PVR ratio can be used to calculate the break-even level of sales revenue for an enterprise.

Example Dash   Fixed cost £9,000   CSR ratio 0.50

$$\text{Break even sales revenue} = \frac{\text{fixed costs}}{\text{CSR}}$$

$$= \frac{\pounds 9000}{0.50}$$

$$= \pounds 18\,000 \quad \text{(which is the revenue from sales of 9000 units)}$$

The PVR is particularly useful when we only have the total revenue and cost figures for an enterprise. Using the PVR ratio it is still possible to calculate the break even level of activity.

Effective communication of the CVP model is important if its full value is to be utilised. The use of graphs is common practice when building CVP models. The graph provides a dynamic picture of the relationship between revenue, costs and volume and can be used to explore the impact of possible decisions. This is illustrated in the following three figures depicting break even analysis in varying situations.

FIGURE 4.1

The break even chart

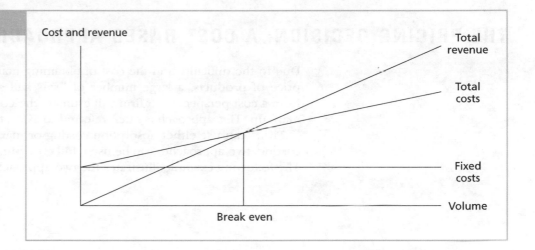

FIGURE 4.2

The break even chart with increased marketing spend

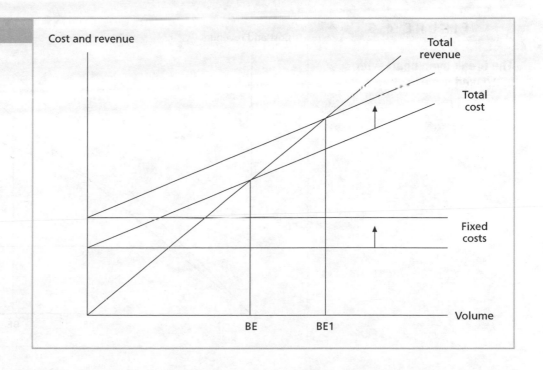

The chart clearly shows the growth in profits as volume increases. The area between the total cost line and the revenue line to the right of BEP is profit at various levels of activity.

The model allows us to test various marketing options. As shown in Figure 4.2 increasing the marketing spend for the coming year has implications for the volume that needs to be sold to break even.

What we can see from Figure 4.2 is that the fixed costs have increased and more units have to be sold to achieve the safety of break even. If we cannot sell more units then we need to increase the price as in Figure 4.3.

As can be seen from Figure 4.3, by increasing the price the slope of the revenue line increases and in this example we are back to our original break even position. CVP analysis is a simple tool but provides managers with a means of testing the implications of possible decisions. In the above example if price remains the same and any volume between BE and BE1 is achieved then value has been destroyed!

THE PRICING DECISION: A COST BASED APPROACH

Due to the difficulty and the cost of obtaining market intelligence regarding the price of products, a large number of firms still approach the pricing decision from a cost perspective. A firm will estimate the cost of a product and then add a mark up. This approach is often referred to as cost plus pricing.

Firms can use either absorption costing or marginal costing. With absorption costing, two approaches can be used, full **cost plus** and manufacturing cost plus. The following example illustrates the two approaches.

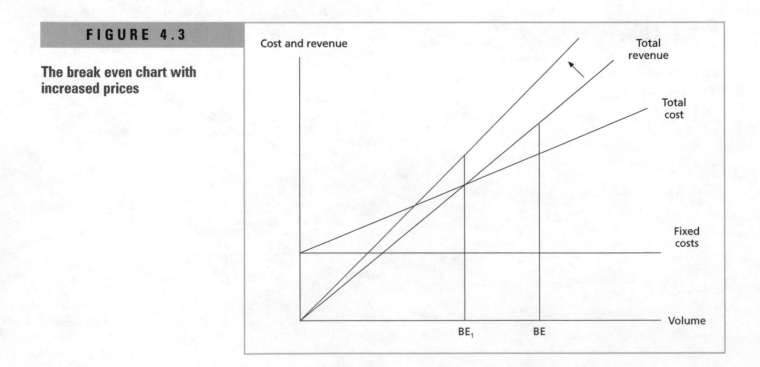

FIGURE 4.3

The break even chart with increased prices

Product A	Full cost plus	Manufacturing cost plus
Variable cost (£)	100	100
Production overheads	50	50
Sales and administrative overheads	50	–
	200	150
Plus mark-up (10%)	20	47% 70
Selling price	220	220

The difference between the two methods is simply the degree to which you attempt to allocate overheads to individual units of production. With manufacturing cost plus no attempt is made to allocate sales and administrative overheads. These overheads are recovered by increasing the size of the mark up, in this case 47 per cent.

The problems with these two approaches are:

■ How do we adjust the price to reflect market and demand conditions?

■ What should the percentage mark up be for the coming period? One solution to this problem is simply to look at the overhead cost and profits as a percentage of the previous year's costs.

■ Apportionment of overheads in 'multi product firms'. This issue was considered when reviewing absorption costing.

■ The circular argument. This is the issue that volume determines cost, cost determines price, if we are using cost plus pricing, and price determines volume! (See Figure 4.4).

To deal with this circular argument the starting point is always the volume estimate, how many units can be sold in the coming period. This information will hopefully come from the marketing department's assessment of the coming year demand for the product and not the accountant's historic record of what the firm sold last year.

FIGURE 4.4

The circular argument

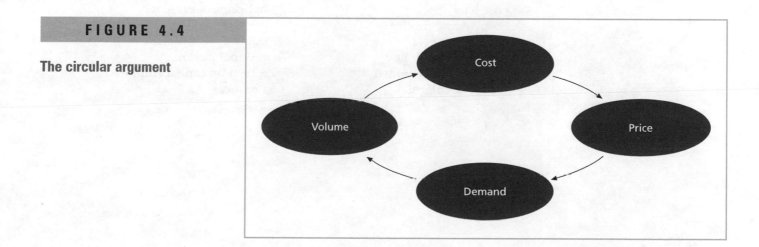

SUMMARY

- In this chapter we have looked at two issues, the problems of measuring performance and the use of financial tools in the decision making process.

- The main objective of any business is to maximise the shareholders'/owners' wealth. If marketing managers are to operate at a strategic level within a company they need to develop the financial skills to demonstrate the contribution marketing strategies make to the business.

- In examining the financial measures of performance it is important that we use techniques that are appropriate to a manager operating within a small or medium sized company, or perhaps at a divisional level of a larger company, and do not simply focus on the value of shares on the stock market.

- Measures used to signal the results of decisions that have already been taken include return on capital employed, residual income and value based approaches such as market value added and economic value added.

- Financial indicators that measure performance are generally referred to as ratios or variances.

- The methods of long term investment appraisal, payback and discounted cash flow are in keeping with EVA because they use a cash flow approach.

- Managers must understand the cost structure and behaviour of costs if they are to effectively make short term marketing decisions. Cost volume profit (CVP) analysis provides the marketing manager with a model of the behaviour of the firm's costs and revenues.

KEYWORDS

absorption costing	fixed assets/costs
break even analysis	investment appraisal
contribution	marginal costing
cost of capital	market value added
cost plus	net present value
cost volume profit	payback
discount rate	ratios
discounted cash flow	residual income
economic value added	return on capital employed
feedback control	variances

CASE STUDY   Fastparts

Fastparts Ltd is a component supplier to the automotive industry. Business is conducted on an enquiry quotation basis. Enquiries are received from the major vehicle assemblers throughout the financial year. The enquiries received tend to be for on the spot orders or for a 12 month contract to supply parts. Obtaining a large contract can be advantageous for Fastparts, as one substantial contract can sustain the business for several months. On the spot orders, whilst welcome, mean higher administrative costs per sale and higher client servicing costs.

The sales team of Fastparts have been working hard for the last 24 months to become the preferred supplier of components to BAF Commercial Vehicles Ltd. To gain the status of preferred supplier they have had to undergo a rigorous vetting procedure where BAF have assessed the entire operations of the company. This has meant a huge commitment has been made by the company both in time and resources in order to gain the status required for BAF to agree to place orders with them. Having achieved the status Fastparts are now keen to get orders. BAF place both spot orders and contracts. To date Fastparts have only received enquiries for spot orders and have had only limited success in converting the enquiries into orders. The orders that have been won to date have invariably been for small quantities and the quantities ordered have always been considerably less than the quantities stated on the enquiries.

The following enquiry has been received from BAF.

Contract for the supply of Part No. 687.
72 000 units per year – 6000 units per month.

Fastparts' design and costing department has produced the following costing and quotation. (The firm used a manufacturing cost plus approach to pricing.)

Cost	£	
Direct material	10.00	
Direct labour	5.00	
Setup costs	1.00	6 hours at £1000 per hour
Total direct cost	16.00	
Production overheads	4.00	40% of direct materials
Total production cost	20.00	
Mark up*	20.00	100% of total production costs
Selling price	40.00	

* The mark up covers both the sales and administrative costs, 70%, and 30% for profit

The sales executive responsible for the BAF enquiry has just returned from visiting the company with the following spot order.

To be supplied by Fastparts
Part No. 687
Qty 600 units
Price £40.00 per unit
To be delivered in 2 weeks*
Payment terms 180 days*

* Fastparts normal lead time is 6 weeks
* Normal payment terms are 30 days

The sales executive is keen to accept the order. To quote 'We must accept this order, the quantity is smaller but we will still make £6.00 per unit profit and it will help us develop our relationship with BAF.'

Questions

1 What financial issues should Fastparts consider in their decision?

2 What strategic issues should Fastparts consider in their decision?

3 Would you recommend that Fastparts accept the order?

Source: Nick Payne, Sheffield Hallam University

DISCUSSION QUESTIONS

1 The firm of Cotton and Co have just published their final accounts for the first year of trading. The following details have been taken from the accounts. The cost of debt finance is 10 per cent, equity finance 15 per cent giving a weighted average cost of capital of 14.5 per cent.

Income statement

Net income after direct expenses	220 000
Less depreciation	−40 000
Less interest	−10 000
Net profit before tax	170 000
Tax	−51 000
Net profit after tax (PAT)	119 000

Balance sheet

Assets	1 000 000
Less depreciation	−40 000
	960 000
Cash	40 000
Net asset value	1 000 000
Less debt	−100 000
Capital employed	900 000
Equity finance	900 000

(a) Calculate return on capital employed; residual income; and economic value added.

(b) How useful is the information calculated in part (a)?

2 A firm of marketing consultants is considering expanding their practice by opening a branch office. The cost of obtaining a lease and refurbishment of a suitable office has been estimated at £610 000. The lease would run for six years, at the end of this period the premises would revert back to the owners. The company uses straight line depreciation for writing off lease and refurbishment costs.
The firm's cost structure for the project is as follows:

Billing rate	£80.00 per hour
Labour costs	£34.00 per hour
Direct materials	£10.00 per hour

Total overhead costs excluding a depreciation charge are £370 000 per year.

15 000 hours are expected to be billed to clients each year.
The firms cost of capital is 14 per cent.

(a) Calculate for the project:

   (i) net present value

   (ii) the payback period

(b) Advise management on how vulnerable the project is to an adverse change of 5 per cent in the number of hours billed to clients and the variable costs of the investments.

(c) By how much would the firm's cost of capital have to change before the project would become viable/unviable?

3 Evaluate the role of cost plus pricing in marketing products and services.

4 You are a product manager for a soft drinks company with profit responsibility for a range of canned drinks sold through vending machines. Fully explain the type of financial analysis you will require and how you will use such information to manage the brands for which you are responsible.

5 Scrumptious Cakes plc supply a ranges of pastries and cakes to supermarkets, delicatessens and tea shops. In search of further growth they are trying to decide whether they should:

(a) adopt a programme of product development and expand their range of products;

(b) consolidate their position with their current products but further develop their sales through new distribution outlets.

Advise them as to how they should evaluate the two options.

REFERENCES

CIMA (2002) *Business Strategy*, Distance Learning Study Pack.

Doyle, P. (2000) *Value Based Marketing: Marketing Strategies for Corporate Growth and Shareholder Value*, Chichester: Wiley.

Drury, C. (2000) *Management and Cost Accounting*, 5th edn, London: Thomson Learning.

McLaren, J.(2003) 'A sterner test', *Financial Management*, July/August.

Wilson, R. (1999) *Accounting for Marketing*, London: Thomson Learning.

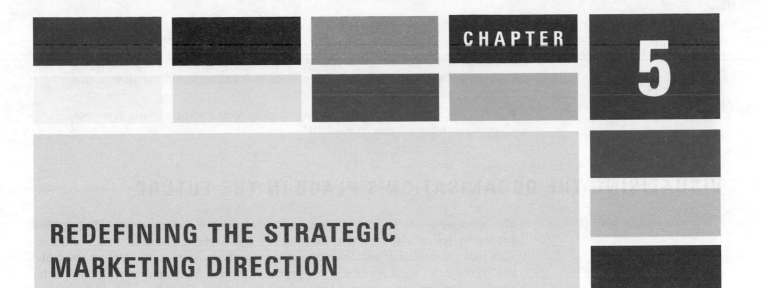

CHAPTER

5

REDEFINING THE STRATEGIC MARKETING DIRECTION

Introduction

The starting point for strategic redefinition is visualising the firm's place in the future. But predicting the future is not an exact science and so is highly risky. Developing possible scenarios for the firm can be helpful, but in the end one view of the future is needed. Because many of the environmental changes, such as technology and the changing boundaries of markets, as we have discussed in the early chapters of this book, have such an impact on the competitive structure of the market, firms must decide from time to time exactly what business they wish to be in and determine whether their current strategy will be successful and sustainable in the future.

In reconfirming the appropriateness of their current strategy, or re-formulating a new strategy, firms should revisit the underpinning generic strategies. Strategic decisions are needed in segmentation, targeting and positioning, choice of competitive strategy and growth ambitions.

Against this background the future business proposition can be developed around the competitive advantage or market gap to be exploited, and decisions taken about the competitive stance that will be adopted by the firm in the market. Specifically this chapter addresses the alternative competitive stances of pioneers, leaders, challengers, followers and market nichers and the decisions they must make to secure or improve upon their market position and performance. The market entry, marketing mix and company capability gaps are then defined in this chapter, before being dealt with in greater detail in later chapters of this book.

Learning objectives

After reading this chapter the reader should be able to:

- Describe the formulation and evaluation of competitive strategies
- Appreciate the importance of a distinctive value proposition in securing the organisation's position in the future and understand the reasons why marketing strategies wear out and become unsuitable for the future

- Evaluate the generic strategies in the context of today's competitive environment and explain the decisions that are required for an effective generic marketing strategy

- Critically appraise strategic marketing decisions for the varying competitive positioning strategies in markets.

VISUALISING THE ORGANISATION'S PLACE IN THE FUTURE

The starting point for the marketing strategy reorientation is **visualising the future** to see whether or not the firm still has a viable position in the market. This may sound harsh and for many managers the answer will be 'most certainly yes'. For others the answer will be 'probably in one form or another'. For a substantial number, however, the answer will be almost certainly 'not in the present form'. In looking forward, the timescale and magnitude of the likely changes affecting organisations will differ substantially. As we said in Chapter 4, what is viewed as the long term can vary enormously between business sectors depending on the length of the market life cycle in that industry. In some sectors an organisation might adopt a planning time horizon of three years, whereas in others it could be five or even ten to fifteen years.

At this point we would add a word of caution or, perhaps, optimism. Changes in the market environments are continually occurring as we have discussed earlier, and in some situations the changes take place faster than managers can cope with, perhaps because of unexpected critical events or unpredictable factors that will affect their decisions. In other business sectors the changes to the market structure and dynamics take longer to emerge. However, often there are visible signals that can be picked up giving a clear indication to the organisation as to what might happen in the future. This is why Drucker talks of the future as already having happened. Organisations and managers with insight will be continuously reflecting and re-evaluating their marketing strategy and deciding what action should be taken to ensure that the firm in some form or another has a robust future.

Against the background of the anticipated changes in their markets, organisations will have to decide which of the following actions are needed:

- Maintain essentially the current role and contribution to the value chain in the sector(s) in which they operate.

- Make some major modifications to their role and contribution to the value chain in the current sector, for example, by vertical integration.

- Carry out a similar supply chain role in a new sector, perhaps through horizontal integration.

- Completely reinvent their role and contribution in a new sector through diversification.

These are visualised in Figure 5.1.

In order to do this the managers in the organisation must agree on the most likely future scenario for what will happen in the market and make a decision on whether the present strategy will deliver satisfactory results, or will require substantial revision.

So far the discussion has been concerned with the impact of changes in the market environment on the future role for the organisation and deciding how radically the organisation must change in order to respond to it. However, the most innovative pioneering organisations drive the sector change themselves. They revisualise their own future and make sweeping changes to their strategy in order to position themselves to take advantage of future growth opportunities. In doing this they force all the players in the sector to reinvent themselves too. Some examples of pioneering firms include Southwestern Airlines, First Direct in telephone banking and Dell Computers.

Such firms, often small and entrepreneurial, are not held back by cautious decision making, traditional and subjective judgements about the sector, internal focus, and wanting to base decisions on the past accumulation of assets. They build their competitive advantage with an external focus, around future activities that will add value for customers and a more objective analysis of strengths, weaknesses and capabilities. Spotlight 5.1 shows how, over the last ten years, two successive CEOs have set out to reinvent IBM.

What business are we in?

Assuming that the organisation does see a place for itself in the future, the next question that needs to be answered is what will be the nature of the added value contribution of the organisation to the business sectors in which it operates now and in the future? In other words it will have to ask, once again, what business are we in? As shown in Spotlight 5.1, as well as responding to the market changes, the organisation's view of its own capabilities, experience and ambition will and should be strong determinants of its future role definition. Often the most difficult challenge is for managers to work out exactly what is their source of competitive advantage that appears in the form of products and services that customers are prepared to pay for.

In addition to asking what business we are in, other questions follow. Which value chain are we part of? And what contribution do we make to that value chain now? Is the nature of the value chain likely to change, and what will be the new roles? And, therefore, what contribution can we make in the future? For example, the removal of block exemption for car manufacturing by the European Union in 2003 led to changes in the role of car dealerships. Block exemption meant that car dealers were tied to a specific car brand that had effective control over the dealership. In the future car dealers will be able to stock whichever car brands they choose. This will lead to car supermarkets and considerably greater power for the dealers but, perhaps, a more limited role too. Already, Mercedes in the UK has responded to this by taking over ownership of its main dealerships.

In the UK the role of certain organisations within the rail travel industry has been altered by successive governments. The relationships between infrastructure providers, train operating companies, maintenance service providers,

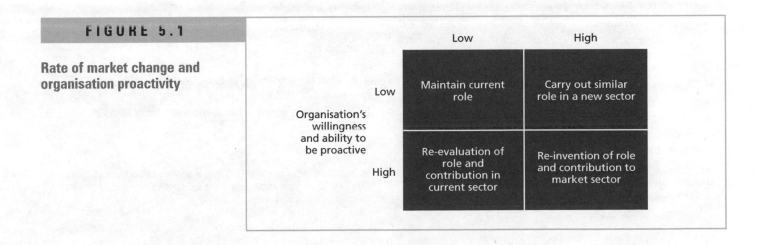

FIGURE 5.1

Rate of market change and organisation proactivity

the strategic authority, regulators and the funding subsidy provider (the government) became increasingly complex and problematic, leading to the withdrawal of one major contractor from the sector and the removal of another firm's operating licence.

There are many examples of organisations that have reinvented themselves. Nokia saw the opportunity in new technology to reinvent itself from a small local manufacturer into a global mobile phone supplier.

It is tempting to believe that whenever change is occurring in a market environment, all organisations in the market must respond by changing too, but a word of caution is necessary. Persuading organisations that change is always necessary sells the books of business gurus and generates huge revenues for business consultants. Moreover, newly appointed chief executives feel that they must prove their worth to the organisation by making sweeping changes. However, no-change strategies or making minor changes can be an appropriate strategic response for niche players and has proved to be successful for many organisations. Some of the most successful firms have made minor rather than major changes to their strategy over long periods.

It requires equally bold strategic marketing decision making to stick to a winning formula and maintain a niche position in the middle of market upheaval. However, the decision to maintain the current strategy must be the result of thorough analysis and quality decision making. In practice too many organisations fail to make the incremental changes necessary to keep them in tune with the market and, consequently, when they do finally need to change, a complete reinvention may be needed to ensure survival.

SPOTLIGHT 5.1 — Reinvention of IBM

IBM has sought to reinvent itself twice during the last ten years. Often the style of reinvention is determined by the chief executive. Lou Gerstner, after spells working for consultants McKinsey, American Express and as chairman and chief executive of RJR Nabisco, took over as chairman of IBM in 1993 after the company had reported losses of US$8.1 billion on revenues of US$62.7 billion. During Gerstner's time at IBM the share price increased from US$13 to US$80 and the sales forecast for 2002 was US$6.7 billion profit on revenues of US$85.9 billion. Gerstner knew little about IT but he did know about marketing, and transformed the company into one that became customer led. The company was reinvented from essentially a mainframe computer manufacturer to a services and solutions business that provided advice for integrating hardware and software.

Gerstner was succeeded by Sam Palmisano, who recognised that with two notable exceptions, Microsoft and Intel, profits in the industry were migrating from the makers of components, such as disk drives, microchips and operating systems, towards suppliers of software, services and consultancy. Palmisano indicated a new direction for IBM by buying the management consulting business of PricewaterhouseCoopers, staffed by 30 000 consultants, for US$3.5 billion. He also laid out his vision for computer systems that are self healing and available 'on demand', like utilities. The opportunity that results from this strategy evolution is business process outsourcing, which is a virtually unlimited market compared to the US$1000 billion a year that companies spend on IT.

An example of this is Procter & Gamble who have signed a US$400 million ten year contract with IBM to outsource the management of its IT infrastructure, as well as other business processes such as relocation services, employee benefits and administration.

Questions

1 To what do you attribute IBM's reinvention?

2 What lessons might other firms learn from IBM's experiences?

Sources: adapted from: Hall, A. 'Curing a sickness called success'. *Sunday Times,* 15 December 2002, and Gerstner, L. *Who says Elephants Can't Dance,* HarperBusiness, November 2002

Sector boundary changes

Trends such as increasing privatisation of what used to be state monopolies, and the deregulation of industries in trading blocs such as the European Union, have led to a changing of boundaries between sectors and sometimes their entire removal. Some years ago petrol retailers saw themselves firmly in the oil industry and never expected to face supermarkets as major competitors. Banks too face competitors amongst supermarkets offering financial services. Supermarkets no longer define their markets in terms of the products they offer but in terms of their consumers and the services and products that they may want. By redefining their markets, as we discussed in Chapter 3, new composite market sectors have emerged, for example, in the home communication and entertainment sectors.

New competition

In defining a new role within the supply chain it is essential that the organisation takes into account the likely future strategies of competitors. As we saw in Chapter 3, the way a company defines its market boundaries also determines how it defines its competitors. If an organisation has a knowledge management capability, it will have identified its indirect and potential competitors as well as its current direct competitors. If a company is to have the capability to make effective strategic marketing decisions it needs a good understanding of who its potential and existing competitors are, and be able to anticipate existing and possible future strategies and capabilities and respond accordingly. Challenge 5.1 shows how the British Council is facing increased competition from new sources in the market for higher education.

The organisation should know how competitors might respond to any of its major marketing initiatives. However, arguably more important for an organisation than being able to anticipate the future actions of existing competition is being able to cope with new competitors from the most unlikely of sources. Organisations can make totally unexpected moves into a traditionally unrelated market sector, or into a country market that is very distant from its home base.

Value chain

In answering the question 'What business are we in?' it is important to recognise that competition is no longer simply between individual firms. As we have already suggested, organisations must define their role and contribution within the **value chain**. The organisation should also consider what would happen to the value chain if it was completely obliterated by a computer virus. How easy would it be for the organisation's contribution to be substituted by others in the supply chain – or would a company's demise not really be noticed or simply accelerate other supply chain efficiencies?

Even if the organisation's contribution within the supply chain is confirmed, in practice the future is secure only if the supply chain itself is effective and performs well, because competition increasingly occurs not between individual organisations but between competing supply chains.

Because of the interdependencies of supply chain working, as well as defining 'what business we are in', organisations must also reconfirm their essential dependencies and partnerships, for example, with component suppliers, service providers, intermediaries and customers that can either secure or destroy their future. They must decide how strong these partnerships are and how successful the supply chain leader is likely to be in the future.

If the organisation is highly dependent on a supply chain it needs to have full confidence in the future competitiveness of the supply chain as a whole, or in the lead player's, as well as its own, capabilities. This should prompt a further dimension to the review of 'what business we are in'.

As a result of visualising the future an organisation will reach conclusions about its role and contribution within the competitive market environment, redefine what business it is in and, if it has critical dependencies within the value chain, decide whether or not they will be reliable.

STRATEGY FAILURE, WEAR OUT AND THE NEED FOR A BRAVE DECISION

Having visualised the future, the next step is to decide whether the existing marketing strategy will secure the organisation's place in the future, or whether the strategy needs to be modified or completely reinvented. However, before

CHALLENGE 5.1

British Council losing ground in competing with Australia and the USA to sell British education

A recent study of overseas students by Mori concluded that the UK remains the first choice for study. Students felt it had the best academic record, UK qualifications are highly regarded and students gave living in a multi-cultural society as a main reason. They felt the UK was safer than the USA and the UK's involvement with the USA in the war on terrorism and the attack on Iraq had little impact on their study intentions. However, a significant number felt the education was expensive, there were too few part time jobs and many thought the teaching was traditional, with insufficient links with commerce and the key thinkers in their chosen field.

The British Council, which markets British education overseas, claims that extra recruitment of non-EU students has generated over £1 billion for the UK and demand could reach 677 000 in the next decade.

However, competition is increasing. The traditional English speaking competitors, such as the USA, Australia and Canada, are becoming ever more proactive in the market. New competition is also coming from Germany, France and the Netherlands, who are offering courses taught in English but with lower fees. Countries that traditionally send students abroad, such as Singapore and Malaysia, are seeking to become regional learning centres themselves. Moreover, student profiles are changing and, with a greater emphasis on the need to combine study with work, the demand for distance and life long learning is increasing.

However, the experience of international students is not what many had hoped for. Universities are facing challenges in increasing pastoral care and English tuition, improving the interaction between UK and foreign students and

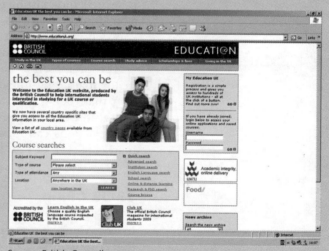

Source: British Council

avoiding high concentrations of a small number of nationalities on some courses.

The British Council believes that the universities need to think of international students more as customers and less as a market in order to ensure the quality of their experience.

Question How has the market for British higher education been redefined? What should British universities do to respond to the market changes?

Source: Adapted from 'UK in danger of losing international study appeal', The *Guardian*, 18 December 2003

thinking about what decisions are needed to create an appropriate and potentially successful marketing strategy, it is important to evaluate the reasons why marketing **strategy wear out** occurs. However effective they are, in practice all marketing strategies have limited lives. The problem is that by the time a particular strategy has outlived its usefulness many customers have already found an alternative supplier.

Strategy failure

There are a number of reasons for strategy failure and it is to these that we now turn.

Poor performance

The most obvious evidence of failure or strategic wear out is if the financial performance of the organisation is unacceptable. The reasons for poor performance could be many. Moreover, it is often difficult to identify specific cause–effect relationships amongst many variables. Each could be the subject of considerable debate about whether major changes in the strategy are required or simply some minor adjustments. This is why signal learning, as we discussed in Chapter 2, is such an important capability within organisations and why the application of financial analysis techniques to monitor and control performance are so critical if a company is to sustain its competitive advantage. If the organisation is underperforming financially it is necessary to ask certain questions. Is failure due to:

■ poor implementation of the right strategy
■ the right strategy being properly implemented but taking longer than expected to succeed
■ A strategy that is not or is no longer appropriate for the market.

If marketing managers are to ensure the strategic marketing decisions made contribute economic value added to a company, they need to understand the reasons behind the poor financial performance of the organisation. However it is important to beware of making over-simplistic assumptions about the reasons for failure. For example, as we have discussed in previous chapters, high market share does not guarantee profitable performance. It may simply indicate that the organisation has charged unrealistic prices to buy market share and therefore failed to add value to the organisation, and what is more it may be unable to maintain the market share achieved if it charges a higher price. In this case the organisation might be well advised to reduce share and concentrate on more profitable business as we saw in the marginal costing example we discussed in Chapter 4.

There are several reasons why companies fail to achieve the level of performance expected:

Operational inefficiency and poor cost control leading to uncompetitiveness: the causes of under-performance can include high production costs, poor use of fixed assets such as buildings and facilities, poor customer service, inefficiency in outsourcing and ineffective financial management.

Poor leadership and management: it can be argued that the problems highlighted above are merely symptomatic of indecisive leadership and weak management leading to lack of direction and control.

Lack of investment: because of lack of direction and a failure to generate profits, organisations fail to invest in projects to secure future growth.

They fail to invest in facilities, equipment, product and service development, brand development and market development.

Inability to cope with market changes: firms in crisis often compound the error by making unwise and inappropriate investments as a panic reaction to the situation.

The nature and intensity of change in the sector environment: different sectors experience change at different rates. For example, change in the industries that are driven by high technology, such as computer hardware and software marketing, is likely to be more dramatic than in industries dependent on well established technology, such as specialist engineering. Over time, industries that are regarded as luxuries experience greater variability in demand than necessities, such as utilities. The level and patterns of demand in the travel sector are affected by the economic situation and unexpected events, such as war and terrorism.

The problems that can contribute to strategy failure are, therefore, the inability to:

- manage an economic downturn, or an industry sector cycle
- anticipate and plan for legislative and technological changes
- cope with slower than expected growth in a key segment, country or product
- cope with slower than expected diffusion of key products and services
- coping with changes in the route to market and distribution channels.

INEFFECTIVE IMPLEMENTATION OF STRATEGIC MARKETING DECISIONS

There are a number of areas where under-performance in the management and implementation of strategic marketing decisions can lead to strategy failure. An important reason is the ineffective use of marketing tools and resources, which will be discussed in more detail in later chapters.

Dependence on one major customer

Smaller firms and especially those that are new starts with one innovative new product or service tend to be over-reliant in the early days on one or two major customers, and in a highly competitive market where competitors can quickly copy new ideas there is considerable pressure to develop new products and services and new customers, whilst also dealing with the normal challenges of developing a sustainable business with limited resources.

In practice, with the increasing concentration of retailers, distributors and manufacturers and the focus on core products, even larger suppliers often become increasingly dependent on fewer large customers and a narrow product range, also putting them at risk or, at best, making them targets for takeover.

Over-dependence on one major product

Smaller firms and especially those that are new starts with one innovative new product or service tend to be over-reliant in the early days on one or two major products. In a highly competitive market, competitors are quick to copy new ideas and thus remove the firm's market lead. Despite their limited resources, they must quickly develop additional or improved products and services in order to build a sustainable business. Even large businesses that provide one component or service in the supply chain of a global company can become vulnerable to the introduction of alternative products.

Change of customer needs and fashion

The main reason for strategy wear out, however, is the failure of organisations to respond quickly enough and adapt to changes in the market and, particularly, to respond to changes in customer needs and fashion, the emergence of a new competitor or changes in the structure of the market. In looking for one over-riding reason for the failure of a marketing strategy, most observers would place the blame firmly on the organisation being too internally and not sufficiently externally focused.

Lack of customer and competitor focus

In this situation managers often fail to spot competitor innovation which changes the nature of the market, or the emergence of a new, unexpected competitor. Senior managers often become preoccupied with managing staff, internal systems, structures and processes rather than using the resources that are available or that could be accessed to add customer value. Efforts should be made to concentrate on the activities that yield the best results for all stakeholders and to avoid the activities that simply maintain the current position or at worst drain resources from more value adding activities in order to try to save dying products and services. A number of failures over the past few years have resulted from this. IBM made the then-largest corporate loss in history in the mid-1990s (see p. 112). Simplifying the problems, their technicians believed that mainframe computers were the answer to future technology developments, whilst newer competitors focused on smaller computers and personal computers. The company simply concentrated on selling what its technicians developed. After the loss and installation of Lou Gerstner as CEO, the firm began a major change programme to become more marketing oriented.

It is not sufficient simply to be marketing oriented. It is important to ensure that efforts be focused upon those activities that will yield the best results and to avoid the activities that at best are simply maintaining the current position or at worst are draining resources from more beneficial activities.

Imminent end of a monopoly

The privatisation of state owned utilities has led to severe difficulties for the organisations being privatised. Often the process of privatisation has been politically fuelled, poorly thought out and structured and with changing expectations of what the organisation could and should do. Often the organisations are overstaffed for their reduced role, and management skills are inappropriate and inadequate for private sector operations. The new competitors do not have the encumbrances of the privatised organisation and are able to compete in lucrative niches, whilst the privatised organisation must remain supplying the full, and often in part unprofitable, customers and products.

Challenge 5.2 shows how Batelco must face the end of its monopoly of the Bahrain telecommunications market.

For the majority of such organisations the difficulty is being unable to change their strategy quickly enough to meet the new competitive situation – a problem that Batelco have so far overcome.

Withdrawal of major sponsor or investor

A number of organisations that are underwritten by a government have a major sponsor or owner and become overly dependent on the protection that this affords. A benign owner or sponsor can cover up the poor performance of an organisation and give it time to correct problems. However this also might allow the organisation to delay taking the drastic action that is needed to create an efficient or profitable business.

Sabena was an inherently inefficient, non-viable business that had support of subsidies from the Belgian government. The events of September 11, 2001 and the downturn in air travel which followed further exposed its weaknesses and the poor performance led to its ultimate failure. Private organisations sometimes sell off assets of either land or a business unit in order to balance the books and support the core business, but this, too, is pointless unless the fundamental problems of the business are addressed.

Strategy wear out

In situations where there is fairly obvious evidence of underperformance, such as low profitability or low return on investment, there is usually external pressure from owners, shareholders or even customers on the organisation's management to take action. Much more difficult are situations where the financial and marketing performance is currently either very good or still acceptable but the under-

---

CHALLENGE 5.2   Batelco and new competition

Batelco was established in 1981 as the sole provider of telecommunications in the Kingdom of Bahrain. Bahrain is an island in the Persian Gulf with a population of around 750 000. Batelco first established fixed line services but more recently has introduced a range of telecoms and IT services including mobile phones, internet service provision and media messaging services.

In the decision taken by the government to open up the market to competition, regulation of the market came under the Telecommunications Regulatory Authority (TRA). The TRA is opening up the market through arranging licenses in nine service areas.

The first license was awarded to MTC-Vodafone to supply the mobile phone market. Batelco reduced its workforce in preparation for the new competitive situation. Inevitably some customers welcomed the introduction of the new service and wished to switch brands straight away and try the new offering. For some of these the new offering did not seem to be as good and so they switched back to Batelco, however a large proportion stayed with the new licensee.

Other customers stayed loyal to the brand either because they were satisfied with the service or because they did not want the inconvenience of switching.

Questions

1 Carry out a detailed analysis of the threats to Batelco in the Bahrain market. What are the main concerns?

2 What actions might they take to retain customers and secure the firm's future?

Source: Robin Lowe

lying forces in the environment are negative. These successful organisations are at the greatest risk because their satisfactory performance means that crucial decisions are delayed, leading ultimately to the need for even more drastic action. In such cases, when it becomes obvious that the strategy needs to be changed, it is a reinvention of the strategy that is required rather than a mere reorientation if business performance is not to be adversely affected. In these organisations there are generally political difficulties. Some managers in the organisation will be aware of the potential problems from the signal learning activities carried out, but whilst results still look attractive or problems can be attributed to business cycles or a temporary downturn, a major reorientation of the strategy will be delayed.

The underlying causes of the future under-performance will have taken hold before it becomes clear to senior management that something needs to be done urgently.

Without clear and decisive leadership in strategic marketing decision making there may be considerable disagreement about the reasons for the problems and, often, no consensus about the solutions either, thus the senior executives of the firm may be either unwilling or unable to make the necessary changes quickly enough.

THE CHARACTERISTICS OF A SUCCESSFUL STRATEGY

Before discussing the decisions that lead to successful marketing strategies it is useful first to consider the characteristics of a successful strategy. Mintzberg (2003) suggests that a strategy is needed when the potential aims or responses of intelligent opponents can seriously affect the endeavour's desired outcome, and suggests five **definitions of strategy**:

Strategies can be intended:

1 **Strategy is a plan**: a consciously intended course of action.
2 **Strategy is a ploy**: just a specific manoeuvre to outwit rivals.

Strategies can be realised in the form of the resulting behaviours:

3 **Strategy is a pattern**: a stream of consistent behaviours, whether intended or not.

Strategic intent is often only partially realised in the form of a delivered strategy. There is often, too, an unrealised part of this strategy which leaves gaps that are often filled by emergent strategies that are not part of the initial intentions.

Strategy can be about external focus:

4 **Strategy is a position**: a unique location for the organisation within its environment achieved by matching up the organisation (internal context) with the environment (external context)

Strategy can also be an internal focus:

5 **Strategy is perspective**: an ingrained way of perceiving the world.

The important question for the organisation is to decide which of these definitions – it can be more than one – best describes the nature of the marketing strategy and whether they will lead to an appropriate strategic approach for the organisation's current and future likely situation.

Mintzberg suggests that a strategy is made up of plans for the future and patterns from the past and also that it comprises a set of objectives, policies and plans that taken together define the scope of the enterprise and its approach to survival and success. He also emphasises that for a sustainable strategy, there must be a strategic fit of the many activities which are fundamental not only to competitive advantage but also to ensuring the sustainability of the advantage. Most critically it is harder to copy intertwined activities.

THE DECISIONS THAT LEAD TO A SUCCESSFUL STRATEGY

The underpinning decisions that need to be made in the development of a successful marketing strategy relate to how managers approach the segmentation of their markets, which segments are to be targeted and how the extra value proposition is to be positioned in the market.

The benefits of making the optimum decisions with regard to segmentation, targeting and positioning are that if these decisions are based on a rigorous analysis and an appropriate understanding of the market they will ensure that managers address the issues that are central to their future strategy, and enable them to make quality decisions about where and how to compete. In the literature the issue of segmentation, targeting and positioning is often addressed as a concept applied from first principles. Many organisations apply their own interpretation of the concept but often, because insufficient thought is given to each of the elements in the process, they find that segmentation, targeting and positioning is not as helpful in driving the strategy as it could be. In strategic decision making, the question is whether the current method of segmentation is helpful and appropriate, whether the segments that have been targeted are the most profitable or can best be satisfied with the existing offering, whether some repositioning is required and, as a result, whether some significant changes are needed to the marketing mix that is applied to the segment.

Before addressing these issues, it is worth reviewing the concept. Customers are individual and have distinctive, individual and diverse requirements and expectations of suppliers, but it is not cost effective or efficient for organisations to try to design an individual marketing mix to satisfy each customer's needs. Consequently organisations identify homogeneous groups (segments) of customers with common needs and characteristics within the total market of potential customers. The groups that are most attractive to the suppliers can then be targeted, so that resources are focused on customers that the organisation is best placed to serve.

The organisation should then position itself appropriately in order to offer the maximum perceived benefit for customers in the target segment in everything that it does. Moreover, the organisation must differentiate its offering from the competitor's offerings. The customer benefits that must be satisfied must include both tangible benefits, as a product or service which delivers the specified requirements, and intangible benefits, such as the imagery created around the corporate identity of the organisation, brand or product, which must be consistent with customer perceptions, standards and values. The organisation's marketing mix must be tailored so that an extra value proposition is created and delivered that appeals to and meets the full requirements of the segment.

Before embarking on the segmentation, targeting and positioning (STP) process it is essential to ensure that the organisation is fully committed to value based marketing and so is committed to being a customer led/marketing oriented business prepared to focus its resources to achieve maximum customer added value and deliver economic value added to the organisation. Without this commitment STP marketing has little real value for the organisation.

The key decision points in the segmentation process are explained in Table 5.1.

Segmentation decisions

To be effective the **segmentation** process requires managers to obtain a deep understanding of their customers and challenge any preconceived ideas they might have, especially when they are dealing with cross-cultural markets They

TABLE 5.1	Key decisions in the STP process
Stages	*Key decisions*
1 Segmentation Choose the variables upon which the segmentation will be based.	Commit to gaining a deep understanding of the customer requirements and purchasing behaviour and reflect this in the variables used. Avoid simple, single segmentation variables that do not achieve precision in targeting and positioning
Create segments for the whole market	Ensure the segments are measurable, substantial, accessible, stable, appropriate and unique. (Wilson and Gilligan, 2004; Dibb, 2003)
Profile the segments and understand their needs and expectations	Ensure the profile is an accurate reflection of the key elements of customer attitudes, values and behaviour
2 Targeting Devise a targeting strategy	Determine the criteria for selecting the target segments, based on a deep understanding of the customers' and company capability
Prioritise the segments and decide how many to serve	Apply criteria that will enable selection decisions to be made on the basis of the segments the organisation is best able to serve or which will be the most profitable. Only target the number of segments that can be effectively resourced
3 Positioning Understand the target segment perceptions	Understand the customers' perceptions of the organisation, brand or products and where they diverge from the organisation's intended image and value proposition

must accept and deal with the diversity of customer requirements, perceptions and expectations and, wherever possible, avoid treating customers as the same. In Chapter 3 we examined the various bases and variables that can be used in segmenting national and global markets. As we saw in that chapter, the segmentation strategy of a company will involve the usage of a combination or hierarchy of segmentation variables, in order to develop a base of understanding about their customers and the structures of their markets on which the company can develop the extra value proposition and distinctive positioning.

In applying the process of segmentation there are a number of key decisions that managers must take which will significantly affect the outcomes. The typical consumer base variables that are used for segmentation were examined in Chapter 3. The decision as to the choice of variables used is important as it represents what is common but distinctive amongst the individual customers that make up the market.

A chemical company supplying carrier chemicals for toiletries and pharmaceuticals (not the active ingredients) observed that its main segmentation criteria were whether the customers were:

- pioneers (innovators, who required R&D support)
- local, regional or global brands
- centralised or localised.

Their strategy was based on supplying decentralised global players, but a high proportion of the market was supplied through distributors to national companies, such as Boots the Chemist in the UK. In Asia many of the smaller national players were growing fast and were expected to be the future regional players, but they only had relationships through distributors, not directly. The company's decentralised account management strategy put the company at a disadvantage as global customers were able to purchase all their requirements at the lowest local price.

Challenge 5.3 shows how a transnational perspective can be taken to segment the market for tourists to Australia and provide a basis upon which to carry out more targeted marketing.

Targeting decisions

Real customer insights can reveal some surprising, apparently insignificant and certainly not 'text-book' points of differentiation between competitor products that probably have a disproportionate effect in the purchasing process. An example might be having somewhere convenient to hold a cup or mobile phone in the car.

If appropriate decisions are made with regard to segmentation, **targeting** and positioning it should help the organisation to be more resource effective by ensuring that the organisation focuses on attractive or profitable segments. It is not possible for organisations to devote resources to all their potential opportunities and so, as we discussed in Chapter 3, managers need to evaluate the profitability and attractiveness of the potential segments and identify the strategic options. They should then make decisions as to which to target in terms of potential economic value added and strategic attractiveness. A focused strategy achieved by targeting the segments that are likely to be the most satisfied will lead to success, profitability and the confidence to then tackle the next highest priority segments.

As we will discuss in Chapter 8 it is essential to measure and evaluate the profitability of each segment and decide whether under-performance of any segments is due to the use of ineffective segmentation criteria, poor targeting and prioritisation, ineffective resource utilisation or a poorly designed marketing mix.

Positioning and repositioning decisions

Having identified and refined the profile of the target segments, the challenge is then to develop the **positioning** of the organisation, brand, product or service. There are two key points in achieving success in positioning:

■ The positioning must be as distinctive as possible and clearly differentiated from the competition.

■ The organisation's image that it wishes to project through all its activities must converge with the customer's perception.

Real customer insights can reveal some surprising, apparently insignificant and certainly not 'textbook' points of differentiation between competitor products, that probably have a disproportionate effect in the purchasing process; two of these are illustrated in Challenge 5.3.

Through the image created to confirm their positioning, organisations make choices. They put a value proposition to customers that makes promises about the quality of the products and level of service they might expect. The organisation also implicitly states that customers like you (with your demographic, lifestyle or behavioural characteristics) buy their products and services. By inference they may also be saying that customers that do not have these characteristics probably do not buy this product or service.

CHALLENGE 5.3   Segmenting the Australian tourism market

The concept of a global segmentation hierarchy can be illustrated by segmenting the visitors to Australia. Some years ago Australia was marketed largely through images of Sydney Harbour Bridge, the Opera House and Ayers Rock and on a country by country basis. This did not really reflect the diversity of experience offered or sought, or the similarity of experience sought by visitors from different countries. The visitors might, therefore, be considered using three types of segmentation base variables:

Benefit and experience sought. The types of experience sought include: excitement from visiting less inhabited places; seeing the famous sights; visiting family and friends; meeting business associates; watching sporting events etc

Visitor characteristics. This would include gap year students backpacking; '5 star' wealthy tourists; business travellers; families etc.

Communication preferences. This is how they might be reached through targeted rather than mass communication, and cross border communication strategies rather than country-based strategies. For example, students might be targeted through university campuses, business people through international travel magazines.

Question: How might this segmentation strategy be used to achieve more targeted marketing through the marketing mix?

Source: Getty Images

Source: Robin Lowe

Organisations must take care with this type of positioning. Particular problems exist where the imagery is created for one target market segment but is unacceptable to another segment. There is a worldwide customer segment that derives benefit from the smell of an expensive perfume. The perfume manufacturer might target a lifestyle segment by promoting a sexy, provocative image. Whilst this might be very successful in many markets, some cultures may find it offensive. Because there is leakage of mass market promotion outside the intended target audience, potential customers from other segments may rethink their purchasing preferences.

Perceptual mapping and distinctive positioning

Given the significance of customer perception in deciding upon a positioning strategy, **perceptual mapping** is used to distinguish between customer perceptions of competitor positioning. Customers are asked to place the relative positions of competitors along a high–low continuum for a number of criteria and these can then be aggregated in a simple two dimensional or a computer generated multi-dimensional matrix. Customer perceptions of the competitive positioning of car brands in two dimensions, quality and price, would leave a cluster of brands such as Ford, Toyota, General Motors, Renault, Mazda and Honda very close together. These two attributes may not significantly distinguish between many of the brands, and so may not help with determining a positioning stance that individual firms might adopt in order to drive their marketing mix strategy. Many firms that have not bothered to obtain real customer insights believe wrongly that such dimensions as quality, service or price are differentiators. The decision that organisations should make is what criteria could be used on the perceptual map axes that would be helpful for positioning. In the car industry the criteria might be applying the high–low continuum to such criteria as sporty performance, being economical, a prestigious image, being family oriented or self assurance.

When an organisation is performing well and there is little serious competition it often will not feel the need to pay too much attention to positioning. As competition becomes more intense the challenge is to find a position on the perceptual map which is unique to the organisation and is based on criteria that are important to the target segment.

Repositioning

If the organisation is under-performing, is not appealing to a sufficient volume of the target segment, is coming under increasing attack from competitors, or the target segments are simply not large enough to sustain a growing business, it may be necessary for the organisation to be **repositioned**. This decision should not be taken lightly as the investment and commitment necessary to carry it through effectively can be huge. Effective positioning is achieving a convergence between customer perceptions and the organisation's positioning delivered through the marketing mix, and this is difficult enough. Effective repositioning requires the organisation to reformulate every aspect of its marketing mix, neutralise old customer perceptions and recreate and influence new perceptions by actions and communications. Changing well entrenched customer perceptions is a very lengthy process, and subtle repositioning communicated through promotional messages is unlikely to be understood by customers who do not have high involvement in the organisation, brand or product.

Spotlight 5.2 on Pret A Manger shows the difficulty of making international growth decisions and the possibility of using repositioning to achieve further growth.

Whilst some repositionings have been very successful, others have left customers confused. Lucozade was successfully repositioned from an energy drink for people that were ill to a drink for sporty people needing an extra energy boost. Guinness was repositioned from an old person's traditional beer to a more fashionable drink for younger age groups. Kylie Minogue has been successfully repositioned for an additional or different audience on a number of occasions. The Labour party in the UK was repositioned from being focused on working class values to appealing to 'Middle England', which led to success in the 1997 general election.

A number of UK retailers, such as Burtons, Woolworths, BHS and Littlewoods spent some time during the 1990s in unsuccessful repositioning attempts.

Confirming customer perceptions

Through their marketing mix activities organisations make promises and deliver their positioning stance. They must test whether their performance delivers against the promises and against **customer perceptions**. If a customer's experience of consuming a product or service does not conform to their perceptions or if the reality of the product or service contradicts the image that they have then they will be disappointed and will not stay loyal to the company, brand or product.

In these cases the marketing mix can then be further tailored to suit customer needs, and this will lead to greater brand loyalty of customers. To achieve this, however, managers must clearly define and communicate the organisation's **competitive stance**, value proposition and positioning. They must explain how the offer differs from that of the competition.

SPOTLIGHT 5.2   **Pret A Manger – retail is detail**

For Julian Metcalfe, founder of Pret A Manger, the cliché 'retail is detail' is a commandment. He admits to being obsessed with every aspect of the business.

Pret A Manger started in 1986, selling sandwiches and drinks. The second shop opened five years later, and by 2003 there were 150 worldwide. The expansion has not always run smoothly. The British business was doing well in 2002, showing profits of US$6 million, but overseas expansion led to the company making an overall loss in the year to December 2002. Metcalfe believed that the overseas expansion was carried out too quickly and this led to the chief executive and deputy chief executive leaving the company. Twenty-two outlets were opened in the USA in one year and Metcalfe questioned why the company was planning a shop in Beijing when it did not have one in Bromley, UK.

Metcalfe believes that Pret should always be aiming to improve in every way. It should have the best carrot juice and the best sausage rolls. He believes that changing the lighting and layout in one store could improve sales by 30 per cent. He also sees the model evolving. Starbucks and Costa have succeeded by creating a café society, by creating the right atmosphere with softer seating and lighting. He believes a similar approach by Pret could allow the company to generate more business later in the afternoon and at weekends, and allow them to open 200–300 new outlets. Growth and international growth can be successful, but they must be managed carefully alongside market development.

Question Do Pret need to consider repositioning themselves if they are to achieve global brand status?

Source: Goodman, M. (2003) 'Pret A Manger puts US growth on a back-burner', *Sunday Times*, 2 November

Future development of STP marketing

Whilst the STP concept has been used by many organisations for many years it has proved difficult to establish quantified benefits on business performance due to the complexity of the business environment. Dibb (2003) also points out that there is little practical guidance on the use of the practice. These two areas would benefit from further research. For these reasons, STP marketing should be regarded not as a marketing tool, but rather a conceptual framework. Its value is in emphasising the need for greater consumer insight and providing a connection to strategic marketing decision making.

The determination and capability of organisations to gain greater customer insights and to manage customer data allows ever smaller sub-segments to be profiled, targeted and served as niche markets. In the limit the sub-segment size can be one, giving rise to one to one marketing, and this is discussed in Chapter 7.

THE VALUE PROPOSITION AND COMPETITIVE STANCE

Through its positioning stance, the organisation states on what basis it will compete and makes an implied value proposition to its target customer segment. As we said in Chapter 1, in developing a value based marketing approach, a company has to *define* value in terms of customer expectations, thus it needs to provide customer benefits, not features. In its value proposition, it has to *develop* customer value and in its marketing programme it has to *deliver* customer value.

At this point it is worthwhile revisiting the first lesson of marketing, that customers buy benefits, not features. It is assumed that organisations surviving in today's competitive environment must offer good quality and service, and many other benefits too, such as competence in consulting or safety and performance in tractor manufacture. Consequently, such benefits as quality and service are no longer differentiators between competing products. They are hygiene factors, so quality and service are not reasons to buy, but if high quality and service are absent then this is a reason *not* to buy.

In the car market Japanese manufacturers were successful during the 1970s and 1980s because of durability, quality and reliability, but the basis of competitive advantage changed during the 1990s to include such factors as design and image, which explains why customers are still prepared to pay more for a Volkswagen than the equivalent Skoda, which contains many of the same components at a much lower price.

Developing sustainable advantage

Earlier, we suggested that some of the greatest organisations have maintained a very consistent strategy underpinned by a clear competitive advantage over many years, sustaining it through refreshment rather than major overhauls. Wilson and Gilligan (2004) emphasise that the problem for many organisations is not developing competitive advantage but sustaining it over a long period of time, thus avoiding the need to continually change the strategy.

Competitive advantages can be identified by taking one of three approaches, according to Wensley (1987):

- those residing in the organisation
- those stemming from functional areas
- those that result from relationships with external entities.

Davidson (1987) identifies eight sources of **competitive advantage** in Figure 5.2, and for a winning strategy he suggests at least one competitive advantage is needed. For above average growth and profits, however, more are usually needed. We would suggest that one competitive advantage suggests a business formula that can more easily be copied, whereas more than one competitive advantage suggests a more complex intertwining of activities that is more difficult to replicate by a competitor.

Ikea has developed competitive advantage in its market through building a number of competitive advantages, but is now being challenged in the UK, see Challenge 5.4.

FIGURE 5.2

Sources of competitive advantage

- A superior product benefit
- A perceived advantage, perhaps created through imagery and effective communication
- Low cost operations
- Legal advantage, because of patents, copyrights or a protected position
- Superior contacts
- Superior knowledge of customers, markets, science or technology and ?
- Scale advantages
- Offensive attitudes, competitive toughness and a determination to win

---

CHALLENGE 5.4   Ikea – no room for complacency

Ikea was created by Ingvar Kamprad 60 years ago as the 'flat pack it high sell it cheap' furniture and homeware retailer. The Swedish company was based on the idea that as long as the price was right customers would be prepared to travel to out of town locations, queue, collect their purchases and assemble the furniture themselves. In 2002 286 million people bought £8 billion of goods. 130 million copies of the Ikea catalogue are printed in 28 languages.

In the UK there has been little direct competition for the Ikea formula and the company has achieved the fastest market share growth in the sector over the last five years to 4.6 per cent, despite an advertising campaign that poked fun at some aspects of British culture.

The UK market for furniture is worth £20 billion and seems to be the next battleground for Britain's leading retailers. In a decade, spending on the home increased as a proportion of the total expenditure at supermarkets from 20 to 23 per cent, whilst spending on food and clothing has declined from 47 per cent to 41 per cent. Supermarket chain Sainsbury's is launching 2500 products in 220 stores, Tesco is entering the market with homewares and furnishings and Marks & Spencer is establishing stand-alone homeware stores. Companies such as Next and the do-it-yourself retailers are also expanding their activities.

New stores are being opened by Ilva (Denmark), Ka (Spain) and a joint venture between MFI, the company with 7.9 per

Source: St Lukes/IKEA

cent, the largest share of the furniture market, and Ethan Allen of the USA. It is, however, Argos, the catalogue based retailer with 5.6 per cent of the furniture market that appears to have recently increased its market share most rapidly.

Question   What should Ikea do to counter the threat of competition?

Source: 'Retail giants home in on arrogant Ikea', *Sunday Times*, 23 October 2003

Alternative competitive stance

In any market it is possible to identify competitors who adopt different competitive stances. The most significant difference is between the market makers, who take the initiative and drive the market forward in new directions, and the market takers, who follow their lead.

Pioneers

Pioneers in a market are those innovative firms that take the market in a new direction, by creating or exploiting a breakpoint, which is discussed in greater detail in Chapter 7. There is evidence from PIMS (Profit Impact of Marketing Strategies) research, discussed by Wilson and Gilligan (2004), that suggests that first movers in a market tend to be more profitable than the companies that follow them. There are many pioneers that have achieved spectacular success and some are discussed in this book. However, many pioneering organisations innovate but fail to capitalise on their ideas. Such firms tend to fail to erect barriers to entry that will enable them to develop a profitable market and defend it against new competitors. Consequently they are soon overtaken by other firms.

Leaders

In most business sectors there is usually one organisation that is the leader. It has greater market share than the others and has the greatest influence on the nature and pace of change of the sector because of its approach to pricing, new product introduction and technological innovation, advertising and promotion and distribution. Its large market share and resources provide the opportunity to make substantial profits.

Challengers

There is often one challenger, or occasionally two, intent upon building market share in the business sector either by attacking the leader directly or by acquiring smaller competitors in order to challenge the dominance of the leader.

Followers

Followers in a sector typically try to maintain the status quo and hence their own stability not by challenging the leaders or challengers, but rather by concentrating on delivering satisfaction to their chosen segment or sub-segment and using resources very efficiently.

Niche

In almost all sectors there are smaller organisations that survive and grow by specialising in certain limited parts of the market, in which they believe their major competitors, the leaders, challengers and followers, will have little interest. Nichers build up very focused expertise, market knowledge and customer relationships that they hope will form barriers to entry and will deter other competitors from attacking them.

Considerable discussion can be found in marketing strategy textbooks of the alternative approaches that might be adopted for each of these types of firm. Given the increasing intensity of competition, a number of writers have used military analogies to attempt to explain why some strategies might be more successful than others. Rather than discuss these approaches and their strategies, we have instead focused throughout this book on some of the types of decisions that need to be taken by organisations in each of these situations.

DEVELOPING THE FUTURE STRATEGY AND GAPS IN STRATEGIC CAPABILITY

The development of a new strategy involves not only building upon the organisation's capabilities but also, in meeting the segment's needs, positioning the brand and product offer through the effective development and delivery of the marketing mix. In determining how future sustainable competitive advantage can be built, it is inevitable that the organisation will identify capabilities and assets that it will no longer use in the new strategy and **gaps in strategic capability** that will have to be filled if it is to be successful in the future. Strategic marketing decisions will be required to ensure that the organisation has the right strategic fit of activities and the capability to deliver these activities. Many organisations fail to implement their marketing strategy effectively because of the gap between their strategic intent, developed during the strategy planning stage, and the strategic reality and delivery capability.

In practice, no organisation has unlimited resources and so the key decisions in the implementation stage are as much about reducing resources and investment in areas that have limited future potential in order to concentrate the resources and investment in areas of future growth. Some important decisions will be needed in a number of key areas:

Nature of the business: the decisions reached about what business the firm is in could well lead to decisions about investments in the value chain, such as manufacturing, distribution, design and development, service provision.

Geographic expansion/market development: the decisions in this area, which will be dealt with in the following chapter, include the market entry and marketing mix strategies, but also need to take account of the ambitions, skills and capabilities of staff in international markets.

Value based marketing investment: the strategic marketing decisions must focus on adding value both to the customer and to the organisation and the judgements that are made about investment options in marketing will reflect this. This is dealt with in Chapter 7.

Outsourcing: critical to the area of value adding are decisions about outsourcing or using in-house services. These decisions may well be essential for the sustainability of the strategy, but could require a major shift in the organisation's role and contribution in the supply chain.

Co-operation and competition alliances and partnerships: the organisation must decide whether it has in place the alliances and partnerships that can further leverage the competitive advantage of the organisation. This is discussed in Chapter 11.

Innovation for reinvention: where a major change is needed in the organisation's activities, the organisation must decide how it can develop the innovative capability to achieve both periodic step change improvements as well as incremental change.

The 7S framework: the 7S framework provides the organisational checklist for managing through change. It focuses upon the organisation 'hardware', the strategy, structure and systems, the 'software', the management style, staff and skills, and, central to everything the organisation does, its shared values.

SUMMARY

- Redefining a firm's strategic direction starts with visualising the firm's place in the future. Predicting the future, however, is not an exact science and so is highly risky.

- Often the most difficult challenge is for managers to work out exactly what is their source of competitive advantage in the form of products and services that customers are prepared to pay for.

- In practice too many organisations fail to make the incremental changes necessary to keep them in tune with the market and, consequently, when they do finally need to change, a complete reinvention may be needed to ensure survival.

- Innovative pioneering organisations have the capability to visualise their own future and make sweeping changes to their strategy in order to position themselves to take advantage of future growth opportunities. In doing this they force all the players in the sector to reinvent themselves too.

- Strategy failure is usually due to either poor implementation of the right strategy, the implementation of the right strategy taking longer than expected to succeed or a strategy that is no longer appropriate for the market.

- The underpinning decisions that need to be made in the development of a successful marketing strategy relate to decisions as to how managers approach the segmentation of their markets, decisions as to which segments are to be targeted and how is the extra value proposition to be positioned in the market.

KEYWORDS

competitive advantage	repositioned
competitive stance	segmentation
customer perceptions	strategy wear out
definitions of strategy	targeting
gaps in strategic capability	value chain
perceptual mapping	visualising the future
positioning	

CASE STUDY — Sainsbury's

Sainsbury's was once Britain's leading supermarket chain, but has recently lost its second place spot in the 'Big four' UK supermarkets to Wal-Mart-owned Asda. Despite bringing in Sir Peter Davis as chief executive at the turn of the millennium and ever-changing strategies and management, Sainsbury's has not kept pace with the supermarket sector and a serious falling out with city investors and analysts has resulted. Sainsbury's is in danger of following Safeway into further decline and losing its independence.

Davis was very active in trying to improve things. He instilled some urgency into the business, and profits rose over the three-year period. However, sales grew hardly at all (like-for-like sales growth of just 1.3 per cent in the fourth quarter of the 2003 financial year compared with 5.3 per cent at Morrison's and 4.6 per cent at Tesco).

Davis had quickly recognised the need to overhaul the systems at Sainsbury's. Within six months he had outsourced the IT function to Accenture, management consultants. He invested £2 billion on refurbishing the stores, opening ultra-modern distribution centres, and upgrading IT systems. This was accompanied by tough cost-cutting, eliminating hundreds of jobs.

Although Davis and his board claimed that their strategy was focused on profits rather than sales growth, many commentators criticised the wisdom of this approach – Sainsbury's has been left sandwiched between discount players such as Tesco and Asda, and the quality players like Waitrose and Marks & Spencer. Investors and analysts started to lose faith in Davis as the share price fell 2.1 per cent during his time as chief executive, whereas over the same period Tesco's share price climbed 17.4 per cent.

In today's economic climate people have become more price conscious. In recruiting TV chef Jamie Oliver to publicise the company, Sainsbury's hoped to appeal to a younger client group, but perhaps simply reinforced the 'southern, middle-class' image of the company.

The Davis plan to unlock value in the group's vast property estate was also disappointing. A proposed joint venture with Berkely (luxury housebuilders) and Peabody (housing trust) to build houses on surplus land around its supermarkets was abandoned.

Sainsburys sold Homebase, its DIY chain, in December 2000 for a reported £750 million. This helped fund their capital investment programme. However, just two years later Permira sold it on for £900 million, which was a little embarrassing!

A number of initiatives have been introduced to try and drive sales across the business with mixed success. A pilot venture with Boots was set up to sell health-and-beauty products in the supermarket but that ended in 2003. Sainsbury's was one of the launch partners in the Nectar loyalty card scheme in autumn 2002, and in June 2003 said they planned to open up to 100 convenience stores on the forecourts of Shell petrol stations.

William Morrison's takeover of Safeway has created a third major force among the EDLP (Every Day Low Prices) players, further complicating Sainsbury's market positioning. They may be forced to go back to the ABC1 'heartland' customers that they have traditionally served.

Davis announced in that he would step up to become chairman from Spring 2004 leaving the new chief executive, Justin King, facing an uphill struggle to reverse the company's decline.

The Sainsbury family still hold 35 per cent of the shares of the company but have failed to take steps to turn around the business. The frustration of investment fund managers at this seemed to reach boiling point in February 2004. Davis announced that he would leave the company in July 2005 and the board announced its intention to appoint Sir Iain Prosser, former chairman of Bass in his place. However, Prosser had a less than dynamic reputation and the city fought against the appointment. Eventually the Sainsbury board decided to back down and look for another chairman.

Questions

1 What do you consider to be the critical success factors for a food retailer in a highly competitive market?

2 What must Sainsbury's do to improve its performance?

Source: Sue Marriott from various public sources

DISCUSSION QUESTIONS

1 Identify the key decision points in developing an effective STP strategy and explain the reasons why many firms fail to gain the full potential that STP marketing offers.

2 Using examples to illustrate your answer explain what criteria you would use to determine if a strategy is in danger of wearing out.

3 Choose an organisation that has recently under-performed expectations. What were the reasons for the under-performance and what decisions might have been taken (and when) to turn around the organisation more quickly?

4 Choose an industry sector that has gone through substantial change. Identify which firms have been the winners and losers and explain the reasons for this.

5 A firm that supplies branded electrical D-I-Y products through large supermarkets is losing out to cheap own (supermarket) brand products. What would you recommend to improve the company's fortunes?

REFERENCES

Davidson, J.H. (1987) *Offensive Marketing*, Harmondsworth: Penguin.

Dibb, S. (2003) 'Market segmentation: changes and challenges', in Hart, S. (ed.) *Marketing Changes*, London: Thomson Learning.

Mintzberg, H., Lampel, J., Quinn, J.B. and Ghoshal, S. (2003) *The Strategy Process: Concepts, Contexts, Cases*, Harlow: Prentice-Hall.

Wensley, J.R.C. (1987) 'Marketing strategy', in Baker, M.J. (ed.) *The Marketing Book*, London: Heinemann.

Wilson, R.M.S. and Gilligan, C. (2004) *Strategic Marketing Management*, 3rd edn, Oxford: Butterworth-Heinemann.

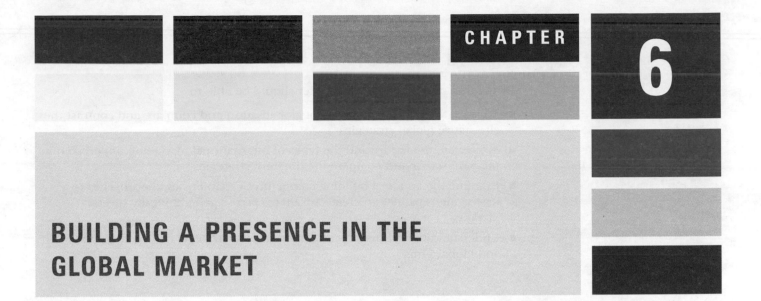

BUILDING A PRESENCE IN THE GLOBAL MARKET

Introduction

As well as making decisions about generic strategies, organisations must make decisions about their position in international markets. A number of organisations and their managers still believe that they are secure in their domestic market and have little to fear from international competition in their sector and so feel there is little point in considering strategies for a global market. However, the performance of even the very smallest organisations is being affected in its domestic or international market by cross-border purchasing activity of some kind.

For the largest firms globalisation provides the driver for development and the means by which organisational performance can be maximised. Customer value can be added and cost efficiencies can be achieved by introducing, where possible, standardised marketing programmes and processes, but, at the same time, adapting certain operational activities, products and services to meet local needs. The problem that such firms face is exactly which aspects of their international activity to standardise and which to adapt because the decisions are often context specific and are affected by the particular factors which drive change within their particular industry. This leads to firms adopting a variety of global strategies, from those that are very similar from country to country to those that are substantially different in each country in which the firm operates. For smaller firms international marketing takes a number of forms ranging from early stage exporting through international niche marketing to global e-marketing. The international development of smaller firms depends not so much on size, the nature of the industry and the environment, as on the firms' ambitions, skills and capabilities.

In this chapter we start by considering the dimensions of the concept of globalisation before considering the alternative strategic approaches and the factors that drive strategic choice. This discussion is then followed by an examination of the strategy implementation issues that MNEs might face in managing their global business and building their global presence. We then focus upon the nature of SME international development, the strategies they adopt and the implications for the management of the company.

Learning objectives

By the end of this chapter the reader should be able to:

- Appreciate the various aspects of globalisation and compare and contrast the alternative global strategies
- Appreciate the nature and the types of international marketing undertaken in the SME sector and compare the different strategies
- Examine the issues of building competitive capability and approaches to leveraging capability to create advantage across geographically diverse markets
- Understand the factors affecting international strategic management in SMEs and global firms

THE IMPLICATIONS OF GLOBALISATION FOR MARKETING DECISIONS

Before considering the implications of increased **globalisation** for marketing decisions, we start by identifying the different possible stances adopted by organisations in a global market.

The organisation's marketing stance in global markets

In today's markets few firms (and individual customers) avoid the effects of international trade and increasing cross-border competition, whether the impact is from the suppliers they use, the physical or virtual presence of competitors, or from international customers, buying in the domestic market, in foreign markets or through e-business.

The starting point therefore is for organisations to decide what their **international marketing stance** should be:

- *Domestic only*: the firm only operates in the domestic market but foreign customers might buy products and services for consumption in international markets.
- *International e-business and direct marketing*: the firm directly markets products and services in international markets from a domestic base through the internet or by direct marketing.
- *Exporting*: the firm markets its products and services across national or political borders.
- *International marketers*: the organisation has marketing activities, interests and operations in more than one country, influence or control comes from outside the country where the products and services are sold and typically profit centres are established in different country markets.
- *Global*: the whole organisation focuses on the selection and exploitation of global marketing opportunities and uses resources from around the world to build global competitive advantage

Strategy implications of globalisation drivers

The increasing globalisation of markets is directly affecting the nature of international marketing strategies. Doole and Lowe (2004) identify a number of

globalisation themes and Table 6.1 shows how these themes drive the development of international strategies.

THE STRATEGIC RESPONSE

Clearly, whilst we have identified the implications of these globalisation themes for global companies, they also create opportunities and pose threats for the other categories of domestic and international marketers too. We discuss the strategic response from smaller firms to globalisation later, but first we focus upon the strategic decisions that the very large firms make against the background of increased globalisation.

TABLE 6.1	Strategy implications of globalisation drivers
Globalisation drivers	*Impact on strategy*
Increased market access	As markets have opened up (e.g. China and Eastern Europe), firms enter higher risk markets to gain a global presence
Increased market opportunities	Deregulation of some industries (e.g. financial services) and privatisation of others (e.g. utilities) has created new opportunities
Greater uniformity of industry standards	Harmonisation of technical and professional standards within trading blocs is increasing the speed and reducing the cost of service internationalisation
Sourcing of products, components and services from a wider range of countries	Global outsourcing of products and services can reduce costs, improve access to technology, ideas and local markets and improves consistency of supply
More globally standardised products and services	Greater commoditisation of products and services means that marketers must achieve lowest cost supply or differentiate their offering by leveraging intangible assets
Common technology used in many more markets	Speed to market and speed of global diffusion of products and services based on new technology become critical
Similar customer requirements	Global segments share common expectations of products and services, and so global consistency with local adaptations is necessary
Competition from the same organisations in each major market	Markets are no longer independent and so international strategies must be cross-border, regional or global in nature
Co-operation between organisations from different parts of the world	Collaborations in the supply chain, through alliances and joint ventures, are essential, but it is difficult to manage a co-operation and competition with different business units of the same company
Worldwide organisation of distribution	Distribution and logistics need to be based on geography rather than national boundaries
Communication generated and received almost anywhere in the world	Consistency is essential for global branding and communicating with global stakeholders

Source: Doole and Lowe (2004)

Globalisation of the organisation's strategy

As major multi-nationals seek to create a worldwide presence, their corporate identity, products, services and communications become all-pervasive. As these globally available products, such as Coca-Cola, Nike and McDonald's become embedded in local markets, albeit sometimes against the wishes of local communities, they become part of the 'new' culture and so contribute to the increasing globalisation trend as well as responding to it. Moreover, international competitors, such as Pepsi, Adidas and Burger King develop strategies that enable them to compete in many of the same geographic markets, whilst local competitors must strive harder to retain their home market.

The consequence of these globalisation effects is to pose a significant opportunity and threat to all firms. It is useful to consider the degree to which a business sector might be considered to be essentially domestic, regional or global. You might think about your own organisation or one that is well known to you, and consider the degree to which the business sector is progressing towards becoming more regional or global and the degree to which organisations in the sector have also progressed to becoming regional or global players. Getting left behind might result in the business being acquired by a competitor or marginalised by customers as loyalties to local companies decline.

No matter how small or large, no matter whether they operate only in domestic markets, a few international markets, or on a global scale, all organisations are facing increased competition. Even those organisations in sectors where there is no perceived competition are subject to competitive pressures. For example, public authorities are benchmarked against those from other nations, poor performance becomes a political issue and managers of the organisation are criticised in the press. In addition organisations must grow within this competitive environment. Their survival and growth is achieved by building competitive advantage through:

■ Improved market effectiveness by adding value for 'internationally aware' customers by providing them with benefits that are significantly better than those of the competitors.

■ Improved operational efficiency and cost reductions through scale and experience efficiencies that will enable the firm to offer better value for money than their competitors.

■ Encouraging and supporting innovations that will add customer value.

■ Creating and extracting value from intangible assets, on a worldwide basis, discussed in Chapter 8.

■ Learning new and more effective ways of running the business.

Standardisation and adaptation

Central to cost saving in global strategies is **standardisation**. The more the elements of the marketing process are standardised throughout the organisation's various geographic locations, the greater the improvement in efficiency that can be made. However, when applying this to individual countries it becomes obvious that consumers may not want a globally standardised product or service due to their own local cultural preferences. Also, it may not be possible to standardise other elements of the marketing activity because of local market conditions, legal requirements and country infrastructure. To maximise revenue, **adaptation** of the marketing mix might be needed, but of course, this can be expensive.

The organisation must take into account these limitations when making decisions about which elements of marketing management it wants and is able to standardise. It is easier to standardise certain elements rather than others as represented in Figure 6.1.

Marketing objectives and strategies are more readily standardised because they are within the control of the firm. Within the marketing mix, products are most easily standardised, promotion less so and distribution and pricing with difficulty.

Distribution channels are usually already well established and price setting in different countries is subject to currency exchange rates. Even where there is a common currency, such as the Euro in Europe, it may not be possible to standardise pricing because of different taxation and the differing ability of customers to pay in countries at different stages of economic development.

Standardisation of marketing programmes and processes

In practice firms adopt a combination of standardisation and adaptation of the various elements of the marketing management programmes and processes by globalising some elements and localising others. At this point it is important to emphasise the difference between **marketing programme and process standardisation**. Efficiencies can be achieved by standardising marketing programmes, for example, by marketing the same products and services using the same new product launch or advertising campaign in a number of countries as shown in Challenge 6.1. Added value to customers can be achieved through familiar worldwide brand names, packaging and design, corporate identity and promotional imagery.

However, customers in some countries may be willing to buy from the organisation but not a standardised product. They may not like a standardised advertising programme, or multi-country packaging and might even be offended by crossborder promotions and imagery. Despite this the organisation can make efficiencies in their global operations through adopting standardised marketing processes rather than programmes. These standardised processes might include planning and managing marketing information and research, local advertising agencies and new product development. It is the standardisation of marketing processes such as these that will integrate the various disparate activities of the organisation's strategic business units around the world, encourage synergistic working and facilitate corporate learning.

FIGURE 6.1

Standardisation and adaptation of marketing activities

Source: Doole and Lowe (2004)

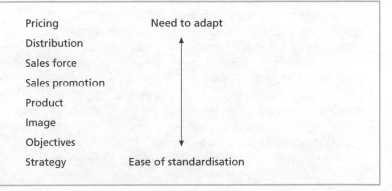

The product–market response

It is against the background of the trend towards globalisation and the need to build a worldwide presence that firms must develop strategic responses which are appropriate to their situation and feasible to implement. For MNEs, the question may be how to rationalise their activities to place greater focus on their products and services with true global potential. For firms that have progressed through the early stages of expansion into new country markets, the next decision is whether or not to progress further and, if so, what strategy they might adopt to enable them to manage their involvement in many countries. Underpinning the growth strategy in either case must be some fundamental decisions about, first, how far the firm's marketing activities can and should be standardised and, second, how the firm will develop its product portfolio and geographic coverage.

The level of geographic development and product strength will determine the strategic options available to a company. Gogel and Larreche (1989) argue that the greater competitive threats of global competition place higher pressures on the effective use of resources. The two main axes for allocating strategic resources are the development of product strength and that of geographic coverage. These two axes have to be managed in a balanced way. Focusing too much attention on product investments at the expense of geographic coverage may result in missed international opportunities. On the other hand, focusing on geographic expansion may result in under-investment in products, weakening the competitive position of the firm.

Figure 6.2 shows the alternative international competitive postures that firms might adopt.

- *Kings*. Because these firms have a wide geographic coverage and strong product portfolio they are in a strong competitive position. They have been able to expand geographically and have not dispersed their resources into weak products. They are in the best position to have an effective global strategy.

- *Barons*. These companies have strong products in a limited number of countries. This makes geographic expansion attractive to them but with greater concentration of distribution and retailing there are fewer opportunities to build the customer base quickly. It also makes them

CHALLENGE 6.1   McDonald's first global campaign

Over the last two years McDonald's has come up against stiff competition from local and global competitors, changing customer tastes away from less fried food and towards better levels of service. It has suffered criticisms from franchisees for opening up too many new outlets that take customers away from existing outlets. In order to revive its fortunes the company has decided to launch its first global advertising campaign in 50 years under the slogan 'I'm loving it'. Its last campaign 'We love to see you smile' largely failed to pay off.

A German agency Heye and Partners, a unit of Omnicom Group, has been hired to start the campaign in Germany.

The campaign consists of five common television spots that will run in most of the 118 countries in which McDonalds operates, but they will be customised with local language and pictures of local customers. The campaign aims to take a youthful approach to selling fast food, by combining music, fashion, sports and entertainment.

Question What is the significance of a global advertising campaign – is it likely to be more effective?

Source: adapted from 'McDonald's launching first global ad campaign', Reuters.com, 1 September, 2003

attractive to companies wishing to supplement their own product strength and therefore they may be takeover targets.

■ *Adventurers*. These have been driven to expand geographically, but they lack strong products. They are vulnerable to an increasing level of global competition. Their challenge is to consolidate their product position which involves internal product development, acquisition or eliminating products to concentrate on a narrower portfolio.

■ *Commoners*. Commoners have a relatively weak product portfolio and narrow geographic coverage. They may have benefited from strong mobility or legal barriers protecting them from intense competition. They are likely acquisition targets, and before any geographical expansion they need to build their product portfolio. A likely international strategy could be one of supplying own brand products to distribution chains or components and services to a major manufacturer.

The key issue for firms is that increasing geographic coverage and product strength compete for resources and each quadrant of the matrix reflects the trade-offs that may become necessary. Whilst the position of a firm on the matrix reflects how it has been able to balance its resources between consolidation and expansion of geographic coverage and product strength, the decision it has made will also have been based on its chosen attitude and commitment to achieving a global strategy.

Part of the problem for firms is that increasing market coverage or generating new products organically takes time and considerable investment. Barons and even commoners are often attractive to predatory kings that want to develop a regional or global presence quickly. The route to becoming a king can either go through the adventurer stage first (e.g. Microsoft) or the baron stage (firms that build a strong domestic market presence and product range through having a large home market), before making significant advances in foreign markets.

GLOBAL MARKETING STRATEGY DECISIONS

For the largest firms the challenge is to achieve a global reach with a significant presence in as many markets as possible. The standardisation/adaptation discussion earlier in the chapter means that there is no common all-embracing strategic approach to exploit global markets.

A number of concepts underpin the alternative strategic options available. At one extreme, the adaptation of the majority of the marketing mix elements leads to the concept of a **multi-domestic approach** in which the firm has a completely different marketing strategy for every single market. At the other extreme is a

---

FIGURE 6.2

The international competitive posture matrix
Source: adapted from Gogel and Larreche (1989)

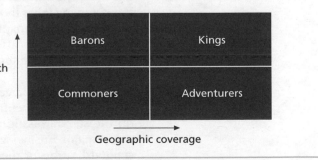

global approach in which everything in the marketing activity is standardised in many countries. In a **regional strategy** largely standardised marketing strategies are implemented in different regions of the world.

The largest, most complex companies in the world use a combination of all these strategies. A **trans-national approach** is one in which the firm has a standardised identity and corporate values throughout but delivers its strategic objectives through composite strategies which contain elements of multi-domestic, regional and global strategies.

Global strategy

A company adopting a global strategic orientation makes no distinction between domestic and foreign market opportunities, seeking to serve an essentially identical market segment that appears in many countries around the world and the customers that make up the segment in essentially the same way. Global strategies are therefore developed to compete with other global firms using the organisation's global resources. They should exploit global market opportunities and deliver short term strategic objectives and goals, but they should also support a broader corporate objective than just the immediate exploitation of another individual country market opportunity.

Sometimes it is necessary to enter an unattractive market which has global strategic significance if, for example, it is the home market of a competitor. The decision to enter an emerging market is justified because of its future rather than current potential. Thus an organisation with such a global focus formulates a long term strategy for the company as a whole and then co-ordinates the short term strategies to support this.

In considering this strategic option, it is important to recognise that the global business environment is constantly changing with many barriers to standardisation being reduced or removed. Some of the globalisation effects, such as economies of scale and the experience effect, have become more significant drivers of standardisation. So too have the high costs of innovation and launching new products; this is coupled with the increasing speed that competitors copy new advances and ever shorter product life cycles.

In practice, however, global firms strike an appropriate balance between the relative advantages of standardisation and adaptation to local tastes. There is little point in standardising programmes for marketing products and services if consumers reject them and only buy the products and services that meet their specific needs.

Multi-domestic strategies

The multi-domestic or multi-national market concept still recognises that foreign market opportunities are as important as home market opportunities. However, the company takes the view that the differences between its international markets are so acute that adaptation to meet market needs is necessary to retain competitive leverage in local markets. Thus the company essentially follows a differentiated marketing strategy with individual marketing mix strategies in many of its world markets.

There are advantages and disadvantages of a multi-domestic strategy to achieve a worldwide competitive advantage, as opposed to a global strategy that is based on the standardisation of marketing activities. However, it is quite clear that for many major businesses there are few benefits to be obtained from widespread standardisation of their activities. Consequently a well organised and managed multi-domestic strategy is an effective method for many companies to develop a global business.

An excellent example of an organisation which can be accurately characterised as having a multi-domestic strategy is Asea Brown Boveri (ABB), discussed in Spotlight 6.1. The firm used a multi-domestic strategy to gain competitive advantage in its target country markets. A key factor in the strategy is encouraging senior managers to be entrepreneurial in responding to local customer needs, industry standards and different stages of economic development. However, after a highly successful period ABB is now experiencing problems, some of which could be described as 'threats from the environment' whilst others might be the result of inadequate management.

A multi-domestic approach is a particularly appropriate global strategy when:

Industry standards remain diverse

For many traditional industries, such as those based upon engineering and particularly those that involve large investment in plant and equipment, the cost of harmonisation of standards is high and the progress to harmonisation is slow. The markets for these industries often involve a country's infrastructure, transport and utilities, and decision making often includes a consideration of impact on the local economy and environment.

Customers continue to demand locally differentiated products

Cultural heritage and traditions still play a strong role in areas such as food, drink and shopping. Whilst there are increasing moves to accept cross-border products, there is still resistance in many cultures.

SPOTLIGHT 6.1   Changes of leader in ABB

The proof that strategies wear out is demonstrated by Asea Brown Boveri. For a decade ABB, which resulted from the merger in 1988 between Sweden's ASEA and the Swiss company Brown Boveri, was widely admired and hailed as a new model of global entrepreneurialism, using multi-domestic strategies. ABB had customers in the process industries, manufacturing and consumer industries, and in utilities (oil, gas and petrochemicals). Percy Barnevik as chief executive was the architect of the model.

He created a head office with 135 staff managing 1300 companies with 5000 profit centres. He applied a 30/30/30/10 rule. He cut 90 per cent of headquarters staff by moving 30 per cent into the SBUs, 30 per cent into free standing service centres concerned with value adding activities and eliminated 30 per cent of the jobs. Similar huge cuts in management were made in the headquarters of the subsidiaries.

The management within the SBUs, which usually had less than 200 employees, were given a substantially enhanced role in managing their business. ABB employed 160 000 staff in 100 countries and a large part of ABB's manufacturing was moved away from the developed countries to the developing countries, including Eastern Europe. By employing people in developing countries ABB was in a position to sell further expertise and services as they helped build the countries' infrastructure.

Jorgen Centremann took over in October 2000 but he lasted less than two years as the company's share price halved. ABB missed its profit targets, it nearly ran out of cash as its debts mounted, and in 2002 it made its first loss of US$787 million. Part of the problem was the liability for huge claims from workers that asbestos had damaged their health.

Question   Do ABB's current problems mean that the concept of multi-domestic global strategies is invalid?

Source: adapted from Doole and Lowe (2004)

Being an insider remains critically important

The perceived country of origin of goods still has a bearing on take up of products and so local manufacturing of goods is frequently necessary to overcome this scepticism.

Global organisations are difficult to manage

In finding ways to co-ordinate global operations, firms decentralise and replace home country loyalties with a system of corporate standards and values. For some companies this proves to be problematic and, in some cases, totally unacceptable to the workforce.

Management myopia

Products and product categories are sometimes candidates for global marketing but managers fail to seize the opportunity. They often believe that the risks in working towards greater standardisation appear too great and local managers can be sceptical that greater standardisation will lead to better performance in the organisation.

Regional strategy

Perhaps one of the most significant developments in global marketing strategy is how firms respond to the rise of the regional trading blocs. Even in global industries, company strategies are becoming more regionally focused. For many companies, regionalisation represents a more manageable compromise between the extremes of global standardisation and multi-domestic strategies

Regional trading groups tend to favour their own MNEs and for companies located outside the region there can be significant tariff and non-tariff barriers. For example, the indigenous manufacturers usually get early warning of new government legislation, as they tend to be part of government decision making. By shifting operations and decision making inside the region an MNE can gain the benefits of insider advantage. This is the driving force behind the Taiwanese companies seeking to locate in the Czech Republic as shown in Challenge 6.2.

The key to developing effective regional strategies is deciding what makes the region distinctive and in what ways the marketing strategy for one region should be standardised within the region and differentiated from other regions.

Transnational strategies

If a firm has sufficient power and resources to exploit all the available opportunities on a worldwide basis, with little need to adapt strategies or involve partners to any great extent, then a simple strategy can be developed. However, many multi-nationals have a wide range of products and services, and marketing activities, such as research and development, communications and distribution, some of which might be suited to global development and others to multi-domestic or regional development. The successful exploitation of these opportunities might require a much more flexible approach to strategic development and market entry, discussed in Chapter 11. It might involve a number of partners in licensing, joint ventures and strategic alliances as well as wholly owned operations.

Trans-national companies integrate diverse assets, resources and people into operating units around the world within a loose, responsive, adaptable but coherent framework. Through flexible management processes and networks, transnational companies aim to build three **strategic capabilities**:

- global scale efficiency and competitiveness
- national level responsiveness and flexibility
- cross-market capacity to leverage learning on a worldwide basis.

In such organisations the ownership of the operations becomes less clear in terms of where any particular product was made, what the nationality of the manufacturing or service provider was, or which firms manufacture and market the product and services.

In practice many of the largest organisations in the world are very effective in global scale efficiency and competitiveness, which are the keys to success in global markets. To achieve this, these organisations frequently adopt a centralised approach to management, in order to keep tight control over resources. As a partial consequence of this they find it more difficult to respond flexibly to local requirements. The increased interest in knowledge management suggests that many organisations recognise the importance of leveraging learning around the worldwide organisation, but find it difficult to share learning without becoming deluged with data.

Ghoshal and Bartlett (1992) argue that the aim of trans-national companies is to further their global scale efficiency and competitiveness in its totality. A trans-national approach is not a particular strategy, but a strategic perspective that evolves as firms and the markets in which they operate increase in complexity.

CHALLENGE 6.2 — Czech stepping stone into Europe for Asian manufacturers

As the Czech Republic was about to become a member of the EU, Asian manufacturers saw it as a launch pad to increase their EU sales. The Czech Republic was at the centre of the wider Europe. It was the closest to Western Europe of the new EU accession states and, because of its good infrastructure, was also close to the East European market too. In 2003 Foxconn, the Taiwanese contract electronics manufacturer, was already moving manufacturing there from other parts of the world, including China, Ireland and Scotland. Set up in 2000 to produce computers for Hewlett Packard, the company grew to tenth place nationally in 2002 with a turnover of US$1.1 billion. The company had taken over the Pardubice Tesla plant of the Tesla communist electronics giant that used to employ 300 000 people.

CzechInvest, the Czech inward investment agency, reported that it was Matsushita's decision in 1996 to build TVs in Plzen that was the start, because Japanese firms tend to follow a move by a big firm. Forty-five Japanese manufacturers moved into the country with many in the electronics sector.

It was not low costs that was the reason for the electronics industry growth in the Czech Republic as labour represents only 5 per cent of total costs. It was the closeness to Western Europe and the availability of existing facilities and labour expertise. LG Philips, the Dutch Korean television tube joint venture set up a factory in central Moravia, close to the old Tesla TV facility.

The Czech Republic, however, is concerned that future growth in investment might be at a slower pace as manufacturers move east and competition from Poland, Hungary and Slovakia becomes tougher. Moreover, the appreciating currency, the koruna, is increasing relative wage and other costs, so bringing them more in line with Western costs. Lower demand had also forced the closure of a two year old plant of contract electronics manufacturer Flextronics (Singapore) and LG Philips had to cut back on production of large TV sets.

Question   Do you think this strategy by the Taiwanese firms will be successful?

Source: Adapted from 'Electronics giants go for Czech launch pad', *Financial Times*, 10 June 2003

Any strategy that is to achieve global competitive advantage for the organisation needs to accommodate some, or all, of the following:

- Simple and complex individual product and market policies, which may be independent or inter-dependent.

- Customer segments that may be specific and unique to a specific market or trans-national and valid across borders.

- Working closely with firms that are customers, suppliers, competitors and partners at the same time, but simultaneously ensuring that the values of the company are maintained and demonstrated to the external stakeholders through establishing clear and unambiguous positioning in all markets.

- Maintaining and building meaningful and added value relationships in the supply chain.

So far we have addressed the fundamental strategic decisions that the largest organisations must make in deciding where and how to compete in the global market. We now turn to where and how smaller firms compete in the same market.

SME MARKETING STRATEGY DECISIONS

Although in this section we deal with SMEs as a whole, in practice the SME sector comprises firms ranging from a single person business up to quite sophisticated businesses employing 250 people that might have a strong domestic market presence and even a significant international presence in a niche market. Furthermore, the fastest growing medium sized international firms will rapidly become large businesses. In considering decision making in SMEs therefore, we do not focus on firms with a particular number of employees but rather on the ownership and management characteristics of smaller firms in general, such as ambition, attitudes, capability and experience, and how these factors affect their decision making on geographic development.

Of the huge number of SMEs only a small percentage, perhaps less than 5 per cent, grow significantly and, of course, there is a very large amount of churn with new businesses starting, and existing businesses failing.

The SME sector is becoming more important as a creator of wealth and employment because large firms have down-sized by reducing their workforce, and have concentrated on increasingly outsourcing their non-core components, often from smaller firms. Employment in the public sector has been decreasing during this same period due to the extensive privatisation of public sector owned utilities and agencies, such as gas, electricity, water and telephones, and the increased volume of public sector services, such as cleaning and catering, which are outsourced to private organisations. In many countries this has left the small and medium sized firms sector as the only significant growing source of wealth and employment.

However, as we have seen in the previous chapters, the international marketing environment is potentially very hostile. It is a small wonder, therefore, that many companies ignore the export potential of their products and services and concentrate instead on their domestic markets.

International marketing in SMEs

In exploiting opportunities to generate revenue SMEs must make decisions about their geographic market development. In this section we review the factors that might affect their decision making process. Before doing so it is useful to consider the alternative approaches for market development.

- *Domestic marketing* is for those firms that have confidence in providing niche products and services that satisfy their loyal, local customer base. They aim to compete locally but see significant barriers in foreign markets

- *Exporting* is primarily concerned with selling domestically developed and produced goods and services abroad.

- *International niche marketing* is concerned with marketing a differentiated product or service overseas using the full range of market entry and marketing mix options available.

- *Domestically delivered or developed niche services* can be marketed or delivered internationally to potential visitors.

- *Direct marketing*, including electronic commerce, allows firms to market products and services globally from a domestic location.

- *Participation in the international supply chain of a multi-national enterprise* can lead to SMEs piggybacking on the MNE's international development. This may involve either domestic production or establishing a facility close to where the SME's new locations are established in other countries.

Domestic marketing

We have suggested that domestic marketing might lead indirectly to international marketing if buyers from foreign markets purchase products and services and export them without any real involvement from the firm. What is perhaps more interesting in domestic marketing is the increased sensitivity to culture, and awareness of the opportunities for cross-cultural marketing in the domestic market, by effectively learning lessons from international marketing. Challenge 6.3 provides an example of this.

Participation in a supply chain

Many firms are part of the supply chain of an international manufacturer or service provider and usually this means domestic marketing of supplies and subsequent exporting by the major company. The only difference for these firms, compared with other domestic marketers, is that supply chain members might 'piggy back' on the internationalisation of their major customer, following them to a new country to supply their operation there. Failure to do this might result in a competitor being created, who will supply the products and services in the new market, and possibly bid for business in the original market too.

Exporting

For many firms **exporting** is the first significant stage in the internationalisation process, as it provides the advantage of considerably expanded market potential with relatively little commitment and limited associated risk. Although considered an early stage of international marketing strategy, exporting, when defined as the selling of goods and/or services across national and political boundaries, usually through agents or distributors, is not solely the preserve of small and medium sized businesses, nor for many firms is it a temporary stage in the process of internationalisation. Many firms, both large and small, particularly those that have highly centralised management, do not progress beyond the stage of relatively limited involvement in international markets. There is an inherent weakness in exporting due to the limited involvement of exporters in the market. This often results in a lack of information and knowledge of the market dynamics and demands and, as a result, can lead to loss of business to a more effective marketing competitor.

Doole and Lowe (2004) discuss the motivations to exporting, which range from government support programmes, attractive profit and growth opportunities, economies resulting from additional orders and the possession of unique products, but they emphasise the importance of an export oriented management team.

CHALLENGE 6.3   Cross-cultural marketing at home

The traditional view of cross-cultural marketing is that it is only necessary to take cultural differences into consideration in international markets – essentially the domestic market is regarded as one culture. In a report in 2003 the Institute of Practitioners in Advertising (IPA) claimed that advertisers in the UK were missing out because they were failing to communicate with black and Asian people, whose combined disposable income was worth £32 billion. In London 32 per cent of people are of ethnic minority origin. The IPA praised a small number of companies, including telecommunications firm BT, and financial services business Halifax, but noted that if the celebrities and sports personalities, such as Thierry Henry – the face of Renault – were taken out, examples of ethnic diversity were few and far between.

Moreover, only 4 per cent of marketing communications staff came from ethnic minorities and 70 per cent of these were in support functions, such as IT and finance. This might partly explain the reason for insensitivity in some advertising campaigns that have been the cause of a number of complaints. However, achieving an acceptable balance is difficult. The advertising regulators even forced the Commission for Racial Equality to withdraw a poster campaign featuring a picture of a black man with the tag line

Renault
Source: Publicis

'Scared? You should be, he's a dentist'. The Advertising Standards Agency (ASA) said the ad was more likely to reinforce stereotypes than to change them.

Question What can cross-cultural domestic marketing learn from successful international marketing?

Source: *BBC Online*

Renault
Source: Publicis

Renault
Source: Publicis

Many companies with export potential never become involved in international marketing. The reasons given by companies for not exporting include too much red tape, slow payment by buyers, lack of competitive products, the danger of payment defaults, a lack of trained personnel and language barriers.

Experienced exporters tend not to highlight these same barriers to exporting, which suggests that they have overcome the problems through managerial pro-activity, for example, by training staff and seeking expert assistance, so that these potential problem areas can be dealt with routinely.

It is tempting to conclude that many exporters are characterised by being product oriented – selling abroad the products and services that are successful in the domestic market. Moreover, exporters often seem to throw away their successful domestic marketing strategies in international markets, preferring instead to effectively delegate their marketing to agents and distributors. In doing this they seem to overlook the alternative market entry and marketing mix strategies, discussed later in this book, that are available to them and instead opt for a strategy of least involvement. In many cases this approach may meet the exporting firm's immediate objectives, especially if, for example, they are simply seeking to off-load excess production capacity, but it does not provide them with a sound basis for substantially increasing their international market presence.

International niche marketing

By contrast with exporters, **international niche marketing** occurs where firms become a strong force in a narrow specialised market of one or two segments across a number of country markets. Brown and McDonald (1994) explain that the segments must be too small or specialised to attract large competitors and true niche marketing does not include small brands or companies that are minor players in a mass market offering undifferentiated products. For the international niche to be successful the product or service must be distinctive (highly differentiated), be recognised by consumers and other participants in the international supply chain and have clear positioning. Niche marketing, therefore, has many of the characteristics of effective global marketing and some suggest that McDonald's and Coca-Cola are global niche marketers in the food industry.

To sustain and develop the international niche the firm must:

- have good information about the segment needs
- have a clear understanding of the important segmentation criteria
- understand the value of the product niche to the targeted segment(s)
- provide high levels of service
- carry out small scale innovations
- seek cost efficiency in the supply chain
- be content to remain relatively small
- concentrate on profit rather than market share
- evaluate and apply appropriate market entry and marketing mix strategies to build market share in each country in which it wishes to become involved.

Niche marketing of domestically delivered services

Suppliers to the travel industry include domestic firms such as hotels, tour operators and leisure attractions that generate substantial foreign earnings for the country by attracting visitors.

With increased international travel and improved access to worldwide communications, a much more sophisticated package and a wider range of services to visiting customers are being offered. Examples include the provision of education, specialised training, healthcare, sports, cultural and leisure events and specialist retailing, for example, luxury goods.

Clearly these activities lead to wealth and jobs being generated in the local economy in much the same way as exporting and niche marketing. The international marketing strategy processes and programmes are similar too in that the products and services must meet the requirements of international customer segments. Consequently issues of standardisation and adaptation of the marketing mix elements are equally important. The additional challenge is that the benefits obtained from the service provided must be unique and superior, and thus outweigh the benefits to the consumer of locally available services as well as the cost of travel that customers will incur in the course of their purchase.

However, such businesses suffer from many of the same international environmental threats that international marketers suffer from, as shown in Challenge 6.4.

In addition to the services designed to be offered to individuals in both consumer or B2B markets, a whole range of additional services which fall into this category of being domestically delivered are concerned with developing solutions for opportunities or problems identified abroad. These might include technology developments, such as research into new drugs, trial and testing facilities, software development and product and packaging design services.

Direct marketing and e-business

A rapidly growing area of SME domestically delivered international trading is direct marketing and, in particular, electronic commerce. Direct marketing offers the benefits of cutting out other distribution channel members, such as importers, agents, distributors, wholesalers and retailers by using a variety of communications media, including post, telephone, television and networked computers. All these allow borders to be crossed relatively easily and at modest

---

CHALLENGE 6.4   Tourism turnaround in Egypt

Tourism is always vulnerable to environmental threats and, particularly, the perceptions that customers have of the safety of their intended destination. However, there is a very strong will to travel. Many customers are quite resilient and ignore the apparent threat and others return as soon as they perceive that the threat is reduced. Egypt attracts 5 million visitors per year with its sun, ancient history and Red Sea diving. Tourism is worth US$4 billion per year, 11 per cent of Egypt's GDP and the main foreign currency earner.

However, this income is vulnerable. Tourism numbers fell after the first Gulf War, again in 1997 when militants massacred tourists at Luxor and again after 11 September 2001. At the start of 2003 tourists had fallen by 25 per cent with the threat of the Iraq war, but this time the recovery was much faster and in August there were 750 000 visitors, an all time high and up 30 per cent on the previous year. The reasons are not entirely clear but could be because of heavy discounting. Italians are the largest single group of visitors, followed by the Germans, British and French. There are more Arab visitors, particularly wealthy Saudis, probably as a result of them feeling less welcome in Europe and the USA. Somewhat surprisingly the number of Israeli visitors trebled.

Question   What are the key factors in successful tourism international marketing?

Source: M.Voss, Egypt's tourism turnaround, *BBC Online,* 7 October 2003

cost without the SME having to face many of the barriers already highlighted in this chapter.

Direct marketing also has a number of disadvantages. Despite the range of media available, communicating can still be problematic and there is always the danger of cultural insensitivity in the communications. Because of the need to manage large numbers of customers it is necessary to use databases which must be up to date, accurate and capable of dealing with foreign languages. Even an incorrectly spelt name can be insulting to the recipient.

Different cultures have different levels of acceptance of the internet and e-business and, if physical order fulfilment is a necessary part of the service, this is prone to the same pitfalls of international marketing too.

Importing and reciprocal trading

Importing is clearly the opposite process to international marketing and as such might be seen as 'exporting' jobs and potential wealth. However, the purpose of raising this issue here is to highlight the nature of international trade as it is today. Rarely do supply chains for products and services involve solely domestic production and delivery. More usually 'exporting' and 'importing' become inextricably linked and so the challenge becomes one of adding value to imported components and services, no matter from where they are sourced, so that they can then be re-exported in order to effectively and profitably meet the international customers' needs.

Importing activity can also considerably enhance the company's potential to network, leading ultimately, perhaps, to reciprocal trading in which, as a result, the supplier might take other products or services in return from the customer.

Alternative SME international development strategies

Before considering the alternative approaches to international development it is useful to categorise SMEs in terms of their strategic capability to internationalise. As we indicated earlier, although size (micro-, small, medium and large) is used to distinguish between firms in some situations, it is inappropriate here. The firm's international ambition, skills and capability are more important in determining the international prospects for a firm rather than size. A useful way of segmenting firms is in terms of their **level of internationalisation** as shown in Figure 6.3.

As their strategic capability increases and their attitude becomes more confident, so firms move from one level to the next, for example, from reactive to experimental, experimental to proactive and proactive to world class. International development is therefore in discrete step changes, not gradual and incremental. Each of these step changes requires a co-ordinated strategy to improve the performance of the firm.

Geographic development of SMEs

For SMEs, country market selection and development of market share within each country is particularly important for growth. Given their limited resources and narrow margin for failure it is vital that their method of country market development is effective. The alternative patterns of SME international development are shown in Figure 6.4.

The conventional approach is that from a sound domestic base SMEs develop either by choosing between expanding into many markets, gaining a superficial presence and accepting a low overall market share, or concentrating their marketing activities in a small number of markets in which a significant market share can be built.

The research in this area is inconclusive about the precise reasons why firms decide on one strategy or another. Katsikeas and Leonidou (1996) found that market concentrators tend, in general, to be smaller firms, because of their greater interest in export profitability and lesser concern with export sales objectives. Typically they make regular visits overseas and this appears to play a key

---

FIGURE 6.3

Level of internationalisation

The passive exporter
- Tends to focus on domestic markets
- Lacks any international focus
- Is relatively new to the export business
- Is often reacting to unsolicited orders
- Does not carry out research or invest in export and has little direct contact with foreign companies

The reactive exporter
- Sees export markets as secondary to the domestic markets but will put effort into dealing with key export accounts
- Does not invest in attracting export orders, but will follow up foreign customers for repeat orders
- May have started to promote its export capacity by visiting overseas clients
- Has only a basic knowledge of the markets and is still undecided about its future role as an exporter

The experimental exporter
- Is beginning to commit to exporting and starting to structure the organisation around international activities
- Is in regular contact with key accounts and is beginning to develop alliances with export partners to build better products and to use their information on their markets
- Is prepared to make product adaptations to suit overseas customer needs and may have appointed dedicated export staff to look after this part of the business

The proactive exporter
- Is focused on key export markets, and devotes substantial amounts of time and resources to entering and developing new markets
- Carries out regular market assessment in the form of desk research and using partners' information
- Produces promotional materials in a number of foreign languages
- Has senior management regularly visiting key accounts to maintain healthy relationships with clients
- May have exporting account for up to 50 per cent of turnover
- Welcomes exporting opportunities and sees them as crucial to the business

The well established exporter
- Knows that exporting is integral to the business and sees the domestic market as just another market
- Generates the majority of its turnover through exports, and significant amounts of time are spent on this activity, with senior and middle managers frequently visiting customers
- Makes substantial investment in training as skills are needed in-house
- Thinking on export markets is both short term tactical and longer term strategic with regular reviews of the overall mission and plan of action
- Has networks abroad which provide excellent information, and quality assured partners deliver on time, every time

role in their strategy for penetrating the market. Concentrators experience more problems associated with product adaptation to the needs of their customers, but pricing and their marketing organisation needs present less of a problem.

Market expanders tend to be larger firms who are more concerned with export sales objectives, do more export marketing research, and have greater overall market share expectations. They place less emphasis on profitability, personal visits are less important and they perceive fewer product adaptation-related problems.

The authors conclude that market concentrators tend, as a result, to be passive or reactive exporters, whereas market expanders tend to be active exporters.

However, a number of firms export almost immediately after they have been formed. For **'born global' firms** to succeed they have to compete with global competitors from the first day, for example in high technology areas or because the distribution method is global, for example, direct marketing and telecommunications based international marketing (e.g. the internet).

The lowering or removal of barriers between countries and the move, for example, in the EU to the harmonisation of standards, the removal of tariff barriers, reduction of non-tariff barriers and the introduction of a common currency within a regional trading bloc mean that, even in their early life, SMEs are more likely to be active in more than one country market because the regional market is considered to be a domestic market.

Many SMEs adopt what appears to be a rather unsystematic approach to country market selection. Their patterns of development tend to be the result of a network approach where the selection of the market is not merely made on the relative attractiveness of the markets and their match with the company capability, but rather on the reduction of the risk of entering unknown markets by working with individuals or companies they know. International development using existing networks of contacts is more typical of Asian firms. Chinese management

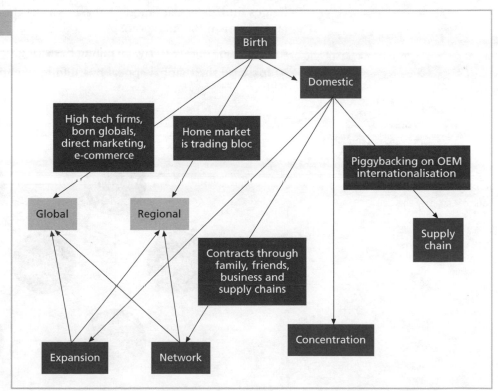

FIGURE 6.4

Geographic development of SMEs

Source: Doole and Lowe (2004)

have been particularly successful in developing a network of family businesses by basing their strategies on Chinese culture and the Confucian tradition of hard work, thrift and respect for one's social network to provide continuity.

Whereas Chinese family businesses internationalise through the family network, suppliers of products and services to supply chains internationalise by following or piggybacking on the international development of the major organisation leading the supply chain.

MANAGEMENT DECISIONS IN INTERNATIONAL MARKETING STRATEGY IMPLEMENTATION

The management of international marketing strategies differs considerably between small and large firms because of the different contexts, nature of the challenges faced and the decisions made.

Large firms are able to apply their huge resources, skills and capability to carry out detailed market analysis, strategy development and implementation systematically and in considerable detail. Smaller firms must compensate for their lack of resources by being more opportunistic, flexible, adaptable and responsive to the potential markets they identify.

Using the **McKinsey 7S framework** in Figure 6.5 it is possible to identify the key decision areas for managing international strategies in small and large firms.

International marketing decision areas in global firms

Strategy

For firms wishing to build a truly global presence there are a number of challenges and principal amongst these is how they might leverage their resources and power in the market to:

- Respond quickly to the changing basis of global competitive advantage.
- Increase their global appeal by building the global brand.

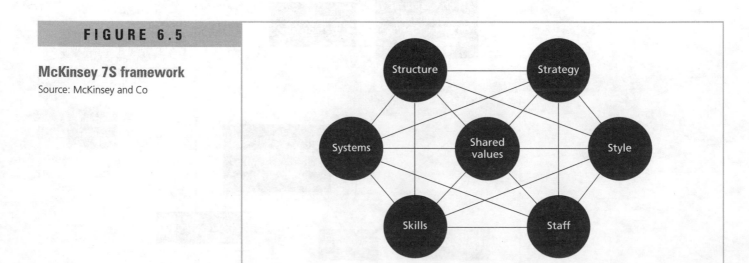

FIGURE 6.5

McKinsey 7S framework
Source: McKinsey and Co

- Create a global presence by achieving global reach, often in partnership with others.
- Manage diverse and complex activities across a range of sometimes similar but often disparate markets and cultures.
- Manage the higher risk associated with entering emerging markets.

Organisation structure

Global firms, by their very nature, are complex and so the organisation structures they create are also complex and specific to the firms' context. The chosen structure must facilitate effective line management and control the performance of the activities and staff of the various business units. A key decision is the degree of centralisation or decentralisation of management responsibility and authority. Centralisation tends to concentrate power, control, and the scope for executive decision making at head office, which is ideal for standardised programmes and processes. However, the result is that the subsidiary business unit staff have little freedom to adapt the marketing strategy implementation to local conditions. Decentralisation pushes decision making out to the local business units and gives local managers greater autonomy, so they are able to manage more creatively. Of course, head office can lose some power and control by doing this.

Large firms often try to reach a compromise by operating matrix management structures with individual members of staff having international as well as domestic company responsibilities and typically reporting to both country and product or brand managers. Sometimes this can lead to a conflict in priorities.

Systems, processes and control

Given the complexity of international strategic marketing in global firms it is essential that an organisation establishes effective processes for the management of its diverse operations, processes and systems to enable managers to share information effectively and make informed decisions to develop and control the business.

Large organisations like to use management tools as part of their processes but as Spotlight 6.2 shows, even these are perceived and used differently in different markets.

Building skills and managing staff

Whilst the skills that are needed in every local functional area and business unit of an organisation are fairly obvious, there are a number of additional skills needed for the effective international management of trans-national business strategies. Highly specialised, closely linked groups of global business managers, country or regional managers, and functional managers are needed to work in networks. These managers must be able to manage in a complex, rapidly changing environment, leverage the organisation's worldwide knowledge, skills and capabilities, and respond quickly and innovatively to new opportunities, wherever they might appear.

They also have to motivate, manage, control and reward staff from very different cultures, often with different expectations, standards and values. These staff may be located at considerable distances from head offices and communications can be problematic.

Management style and shared values

In trans-national organisations with composite strategies, the shared standards and values of the organisation may be the only common aspect that binds the various parts together. However, it should also be recognised that, although global businesses are diverse, the chief executive can still have a major effect on the business. The personality of entrepreneurs, such as Bill Gates, Steve Jobs, Michael Dell and Richard Branson, shapes the management style and shared values of the businesses they create from their early days, and influential managers, such as Jack Welch at General Electric, Lou Gerstner at IBM and Chris Gent at Vodafone have driven existing businesses in new directions.

International marketing management in SMEs

In contrast with large firms SMEs must make up for their lack of resources by responding quickly, innovatively and flexibly to new opportunities. Consequently their strategies are usually emergent and are frequently adapted to exploit new opportunities and combat threats.

Systems and support networks

Typically, SMEs tend not to have sophisticated systems and support networks for managing their international operations, as is the case for large firms. Of course, advances in technology and the lower cost of IT systems are enabling SMEs to develop more advanced systems than they have had in the past. However, SMEs tend to rely on more informal, 'soft' systems and support networks that are based on personal contacts with family, friends, other business managers and officials for support, advice, information and knowledge.

SPOTLIGHT 6.2   **The use of management tools**

Much is written about the importance of management tools and a survey in 2003 by US consulting company Bain and Co (www.bain.com) suggested that in the USA there had been a dramatic increase of 60 per cent in the number and types of management tools compared to two years previously. Bain believed that the reason for this was the difficult economic climate and, in response, managers were trying to preserve customer revenues, prepare for growth, prepare for contingencies and focus on ethics. CRM, contingency planning and knowledge management had shown particular increases in usage and satisfaction.

The survey showed interesting differences between regions. In Asia managers focused more on CRM and customer segmentation, whilst those in Europe put greater emphasis on change management and knowledge management. In North America the focus was not so much on revenue growth as cost cutting, using methods such as down-sizing, outsourcing, re-engineering, stock buy-backs and contingency planning.

Bain concluded that management tools should be used because they help the company perform better, not because they are fashionable.

- All tools have pluses and minuses, so the users must understand them fully.
- The focus should be on enduring strategies not fads.
- The right tools should be chosen for the job.
- Tools must be adapted for the organisation's business system, the organisation should not adapt to the tools.

Question Should managers depend on management tools – what are the advantages and disadvantages?

Sources: adapted from FT Information, Global News Wire, Asia Africa Intelligence, Wire Syndications Today, Business Today (India), 23 November 2003

Organisation structure

As an SME increases its involvement in international markets, so it needs to set up an organisation structure that will enable the leadership and management to effectively support, direct and control its often widespread and growing organisation.

For a firm starting out in export markets, the decision is relatively simple. Either the international business is integrated within the domestic business or separated as a specialist activity. Setting up a separate activity, such as concentrating the international marketing skills and expertise in one department, avoids a situation where the international business is 'low priority', and allows the department greater independence to look specifically at international marketing opportunities.

There are, however, some disadvantages too, as a separate department may be seen as less important by senior managers and could, as a result, create possible conflicts between domestic and international market demands.

Staff skills and management style

SMEs tend to be much less formal about defining the skills and types of staff they require and, instead, expect staff to adapt to the company's needs and particular management style. The way that the firms are managed often reflects the personality of the owner or chief executive and this style is often carried through to relationships with customers and other stakeholders too, even when the customers are in far distant locations.

Ethical behaviour

One of the aspects of management that is particularly important in global marketing in both small and large firms is ethical behaviour. We consider this in greater detail later in this book but it is one of the aspects of the De Beers case study at the end of this chapter.

SUMMARY

- Global firms have both contributed to globalisation by developing a worldwide presence and strategy and offering similar products and services, and responded to it, through market development.

- Global strategies are determined by the industry context and corporate style and ambition. Therefore, strategies range from multi-domestic strategies, in which each market is seen as separate and individual, through to globally standardised strategies, in which the firms identify one global segment with similar needs. Trans-national firms use a combination of different strategies to build global efficiency, local effectiveness and knowledge assets.

- SMEs adopt a range of different approaches to international markets to enable them to compete alongside global players. Their strategies and approaches to geographic development fit with the industry context, their own skills, capabilities and ambitions.

- To enable managers to set and control the operations of the business, an appropriate organisation structure is needed. International managers must also be able to recruit and develop the right staff with the skills necessary to deal with the complexity, diversity and conflicting challenges of global business development.

- In global markets with many different aspects to the international marketing strategy, it is the shared values of the organisation that bind it together.

KEYWORDS

adaptation
'born global' firms
exporting
global approach
globalisation
globalisation themes
international marketing stance
international niche marketing
level of internationalisation

marketing programme and process
  standardisation
McKinsey 7S framework
multi-domestic approach
regional strategy
standardisation
strategic capabilities
transnational approach

CASE STUDY — Changing the business model at De Beers

De Beers sells 80 per cent of the world's rough diamonds. It is 45 per cent Anglo-American owned with the remainder owned by the Oppenheimer family and government of Botswana. In 2003 it reported results that showed that the company had achieved a significant turnaround. A strategic review in the company in 1999 showed that against two benchmarks, GDP and the performance of the luxury goods market, De Beers was under-performing. Diamond jewellery consumption had been declining during the previous ten years at a compound annual rate of minus 2.5 per cent.

History

For most of the century, as well as mining the vast majority of diamonds in South Africa and Botswana, De Beers had sought to maintain their value by guaranteeing to buy any other rough diamonds that they were offered. Indeed, it would recruit French speaking graduates, train them to value rough diamonds and send them into equatorial Africa with large amounts of money to buy diamonds. The largest flawless diamond yet discovered, the Millennium Star, was bought from villagers in the Congo. This strategy was successful whilst De Beers operated all the commercial mines. However, when diamonds were discovered in Russia, Australia and Canada it became impractical. One of the consequences of this was that De Beers had stockpiled US$5 billion of rough diamonds, which paid no interest and were an inefficient use of capital.

The old model was also attracting the attention of the EU regulatory authorities, concerned about De Beers' control over the market. Moreover, De Beers had a charge of price fixing instigated by the US Justice Department in 1994. Whilst a similar charge against General Electric has been dropped, the charge against De Beers has not, which means that senior executives of De Beers cannot travel to the USA because of the fear of being arrested, and this has

constrained the company's development in the world's biggest market.

A further concern is that new synthetic diamonds have been developed, and it is claimed that they cannot be distinguished from naturally occurring diamonds.

Turnaround

In the three years to 2003 the annual growth rate in the diamond market reversed from decline into 3 per cent annual growth, and was largely attributed to De Beers. The reason for the turnaround was a fundamental change to De Beers' old business model. De Beers decided to stop trying to control the market and instead aimed to stimulate demand.

About 60 per cent of the US$8 billion sales of rough diamonds take place at ten week long sales, called 'sights', at which 120 invited buyers, called sight holders, are offered graded packages of diamonds on a take it or leave it basis. These buyers must commit to invest in marketing and developing brands for diamonds and trade the stones or cut and polish them for manufacture into jewellery.

De Beers helped to generate US$180 million marketing spend in 2002, double the previous year, and itself became more proactive in marketing. It formed a joint venture with luxury goods group LMVH to create a string of upmarket shops, starting with one in Bond Street, London. In July 2003 it reported first half year sales up 2.75 per cent to US$2.92 billion and profits up 34 per cent to US$414 million.

Brand image and conflict

De Beers spends its brand marketing money on associating diamonds with love and purity. The model Iman is the face of De Beers in promotion. However, De Beers is worried that diamonds might become too closely associated with conflicts in many of Africa's diamond producing countries. Diamonds from war zones are often mined by slave labour, smuggled out and sold to pay for arms.

Now De Beers tries to avoid buying diamonds from conflict areas by only selling stones mined by the company or by its Russian partner, Alrosa. Fifty diamond producing and trading countries have agreed to a set of minimum standards and signed up to the Kimberley Process, a scheme to prevent such diamonds entering the trade. However, De Beers is concerned that many of the signatory countries cannot uphold law and order and smuggling will continue.

Countries that do not sign up to the Kimberley Process will be barred from trading and this might include some of the poorest countries, where achieving the minimum standards might take longer.

Questions

1 What are the factors that are influencing decisions about De Beers international marketing strategy?

2 Have De Beers made the right decisions – what else could they do?

Source: Adapted from Simpkins, E. (2003) 'De Beers wins a gem of a gamble', *Sunday Telegraph,* 24 August

DISCUSSION QUESTIONS

1 How does increased globalisation affect the international marketing strategies of global firms? In an industry of your choice explain how a global firm is developing a very proactive strategy to build upon some of the drivers of globalisation.

2 How can a small firm compensate for its lack of resources when competing in international markets? What do you consider to be the critical success factors for an SME international marketing strategy?

3 What are the alternative strategic approaches to global markets other than a multi-national company? Using examples to illustrate your answer, explain when these strategies should be used.

4 What advice would you give to a successful, 300-employee, niche food processing business that has been successful in its domestic market but now wants to market its products abroad. Explain the alternative approaches that it should consider in its geographic development.

5 How does the management and control of a global marketing strategy differ from the management and control of a domestic strategy? What specific skills do international managers need?

REFERENCES

Brown, L. and McDonald, M.H.B. (1994) *Competitive Marketing Strategy for Europe*, Basingstoke: Macmillan.

Doole, I. and Lowe, R. (2004) *International Marketing Strategy*, London: Thomson Learning.

Katsikeas, C.S. and Leonidou, L.C. (1996) 'Export marketing expansion strategy: differences between market concentration and market spreading', *Journal of Marketing Management*, 12: 113–34.

Ghoshal, S. and Bartlett, C.A. (1992) 'What is a global manager', *Harvard Business Review*, September–October.

Gogel, R. and Larreche, J.C. (1989) 'The battlefield for 1992: product strength and geograhical coverage', *European Journal of Management*, 17: 289.

INTEGRATIVE LEARNING ACTIVITIES

An introduction

Decision making is at the heart of the marketing strategy process. Decisions are taken by managers at all levels that serve to reinforce, adjust or completely change the direction of the organisation's marketing strategy.

The focus of this book is on building the capabilities to make strategic marketing decisions and making quality decisions within the overall planning process.

The chapters in this book focus upon providing the underpinning knowledge to support the process of strategic marketing decision making. The purpose of the two integrated learning activities at the end of each of the two parts is to integrate the six chapters that make up each of the parts. More important, however, is that together, the two activities provide a framework for strategic marketing decision making and give the opportunity for readers to consider the practical issues involved in a value based marketing approach to competitive marketing strategy.

Learning objectives

On completing the integrated learning activities the reader should be able to:

- Critically analyse the requirements of the strategic marketing decision process
- Identify strategic options and critically evaluate the implications of strategic marketing decisions in relation to shareholder/owner value
- Apply relevant concepts and models to each of the stages of the decisions required in developing an extra value proposition for customers which also delivers economic value added to shareholders/ owners
- Demonstrate the ability to develop innovative and creative solutions to enhance an organisation's global competitive position
- Demonstrate the ability to reorient the formulation and control of cost effective competitive strategies, appropriate for the objectives and context of an organisation operating in a dynamic global environment

The aims of the integrated learning activities (ILAs) therefore are much wider in scope than the short case studies found at the end of each chapter. The objective is to provide a vehicle through which the reader is able to develop practical skills in strategic marketing decision making. In completing these activities you will need to synthesise the various strands and themes explored throughout the book and apply them to a practical situation. To complete each of the activities the reader must move well beyond the boundaries of the textbook, researching new material and exploring the interplay of the concepts discussed in the text and possible solutions to the practical problems identified in each activity.

Each of the ILAs depicts very different scenarios.

Part 1

In this activity we examine the strategic choices made by Cable and Wireless in the context of dramatic change in the global telecommunications industry and evaluate the strategic decisions they made in responding to the changing demands of their global market.

Part 2

In this activity we examine strategic marketing decision making in an organisation of your choice by examining the areas where decisions are required to develop and implement new, innovative strategies that will create value for customers, organisations and other stakeholders.

In each of the activities a series of questions is posed, together with suggestions on how to get started, a framework depicting the key factors to consider in completing the task and suggested web sites you may find useful.

Additional observations are also made that will assist you in addressing the key issues and show how you could develop the activity further.

In each of the activities we have provided only outline information on the scenarios. A key skill in strategic marketing decision making is finding information about markets, analysing it, deciding what is most important and preparing a structured, logical rationale for the decisions that must ultimately be made. In each activity, therefore, you will find information outside the case to complete the task. Much of the information you can use is available on-line. You should not have to approach staff in the organisations depicted for further information to complete the task.

Strategic decisions in an unpredictable world

Introduction

Arguably the most significant changes in the global competitive landscape over recent years have been the growth of multi-national, global and, recently, transnational approaches to strategic development. In this activity we consider a market which has moved from a multi-domestic market dominated by national players in protected markets to one which has become truly global and highly competitive. The basis of the competitive advantage of the firms involved has changed due to shifts in market structures and technological innovations, as well as rapidly changing customer expectations. This has had the impact of altering the competitive landscape of the global telecommunications market and changing the way companies now struggle for a global competitive advantage. The basis of the competitive advantage of the firms involved has changed due to shifts in market structures. In this activity we examine the strategic choices made by Cable and Wireless in the context of dramatic change in the global telecommunications industry, and evaluate the strategic decisions they made in responding to the changing demands of their global market.

Learning objectives

After completing this activity the reader should be able to:

■ Critically evaluate the difficulties associated with strategic choice in the technology industry

■ Apply the lessons of organisational learning to effective decision making

■ Use appropriate concepts and analysis to examine and critically evaluate the competitive strategies pursued

The scenario: Cable & Wireless – and the burst telecoms bubble

Cable & Wireless (C&W) began life as the Eastern Telegraph company, laying cables to link Britain to its empire in the late nineteenth century. Now Cable & Wireless is an international telecommunications company, with customers in 80 countries. Arguably, it has changed more since the year 2000 than at any other time in its history.

In September 2000 Cable & Wireless – led by Chairman, Graham Wallace – was being lauded for its focused global strategy.

Cable & Wireless bucked the trend of the telecommunications industry – which at the time was about global scale, acquisitions and mergers – by concentrating on one market. 'The value of focus is not just a myth of the financial markets. For fast-growth businesses in rapidly expanding markets, it's essential,' Wallace said in September 2000.

Wallace decreed that Cable & Wireless would concentrate solely on the data requirements of global business customers. This involved disposing of assets no longer regarded as 'core' to their strategy: British mobile operator, One 2 One (now T-Mobile), the consumer part of the cable division (to NTL), and Hong Kong Telecom, Hong Kong's incumbent carrier (to Richard Li's PCCW). The HKT deal netted nearly £10 billion in cash and shares. Yet waving goodbye to the source of 32 per cent of the group's 1999 revenues took some courage, as did pulling out of wireless and broadband, perceived as glamorous businesses.

Wallace admitted to no backward glances – stressing the benefits of this new focus. 'I can't tell you what a release it is to know absolutely who your customers are. It makes running this business a great deal more simple.' Instead of trying to imagine what television channels elderly ladies in the north of England might

Source: Simon Kelly, Sheffield Hallam University

want, or to get into the minds of mobile phone toting teenagers, Wallace could eat and sleep the new data services demanded by business customers. Although traditional voice services still represent 60 per cent of C&W Global, it is estimated that by 2010 higher margin revenues from IP and data, growing by over 30 per cent a year, should make up more than 80 per cent of the total revenues of C&W.

With at least £5 billion of cash now anchoring the balance sheet (in contrast to its newly debt laden rivals) the strategic decisions made were described by commentators as 'the greatest transformation story in European telecoms'.

What a difference two years makes. By December 2002 the fortunes of C&W had taken a very different turn. On 6 December, Moody's, a credit rating agency, downgraded C&W's debt to junk status.

A tart research note from analysts at Dresdner Kleinwort Wasserstein suggested that investing in the company 'was like buying what appears to be under-valued real estate at the foot of an active volcano'.

What made C&W's implosion so tragic was that it could all have turned out so differently. At the start of the telecoms boom C&W found itself in the unusual position of owning both a worldwide cable network and a collection of local telephone firms in Britain and its former colonies, a hangover from C&W's historical roots as operator of the British Empire's telegraph and telephone networks.

The conventional wisdom in the boom was that the future lay in providing high speed data connections on a global scale. So C&W duly sold its local access firms in Britain, Hong Kong and Australia, and invested the proceeds in long haul data capacity and related services for large companies. It bought an American network, built a European one and beefed up its undersea cable network.

The problem, of course, was that many other firms were doing exactly the same thing, resulting in a capacity glut and tumbling prices. Former national monopolies such as British Telecom and Deutsche Telekom responded to the ensuing crash by retrenching to their home markets, where local access networks provide reliable revenues. But C&W had lost that option and had no choice but to forge ahead with its global strategy, alongside WorldCom, Global Crossing, 360networks and other troubled operators. It even branched out into the web hosting business – just before it collapsed.

By 2003 industry revenues had increased to a high of US$1.37 billion according to the International Telecommunication Union (ITU). There are now 1.2 billion fixed telephone lines, 1.3 billion mobile phone users and 665 million people with internet access. Consumer spending on communications is growing faster than spending in any other category. Surely that makes telecoms a vibrant and successful industry?

It does not. Despite all these apparently healthy signs, over the past couple of years the industry has become notorious for fraud, bankruptcy, debt and destruction of shareholder value. Exactly how much money has gone down the telecoms drain is hard to quantify, but many estimates hover around the US$1 trillion mark. Dozens of firms have gone bankrupt, including Global Crossing, 360networks, Williams Communications, Viatel and WorldCom, whose bankruptcy in 2002 was the biggest ever. Hundreds of thousands of workers in the industry have lost their jobs. What explains this paradox of an industry in chaos amid strong demand, growing traffic and record revenues?

The short answer is that although the industry has continued to grow, it has not done so in the manner, and above all, to the extent, that those in the industry expected. Telecoms is an infrastructure-intensive business, and because infrastructure takes a long time to build, telecoms firms have to make bets on the level and nature of future demand. Cable & Wireless laid their money firmly in the global IP and data market. As it turned out, the bet, like many made during the technology bubble of the late 1990s, was spectacularly wide of the mark.

In particular, the mania that accompanied the rise of the internet persuaded many investors that demand for data network backbone capacity, to pipe internet traffic across continents, was about to explode. Since 1997, internet traffic has roughly doubled every year. Much of the industry, however, was convinced that traffic was doubling every 100 days. This widely quoted statistic became an essential ingredient of business plans and conference presentations during the bubble. Dozens of firms rushed to build new fibre optic networks in America, Europe and Asia. But apart from a brief period in 1995–96, the figure was simply wrong.

This mania was spurred on by bullish investors and led to the creation of a number of start-up firms who splurged on vast infrastructure investments; the incumbents followed suit. The former national monopolies in Europe, AT&T in America and NTT in Japan all tried to transform themselves into global operators. They built new networks and bought stakes in foreign operators. European companies gambled that the supposed surge in demand for fixed communications capacity would be followed by a similar leap in demand for mobile capacity, and they paid over €100 billion (US$90 billion) for licences to run 'third generation' (3G) mobile networks. In the process, they ran up huge debts.

Between 1998 and 2001 the amount of fibre in the ground increased five-fold. Meanwhile, advances in the technology of feeding signals into fibres at one end and extracting them at the other increased the transmission capacity of each strand of fibre 100 fold. So total transmission capacity increased 500-fold. But over the same period, demand merely quadrupled.

In the United States, more than a dozen national fibre backbones were constructed; a similar duplication happened in Western Europe. Telecoms firms were betting on an overnight transformation that would translate into a sudden leap in demand.

When it became clear that the industry had bet on an increase in demand that was not likely to materialise in the near future, ferocious competition and frantic price cutting ensued. Equipment vendors' sales dried up. And some firms resorted to fiddling to conceal the lack of revenue.

There is no shortage of traffic growth. Internet traffic is (reliably) said to be doubling every year, and voice traffic on both fixed and mobile networks is rising. But as the industry has found to its cost, traffic growth does not translate into revenue growth. Moreover, in the rich world at least, markets are saturated. So new revenue cannot come from new subscribers either, which is what has recently fuelled the mobile phone industry. Instead, it will have to come from new services for which customers are prepared to pay.

But the lesson of the past few years is that the industry is notoriously bad at gauging demand for its services. The two most successful new telecommunications technologies of the past decade – internet access on fixed networks, and text messaging on mobile networks – were both unexpected breakthroughs that emerged in spite of, rather than because of, the industry's best efforts. So, once the smoke has cleared and the dust settled, expect the telecoms revival to come riding on the back of an unexpected technology that nobody in the industry has yet heard of.

Back at Cable & Wireless CEO Francesco Caio has declared himself 'not dissatisfied' with the first nine months of his tenure which began in April 2003. Much remains to be done after their near-death experience last year. The main challenge remains turning round its key UK business. Even assuming a sharp cyclical upturn, domestic profitability is threatened, not least by the spread of internet telephony among large corporate clients. C&W needs to do very well in selling wholesale capacity merely to compensate for the decline in its legacy business. However, it looks as though the operator has made some progress. The new focus on short term wholesale contracts seems to have made up for revenue weaknesses in other areas. There are also indications that the company is aggressively pursuing its restructuring plan and that cash generation is picking up. In the Caribbean, C&W continues to suffer from the aftermath of deregulation and aggressive competition from new entrants. But at least, ignoring exchange rate fluctuations, it seems that the bleeding has stopped. The share price has long anticipated as much, having almost tripled over the past 12 months.

The tasks

1 Critically analyse the strategic choices made by Graham Wallace in the context of the changing competitive landscape of the global telecommunications market?
2 Evaluate the learning capabilities Cable & Wireless need to develop in order to make quality strategic marketing decisions in the future.
3 Assess the difficulties associated with making strategic choices in the global technology market.
4 Outline the strategic choices available to Cable & Wireless today.

Sources

www.economist.com
www.ft.com
www.forrester.com
www.cw.com

Useful websites

www.cw.com
www.totaltele.com
www.icclaw.com
www.arcchart.com/wallcharts/coml_telecom.asp
www.netlondon.com
http://globalcomms.evolutionsltd.com/
www.economist.com
www.ft.com
www.forrester.com

Getting started

In this activity we have examined the strategic choices made by Cable & Wireless in the context of dramatic change in the global telecommunications industry. You should use this case study to obtain an understanding of the industry and the competitive position of Cable & Wireless as well as for general background information. To complete the learning activity, however, you will need to access a range of research material from libraries and web based sources, as well as, perhaps, external sources of information.

In task 1 it is important to consider the key trends affecting the development of the telecommunications market, the competitive positioning of the global players and how the changes occurring impact on the way the market is structured. In light of these you then need to evaluate the strategic choices made by Cable & Wireless and assess whether they were appropriate in the context of the changes occurring in the global telecommunications market.

In Chapter 2 of this book we examined the learning and knowledge management capabilities required by companies in order to make effective strategic marketing decisions. The starting point of tasks 2 and 3 is therefore to consider the principles discussed in this chapter. In light of this learning you need to evaluate the learning capabilities Cable & Wireless should develop in order to make quality strategic marketing decisions in the future and then assess the reasons why the decisions made resulted in the apparent difficulties Cable & Wireless faced in sustaining their competitive advantage in the global technology market

In task 4 you are asked to outline the strategic choices available to Cable & Wireless today. In doing this you will need to consider the strengths and weaknesses of the strategy pursued by Cable & Wireless to date. Against the background of the firm's capabilities, the competitive landscape and the trends identified in the market, you should consider the strategic options available to them if they are to develop and sustain a global competitive advantage whilst delivering value to customers and economic value added to their shareholders.

In summary, in completing the tasks you need to ensure you consider the following key factors.

The element of the plan	Some concepts, models and issues to be addressed
Analysis	• The key international trends impacting on the development of the market • An assessment of the structure of the global market • The competitive positioning of the key global players • Assessment of strategic choices made
Strategic choices	• Identification of the key strategic marketing issues the company needs to address to compete effectively in the global market • Realistic long term marketing strategic options available

- The potential added value of strategic options to customers and to shareholders
- Recommendations as to which strategic option to pursue
- A clear and logical link between analysis and response
- Innovation and creativity in the response
- Coherence and justification of recommendation

The way forward

The tasks in this activity show how the complexities encountered in strategic decision making in global markets make it a fraught and complex process. Making effective strategic marketing decisions needs capabilities in knowledge management and learning but also requires the decision makers to evaluate the signals from the marketplace appropriately if the reformulation of their strategy is to be effective. After studying Part 2 of the textbook you may wish to revisit the solutions you have recommended in this activity and consider how your recommendations could be successfully incorporated into a strategic marketing plan.

In doing so you may wish to consider such aspects as: What is an appropriate generic strategy for Cable & Wireless? How can you ensure future decisions are made based on an appropriate analysis? What are the implications in terms of the marketing programme that should be developed in order to meet the objectives set? How can Cable & Wireless make certain they have appropriate systems to ensure the managers around the globe respond to the challenges identified? All of this is hard to achieve in strategic decision making in a global market. For senior managers, the problem is how to maintain a coherent worldwide strategy, retain a unique vision and purpose, and yet at the same time create an operation which delivers value to consumers across the globe and adds economic value to the company. For most firms the decision making process is concerned with managing a number of tensions and ambiguities. It is how you would resolve such tensions that you may wish to consider on completion of Part 2. There is a need to adopt a regular, thorough and systematic sequence, but at the same time provide the flexibility which allows innovative and creative solutions to address problems when and where they occur. Whilst detailed analysis is necessary to fully appreciate the complexities of a situation, there is also a need for a clear uncluttered vision that delivers value to all stakeholders.

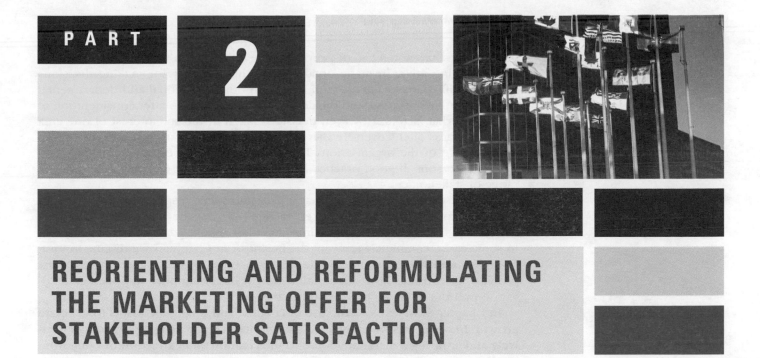

PART 2

REORIENTING AND REFORMULATING THE MARKETING OFFER FOR STAKEHOLDER SATISFACTION

Part 1 of the book was concerned with building the capabilities needed within an organisation to make effective strategic marketing decisions and then deciding on the organisation's future competitive stance in terms of its customers and markets. In Part 2 we now turn to reorienting and reformulating the marketing offer to build stakeholder satisfaction through the the strategic marketing implementation decisions that must be made in order to deliver a viable and sustainable strategy for the future.

Decisions in many of the areas usually referred to as 'strategy implementation' are not simply about strategy implementation but, instead, can have a very significant effect on the future strategic direction of the organisation. For example, changing any part of the marketing offer, for example with new products, distribution channels and communication strategies, has often turned around failing organisations.

One of the main criticisms of marketing strategy implementation in the past has been that too often each of the elements of the marketing mix has been managed almost in isolation. Whilst product, brand or marketing managers have had the responsibility for managing the marketing mix overall, the finance, research and development, production, distribution, sales and customer service departments have often had disproportionate influence on their particular part of the marketing mix. In many organisations the authority for making decisions about specific parts of the mix still rests with other functional and departmental managers in the business, and the decisions are often taken after consideration of largely internal factors. However, decisions taken in the self-interest of one area of the business often adversely affect another part of the business and the overall performance of the organisation. This can result in the organisation failing to share the lessons of good practice and losing sight of the need to satisfy its full range of stakeholders.

In Part 2 we discuss the ways that organisations can respond innovatively and decisively to changes in the market, technology and the environment by fully using their assets, skills and capabilities to either change part of their activities or, in some cases, completely reinvent the business. In Chapter 7 we discuss innovation that enhances the organisation's competitive position and leads to fast growth. We consider how organisations might better support and manage innovation in order to create new opportunities.

In Chapter 8, we explore the use of tangible and intangible assets to generate growth. In doing this we emphasise the importance of managing branding effectively and applying a marketing focus to the creation and extraction of value from intellectual property.

In Chapter 9 we consider the decisions that are needed to reformulate the portfolio of products and services and develop pricing strategies that support portfolio development to ensure that the organisation's future profitability will be delivered. In Chapter 10 we examine the use of integrated communications to deliver the organisation's various messages to customers, and build strong and mutually beneficial relationships with them.

Throughout Part 2 we emphasise the need for the organisation to be customer led rather than internally driven by adding stakeholder value through implementation activities. In Chapter 11 we take this further by exploring how decisions might be taken to build value adding activities in the extended organisation, through supply chain management, choice of route to market and by using collaborative partnerships.

Finally, in Chapter 12 we examine the decisions a company has to make in deciding how to approach its evaluation of marketing performance. We also explore the wider dimensions of strategic marketing decision making and discuss the goals and expectations of stakeholders and the impact they have on strategic marketing decisions and the achievement of a sustainable competitive advantage.

CHAPTER

7

ACHIEVING FAST GROWTH THROUGH INNOVATION

Introduction

In the previous two chapters we have discussed the strategic marketing decisions that are needed to define or redefine the organisation's competitive stance on a generic and geographic basis. The impact of these decisions could be significant and, as a consequence, may require changes to many aspects of the current marketing strategy. The firm may need to more rapidly build, adapt or reinvent the **business model** in order to exploit new opportunities that will deliver the organisation's growth aspirations, respond to under-performance, or address imminent market or environment threats or opportunities.

In this chapter we focus in particular upon how the organisation might make bolder and more innovative strategic marketing decisions. In doing this we start by looking at the nature and impact of innovation, and particularly how new technology can both be a major threat but also provide an opportunity to re-invent the business model or marketing strategy.

We then go on to discuss the way small and large organisations manage innovation and develop more entrepreneurial, fast growth marketing strategies. Specifically we consider how they seize and exploit opportunities on a worldwide basis.

Perhaps the most significant innovations that have provided opportunities for adapting, building or reinventing the business are based on the application of new information and communications technology. We discuss the impact of e-commerce on the strategic marketing decisions that relate to the development of new opportunities and routes to market.

As a result of the introduction of new technologies it is increasingly recognised that the effectiveness of organisations in managing knowledge is likely to be a major determinant of competitive advantage and future performance

Learning objectives

By the end of this chapter the reader should be able to:

■ Explore the sources of innovation and apply the techniques to identify new opportunities

- Demonstrate the ability to develop innovative and creative marketing solutions to enhance an organisation's global competitive position
- Understand the characteristics of fast growth and apply some concepts of entrepreneurship to exploit fast growth opportunities
- Critically appraise innovative marketing strategies in small and large companies operating on global markets
- Identify the process elements needed to manage innovation and the risks associated with it
- Evaluate the use of e-business in delivering innovative marketing solutions.

THE NATURE, SOURCES AND IMPACT OF INNOVATION

In this chapter our focus is upon the major innovations that affect all aspects of the business by bringing about significant changes in performance or even a complete reinvention of the business. However, innovation also takes the form of incremental improvements that are part of continually updating the business and which are considered at various points in this book. For example, new product development is used to continually refresh the organisation's portfolio and is discussed in Chapter 9.

The nature of innovation

In looking at the nature of innovation, it is easy to assume that technology is the main driver for major change. Technological or scientific research can lead to an invention that can result in a 'great leap' forward. However, the major changes in an industry sector are not solely the result of technological advances, but instead can be the result of an entrepreneur spotting opportunities created by changes in the market environment and exploiting them, often using a mix of existing and new technology and techniques in a new context.

Industry breakpoints

The step changes in industries are referred to by Strebel (1996) as **industry breakpoints** and have the effect of either significantly increasing customer or organisation value through cost reduction. The personal computer market has been the subject of a number of breakpoints including:

- the introduction of PCs alongside mainframe computers, catching IBM off guard
- the growth of more affordable PCs from Asia
- new distribution channels (PC supermarkets, direct marketing, on-line sales, etc.)
- the introduction of laptops
- the introduction of the internet and linking PCs to the telephone network
- the introduction of games
- the use of PCs as multimedia centres.

Whilst many of the breakpoints were technology driven it was often entrepreneurial behaviour that exploited the breakpoint opportunities.

Strebel (1996) identified two types of breakpoints:

- Divergent breakpoints are associated with sharply increasing the variety of competitive offerings, resulting in increased value for the customer.
- Convergent breakpoints are the result of improvements in the systems and processes used for the delivery of the offerings, leading to lower delivered costs.

Between the breakpoints continuous development can result in refinements and developments to the product, service or process offerings that add value and maintain the customers' interest. For example, whilst working towards the next major technological advance in home entertainment Sony launches a stream of new products based on existing formats with improved design and additional features.

Technology discontinuities

The relationship between the continuous small improvements in a sector and the **technology discontinuity** is shown in Figure 7.1.

The '**S**' **curve** shows the relationship between the cumulative investment in the product or technology and the resulting improvements in performance. Continual investment in product, service or process development produces a stream of small performance improvements. At the top of the 'S' curve, however, even for quite large amounts of investment made there is little further improvement in performance. The product, process or technology has now reached the mature phase of the life cycle and, probably, the status of being a commodity. Clearly, this may be one reason for strategic wear out as the organisation, for which this is a cash cow, may be totally committed to the technology or product and have considerable assets tied to this particular process. As a consequence the organisation may be unwilling to aggressively seek a replacement that might require huge investment in a new development and marketing to support it. It may upset current purchasing behaviour and revenues, and could result in cannibalisation of the existing business.

At the point of discontinuity in the 'S' curve an entirely new, breakthrough technology, product or process can be introduced. Quite often the organisation

42593 · THOMSON · STRATEGIC MARKETING DECISIONS · DOOLE AND LOWE · SEGN 9

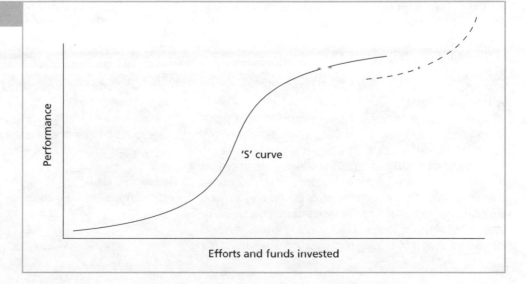

FIGURE 7.1

R&D effort and discontinuity
Source: Foster (1986)

pioneering the new innovation will be unknown in the sector and not one of the usual competitors. It may be based in a far distant region of the world and the significance of its activities may not be obvious. In the early stages, the new organisation and its innovation might even be treated with contempt and not be seen as a serious threat by the current organisations in the market, with the result that when it becomes established the existing firms in the industry will have to play 'catch up'. Dyson introduced new technology to create innovative household cleaning products, the low cost airlines compete with major airlines and on-line retailers, such as Amazon, challenge traditional retailing processes.

The breakpoints can be traced in the photography market, and Challenge 7.1 shows the decision made by Kodak in response to the latest breakpoint.

Categories of innovations

There are three **categories of innovations** (Robertson 1967), according to the disruption they cause to customer buying and usage patterns. The implication of this is that if buying and usage patterns change there is a greater need for marketing to re-educate consumers as to why the products should be bought and how they should be used.

Continuous innovations

Continuous innovations cause negligible or slightly disruptive effects upon the purchase and consumption of the product, requiring little customer re-education. For example the introduction of fluoride in water, additives in food, new chemicals in fertilizers or the use of CFC free refrigerants in refrigerators has no significant effect on the purchase process or use of the product, at least as far as the consumer is concerned. Flat screens have not changed the use of televisions, other than to make the living space more aesthetically pleasing.

CHALLENGE 7.1   Kodak – smile please, we've gone digital

In 2003 Kodak announced its decision to stop production of traditional cameras in Europe and America. In the USA in 2003 12.5 million digital cameras were sold, overtaking the traditional technology for the first time. Kodak will concentrate its production of the film format in Asia, Latin America and Eastern Europe where growth is still in double digits. In China too, it is estimated that 60 million people have yet to buy their first camera.

The diffusion of the digital revolution has been rapid. The first cameras from Sony and Canon only came onto the market in the early 1990s. By the mid 1990s, however, sports and news photographers could already see the benefits over the awkward and time consuming process of developing film. The responses of fashion, portrait and advertising photographers to the new technology, however, illustrate the diffusion curve. Lord Lichfield enthusiastically changed to digital in 1998, not least because he saved £70,000 per year. John Swannell, a fashion and portrait photographer, uses both, digital for speed and economy but film for reliability when shooting in more remote locations. Terry O'Neill, famous for glamorous photographs of film stars and politicians, thinks only film will do, believing digital to be all gimmicks and not proper photography. He is not prepared to let art directors use computers to put the images together.

Recent research shows that only 14 per cent of digital pictures are printed, the rest are discarded, downloaded to PCs or e-mailed to family and friends

Question How appropriately do you think Kodak is responding to the new challenge?

Source: *Daily Telegraph* 15 January 2004

As consumers become more knowledgeable, however, there is no guarantee that products that are going be consumed in the same way but with substantially changed ingredients will automatically be acceptable to consumers. The introduction of genetically modified (GM) foods has raised fears in consumers' minds and reluctance to purchase.

Dynamically continuous innovations

Dynamically continuous innovations have a more disruptive effect on the way that products and services are used. For example, the introduction of the fax machine required some changes in office routine to ensure that it was used effectively. A digital camera can fall into both this and the following categories. If a digital camera is used to take pictures and the memory card is then taken to a photographic shop for processing, it has little effect on use and purchasing but, against substantially falling sales, processing companies have had to explain that their services extend to digital photography too.

Discontinuous innovations

Discontinuous innovations have a highly disruptive effect upon usage and purchasing patterns, and require a high level of marketing to explain the benefits and to educate consumers about how the product should be used. Video players and microwave ovens have had a significant effect on customer lifestyles. MP3 players for music downloaded from the internet and digital cameras that are used by the customer in conjunction with a computer or special printer for processing have a more disruptive effect on purchasing and usage.

The more disruptive the innovation is to the customers' normal purchasing, consumption, and disposal patterns, the greater the investment that is needed to educate them in respect of why they need the innovation, how they will benefit from it and how they should use it (and not use it). In the early days of microwave ovens, for example, suppliers omitted to tell consumers that they were unsuitable for drying cats after they had been out in the rain!

If the innovation requires a radical change in the firm's management processes such as manufacturing, the distribution channel and marketing, then a reorientation or even a complete reinvention of the firm's business model might be needed.

Impact of technology

Many of the major steps forward in recent years have been associated with the introduction of technologies such as those that support e-commerce, information management, telecommunications, computer aided design, process, inventory and logistics management. These are the enabling technologies in marketing that provide the solutions to old problems, such as, how can customers in remote locations around the world contribute to the design of a new global product as much as the customer next door, and how can a ten-person business market its products or services to its potential customers in 40 or 50 counties? Managing market entry in so many countries through agents and distributors would probably be beyond the resources of most small businesses.

Technology does not change the elements, challenges and dilemmas associated with the marketing decision making process, such as the impact of culture on international marketing and the need to achieve a balance between the standardisation and adaptation of the marketing process and programmes, but it does have a major impact on the nature of the marketing strategy that is used and the solutions that are developed.

Whilst we have discussed some of these challenges in previous chapters it is useful to focus specifically upon how technology helps firms and their managers to address these challenges. Technology both drives change and provides a means of responding to change. The development of new and existing technology allows things to be done better and faster than before. At the outset, however, it is important to emphasise that technology is of no value until it has a practical application. As illustrated in Figure 7.2, the **pioneers**, those firms that are first to successfully embrace a new technology and find a practical application for it, for example Amazon in book retailing, in creating a new product or service or a new route to market will gain a new source of competitive advantage. However, this might well set new standards for the industry sector that will mean competitors, such as Barnes and Noble, will also have to achieve those standards if they wish to compete in the future. So all competitors in the sector will have to catch up by embracing the new technology. Consequently, the innovative firm again has to find a new innovation or technological advance that allows them to get ahead again. Dell Computers is an example of a firm that has continually striven to embrace new technology throughout its business to find new competitive advantage and customer oriented applications.

Communications technology helps people around the world to become more aware of changes in the market environment and of the various responses of companies around the world to those changes. Customers are easily bored with their existing products and services and are always looking for innovative new products and services that will regain their interest. They are less brand loyal, and if one firm does not meet the needs of international customers then a competitor will. Customers find out about the development of new products or new ways to reach the market and they want to benefit from the changes. Customers want it and want it now!

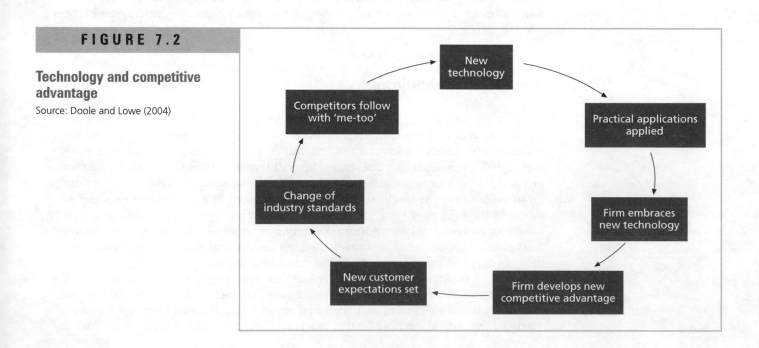

FIGURE 7.2

Technology and competitive advantage

Source: Doole and Lowe (2004)

Sources of innovation

Whilst new technology might be created by an organisation, the opportunities to market the new products and services emerge from the market environment in the form of customer needs. Accordingly the organisation must identify a source of opportunity and then respond more quickly than competitors in order to gain competitive advantage.

Two views about the **sources of innovation** come from Ansoff (1965) and Drucker (1985). Ansoff emphasised the effect of shock events on innovation. He suggested that shock events arrive suddenly, pose novel problems and raise the prospect of major business loss. A recent example of this has been the downloading of music files using a computer and playing back the files using an MP3 player. Pirate websites allow customers to share music files and so avoid paying for copyrighted music. Apart from the artists who have lost royalties, the big losers have been the record companies, such as Sony, Universal, Warner Brothers, EMI and Bertelsmann, who initially responded very slowly to the increasing threat (and opportunity) and as a result suffered substantial losses in revenue. Many players are now competing directly or through competitive alliances involving the hardware, software and retailing giants, such as Apple, Dell, Hewlett Packard and Wal-Mart (Schwartz and Markoff 2004).

Drucker (1985) identified factors such as:

- The unexpected event that triggers off a new demand (for example, potential oil shortages and climatic changes).

- An incongruity between what is available and what is needed by consumers (for example, the introduction of telephone banking).

- A process need to fulfil a major new demand by consumers (for example, security software for e-commerce). An example of this is illustrated in Challenge 7.2, for managing the huge increases in currency transactions.

- A change in the industry structure (for example, the increased deregulation of financial markets).

CHALLENGE 7.2   Continuous Link Settlement Bank (CLS)

One result of increased globalisation has been the huge growth in financial market activity and it is estimated that the value of foreign exchange (FX) trades settled every working day is US$3500 billion. If the settlement of both sides of the major FX transactions does not occur simultaneously, then the resulting settlement risk could be so great that it exceeds a bank's capital. Although bank failures are rare, they do tend to cause a so-called domino effect on other banks.

As a result CLS was set up in 2001 to manage simultaneous settlement of FX transactions. Each day it knows before the start of daily activity which trades are due for settlement and calculates members' net positions in each CLS currency (principally US dollar, pound sterling, euro, Swiss franc, Japanese yen and Canadian dollar). The members then pay into CLS amounts in currencies that they are short of and CLS balances its books.

The Bank has headquarters in New York and was set up with 66 shareholder banks and the opportunity for additional banks to be third party users. Its operations are based in Canary Wharf, London, where it has less than 200 staff. IBM manages the IT, while Swift provides the network for handling messages.

Question There is a high level of collaboration between organisations in this new venture, what do you consider to be the advantages and disadvantages?

Source: adapted from 'Settlement risk: Here comes CLS', *Banking*, 27 June 2000

- A change in demographics, (for example, the increasing number of elderly people in developed countries is providing the opportunity for new products).

- A change in the perception or mood of the community (for example green marketing).

- The development of new knowledge (for example, bioscience).

Techniques to identify opportunities

It is clear that technology acts as a catalyst for major change, but innovation does not only depend on inventions or major technological advances. Many entrepreneurial organisations have made major innovations in non-technological areas. At this point it is worth considering how opportunities for innovation might be identified, assessed and developed commercially.

A number of writers have discussed techniques to identify opportunities. These include:

- *Scientific exploration* that is curiosity driven and starts with no immediate, obvious application or customer benefit in mind. Universities and small bioscience exploration companies, often funded by the multi-national pharmaceutical companies, are examples of this.

- *Analysis of current and anticipated customer needs* is an obvious starting point. Asking customers what they want usually identifies new product and service developments, that will be discussed in Chapter 9, but it is often difficult for customers to articulate what they do not know is possible. Forty years ago few customers would have been able to explain that they would want to buy products and services electronically.

- *Segmenting markets further* than they have been segmented before leads to developing products and services to more effectively meet the needs of sub-segments of customers. Sometimes the sub-segmentation can lead to a mass market opportunity, as in the case of multipurpose vehicles (MPVs).

- *Identifying a new emerging segment* that is born out of changes in the mood, attitudes and expectations of customers and dissatisfaction with current offerings. Successful exploitation requires the innovator to be able to anticipate this before the situation is fully articulated and documented in the press. This is frequently difficult to achieve successfully as often moods and attitudes change significantly in the early stages of development and so the final commercial opportunity is often rather different from the one originally envisaged. The Bodyshop timed its market entry correctly to reflect the mood at the time.

- *Applying existing techniques in a new sector.* Managers can make connections between seemingly unrelated ideas or apply a technology, process or technique from one business sector in another, often through inter-sector partnerships.

- *Vertical integration* of the supply chain of an organisation can eliminate one link in the chain or create a new, better value route to market. Disintermediation in the supply chain is discussed later in this book.

- *Business rationalisation* or mergers often lead to the termination of some products and services, and this can leave behind an unfulfilled market requirement or the possibility for an entirely new configuration of products and services.

- *Spin outs from existing business.* Sometimes innovations do not fit with the core business of firms and so the business is spun out separately, for example, Lexmark from IBM and the low cost airlines Go from BA, eventually taken over by easyJet, and Buzz from KLM, taken over by Ryanair.

- *Innovation in mature sectors.* The most successful innovations have often taken place in mature sectors by offering customers a **quantum leap in value**.

Creative thinking techniques

Creative thinking techniques can be applied by managers in an existing organisation to observe trends, understand the underlying causes of common complaints, apply leading edge knowledge and expert ideas in the sector, and spot market gaps and unfulfilled requirements. Structured brainstorming by a selected group of staff and experts can be used.

One of the problems of many of the approaches discussed so far is that innovation is often conditioned by staff and experts' traditional view of the industry. Kim and Mabourgne (1997) proposed that high growth success resulted not from trying to beat competitors but from making them irrelevant by offering customers a quantum leap in value. Essentially this required the innovators to think about the industry in a completely new way by asking the questions:

- What factors that your industry takes for granted should be eliminated?

- What factors that your industry competes on should be reduced well below the standard?

- What factors that your industry competes on should be raised well above the standard?

- What factors should be created that our industry has never offered?

If these questions are applied to industries before recent breakpoints, such as the introduction of telephone banking and low cost airlines, it is understandable why the new initiatives did not come from the traditional suppliers to the market, who believed the existing business model should be retained. It is also clear why new businesses were able to come into the market and satisfy customers more than their traditional competitors.

Making successful innovation decisions

So far we have presented some conceptual and perhaps rational methods for looking for opportunities in the market. However, innovation does not necessarily follow rules and the way that entrepreneurs and enterprising organisations identify and develop opportunities is often very subjective and personal, rather than objective and rational.

Frequently organisations believe that an opportunity which is clear and obvious to them must be equally clear and obvious to many other organisations, but this is often not the case. The same opportunity is not always obvious to everyone and quite often a simple idea can be introduced without immediate competition. Even if there is competition, exploitation of the elements of the total product offer can provide a unique edge. For example, Starbucks runs coffee bars, which are part of what is essentially a commodity market. Although they have considerable competition they provide a differentiated product that is valued by customers, even though they have to pay a relatively high price for the product.

Opportunities do not seem the same for everyone and not everyone will pursue what appear to be obvious commercial opportunities. Often the innovator has in mind a very specific product or service offer to fill a market gap but customers might not accept the solution in that particular form. Therefore it is vital for the innovator to focus on the opportunity or market gap and be flexible in the product or service offering. In thinking about this, for example, the rule that innovations must create value for the customers can be interpreted by innovators in different ways. Different companies will create different value propositions to exploit the same market opportunity.

The exception to this is when competitors spot the same opportunity in high profile growth markets that have received high coverage in the press.

Products and services developed to exploit complex opportunities often break down because it becomes difficult to explain the benefits to customers. The most important factor in making successful innovation decisions is recognising the importance of educating customers through marketing communications. No matter what the breakthrough is, and what the potential benefits are for customers, they must be explained in a clear and simple way.

Evaluating and exploiting market opportunities

In making decisions to evaluate and exploit market opportunities there are a number of considerations. In general it is better to focus on creating customer value rather than on lowering costs, as lowering costs can simply lead to a price war, erosion of value and customer dissatisfaction. There are exceptions, for example, where existing suppliers in the industry have built unnecessary costs into the operation. Low cost airlines and value food retailers, such as Lidl, Aldi and Netto, are examples of the exploitation of a market opportunity, in which a customer segment is seeking added value in the form of low price products and services, with 'no frills'.

In making innovation decisions it is essential to address a number of key questions:

■ Who are the customers?
■ How clearly and simply can the value proposition be explained to them?
■ How many customers can you switch?
■ How quickly (the diffusion curve)?
■ Who needs to be influenced (the customers and the distribution channel)?
■ What are the routes to market?
■ What are the barriers to introduction?
■ How will competitors react and will you be a threat?

The emphasis in the identification of opportunities should be in adding value from the customer point of view. It is important to stress that many products have been launched into the market without really taking into account the customer perspective. The Sinclair C5 and third generation mobile phones are examples of innovators being 'in love' with the technology rather than understanding how customers might value (or not) the product.

The emphasis on innovation should be on value added product introductions priced even higher than the competitive products they are aiming to replace. Gillette introduced Sensor razor blades as a breakthrough product in a commodity market. Customers were prepared to pay considerably more for real benefits – in this case a closer and more comfortable shave – and Mach 3 has been introduced as a further development.

Steve Jobs at Apple (see Spotlight 7.1) has consistently exploited new opportunities and used creative marketing to add an extra edge.

ENTREPRENEURIAL, FAST GROWTH STRATEGIES

Having considered the nature and sources of innovation we now turn to how the strategies of organisations respond to the opportunities and threats that result from innovation. There is a substantial difference between organisations that can be described as follows:

- *Pioneers* track environmental changes, spot market gaps and opportunities and endeavour to be first in.
- *Second in* firms watch the market pioneers and follow their leads in innovation, learning from their mistakes and attempting to improve upon the pioneer's initial offering.
- *Imitators* (me too) firms simply attempt to copy the products and service innovations and offer 'value for money' alternatives.
- *Defensive* firms tend to follow their own path and only respond to innovations in the market when it is absolutely necessary.

We are concerned here with pioneers, but there are differences between the two types of organisations that achieve above average performance.

SPOTLIGHT 7.1   **Steve Jobs at Apple Computers**

'The genius of Apple is that the brand has come to embody a lifestyle.' Despite the computer industry being dominated by two or three giants, Apple, the underdog, still manages to capture the imagination of customers across generations and lifestyles, from teens to technology geeks to middle aged business executives, and achieve very high levels of brand loyalty. From the sleek titanium Powerbooks to its best selling iPods (the leading portable digital music player)

Steve Jobs
Source: Courtesy of Apple Computers, Inc. (photographer: Gary Parker)

and iTunes software, Apple uses design, an innovative retail strategy and grassroots marketing to appeal to its customers. In 2003 Apple was *Advertising Age*'s 2003 Marketer of the Year.

Steve Jobs is the iconic CEO, whose marketing genius comes from his goal to make things that change people's lives. In his work he adopts a very hands-on style and this is transferred to Apple's way of marketing, which is accessible. The company talks to people. The company focuses on building relationships with the media and editors in order to gain the maximum publicity and has worked on joint marketing with companies including Volkswagen and Pepsi.

The weakness of Apple is associated with its strengths and the company has made a number of mistakes. Perhaps the reason is partly Jobs himself. He is passionate, not the most politically correct and has not always had a professional management team around him that could make the best of his genius.

Question   What are the critical factors for success in a business run by a very entrepreneurial chief executive?

Source: adapted from A. Cuneo (2003) 'Marketer of the Year: Apple', AdAge.com

Fast growth organisations

Fast growth organisations have an effective strategy, are well managed, customer led and innovative throughout the organisation. Customers choose to buy from them rather than competitors. Their characteristics are:

- superior product or service
- customer perception that the offering is better than those of competitors, often because of the brand
- global skills, competencies and speed of learning
- greater assets and resources
- legal advantages over competitors
- value and quality advantages
- scale economies and a lower cost base
- better relationships with key stakeholders
- positive leadership and a confident approach to management.

Entrepreneurial organisations

Entrepreneurial organisations:

- *Exploit and create the market breakpoints*. Periodically some firms do this by offering customers a quantum leap in value (for example, Dell, Microsoft, Virgin and Dyson), sometimes through technological innovation and sometimes through entrepreneurial activity.
- *Think about customers differently*. Some organisations have anticipated what customers might need in the future, often without customers being able to articulate it themselves (for example, Sony did this with the Walkman and Napster made downloading music a high profile reality).
- *Manage customers and customer experiences at a much higher level*. Most of the early success of the Disney theme parks was the result of exceptional levels of service and 'people' processing.
- *Think about the organisation differently*. These companies use their relationships and partnerships with other organisations to leverage value in a completely different way. Alternatively they develop new business models that create customer value (for example, eBay and Lastminute.com).

Entrepreneurial marketing strategies

Entrepreneurial management and marketing is required in both small and large organisations to set up, reorient or reinvent the organisation. More conventional fast growth management and marketing is needed during periods when market building through incremental growth or consolidation after a period of change is needed to ensure a potentially winning idea has the time to become fully established. Whilst many organisations might fail to spot the need for reorganisation and reinvention, many more miss the opportunity to build a sustainable and secure organisation because they lack the strong management that can resist the urge to continually embark on unnecessary, expensive and unproductive internal restructuring and instead focus on building revenue-generating internal and external relationships.

Bolton and Thompson (2000) focus on entrepreneurial strategic development, as shown in Figure 7.3. It requires entrepreneurial management to recognise a window of market opportunity and the strategic capability to position the offering in the market in such a way that appeals to and will benefit customers. To build the new innovation into a sustainable business the organisation must be willing and able to change in line with the needs of the growing business.

An example of an organisation that has been created in this way is Dyson, discussed in Spotlight 7.2. Dyson illustrates the first **visionary leap forward**, supported by effective **strategic positioning** and continuous operational improvements shown in Figure 7.4 and discussed earlier in the chapter. The Dyson case also shows that another breakthrough will be needed in the future to maintain momentum. The washing machine has not really caught customers' imagination.

Diffusion of innovation

Having launched the innovation, the critical success factor is how quickly the innovation can generate a positive cash flow. Negative cash flows result from the high cost of research and development, reconfiguring the operations, and launch and ongoing marketing costs, but then, hopefully, cash flow becomes positive, as sufficient customers begin to buy and re-buy the new offer.

The purchasing of new products and services tends to follow the **diffusion curve** shown in Figure 7.5.

Some potential customers are innovators, always keen to try any new development, and they will be the first to engage with the innovation and be persuaded

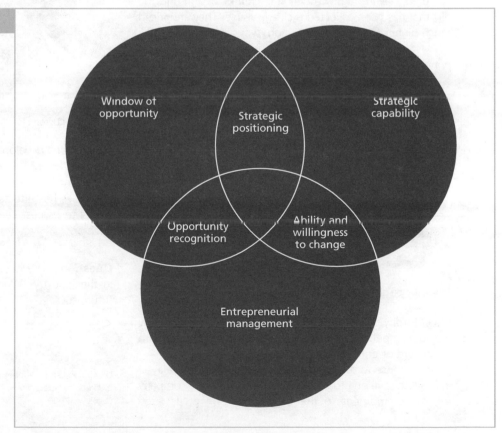

FIGURE 7.3

Entrepreneurial strategic development

Source: adapted from Bolton and Thompson (2000)

Window of opportunity

Strategic positioning

Strategic capability

Opportunity recognition

Ability and willingness to change

Entrepreneurial management

to make the purchase, but the question is how quickly the early adopters and early majority will buy. Sales and marketing staff are frequently over-optimistic about how quickly they can convince the mass of customers of the benefits of the innovation, because customer inertia and staying loyal to a product they are familiar with may reduce the speed of switching. Customers are often unwilling to spend their hard earned cash on something that may not be completely proven. Of course, if the innovators are not convinced about a new product the early majority will not follow and the product or service may die.

The more disruptive the innovation on purchasing and consumption patterns, the more expensive it may be to educate customers and persuade them to buy. A complex new product or service may require more explanation, greater trust and a big leap of imagination on the part of the customer before they will purchase from the organisation. Moreover, products and services that are based on a significant new technology that does not really offer discernable customer benefits, when compared to existing products and services, may also not attract customers quickly enough. Success might be even more difficult to predict if the innovation is also dependent on the availability of complementary products. Perhaps part of

SPOTLIGHT 7.2   Dyson, still cleaning up?

In 1993 James Dyson introduced his no loss of suction vacuum cleaner onto the UK market. It revolutionised the vacuum cleaner market by dispensing with the need for a bag and using patented Dual Cyclone technology. The cleaners are also a change from convention. They are brightly coloured, have a highly functional, chunky design and the dirt that has been collected is clearly visible. They are priced much higher than the competition, typically around £200.

Dyson's management style is based on James Dyson's principles and is also different from many competitors.

Source: Dyson plc

Dyson bans smoking and ties and has little time for memos and e-mails, which he considers to be a way of passing the buck. The majority of staff are young, often straight from university. The company emphasises quality throughout and James Dyson is very much the high profile face of the company, featuring prominently on the website.

The company grew rapidly during the 1990s reaching over 40 per cent of the vacuum cleaner market by volume. However, competitors, such as Electrolux of Sweden and Glen Dimplex (the Morphy Richards brand), are fighting back and low priced competitors, such as LG and Samsung of South Korea, are offering products for less than £100.

In response to this Dyson moved production to Malaysia in order to save on production costs. However, the company retains commitment to the UK in the form of its large

Source: Dyson plc

research and development department, which forms 25 per cent of the 1200 UK workforce. Some critics have suggested that the move, which resulted in 600 manufacturing job losses has affected their sales in the UK, but the firm points to its best ever sales in 2003 as justification for its decision.

Question In what ways has Dyson created a breakpoint in the industry? What should the company do to ensure future success?

Sources: adapted from M. McCourt, Letters to the editor, *Financial Times*, US edition, 22 December 2003; P. Marsh, 'Dust is settling on the Dyson market clean-up', *Financial Times*, 12 December 2003; S. Crainer and D. Dearlove (2000) *Generation Entrepreneur*, Pearson Education

the reason for the failure of third generation mobile phones to take off was the lack of suitable internet services. Adoption rates that are much slower or faster than forecasted can be problematic for cash flow. In practice forecasts are rarely accurate and whilst it is more important to forecast as accurately as possible it is also essential to have contingency plans for when sales do not follow the forecast. If the products are underperforming (Figure 7.6) the decision options are to withdraw a 'loser' from the market, try harder to persuade customers to buy a product that might be a technical success or consider modifications to the offer.

FIGURE 7.4

Entrepreneurial strategy development

Source: adapted from Bolton and Thompson (2000)

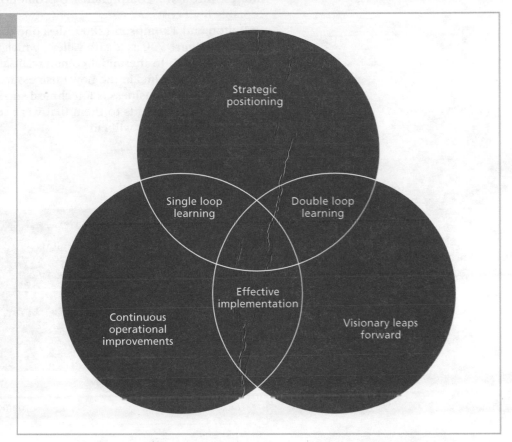

FIGURE 7.5

The diffusion curve

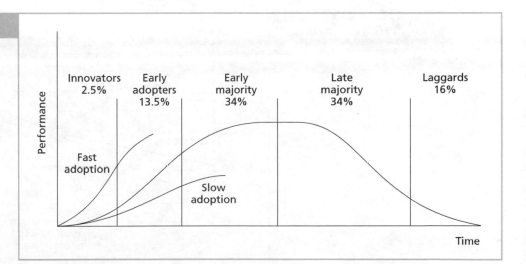

The question then becomes: how long should the offering be given before modifications are made?

Large MNEs may need to launch a comprehensive range of new products and services simultaneously into many markets. Their considerable resources allow them to tolerate large negative outflows over longer periods. By contrast smaller organisations need a positive cash flow as quickly as possible merely to survive. They need to keep their fixed costs as low as possible in order to reach the break-point quickly (Figure 7.7). This may mean that their launch and marketing programmes need to strike a careful balance between creating awareness and interest through a comprehensive promotional programme and incurring unacceptably high costs.

Bolton and Thompson (2000) describe the period up to the break even point, shown in Figure 7.8, as 'death valley', which must be crossed before reaching the 'land of plenty'. In the initial commercialisation period for any innovation there are two critical points in the new business model, shown in the figure. The first is whether the new business is a technical success – does it work for the customers and deliver the benefits to them that were set out in the original brief? If it does not then the business will fail.

FIGURE 7.6

Decision areas

Source: adapted from Bolton and Thompson
(2000)

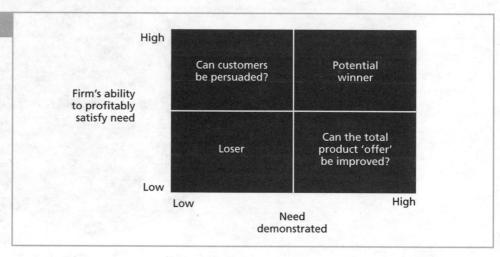

FIGURE 7.7

Break even

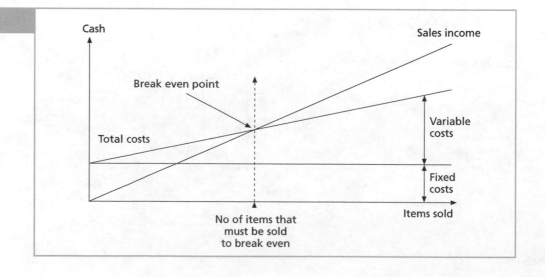

The second point is whether or not the new business is a marketing success – in other words, will sufficient customers from the target segment buy and repeat buy to generate the necessary cash flows? If not the business will again fail.

It is worth re-emphasising that the organisation should focus on the opportunity to generate revenue from the market gap rather than try to sell a specific product or service. Famously, Honda started up in the 1960s in the USA trying to sell large motorcycles to compete with Harley Davidson. Initially they failed, but they noticed that they had raised interest in 50 cc bikes and, instead of withdrawing, they changed their plan and marketed 50 cc bikes. Forty years later they are the leading motorcycle company in the USA.

The problem for decision makers is how long the initial product or service offer should be supported before making a significant revision. A further problem is created if a product or service is successful in some less important country but fails in the major markets.

THE INNOVATION PROCESS AND RISK MANAGEMENT

There are many examples of well respected high profile organisations that employ well qualified staff but fail to innovate. Small organisations have to innovate to survive but large organisations can live off past successes and their huge resources for some time before they are in difficulty. In this section we explore why large firms often fail to innovate, different attitudes to risk, and what is considered good practice in managing innovation.

The reasons why large firms fail to innovate

Most organisations want to create new products, services and processes in order to develop their business and achieve improved performance, but large organisations tend to believe that controlling their resources and using them efficiently is

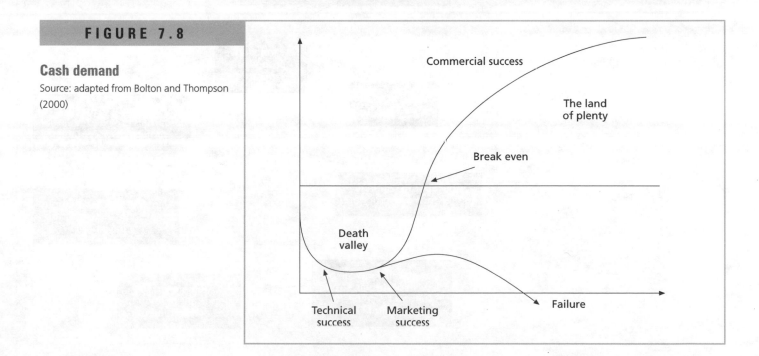

FIGURE 7.8

Cash demand
Source: adapted from Bolton and Thompson (2000)

the main reason for success. However, as Figure 7.9 shows, achieving improved performance requires the organisation to do things in new ways, but this is in direct conflict with many organisations' management culture of controlling resources by using tried and tested methods. Inevitably, controlling resources leads to a risk averse approach, in which innovation is only tolerated if the innovators follow company rules, all important decisions are taken by senior managers and success can be virtually guaranteed.

In practice innovation in many large firms often follows the sequence in Figure 7.10 with the consequence that the organisation develops a 'blame culture' and a scapegoat is blamed when innovations fail. Consequently few members of staff volunteer new ideas for fear of failing.

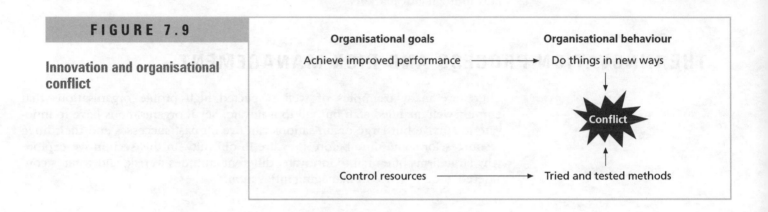

FIGURE 7.9

Innovation and organisational conflict

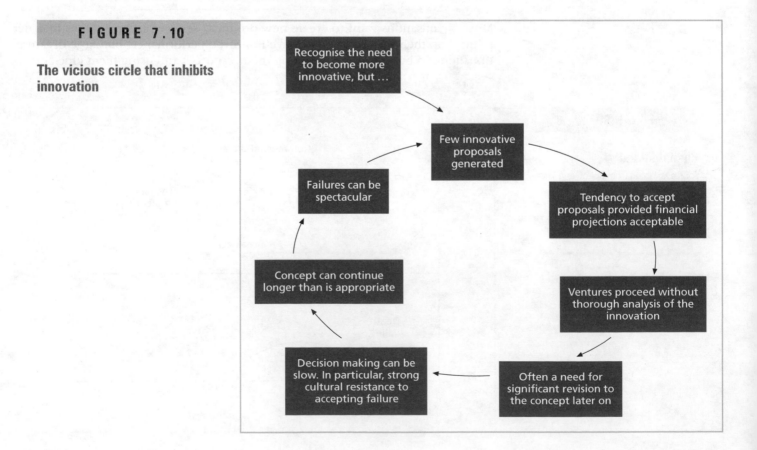

FIGURE 7.10

The vicious circle that inhibits innovation

The contrast between entrepreneurial and administrative management

Stevenson (2000) contrasts the administrative management approach of large organisations with the entrepreneurial management approach in small firms and emphasises the differences as follows.

The organisation's strategic orientation and management structure

- Entrepreneurial management focuses on the opportunities created through the rapid changes taking place, whereas administrative management focuses on planning systems, cycles and performance criteria.
- Entrepreneurial management structures tend to be flat and informal, whereas administrative management has clearly defined authority.

Its commitment to the opportunity

- Entrepreneurial management is action oriented, makes fast decisions and manages risk, whereas administrative management has multiple layers of decision making and seeks to reduce risk.

Its approach and commitment to the use and control of resources in pursuing the opportunity

- Entrepreneurial management tries to limit its use of resources to what it needs and maintains flexibility by arranging to use, rather than own, resources, whereas administrative management tends to think that risk is reduced by having excess resources and formal planning. Power and status in administratively managed firms are associated with having resources to control.

The key differences seem to be that entrepreneurially managed firms take risks but also manage risk, whereas large organisations often attempt to avoid risk, perhaps because many managers believe that avoiding failure improves their career prospects rather than trying to innovate and risking failure. This often results in firms simply extending their existing range or broadening their market coverage, as shown in Tasker's matrix of relative risk in Figure 7.11, rather than pursuing more risky new product developments or new market developments.

FIGURE 7.11

Tasker's risk matrix

		Newness of product			
		Same	Extended range	Redesigned/ improved	New
Newness of market	Same	1	2	4	8
	Broader coverage	2	4	8	16
	New but related	4	8	16	32
	New	8	16	32	64

The challenges in managing innovation

Regardless of whether the organisation is large or small there are a number of challenges in managing innovation including:

- picking winners from the ideas suggested
- developing appropriate organisations
- developing stimulating climates
- deciding how much to spend and when to terminate projects
- meeting timescales and being first to market
- handling the marketing/R&D interface
- coping with uncertain technologies.

Supportive innovative management

The pioneering, innovative firms tend to have certain characteristics including:

- a fundamental and sustained commitment to innovation
- a willingness to accept risks
- an ability to protect the product by patents and/or aggressive marketing behaviour
- an ability to target and capitalise upon high margin markets
- an ability and willingness to commit resources
- a degree of flexibility
- top management commitment
- a previously successful track record.

The successful innovators:

- understand user needs
- pay more attention to marketing, user needs and after sales servicing
- carry out more thorough development and design work
- employ external technological expertise
- give individuals more responsibility for new product development
- are committed to innovation
- see innovation as a corporate wide task
- communicate internally and externally

The question, therefore, is how large firms can build in some of the innovation characteristics of small firm entrepreneurial management and market orientation, particularly building a supportive culture which tolerates and learns from failure. Many large firms are successful innovators and part of the solution is deciding how to organise and manage innovation. Firms adopt different solutions to managing innovation as shown in Challenge 7.3.

THE CONTRIBUTION OF E-COMMERCE INNOVATION TO FAST GROWTH

Whilst much of the innovation discussed so far has been specifically related to an organisation or industry, e-business innovation has affected most businesses.

During the dotcom boom at the turn of the millennium many organisations believed that the decision to embrace the new technology alone was almost guaranteed to deliver spectacular results. It was only some time later that these same organisations reluctantly realised that technology provides solutions for some business problems but does not, in itself, create a new business. Underpinning the technology there must be a sustainable business model with the usual dynamics of revenue generation, appropriate and manageable costs and customers that are satisfied with what they have received for the price they have paid. E-commerce can reduce costs, for example, by cutting out intermediaries in the supply chain, enabling easier access and management of suppliers, and providing

---

CHALLENGE 7.3   Models of new product innovation

One of the challenges for firms is how to organise their new product innovation in order to get the greatest creativity and generation of new ideas, and the most effective contribution from all departments in developing and commercialising the idea. The decision is which department should be responsible for the new product development (NPD) process.

Research and development department

In the 1970s NPD was handled in R&D laboratories and was more concerned with what could be produced rather than what customers wanted. As the concept of marketing became much more embedded in the 1980s the responsibility for NPD was passed to marketing departments.

Brand marketing manager responsible for new products

In some firms brand teams take responsibility but there can be a tendency to concentrate on building the brand and gaining more shelf space and so the NPD can be focused on short term adaptations. This is referred to as the 'low hanging fruit' strategy. Kraft, Unilever, Bestfoods and Procter & Gamble take this approach.

Cross-functional teams

Alternatively cross-functional teams are set up to allow the many parts of the organisation, such as R&D, manufacturing and supply chain, to become involved but this can result in the process becoming too bureaucratic and the NPD process is likely to stall.

The innovation team reports to marketing director: examples include McVities, Diageo and Nestlé.

The innovation department reports to the board: Coca-Cola Great Britain is using this approach to relaunch brands and develop more UK originated brands.

Global companies hand responsibility to one country: Lever Fabergé

Unilever has a focus on its global brands and gives each country responsibility for their development. The UK handles deodorants, such as Lynx, while France handles the shampoo sector, such as Sunsilk. Products are developed and then handed over to the local country operation to be launched.

Skunkworks

A number of companies have set up 'skunkworks' as entirely separate units physically outside the company to maximise creativity. Unilever set up Unilever Ventures to encourage employees, scientists and entrepreneurs by giving one-off payments or the opportunity to work with brand teams to develop their ideas.

The question is: how separate should the products be from the parent company? The first product of GlaxoSmithKline's (GSK) thefuturesgroup was Plenty, a juice drink. The question for GSK was whether to launch under a new brand, The Ealing Juice Company or the GSK brand, which it ultimately did.

Question   What are the arguments for and against the various types of innovation organisation?

Source: Adapted from Murphy, C. (2003) Innovation masterminds, *Marketing*, 15 May

better targeting, servicing and management of customers. However it may also require higher infrastructure investment and incur additional costs of running the business.

In seeking to use e-commerce as the mechanism for reorienting and reinventing the business, either to exploit new opportunities or to cope with an imminent threat, the strategic marketing decisions that managers must consider:

- What is and will be the future role of e-commerce in the business sector?
- How might e-commerce be used to better integrate some of the external and internal processes that drive the organisation?
- What should be the purpose of the organisation's website?
- What will be the successful business models of the future?
- What development is needed for the website to be integrated within the overall business model?

A key task is to decide how innovation in the website and business model might help business development. However, before discussing different websites and business models it is worth reviewing the **six Is** characteristics of the internet that underpin the strategic marketing decisions (see Table 7.1).

Challenge 7.4 illustrates the use of websites and international partnerships for on-line job and home searches.

TABLE 7.1	The characteristics of the internet – the six Is
	Characteristics
Interactivity	• Customer initiated contact by seeking information • Marketer has 100% customer attention, collects and stores all responses and can improve future dialogues
Intelligence	• Can continuously collect and analyse information and make individually focused offers
Individualisation	• Building on the intelligence stored in databases, marketing communications can be tailored to meet individual needs so achieving mass customisation
Integration	• Managing integrated marketing communications and mixed mode buying, where customers might switch channels during the purchasing process
Industry restructuring	• Disintermediation involves removing the traditional intermediaries from the distribution channel • Reintermediation involves gaining a presence on websites that might fulfil the role of intermediary
Independence of location	• Reach can be extended into countries where it is not viable to locate a significant sales support activity

Source: Deighton (1996)

The purpose of websites

Websites are used for many purposes but for strategic marketing decision making they fall into four main categories (Lindgren 2003). The managers must decide how they wish to use the website:

- as an organisation site
- to provide service on-line
- to provide information on-line
- to facilitate business transactions on-line.

Organisation sites

At the most basic level websites provide organisation information to stakeholders ranging from the organisation's origins, business mission and areas of activity, standards and values, brands, financial performance, job opportunities and contact points through to quite specific information about products and their applications. As these websites are freely accessible, firms appealing to global customers must consider the degree to which their websites should be offered in multiple languages.

As well as providing information about products some sites take customers through the purchasing process and options. For example, customers can design their new car from a range of options, such as whether to have cruise control,

---

CHALLENGE 7.4   On-line joint venture to improve new job and home searches

Searching for a new job, home or a car is now increasingly done on-line and in 2003 a joint venture, FinnTech, was set up with the aim of creating an industry standard technology to power the classified websites of regional newspapers across Europe. The partners in the venture are Norwegian classified operator Finn.no (50 per cent), fish4.co.uk (25 per cent), and Associated New Media (25 per cent). Finn is

Source: Fish4homes

Norway's largest portal for real estate, jobs and car adverts, controlling 70 per cent of the print market and 85 per cent of the on-line market. Associated New Media is part of the *Daily Mail*, *Evening Standard* and *Metro* media group and publishes successful websites, such as www.thisislondon. co.uk, www.thisismoney.co.uk and www.femail.co.uk. Fish4 is owned by Northcliffe newspapers, Newsquest media, Trinity Mirror and Guardian media and provides a gateway, linking a network of 177 regional sites, featuring sport, news and local information. It runs the UK's number 1 recruitment site, www.fish4jobs.com as well as www.fish4homes.com and www.fish4cars.com.

These companies are all owned by leading newspaper groups that together print and distribute 79.4 million newspapers in Europe every week. It is intended that the joint venture will improve the speed and accuracy of searches by creating off-the-shelf solutions to power existing websites or create completely new on-line classified sections.

Question   What are the sources of competitive advantage for on-line service providers of this type?

Source: adapted from M2PressWIRE, 21 May 2003

petrol or diesel, metallic paint and alloy wheels, but then are referred to the local dealer to complete the purchase.

Service on-line

On-line banking puts customers more in control of their accounts from anywhere in the world and allows them to make transactions any time of the day or night. The saving for the bank is in being able to reduce the cost of bank branches, service centres and individual banking transactions. By providing an on-line tracking service around the world Federal Express have been able to make huge savings on staff employed to answer queries from customers about where their package is. The system involves applying bar codes to the packages, which are then scanned each time they progress past a key point on the journey. This information can then be transferred to the website and accessed by customers worldwide.

Information on-line

Many media organisations, such as newspapers and television stations, provide websites that enable customers to access current and archived past files of news, data and images. Often, such sites provide one level of access free, but may charge a subscription for heavier users or may require payment for more valuable information. As this information is in digital form it can be accessed and delivered on-line anywhere in the world.

Business transaction on-line

Business transactions on-line are the most significant recent development in marketing. However, it is the interactivity of the internet that is not only capable of providing rapid transfer of information that supports business transactions but is also the platform for sophisticated e-business models whether they are business to consumer (B2C) or business-to-business (B2B) market or are one of the other business model variants Timers (1999) identified and shown in Table 7.2.

Business to consumer (B2C)

The internet has allowed individuals and businesses of any size to set up a website as a virtual shop – an on-line showcase for their products and services and an interesting alternative to purchasing through traditional retailing. Some of the decisions include:

- How potential customers might be offered security and confidentiality in transactions.
- The choice of which language they wish to communicate in and sensitivity to the local culture and legal frameworks.
- The degree to which on-line buying is provided and on-line product 'offer' comparison with offers from competitive websites is encouraged.
- The ease of transferring customers, who are not prepared to use the internet for purchase, to other modes of buying, such as a physical store and whether the offer will be the same.

■ Whether the products and services lend themselves to on-line retailing. Products that require low customer involvement in the purchasing process may be ideal for on-line purchasing whereas high involvement products and services may not. Products that are sold on the basis of their design or quality of manufacture may not be seen to their best effect without allowing customers to smell, feel and touch them. Services that involve considerable negotiation between supplier and purchaser may also be unsuitable.

■ Whether the fulfilment of the order depends on more traditional distribution, the associated limitations of the existing infrastructure and the availability of appropriate logistics in each customer's country. Large physical or perishable goods require a commitment by the firm to set up or outsource a suitable distribution method to deliver the goods to the consumer. Small items, such as CDs and books can be posted but delivering valuable goods or very bulky goods, such as furniture, directly to the door also requires arrangements to be made for the customer to receive them.

Business to business (B2B)

The transactions between businesses in the B2B market are often much more complex. Interactions involve the exchange of significant amounts of information between the seller and customer before, during and after any transaction. The information includes such things as specifications, designs and drawings, purchase contracts, manufacturing and delivery schedules, inventory control, negotiation of price and delivery. Other B2B transactions are relatively routine repurchases or reorders often of commodity items. Some of these purchases will be core to the business, such as raw materials and essential maintenance services, and others will be occasional or peripheral, such as facilities management or purchase of office equipment.

The internet enables a far wider range of data to be exchanged without restriction on the number of participant organisations. The mechanisms by which the

TABLE 7.2	Internet business models	
Models	*Role*	
e-shop	Web based marketing of a shop or company	
e-procurement	Electronic tendering and purchasing	
e-malls	Collection of e-shops	
e-auctions	C2C, B2B and B2C auctions	
Virtual communities	B2B and B2C communities	
Collaboration platforms	Collaboration enablers for businesses or individuals	
Third party market places	Exchanges or hubs for buyers and sellers	
Value chain integrators	Provide services across the value chain	
Value chain service providers	Provide specific value chain services, e.g. logistics	
Information brokerage	Provide information for consumers and businesses	
Trust and other services	Authenticate the quality of service	

Source: adapted from Timmers (1999)

exchanges take place and business can be transacted are web portals. These are 'hubs' where all the interested participants congregate. Typically there are two types of hubs:

■ industry specific hubs, such as automobile or aerospace manufacturing
■ function specific hubs, such as advertising or human resource management.

Using e-hubs firms can improve the efficiency of the processes of transactions and thereby lower costs. The hubs can reduce the transaction cost by bringing together all the purchasing requirements of many hundreds of customers world-wide (Kaplan and Sawhney 2000). E-hubs attract many buyers who are able to negotiate bulk discounts on behalf of a range of smaller individual buyers.

If the products are commodities with no need to negotiate specifications then the dynamic nature of the e-hubs enables buyers and sellers to negotiate prices and volumes in real time. In sectors such as energy purchasing the peaks and troughs of supply and demand can be smoothed. However, blackouts in the USA and Europe, due to the inability of power companies to supply, have raised the question of whether a system which is highly efficient in normal times can also leave insufficient in reserve to deal with abnormal demand or unforeseen conditions.

The USA still leads in electronic B2B and much of the innovation in B2B has come from the USA, but firms around the world recognise that the potential savings can be quite significant and a number of countries, particularly in Europe are catching up. Once major supplying countries such as China develop their e-business processes, the internationalisation of sourcing and supply chain management will be increased.

A culture change in attitude is needed, as firms that would normally compete will have to co-operate for the mutual benefit of reducing costs, and increasingly these will often be cross-border co-operations. Competing car makers have set up Covisint.com for purchasing and Steel24-7.com has been set up for steel buyers. It is easy for firms to fall into the trap of believing this is simply an additional form of buying and selling. Firms that decide to trade in this type of market-place must consider the serious implications to their whole business strategy and operations.

The benefits of e-procurement, such as convenience and cost saving through group purchasing, appeal to governments for public sector and private–public sector purchasing, but often progress is much slower than in private business. The European healthcare sector has been slow to migrate to e-procurement as healthcare authorities are conservative, have a very proscriptive approach to purchasing and are unwilling to change processes. There are fears among healthcare professionals about data security and hospitals are driven by clinical need, not profit.

Consumer to consumer (C2C)

The concept that underpins this model is that consumers sell to each other through an online auction. EBay is the most successful site for trading between individuals who buy and sell antiques, collectible items and memorabilia by virtual bidding. This type of buying and selling tends to become almost a hobby in itself for customers. EBay takes a fee to insert the advertisement and a fee based on the final value. EBay has competitors, such as QXL, but is taking the lead internationally and demonstrating fast growth, often powered by publicity from the increasingly bizarre items sold on its site.

Consumer to business (C2B)

This works in reverse to the normal type of auction as consumers join together to reduce the prices they pay through bulk buying. A final date is set and the price falls as more customers join the buying group. While this is an established model in the business to business sector it is less well established in C2B. Sites such as Letsbuyit.com facilitate the process but have struggled to develop a viable business model. Priceline.com is similar but provides a mechanism for consumers to say what they are prepared to pay for a product or service, such as an airline flight. Suppliers decide whether they are prepared to accept the offer.

INNOVATION IN WEBSITES AND E-BUSINESS MODELS

Smith and Chaffey (2002) explain that in making decisions in e-business models managers should take four perspectives:

Buy side perspective, which includes new supply chain and procurement models.

Sell side perspective, which includes new distribution, communication and customer management models.

Internal organisation perspective, which includes new internal systems, processes and structures for the organisation.

Value chain perspective, which is the integration of the above three perspectives with the external network of the extended organisation to add stakeholder value.

Suitable models are then required to optimise overall performance. However, a report by Durlacher (2000) suggests that once the models have been decided, they should not be regularly changed but, instead, innovation should be achieved through exploiting flexibility within the model, for example in marketing and partnerships.

There are a number of reasons why new, more flexible models must be developed, to respond to changes in buying patterns, for example customers who do not watch TV, browse in shops or respond to traditional advertising and distribution channels. There are also those B2B customers that are exploiting the benefits of a much more dynamic, flexible supply chain and seeking multiple sources of supplies. There are those B2B and B2C customers who accept the commoditisation of some products and want to buy at the lowest price or greatest convenience, provided that the quality, quantity, and delivery time are right.

The dynamics of customer internet navigation need to be clearly understood so that managers can make decisions about website innovation and promotion in order to increase the traffic through the site. The main task, as with all communications, is to ensure that activities are integrated and measured. Before considering the methods of doing this it is important to emphasise that managers must be able to evaluate the cost of acquisition of site visitors, leads and actual sales from the methods.

Search engines are still used by an estimated 80 per cent of web users for information, and so it is critical for marketers to be registered. Moreover it is essential to ensure that the offer will be in the first 20 'hits' for a keyword as potential customers rarely scroll down further. There are other mechanisms for promotion, such as directories, links to other partner websites, banner advertisements and off-line traditional advertising.

Emerging e-business methods

Whilst it is not our intention here to predict developments it is useful to identify the new technologies that could indicate some new routes to the e-business market. They include:

- Interactive digital TV, which not only allows purchasing using the TV remote control, but allows a vast range of other activities, such as banking, gambling, voting and programme participation.

- Digital radio is available via the web, where advertisements can be provided.

- Mobile phone technology is advancing all the time, with phones becoming miniature computers that play back video, audio and images. Text messaging can be linked with global positioning systems to direct customers to an offer available close to them. Bluetooth wireless connection can increase capacity and voice recognition can increase functionality.

- Interactive kiosks have been set up in convenient locations to provide many interactive services at low cost.

Inevitably it is the integration and application of these enabling technologies along with traditional technologies that provide a myriad of flexible opportunities that will enhance the business model. Siebel Systems (discussed in the case study at the end of the chapter) is an example of a firm that has built a business around integrating relationship marketing activity in the form of e-CRM.

SUMMARY

- Technological and non-technological innovation both drive change in markets and provide the means of responding to changing environmental factors, competition and customer requirements and expectations.

- Breakpoints are step changes that occur in industries and offer the opportunity to significantly add customer or organisation value.

- There are categories of innovation from 'new to the world breakthroughs' of minor adaptations to products and these pose different challenges for marketing, but the most successful organisations combine breakthroughs with incremental improvements throughout the marketing process to retain customer interest and loyalty.

- An effective innovation process is essential, from identifying and exploiting the sources of opportunity through to effectively managing diffusion of the innovation into the market.

- A supportive culture is needed to encourage risk taking, but innovation should be carried out within a process that is designed for managing risk too. The lessons from research into good practice suggest that the process should focus particularly on a marketing orientation and effective marketing management.

- When compared with average performers the characteristics of the fastest growth organisations that are the most proactive in the market show differences in ambition, attitudes to business, management style, awareness of customer value, and approaches to dealing with competition.

■ Fast growth firms orient the organisation to achieving initial growth but then rapidly build distinctive positioning and a management approach that embraces change in order to build a sustainable future.

■ In internet marketing, technological innovation supports new customer communication methods through the website and enables new business models that provide a platform for adding customer value.

KEYWORDS

business model	pioneers
categories of innovations	quantum leap in value
diffusion curve	'S' curve
entrepreneurial management and	six Is
marketing	sources of innovation
entrepreneurial organisations	strategic positioning
fast growth organisations	technology discontinuity
industry breakpoints	visionary leap forward

CASE STUDY	Siebel Systems and CRM

In 1993 Tom Siebel spotted a gap in the market. Companies that had multiple distribution channels and points of contact with customers needed a system to ensure that customers received co-ordinated communications and the company's customer facing activity, such as the sales force, was managed effectively. For many Siebel has become synonymous with customer relationship management (CRM).

Siebel grew spectacularly for just under a decade and in 2002 Tom Siebel was named CEO of the year by *Industry Week* magazine. However, as with the majority of IT businesses Siebel suffered a dramatic fall in 2002 with revenue declining from US$2.5 billion to US$1.64 billion. By 2004 the company employed 7400 in 32 countries. Forty-three per cent of its revenues came from CRM software and 57 per cent from consultancy and maintenance.

Siebel's growth came through a strong focus on application development in response to customer needs and selling the business solution to a wide range of customers. Having established a strong leadership in selling CRM applications Siebel is now coming under attack from other competitors, who have started to attack the market more aggressively. SAP is starting to cross-sell its own CRM system to its Enterprise Resource Planning customers.

In response to this Siebel must become more customer-led rather than technology driven. Ultimately it is Siebel's customers' customers who will either be satisfied or dissatisfied with the level of customer service they receive as a result of the effectiveness of the CRM systems. It is essential therefore that not only is the IT system efficient but Siebel's immediate customers must also be able to fully exploit its potential.

Tom Siebel manages the company in a very hands-on way and is involved in all the key decisions. As with a number of IT companies the products and services are largely designed in the USA. However, Siebel has developed substantial sales outside the USA:

USA (62 per cent)

Europe (28 per cent)

Asia (5 per cent)

Others (5 per cent)

The Siebel operations around the world have the responsibility for marketing, selling, installing and servicing the systems. In response to customer needs Siebel has developed other business applications software. One difficulty companies have is managing the complexity of their IT systems, so Siebel has developed its Universal Applications Network (UAN) to more easily integrate disparate IT systems.

Siebel's challenge is to grow the market and to do this it must become even more customer-led and avoid the criticism of many technology companies of being too technology focused. It must also adapt to meet the needs of its customers in different countries in order to build up long term relationships.

Questions:

1 What changes in the market and environment (positive and negative) are likely to have the greatest effect on Siebel over the next few years?

2 What should the company's management do in order to maintain its growth, especially in overseas markets?

Source: various public sources; www.siebel.com

DISCUSSION QUESTIONS

1 What do you consider to be the critical stages in taking an opportunity or idea from concept through to a sustainable business? What challenges does this pose for the marketer?

2 Having been recruited to a key management role in a business that is excellent at technical innovation but has so far achieved only modest market growth, what steps would you take to achieve the fast growth that the company is capable of? How would you manage the associated risks?

3 What do you consider to be the principal reasons for the under-performance or failure of many companies that start off with a breakthrough idea? Choosing a successful organisation as an example, explain what lessons can be drawn to guard against under-performance.

4 What makes it difficult to be an entrepreneurial marketer in most large organisations? How can a more supportive culture be created?

5 Using examples to illustrate your answer, explain how e-commerce innovations have changed the basis of competition in a sector of your choice.

REFERENCES

Ansoff, I. (1965) *Corporate Strategy*, New York: McGraw-Hill.

Bolton, B. and Thompson, J. (2000) *Entrepreneurs, Talent, Temperament, Technique*, Oxford: Butterworth-Heinemann.

Deighton, J. (1996) 'The future of interactive marketing', *Harvard Business Review*, November–December: 151–62.

Drucker, P.F. (1985) *Innovation and Entrepreneurship*, Oxford: Butterworth-Heinemann.

Durlacher (2000) 'Trends in the UK new economy', *Durlacher Quarterly Internet Report*, November: 1–12.

Foster, R. (1986) 'The S-curve: A New Forecasting Tool'. Chapter 4 in *Innovation, The Attacker's Advantage*, New York: Summit Books, Simon and Schuster.

Kaplan, S. and Sawhney, M. (2000) 'E-hubs: The new B2B marketplaces', *Harvard Business Review*, 78(3) May–June: 97–103.

Kim, W.C. and Mabourgne, R. (1997) 'The strategic logic of high growth', *Harvard Business Review*, 75.

Lindgren, J. (2003) *E-marketing in Marketing Best Practices*, Mason, OH: Thomson South-Western.

Robertson, R.S. (1967) 'The process of innovation and the diffusion of innovation', *Journal of Marketing*, 3(1): 14–19.

Schwartz, J. and Markoff, J. (2004) 'Power players', *New York Times*, 12 January.

Smith, P.R. and Chaffey, D. (2002) *eMarketing Excellence*, Oxford: Butterworth-Heinemann.

Stevenson, H. (2000). 'The six dimensions of entrepreneurship', in Birley, S. and Muzyka, D.F. (eds) *Mastering Entrepreneurship*, FT Prentice Hall, pp. 8–13.

Strebel, P. (1996) 'Breakpoint: how to stay in the game', *Financial Times Mastering Management*, part 17, pp. 13–14.

Timmers, P. (1999) *Electronic Commerce Strategies and Models for Business-to-Business Trading*, Chicester: Wiley.

ADDING VALUE THROUGH LEVERAGING TANGIBLE AND INTANGIBLE ASSETS

Introduction

In recent years increasing focus has been placed on the need to make effective strategic marketing decisions that add value for stakeholders. The reason for this is that increasing competition in business and pressure on costs means the ultimate consequence of not adding value is bankruptcy. The rationale is that by focusing on increasing stakeholder value organisations can improve effectiveness, reduce their vulnerability to competitive threats and so increase the robustness and sustainability of the business.

The value based marketing approach has led to considerable debate about whether marketing should focus on narrow definitions of value, especially shareholder value, or on broader definitions of value for all the organisation's stakeholders. Here we take the broader view and particularly emphasise the increased strategic options that result from greater emphasis being placed upon intangible as well as tangible assets.

In adding value many organisations focus largely upon growth through the use of their tangible, owned, often traditional assets, for example maximising the use of their production equipment and factory capacity, selling existing and improved products to the same customer segments. By deciding to compete using traditional business models and competing on factors, such as price, conformance to requirements and service, they are often vulnerable to newer, cheaper and more flexible competitors. Successful organisations consider the strategic options that result from adding value by leveraging both the range of tangible and intangible assets that they possess and the assets that they do not own, but that can be leveraged through the supply chain from suppliers, partners and distributors. Later chapters build upon the discussion of these topics.

In this chapter, therefore, we focus on making effective use of the range of owned assets that the organisation can utilise to generate value and growth. First we discuss how the tangible assets can be made to work hard to deliver the maximum performance and growth that is possible within the constraints of the firm's existing operation. We then discuss the use of the intangible assets of the firm and, in particular, brand management and intellectual property creation and extraction.

Learning objectives

After reading this chapter you should be able to:

- Achieve growth by adding stakeholder value using the tangible and intangible assets of the organisation

- Recognise brands and intellectual property as key exploitable assets and, in conjunction with other resources, use them to extract value

- Identify good practice in investing in and managing brands effectively in order to improve customers' perception

- Understand the value of intellectual property in the marketplace and appreciate how value can be obtained from it through effective marketing

MARKETING APPROACHES AND THE RESOURCE BASED VIEW

As the world has moved from a situation of excess demand to excess supply so the strategic marketing options have also changed. The views of the 1980s, typified by Porter, suggested that understanding industry dynamics and characteristics was critical to successful marketing and business performance, whereas in the 1990s, writers such as Prahalad and Hamel (1990) focused on the ability of the organisation to exploit core competencies. This led to greater focus being placed upon **intangible assets**, such as branding, staff knowledge, skills and competencies and knowledge management.

The starting point in this discussion of value adding through leveraging the **tangible assets** and intangible assets is a review of the three familiar marketing approaches identified by Hooley et al. (2004):

Approaches to marketing

- *Product push marketing* is typified by organisations that focus on persuading customers to buy the products and services that they can produce, deliver and improve easily, largely using their existing realm of knowledge and resources. The weakness of this marketing approach is that satisfying increased customer requirements is considered secondary to focusing on what the organisation is capable of delivering.

- *Customer led marketing* is typified by those organisations that do everything they can to satisfy customer needs. Some organisations have taken this to extremes and set out to deliver customer needs almost irrespective of cost.

- *Resource based marketing* is considered to be a balanced strategy between meeting the market requirements and exploiting the organisation's capabilities to serve the market. **Resource based marketing** takes into account the competitive situation, the full range of assets, skills and competencies of the organisation and aims to exploit the organisation's role within the supply chain. It is illustrated in Figure 8.1.

Whilst considering alternative marketing approaches it is worth commenting on another traditional approach that was referred to in Chapter 7, entrepreneurial marketing, and a newer concept, network marketing, which is concerned with greater co-operation with external organisations.

- *Entrepreneurial marketing.* Entrepreneurs tend to focus on the opportunity or market gap, irrespective of whether or not this will make use of existing assets.

Entrepreneurial marketing takes the form of a new business start or step change innovation within an existing firm. Although there are different views of how to manage corporate innovation, many large organisations appear to prefer to manage diversification through setting up separate entrepreneurial ventures, rather than placing them within the existing organisation structure.

■ *Network marketing* is becoming increasingly significant as organisations, desperate for growth, use connections through alliances, partnerships, and equity participation in other organisations to exploit opportunities that are not deliverable through their directly owned assets. The rationale for **network marketing** is that an organisation can increase its revenue not by increasing its own market share or sales through its own market development but rather by taking a share of the increased potential revenue for the network of organisations.

The first three marketing approaches are often conceptualised as being on a continuum, with product push marketing and customer led marketing at the extremes, and resourced based marketing in the middle. However, in practice most organisations cannot base their strategy on one marketing stance to the exclusion of the others. Most organisations aim to be customer led, albeit not at any cost. Most organisations also aim to maximise the return from existing products and, where appropriate, optimise the use of existing facilities and equipment. Most organisations, perhaps with varying degrees of success, are trying to become more entrepreneurial and opportunity focused, and many are beginning to take a resource based approach by more comprehensively evaluating their resources and exploiting those that add greatest value.

Organisations must decide which of the alternatives is right for the particular context at a particular point in time. For example, Chinese firms are usually

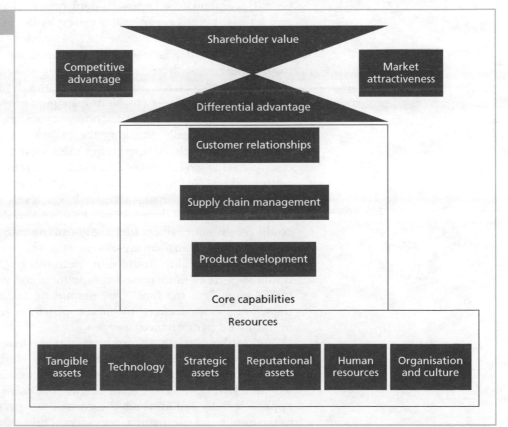

FIGURE 8.1

Intangible assets and the resource based theory of the firm

Sources: P'eterlaf (1993); Collis and Montgomery (1995)

tightly managed, family owned and passed down between generations. Many concentrate on manufacturing quality components and products at low prices in relatively stable markets and so product push is likely to be the most appropriate strategy. Western entrepreneurs do not have the benefit of low cost operations and labour and must instead focus on market opportunities, often sourcing products and services from low cost providers to supply those opportunities through third parties. Suppliers of commodities with no differentiation have little option but to try to become ever more customer led. Businesses in the technology and healthcare sectors must have a resource based marketing approach.

These marketing approaches are extremes and snapshots of businesses at a particular point in time. Rather than think about which one marketing approach is ideal, organisations should be thinking of which will be appropriate to generate cash flow and profits today, tomorrow, and in the future. Past events and traditional assets can contribute future value but there is a need for balance. There can be a strong pressure from some managers to rely on value contributions from the past and tried and trusted products and methods. Other managers, keen to make their mark, often want to scrap everything from the past, which they consider to be worthless in the future markets.

INCREMENTAL VALUE CREATION THROUGH GROWTH

The starting point is to consider the growth and future profitability targets and aspirations of the company. They will depend upon the context of the organisation and the ambitions of its management and internal and external stakeholders. Each will have a different view of value and growth possibilities.

In strategic marketing decision making there appears to be a general belief that growth is essential for improved performance. Indeed an ambitious entrepreneur and a not-for-profit organisation driven by beliefs and idealism will both wish to grow their activity or increase their influence. If the business model stays the same, the cost base is essentially unaltered but revenue comes under pressure from competition, then growth is the only route to improved performance, especially in the short term. Spotlight 8.1 shows, however, that some managers have very difficult decisions to make in managing growth, pricing and costs.

However, before the organisation pursues growth strategies it is worth deciding whether radically changing the business model and cost base rather than focusing exclusively on increasing sales would improve shareholder value. For example, changing the route to market by franchising or licensing, rather than setting up wholly owned subsidiaries, could improve value added and return on investment for the organisation at lower levels of direct sales. Removing intermediaries from the distribution chain and replacing them with on-line selling could create value, albeit after significant investment has been made.

In practice many organisations still see increased sales as the route to increased profitability. In the short term this might be deliverable, but against an underlying trend of increased competition and reducing margins it may not be a viable long term solution. Care should be taken to analyse the true situation, therefore, before deciding to pursue growth as growth may not necessarily result in improved performance.

Within the portfolio of products and services there will be different cost and price trends for different product categories. Moreover, the ability of marketing to add customer value will differ from product category to product category and it will not always be possible to rescue lost causes. In practice a more objective approach is needed in which the growth prospects are fully evaluated in the light of customer and competitive pressures. This is likely to lead to the rationalisation of some products and services and the greater concentration of resources, both financial and non-financial on the products and services with true potential for profitable growth.

It is necessary to see if continuation of the current strategic marketing approach and the consequent incremental improvement in added value for the organisation will be sufficient to deliver the desired performance or whether a more creative approach is needed. In Figure 8.2 path A is based upon the incremental growth from current activity and is largely achieved by leveraging the tangible assets of the organisation. Path B is needed to achieve the desired targets of, for example, return on investment. It requires a more radical change to the marketing approach and depends on leveraging some of the assets of the organisation that have not been fully exploited before to fill the growth gap. In some possible future scenarios the gap could become much larger if the organisation is only able to achieve the contribution path (C) as competitors increase volume by charging lower prices, higher prices through innovation and achieving better

---

SPOTLIGHT 8.1   **Channel tunnel**

Richard Shirrefs, chief executive of the Eurotunnel, the Channel tunnel high speed rail link between France and England, appeared to have an almost unsolvable dilemma. In July 2003 the company reported operating income down 7 per cent to £272 million and a loss of £77 million, with revenue from Shuttle trains down 11 per cent to £149 million. The number of passengers on the Eurotunnel high speed trains fell by 11.5 per cent to 2.85 million, compared with the forecast of 13 million per annum when the tunnel was built. Eurotunnel is laden with debts of £6.5 billion and had hoped, but failed, to reach 'cash break even', generating enough income to meet repayments on borrowings.

There are many problems. In order to reverse the declining revenues, Eurotunnel slashed its prices to as low as £9 for a return trip to Calais to try to compete with ferries and

budget airlines, but this appears not to have worked and analysts criticised the company, saying it should stick to premium pricing. Eurotunnel hopes that a high speed train link through Kent will increase passenger numbers and a new freight terminal at Folkestone could help increase freight but there seems little chance of an improving situation in the near future.

A shareholder revolt in April 2004 led to the replacement of the board.

Question   What should Jacques Maillot the new chairman do?

Source: adapted from A. Clark (2003) 'Channel price war hits tunnel operator', The *Guardian*, July 22 and *BBC News Online*, 8 April 2004

FIGURE 8.2

Contribution gap
Source: adapted from Doyle (2000)

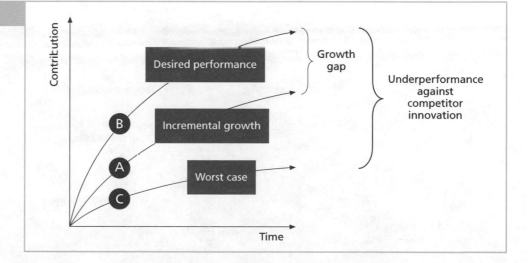

than expected productivity . The only response would be a radical restructuring of the organisation in order to save costs, focus resources on products and services with growth potential and so retain existing customers.

The actions that can be taken to achieve growth are shown in Figure 8.3, and the organisation must decide on the priorities which will compete for funds.

An organisation will need to decide which of these options will provide the best return for its efforts by analysing both the investment required in financial and human resources and anticipated performance improvements (shareholder value added), and carrying out a risk assessment of the likelihood of success and the possible consequences of failure. The key to success is focusing the growth strategies in markets that are increasing in attractiveness and in which the organisation is able to develop competitive advantage through distinctive positioning.

Challenge 8.1 shows that Harley Davidson must reach some decisions in the future about repositioning to maintain growth, and deciding where investment might be made.

The twin objectives for business are therefore based largely around increasing volume and improving productivity. The actions that can be taken to deliver these improvements are shown in Table 8.1.

FIGURE 8.3	
Actions to achieve growth	• Increase customer retention • Increase the share of total customer purchases • Gain new customers • Develop new products and services • Enter new markets or business sectors • Find new, lower cost or more value adding routes to market • Accelerate international market growth • Grow into new sectors • Make acquisitions or form alliances and joint ventures

TABLE 8.1 — **Volume and productivity improvements**

Strategic objectives	Marketing strategy objectives	Marketing task areas
Improve productivity	• Raise prices	• Better segment pricing
	• Cut costs	• Variable costs • Fixed costs
	• Improve sales mix	• Emphasise more profitable products
Increase volume	• Expand market	• Convert non-users • Enter new segments • Increase usage rate
	• Market penetration	• Win competitors' customers

Source: adapted from Doyle (2000)

ADDING VALUE THROUGH THE INTANGIBLE ASSETS

So far we have discussed the traditional concepts for achieving growth in the market. Many organisations base their growth strategies around these approaches and the easily identified, tangible assets of their business. Indeed, firms are mainly valued by their tangible assets and resources. However, the emergence of the information age has meant that tangible assets represent an increasingly small proportion of the total market value of the organisation. For example, Doyle (2000) observes that the ratio of the market value to book value of the Fortune 500 averaged 8, implying that tangible assets represent only 12 per cent of the organisation's total assets. Organisations that are smaller than the Fortune 500

CHALLENGE 8.1 **Repositioning Harley Davidson for youth**

Harley Davidson's elderly rockers

Harley Davidson held its 100th birthday party, celebrated by 350 000, at its home in Milwaukee. Similar celebrations were held in Sydney, Tokyo, Barcelona, Atlanta, Hamburg and Los Angeles. In the same year Harley was reporting record performance with 263 653 Harleys and 10 943 Buell motorcycles generating worldwide sales of US$4.1 billion, 20 per cent up on 2001. This was the 17th year of record sales and earnings achieved by sticking to the successful formula of heavyweight bikes for touring and cruising from one of the world's best known brands.

Unlike the British motorcycle industry, which in the 1960s, with names like Triumph, BSA and Norton, was the UK's third largest export, Harley has managed to fight off Japanese competition. The exception is Honda, the leading US bike manufacturer. In the 1970s Harley almost went bankrupt as sales dropped to a third. AMF, an American conglomerate, rescued Harley but ten years later lost interest and the company was bought by its management. The management made major strategic changes to secure Harley's future and were helped as the US government imposed tariff barriers on Japanese bikes for a period.

The biggest cloud on the horizon for Harley is probably best illustrated by the only things that seemed to go wrong at the birthday party. Rumours went round the crowd that the finale and headline act would be the Rolling Stones, a

Source: Harley Davidson

perfect fit with the rebellious past for many bikers. Imagine the disappointment when Elton John walked on. The Milwaukee police were quite happy, however, as the crowd left in droves and so there was a peaceful, staggered end to the event.

The real question for Harley is who their customers are now and who they will be in the future. At the moment they are the 'baby boomers' from the increase in birth rate just after the Second World War – the average age of customers is 43 as against that for the industry of 36. Coming from all walks of life, male and female, they include wealthy accountants, solicitors and company directors, wanting to relive their youth by using bikes for a weekend jaunt.

Harley do not have a problem at the moment, but eventually the company must reposition itself to appeal to the next generation.

Question Does Harley have a problem and will the company need to reposition itself eventually to appeal to the next generation?

Source: 'Harley revs up for the youth market' *Sunday Times,* 30 November 2003

Source: Harley Davidson

might learn the lessons and focus particularly on their intangible assets as a way of growing and adding shareholder value.

In addressing the question of what constitute the intangible assets that might be leveraged to enable the organisation to grow faster, it is useful to consider the implications for the organisation of the resource based theory illustrated in Figure 8.1. In the resource based view (Peterlaf, 1993) there are five types of assets and the characteristics of these are shown in more detail in Table 8.2.

The next section is a discussion of how brand assets might be leveraged. This is followed by a consideration of how technology assets might be used to create value and particularly the role of marketing strategy decisions relating to intellectual property protection and management.

Before discussing these it is useful to briefly consider the remaining assets. Strategic assets such as monopolies or licences that restrict competition allow firms to maximise their profitability and thus add considerable shareholder value. If the firms are well run they will also add customer value, but in practice many monopolies seem to place higher importance on such things as employee job security and meeting government political ambitions rather than on delivering better managed services. The problem arises when sectors such as utilities and communications are opened up to new competition. Not only are existing monopolies forced to compete with aggressive new market entrants but they have to manage an inevitable decline in revenue and a decline in morale associated with job losses that is an inevitable consequence of the privatisation. Rather than operate a 'level playing field', some regulatory authorities are so keen to create equal competition that they severely limit the scope for development in the old monopoly and give disproportionate incentives to the new business. Batelco in Bahrain is one example of an organisation whose monopoly was ended at the start of 2004 (see Challenge 5.2).

TABLE 8.2	Asset types and their characteristics in the resource based firm
Types of assets	Characteristics
Reputational assets	• Name of the company and brands that convey the reputation of its products and services and fair dealings with stakeholders
Strategic assets	• Licences, natural monopolies or other privileges that restrict competition
Technological assets	• Proprietary technology in the form of patents, copyrights and trade secrets or special know-how in the application of technology
Human resources	• Skills and adaptability of employees
Organisation and culture	• Values and social norms that shape the commitment and loyalty of employees

Source: adapted from P'eterlaf (1993)

LEVERAGING BRAND ASSETS

Of the intangible assets of the firm, the brand is the most critical in influencing strategic marketing decisions. Of course, the importance of the brand differs between the sectors and contexts. Moreover, the relative importance placed by organisations upon the brand differs. The Japanese retailer Muji even makes a virtue of no brand, but perhaps this simply reinforces the Muji brand. For many years Marks & Spencer avoided using any branding in its stores apart from its St Michael brand, which was little more than a quality mark. Under pressure from market and financial forces the firm has had to introduce some branding in its stores. However with sales of clothing still declining in Summer 2004 the threat of takeover was again looming.

Brands as assets for investment or milking

The fundamental question for an organisation is whether it should make a strategic marketing decision to provide investment to specifically support and build the brand. In making the decision the organisation must answer the following questions:

- Is it necessary to brand at all?
- Does the organisation regard the brand as a significant asset or simply a name that is applied to products and services?
- How does the organisation's brand currently contribute value to the business?
- With support, how could the brand add greater value for the business in the future?

Spotlight 8.2 shows an interesting cross border strategy for brand building through sponsorship that will appeal to potential customers

Many of the world's most valuable brands have received heavy and sustained investment over decades in every aspect of their marketing strategy, from customer research, segmentation and positioning through to every aspect of marketing mix activity. Usually the investment includes a large commitment to advertising but other factors, such as totally consistent quality, reliability, continuous innovation and total staff commitment, are just as important to achieve widespread customer loyalty and recommendations.

Careful consideration should be given to whether a new or improved product, line extension or modification will enhance the overall brand as well as helping with the initial sales of the product. It has been suggested that the strongest brands convey a core value to all their customers by the associations that are made with their name. By adding '-ness' to the brand names consumers instantly associate values that are globally recognised. Levi's launched a range of smart casual clothing under its Levi's brand, but the products were not made from denim. The products failed to sell, perhaps because this range did not support and add to the brand that is closely associated with denim. The question is whether the products had 'Levi-ness'. Some years later Levi's relaunched the products under the Dockers label.

However in many less sophisticated organisations, managers use the name or brand on new products, line extensions or modifications without any real thought to whether the name will enhance or reduce the value of either the product or the firm's overall reputation. Their purpose is often very short term. They simply want customers to buy a product or service presented under the brand name. These kinds of decisions at best do little to enhance the brand and at worst are a drain on the brand. Even with well known brands there are many examples of inappropriate brand extensions and product modifications.

The purpose of brands should be quite simple. When applied correctly they should create value for customers by helping them to make purchasing choices from the increasing range of competitive offerings available and help to reduce the risk of choosing the wrong product or service.

Customers expect brands to 'guarantee' customer satisfaction or, if it is a corporate brand, with the organisation too. With a brand, customers should at least know what they are going to get and ideally be delighted with the offer. Customers expect the brand to guarantee satisfaction right the way through the purchase decision making process and, of course, in some sectors customers do not differentiate between the brand owner and the brand distributor. For example, customers would not expect a car dealer to dissociate itself from the brand values of the manufacturer of the car it sells.

Adding value through the brand

Brands have the potential to add value to the organisation by providing the following benefits:

Price premium: they should allow higher prices to be charged than products that have an equivalent specification but no brand.

SPOTLIGHT 8.2   **Chinese phone maker sponsors Everton**

Kok Kin Hok owns a local football team in Shenzhen and the mobile phone firm he heads, Kejian, sponsors Chinese mid-fielder Li Tie's contract at Everton in exchange for publicity in China and the firm's name on the Everton shirts. A Chinese journalist in Liverpool produces stories that appear prominently on Chinese TV stations and sports websites. In this way the firm avoids the huge costs of TV advertising. The strategy is effective because English Premier League games are the most watched sport in China, attracting audiences of between 100 and 360 million and there are few Chinese players currently playing at this level.

Li Tie
Source: image supplied courtesy of Everton Football Club

Kejian has only 3 per cent of the China mobile phone market, which is the world's largest with 250 million subscribers. It is one of 30 handset makers, 20 of which are Chinese, so the market is competitive and quality and price conscious. Analysts have estimated that local manufacturers increased their share of the market from 10 per cent to 50 per cent in the two years up to 2003. Most of this improvement has come from better inland distribution where a 'push strategy' has worked better than the successful high budget 'pull strategy' used by foreign brands in the big cities. Kejian sees the production of handsets as essentially the assembly of kits. It has a joint venture for technology and assembly and the company has chosen to use Samsung for its quality components and trendy styles.

Samuel Lam, the marketing chief of Kejian, who joined from Samsung, sees brand image as the critical success factor, and wants a healthy, energetic, upmarket look appealing equally to men and women. Football is central to its image at the moment but the Beijing 2008 Olympics will offer the opportunity to further build the sporty image. The company already appears to be a pathfinder in the new sports sponsorship market in China.

Question   What do you consider to be the advantages and disadvantages of this brand association?

Source: adapted from M. Hennock, Chinese phone maker's fancy footwork, *BBC News Online*, October 27, 2003

Higher volumes: branded products can. generate higher volumes than non-branded products if they are priced at market rates, rather than at a premium.

Lower costs: high volumes should lead to cost reduction from the economies of scale and the experience effect.

Better utilisation of assets: the predictably high level of sales should lead brand managers to make effective use of assets, such as equipment, the supply chain and distribution channels.

Customer perception of brands

Brands add value to the organisation only if customers believe the brand adds value for them. The organisation needs a sufficient volume of customers to be prepared to pay a price premium to create the value to offset the investment that is made in the brand. Whilst organisations try to create a distinctive, positive image in consumers' minds through their marketing activities, ultimately customers make up their own minds and build their own individual perception of the brand.

The customers' positive perception of the brand is built from various sources:

Experience of use of the product before and satisfaction with its performance.

Personal referral from friends and acquaintances. Peer pressure, for example, wearing the 'cool' brand can be critical.

Editorial and other public sources, such as the media, consumer reports and endorsement by experts or fashion gurus.

Communications by the organisation both through interactions between its staff and customers and promotion by using the marketing mix.

The real question and the subject for the remainder of this section is how can the brand value be leveraged to add value for customers and the organisation in the future, and how can reduction of value be avoided.

Brand categories

There are three brand categories (Doyle 2000):

Attribute brands are created around the functional product or service attributes, such as quality, specification and performance to build confidence amongst customers in situations where it is difficult for them to evaluate the difference between competitive products. The brand provides a 'guarantee'. Examples include Volvo for safety, Asda Wal-Mart for every day low prices and Intel for computer processing.

Aspirational brands create images in the minds of customers about the type of people who purchase the brand and convey the standards and values that the brand is associated with. Such brands do not simply deliver the customers' functional requirements of the products and services, such as high specification and quality, but also deliver status, recognition and esteem that are associated with the brand. Examples include Ferrari, Rolex and high fashion.

Experience brands focus on a shared philosophy between the customer and brand and on shared associations and emotions, but not necessarily on claims of superiority. Examples include Nike, Virgin and easyJet.

The appeal of these different types of brand varies according to the context of the purchasing decision. Challenge 8.2 illustrates an example of a brand that has dominated its niche market for a century.

In luxury product markets aspirational brands are likely to be most successful, whereas in consumer markets, where there is little to distinguish between the attributes and performance of products, experience branding is more appropriate. In business-to-business markets where the purchasing process should be more rational, objective and based on specifications, attribute branding would be more appropriate.

In global markets, too, because of different cultures, customer expectations and market sophistication the appeal of a particular branding approach might be more relevant for a similar product. For example, in some cultures the attributes,

---

CHALLENGE 8.2   Bisto – 100 years of lump free gravy

Bisto is a classic, nearly 100 year old brand survivor that has 62 per cent of its market. In 1908 two housewives wanted a product that would guarantee perfect lump free gravy for the great British roast. So Bisto, the powder that 'Browns, Seasons and Thickens in One' was created. The secret of Bisto's success is the heritage associated with the brand created through sustained investment in advertising and marketing, backed up by in-depth understanding of changing consumer trends.

The main change over the last 25 years has been that the family are no longer likely to sit down together for the traditional roast and instead want something to eat quickly and separately, and so instantly dissolving Bisto granules were introduced in 1979. In the 1990s Bisto Best was introduced as a premium product, sold in jars. More recently there has been a revival of the British dinner classics, such as cottage pie and sausages and mash. Bisto now has to cater for both 'start from scratch' as well as 'instant pour-on' cooks.

Advertising has been the key to developing the brand. The Bisto Kids, introduced in 1919 as mischievous cartoon characters with their cast-off clothes became instantly recognisable in the 1920s and 1930s and the slogan 'Ah, Bisto!', which reflects the main thing about the product, the smell, is synonymous with the brand even today. Key times for advertising are Christmas and Easter, when people eat more roasts and need to be reminded about how strongly they feel about the brand.

For some time Bisto used sales promotion campaigns including 'Roast Britanniaah' at the point of sale to help to ensure customers remained loyal, but the firm was concerned that it might not be getting the best return on its investment and it noticed that promotions of one size of pack could cannibalise sales of larger or smaller packs. As a result it called in consultants Billetts to better understand

These images have been reproduced with the permission of Centura Foods Ltd; BISTO and the Bisto Kids are registered trademarks.

the dynamics of promotions. After a detailed analysis the consultants were able to develop a model that made strong recommendations about the type and value of sales promotions that should be undertaken and what should be the right balance between promotions and advertising. An important additional benefit of this consultancy was that the various internal departments also co-operated much more on the marketing model, which they perceived to be robust, reliable and based on facts.

Question What do you consider to be the critical success factors for brand longevity?

Sources: adapted from 'Lunch lesson 6 – brand management', *BBC News Online* 16 October 2003; 'MCA awards 2003: new recipe hits the spot', *Guardian*, 6 February 2003

functionality and specification may be more important, whereas in others aspirational branding might be more appealing.

Different interpretations of the brand

De Chernatony (2001) has carried out research amongst consultants and highlighted the different interpretations of the brand that are made:

- *The input perspectives*: these include the following: logo, legal instrument, company, shorthand, risk reducer, positioning, personality, cluster of values, vision, adding value and identity.
- *The output perspectives*: image and stakeholder relationships.
- *The time perspective*: the brand as an evolving identity over time.

A number of these interpretations are considered in terms of assisting in brand building and management.

Brand communications

Shrimp (2003) explains that customer brand knowledge and response, which are central to brand value, depend on brand awareness and brand image as shown in Figure 8.4. Brand awareness to generate recognition and recall amongst customers requires long term commitment to an integrated communication strategy. Brand image, of course, can be positive or negative and while positive brand associations can be made, negative associations can have a very detrimental effect. As we discuss in the next section, these negative associations can be the result of either unanticipated, uncontrollable events in the environment or poor management.

Figure 8.5 shows the dimensions of brand identity. They include:

- Physical: the appearance of the brand (colours, logo and packaging).

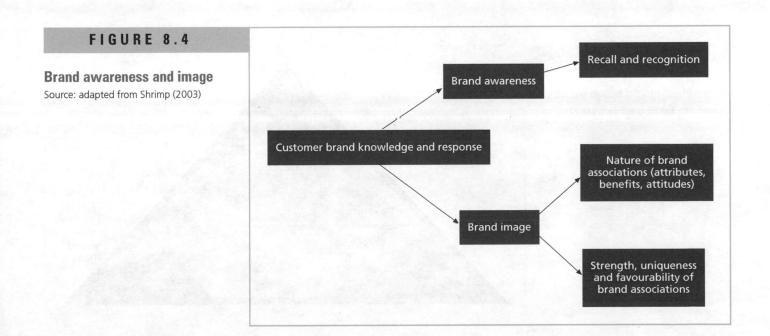

FIGURE 8.4

Brand awareness and image

Source: adapted from Shrimp (2003)

- Reflection: the image of the target audience reflected in brand communications. Coca-Cola and lager advertisements often show young people but, of course, the total market includes other segments.
- Relationship: the brand relates to its customers in a distinctive way, for example, Harley Davidson (Challenge 8.1).
- Personality: the character of the brand, for example, Apple (Spotlight 7.1).
- Culture: the background and values of the brand, for example, the country of origin effect and Nike's 'Just do it'.
- Self-image: how the customer sees herself or himself.

Brand management

Brand management is primarily concerned with making decisions to build, eliminate, reposition or revitalise brands in much the same way that product portfolios are managed. This is discussed in Chapter 9.

Branding strategies and the brand portfolio

The first decision is to choose between the alternative branding strategies that can be applied to the brand portfolio. The alternatives are as follows:

- *Umbrella brands* occur when one brand supports several products, as is the case with Philips electrical products.
- *Product brands* For example, Unilever, Procter & Gamble and pharmaceutical firms give each product a unique and distinctive brand.
- *Line brands* occur where a company has a number of complementary products sharing the same brand concept. L'Oreal sells haircare products under the Studio Line brand.
- *Range brands* are similar to line brands but include a broader range of products. Heinz uses WeightWatchers and Nestlé uses Findus for frozen foods.

FIGURE 8.5

Brand identity and brand pyramid
Source: adapted from Kapferer (1997)

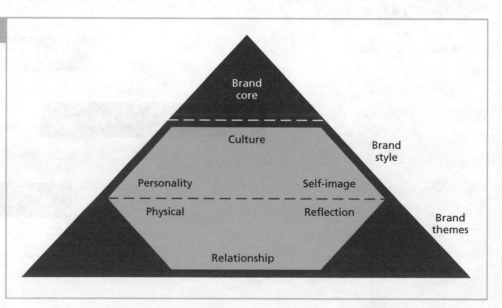

- *Endorsing brands* are a weaker association of a corporate name with a product brand name and are often used after acquisition. Over time, Nestlé has gradually increased the size of 'Nestlé' on the packaging of its acquired brands, such as Kit-Kat. This may be one step towards umbrella branding.

- *Source brands* occur where products are double branded with a corporate or range name and a product name, for example, Ford Mondeo.

Essentially the decision about which strategy to use is determined by whether the benefits of a shared identity outweigh the importance of differentiation between the individual product brands.

In managing the portfolio it is then necessary to make decisions in the following areas.

Brand extensions

Involves applying the brand to new product lines (for example, Persil washing up liquid as well as washing powder) and different product categories – an approach favoured by experience brands, such as Virgin and easyJet (see Spotlight 9.1), to make a brand appeal based on a common philosophy.

It is the brand perception of the customers that will ultimately determine how far the brand will stretch.

Brand positioning and repositioning

In order to make the brand relevant to the new market and changing customer needs, brand positioning needs to be updated occasionally. Ideally this should be incremental and based on adjustment rather than major change because consumers appear to respond best to consistency in brand identity. Whilst most brands need to be refreshed from time to time, some brands need a more significant repositioning, perhaps because the market no longer exists or the business model needs to change substantially.

Exploiting brand potential

Many brands are under-utilised and have greater growth prospects than their managers believe. The brand growth prospects could be in new market segments, for example, international markets, new products areas or finding new uses or new users for the existing product or service.

Brand elimination

Supporting brands fully with investment in communications, innovation and channel management can be hugely expensive. Many companies simply have too many brands, often the result of acquisitions. A number of companies have carried out brand culling so that they can support their priority brands more effectively. It is often at the time of new acquisitions that organisations need to make the elimination decision. The strategies for brand elimination and focusing on a smaller number of brands extend to dropping the name completely but this can be risky and can lead to loss of market share if customer perceptions are not managed. The remaining strategies are phasing out the brand gradually over an extended period or co-branding using the brand name of the acquired and acquiring companies.

Global branding

Success in building a global brand depends on both the external (uncontrollable) factors and internal (controllable) factors. Customers ultimately determine the success of a brand, and their perception of the brand is affected by the appeal of the total product and service offer and the supporting marketing mix, for example communications, distribution and pricing. But customers are also affected by many environmental factors, such as the sensitivity of the brand managers to different cultures. So consistency of customer perception of the brand is required but at the same time the brand must be sensitive to cultural differences.

There must be consistency and clarity of brand positioning in different countries and this is achieved by consistency of the corporate identity, logo, design and identity achieved through effective communications and standardisation of the marketing mix as far as possible. The brand must be continually supported through innovations, investment in promotion and appropriate band stretching.

Sometimes consistent positioning is difficult, for example because of the different price positioning that is necessary due to customers from different countries having differing abilities to pay, because the countries are at different stages of development.

Inevitably crises affect the brand from time to time and, perhaps the best test of a global brand is whether problems are managed effectively and whether the brand suffers long-term by malicious actions.

Country of origin (COO) effect

An important aspect of global branding and, indeed, unbranded products too, is the COO effect. Brands give confidence to buyers in situations where knowledge about the product is limited, for example because the technology is not understood. In such situations the **country of origin** perceptions can influence buying decisions by creating trust in the particular expertise of firms and workers from that country.

Consumer perceptions of COO are usually based on national stereotypes, for example Japanese products tend to be regarded as high quality, reliable and 'miniaturised' and German products as 'well engineered', whereas US products are often perceived to be big and 'brash'. The COO effect can have a negative or positive effect on value. For example, British products are often seen as traditional and reflecting heritage, which may not help the dynamic organisations with leading edge technology that want to market their newly developed products globally. Over the years some brands, such as McDonald's, have been associated with the heritage of the country of origin. Of course, in times of trouble customers can become angry at the actions of a country and this anger can be vented, at least in the short term against the brand. From time to time the premises of American brands around the world, such as McDonald's, have been attacked by people protesting against American foreign policy.

Products from developing countries are often seen by Western consumers as low quality, unreliable and usually copies of products from developed countries. This was the perception of Japanese products too some decades ago and shows that it is possible to change consumer attitudes. Overcoming these stereotypes is often the first challenge for international marketers who must prove that their product does not reinforce negative stereotypes.

There are significant differences between countries in the willingness of consumers to buy locally produced products. Usually this appears to be related to the feeling of nationalism that exists in the country at the particular time the assessment is made. In developing countries, such as China, Ho (1997) found that nationally produced goods are often seen to be inferior to foreign goods.

Increasingly, of course, the MNE's headquarters, the brand's perceived 'home', the location of product design and places of manufacture may all be in different countries. Consumers are becoming much more aware of these differences and make increasingly sophisticated decisions based on COO. For example, brands such as Nike and Gap that use garment making contractors in emerging countries provide the 'guarantee' of the quality of merchandise from those countries. The brand guarantee supersedes the possible negative country stereotype.

Erosion of brand value

Brands can, of course, under-perform expectations or decline in value from time to time for a variety of reasons. For example, a failure to understand customer expectations (Marks & Spencer), inappropriate brand stretching (a number of the top fashion brands), a failure to reposition quickly enough in response to market decline (e.g. Levi's) or failure to respond to new competition (Pan Am and many of the European and American car manufacturers at some point in their recent history) can severely affect the brand value.

Private branding is used widely in retailing and, as the major retailers have become more powerful, so the private brand share of the market has increased significantly, especially during recession. This is because consumers perceive private brands as providing 'value for money', and this has been encouraged as retailers have continually improved the quality of their own label products. Supermarket labels and low priced 'fighting brands' are gaining an increasing share of the market and reducing the demand for brands. Supplying supermarket private labels has long been a viable business venture for efficient producers with good relationships with the supermarket product. The question for branded producers is whether or not they should also make private label brands.

Whilst the organisation tries to influence how customers build more positive perceptions of the brand, it is important to point out that there are many factors that can have a negative effect on the brand value. Whilst bad management and poor brand decision making are the main reasons for declining brand value, other factors that are outside the organisation's control, or unexpected events that are poorly managed, can also seriously affect customer perception of the brand.

Brand piracy

One of the most difficult challenges for brand management to deal with is **brand piracy**. Research suggests that the problem of forgery of famous brand names is increasing and many but by no means all of the fake products have been found to originate in developing countries and in Asia. It is important to recognise the differences between the ways in which forgery takes place. Kaitiki (1981) identifies:

Outright piracy in which a product is in the same form and uses the same trademark as the original but is false.

Reverse engineering in which the original product is stripped down, copied, then undersold to the original manufacturer, particularly in the electronics industry.

Counterfeiting in which the product quality has been altered but the same trademark appears on the label. Benetton, Levi's and LaCoste have all been victims.

Passing off involves modifying the product but retaining a trademark which is similar in appearance, phonetic quality or meaning – for example Coalgate for Colgate and Del Mundo for Del Monte.

Wholesale infringement is the questionable registration of the names of famous brands overseas rather than the introduction of fake products. This might be considered to be brand piracy but is entirely within the law, and has been very prevalent in e-business with the registration of dotcom sites by individuals hoping to sell the site later, at substantial profit, to the famous name.

The issue of brand piracy clearly is affecting MNEs badly through lost revenues and the USA has led the way in insisting that governments crack down on the companies undertaking the counterfeiting. However, such firms have sophisticated networking operations with much of their revenue coming from sales to consumers in developed countries. Trying to reduce or eliminate their activities is costly and time consuming and unlikely to be a priority for governments in less developed countries. Moreover, pursuing legal action in foreign markets can be expensive, particularly for small companies, and can result in adverse publicity for larger companies.

Grey marketing

Grey marketing is the use of channels unauthorised by the brand owner to supply products into a market. Usually a legitimate dealer sells products obtained for one market into another at a much lower price, often giving customers the impression that they are being overcharged by the official channels. In Europe different country pricing of some car brands led to cross-border purchasing through the grey market by individual customers, who were able to buy at much lower prices. This resulted in considerable criticism of the car companies' policies. Doole and Lowe's (2004) *International Marketing Strategy* provides a fuller discussion of grey marketing.

Brand associations

As we discussed earlier, brand association is used to communicate brand image to consumers. The most obvious **brand associations** are with the owners of the brands, such as Richard Branson with Virgin and Bill Gates with Microsoft. For some customers such figures are heroes and are the very personification of the brand. To others such figures are arrogant and exploitative and would be a significant reason not to buy the brand. Celebrities, such as media or sports personalities that can communicate the values associated with a particular brand can be effective in enhancing brand equity as shown in Challenge 8.3, but this needs to be done carefully. There can be damage to the brand if the celebrities are inappropriate or engage in undesirable behaviour. Product or corporate brands can also become too closely associated with inappropriate sponsored events or organisations. Their public relations activity that is designed to achieve a better relationship with governments and politicians can backfire and have a negative effect on brand value if the politicians or civil servants are corrupt. It is therefore vital to take care when making strategic marketing decisions in these areas.

Unacceptable business practices

A number of brands have been accused of unethical business practices such as pollution of coasts by oil companies, exploiting child labour in garment making, and pharmaceutical companies charging high prices for drugs in LDCs. These practices might be carried out either directly by the organisation or indirectly through third parties, such as contractors for famous brands. Nike, Levi and Gap have suffered negative publicity in the past. Of course, what is acceptable and unacceptable is often a very personal view and is affected by differences in stakeholder situation, culture, affluence levels and understanding of business practices.

Unexpected crises

From time to time events occur that are largely outside an organisation's control but can damage the organisation's reputation. Disaffected employees have tampered with products from Heinz and Johnson & Johnson, hackers have attacked Microsoft's operating system and anti-company propaganda has been publicised through protests and websites. The Firestone brand was damaged when tyres fitted to the Ford Explorer were associated with accidents in the USA. Oil spillages and ferry and plane crashes have all damaged well known brands, too.

Customers expect companies to have systems in place that will prevent many of these events. Even where no blame can be attributed to the firm directly there can still be some damage to the brand value. In such situations it is essential that firms respond fast to deal with the crisis before the media take control and the brand damage becomes worse.

CHALLENGE 8.3   Luxury brands – just too common

Luxury brands succeed because of their exclusivity. Customers buy them because others cannot afford to – 'if you have to ask the price, you cannot afford it'. In July 2003 Domenico De Sole, CEO of Gucci, complained that the previous three months had been the worst in memory for the luxury goods business – SARS, the war in Iraq and the rise of the euro against the dollar being largely responsible.

Other commentators, however, see the problems originating from inside the industry rather than the environment. The industry sees the opportunity to increase revenues by taking fashion to the masses and selling more without reducing prices. In doing this, however, the brands lose their label of exclusivity in brand positioning and their identity becomes confused, because the luxury brands no longer have control over the type of customer that buys the product. An extreme case was when football hooligans adopted Burberry as their uniform.

The links to the mass market for luxury brands are usually product placement and celebrity endorsement, sometimes intended and sometimes not. Girl band Missteeq brought exclusive Cristal champagne to a wider audience by saying they only drink Cristal. Companies have given away products to celebrities and they in turn have opened up a new market, for example Victoria Beckham for Gucci, Oasis for Adidas. Other celebrities have been signed up to promote brands to the masses, for example Burberry used Kate Moss to revitalise its flagging sales. Of course, everyone has his or her own agenda. Kylie Minogue made a catwalk appearance for Chanel, prompting speculation that this might be Chanel broadening its appeal or part of Kylie's strategy for repositioning herself.

In the 1990s UK consumers seemed to use the brands to show off, and in response to this many brands offered individual low price items within their range, for example a Gucci bracelet for £65, or they placed brands on a very wide range of unconnected products – in the case of Ralph Lauren's Polo on tins of paint and golf balls. But lower end brands have improved their quality and consumers have now become more comfortable with brands at both ends of the scale and mix and match. They are quite happy to carry a Prada handbag or wear Gucci shoes along with a shirt bought from low price clothing retailer, Matalan, or even supermarkets, such as Asda Wal-Mart.

Question Is it possible to maintain brand exclusivity whilst expanding sales in the mass market?

Source: adapted from *The Scotsman*, 9 July 2003

Brand building and management

As a valuable existing asset and a potentially even more valuable future asset, it is essential to manage the brand to create additional value for the organisation by attracting new customers, increasing sales to existing customers and maximising the sales of the existing and new products and services, together with managing problems. However, in order to create future brand value the marketing activities undertaken must also enhance customers' brand perception. Marketing activities that use but do not enhance the customer perception of the brand ultimately devalue it. For example, in the 1970s the MG car brand was applied to undistinguished family cars and its sports car heritage was undermined.

The recession of the early 1990s sparked off the first real challenge to the power of the biggest global brands. Before then, apart from a few exceptions, they had relentlessly increased their dominant position steadily and consistently over decades. However, at this time brands came under pressure more than ever before and, by understanding the reasons for this, it is possible to build more robust brand management strategies for the future.

Khashani (1995) draws attention to changes in a number of factors that affect brand performance. Customers are better educated, better informed, more sceptical, more willing to experiment, less brand loyal, much more media aware and have higher expectations of the total brand package. Competition is more aggressive with more rapid launches of higher quality 'me too' products. Retailers have greater awareness of brand performance. In response to better consumer information, they have introduced better quality private labels.

These changes in the brand market environment have been compounded by weaknesses in brand management including low investment, poor consumer communication, an emphasis on quick returns rather than long term brand building, inadequate innovation and an emphasis upon small modifications. Khashani criticises brand managers for lazy pricing, insufficient attention to value creation, pricing arrogance, insufficient product differentiation, poor value for money and tolerating high cost bases. He summarises much current brand management in terms of complacency and acceptance of a comfortable status quo, with little long term vision, little innovative thinking and insufficient interaction with customers and distributors. Brand management has typically been bureaucratic and risk averse, and has taken a short term view. In brief he feels that brand managers have lost the killer instinct.

Khashani's solution is to get lean, avoid the temptation to live off past successes, cut costs to improve cost structures and provide a basis for aggressive pricing. He advocates pruning weak brands and reallocating resources, investing and innovating in the product and service and creating more consumer value. It is essential to listen to the market and get closer to customers. He stresses the need to be bold and think creatively, setting new market and performance standards and taking risks. The aim must be to think globally, launch products and services sequentially and rapidly across markets and build world brands.

Business to business branding

So far the discussion has focused on global consumer branding but branding is important in business to business marketing too. Purchasers and users value the commitment of suppliers to the product and service, and the benefit from dealing with a high profile firm. In some situations benefits can be gained from an association with globally recognised branded components such as Intel microprocessors in computers.

In business to business branding firms have similar brand naming options to the consumer market. Whilst firms such as IBM and Microsoft emphasise the corporate brand, other firms, such as GlaxoSmithKline and AstraZeneca in the pharmaceutical industry, promote individual product brands.

Ultimately, the rationale for the existence of brands in business to business marketing is the same as in consumer goods marketing, to avoid commoditisation of products which leads to decisions being based only on price.

LEVERAGING VALUE FROM INTELLECTUAL PROPERTY

The intellectual capital of an organisation covers a considerable range of knowledge, skills and capabilities within the firm. We discuss knowledge acquisition, creation, extraction and management at various points in this book. Knowledge management will be a critical intangible asset in the future because it increases future strategic options and reduces dependency on traditional business models and income streams that are constantly under attack from competitors.

Knowledge acquisition and creation occur throughout the organisation in an often *ad hoc* manner, sometimes at high cost. Value extraction only occurs when a customer or commercial application is identified for the knowledge. Intellectual property management is a key aspect of this for many firms.

Intellectual property (IP) management

For many organisations an important intangible asset is **intellectual property**, whether it is Coca-Cola's secret recipe for Coke or the patents on pharmaceuticals that provide a company with an essentially protected income stream during the life of the patent before competitors are able to offer generic equivalents. This is discussed in the case study at the end of Chapter 9. Many organisations still regard IP management as the responsibility of the legal department, the R&D or technology department. The role of marketing management in IP management is often ill defined.

In practice, however, marketing management should play a key role in the process for a number of reasons, mainly that it is the task of marketing to maximise the benefits for the organisation that accrue from patents and copyright protection, by using them to assist in generating income and to defend the organisation from competitors using similar intellectual assets.

Value generation from IP

Sullivan (2000) proposed that a firm is not simply what its final report states but is in fact a bundle of intellectual and structural capital together with complementary assets, and it is the intellectual capital that is at the centre of value creation. All the other assets are there to help convert the intellectual capital into profits as shown in Figure 8.6. In contrast to the way that it is regarded in many firms, IP must provide extra value and not be simply considered as a 'by-product' of the innovation process. Sullivan proposes the hierarchy shown in Figure 8.7.

Consequently this view of IP leads to the concepts of value creation and value extraction roles within the firm. A considerable investment is made by many firms to create IP through R&D with varying degrees of market focus, from curiosity driven research with no market application in mind through to solving customer problems.

Davis and Harrison (2001) discuss the importance of extracting value from IP and identify offensive, defensive and strategic roles. Offensive roles are usually concerned with new product development (NPD), improving products and providing the opportunity for strategic alliances and joint ventures. This also includes licensing, selling and donating IP in order to generate income, directly or indirectly.

Defensive roles relate to establishing areas of IP in order to increase design and development freedom, cross-licensing and litigation bargaining power, so preventing other organisations from making identical products or using the same processes or intellectual property for value creation.

There is also a strategic role for IP in building the reputation and image of the organisation as a 'leading edge' technology firm and using multiple patenting to block competitors from broad areas of technology.

Of course, to obtain value from the defensive role, the organisation must be willing and able to identify infringements of the patents or copyright, and be prepared to take transgressors to court. This raises a number of questions:

FIGURE 8.6

Value from the firm's intellectual capital

Source: adapted from Sullivan (2000)

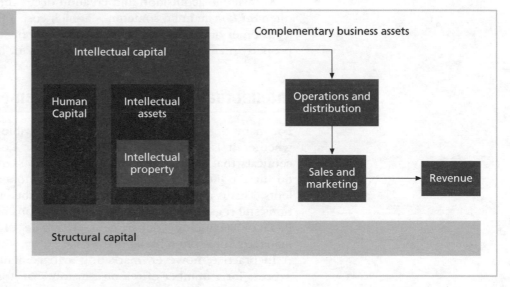

FIGURE 8.7

Integrated IP management

Source: adapted from Sullivan (2000)

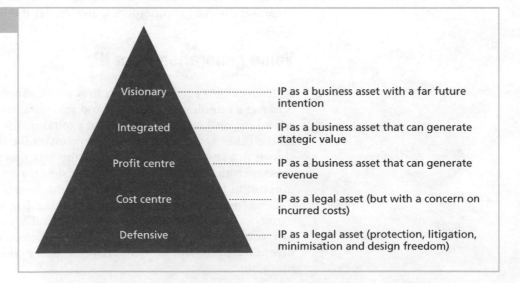

- Whether the IP protection is strong enough to win in court.
- Whether the organisation has enough resources to take the transgressor to court.
- Whether the organisation can prove infringement. It is easier to prove infringement of a patent that describes a final product that is on the open market than a manufacturing process that might be carried out within the secrecy of the transgressor's own facilities.
- Whether it would be more cost effective for the organisation to compete on better marketing rather than rely on IP protection through the courts.

These issues present real problems for small firms. Publishing a patent provides a publicly available, detailed explanation of the intellectual property claimed. It also explains what is not being patented and allows competitors to work out how they could circumvent the patent and copy the idea, particularly if the patent is not well written. Often, therefore, it is not worthwhile for the smaller firm to patent ideas, as there is a risk that they will inadvertently tell competitors how to copy the idea but not have adequate funds to take to court those infringing the patent.

CHALLENGE 8.4   Intellectual property and the semiconductor market

There are around 40 companies, including Philips, STMicroelectronics, Motorola and Texas Instruments, in the semiconductor market. They all have relatively low shares so that no one company can dominate the market. Some niche companies, such as ARM, design and develop but do not manufacture. Semiconductors are used in many applications including washing machines, TVs and computers. Change takes place slowly in some markets but in others, such as mobile phones, the developments are occurring very rapidly.

There are three main areas of concern for intellectual property protection in this market:

Process: the manufacturing process is complex and takes place in clean conditions. The main IP developments are in removing cost from the manufacturing process and finding innovative processes to integrate the different functions that semiconductors perform.

The device: technology can change the structure of the devices in order to improve performance, miniaturise and perform multiple functions.

Applications: new methods of applying the devices to products are developed by working with customers.

Patents are designed to protect the idea, but by publicising the process others can find ways round the patent. They might also deliberately infringe the patent if there is little chance of them being taken to court.

IP protection can be extremely costly, with a full international patent costing well in excess of £25 000. IP is usually managed either by the organisation's legal department, because the main purpose of patenting is to stop others using the IP, or by the R&D department, who are the main generators of IP. But patents improve a scientist's CV – even when they may be of little use to the firm – and so there is a danger of unnecessary expenditure being incurred if scientists exaggerate the importance of their invention.

Some suggest that IP protection should be managed by the marketing department as a marketing asset. IP can enhance the firm's reputation in the city as a 'leading edge' technology firm – here the number of patents is more important than quality! IP can provide an income through licensing. But much of the cost of patenting is wasted as there is little point taking out a patent unless the organisation is willing and has sufficient resources to be able to take to court companies that infringe the patent. For example, it is difficult to know what manufacturing processes are being used within a competitor's factory. Increasingly, manufacturing is being done in China and other parts of Asia, where it would be very difficult to win a court action using process patents. It is even difficult to collect device patent license fees, unless the products are sold into Western markets. Moreover, small firms often do not have the money to resource a court case to protect their IP.

Question What should be the main considerations when developing a strategy for IP protection?

Source: Milton Jorge Correia de Sousa

The decisions therefore should be 'marketing based'. As Challenge 8.4 shows, larger organisations can also usefully adopt a more marketing based approach to IP management.

Intellectual property and knowledge extend to many areas of activity. Creativity and imagination are a key asset for Urban Splash, the subject of the case study at the end of this chapter. Companies that have these assets are able to attract partners who can contribute complementary assets to complete joint projects.

SUMMARY

■ Stakeholder value is added through tangible and intangible assets and the approach that the organisation adopts to marketing reflects their view of the value of the assets.

■ Most organisations recognise growth as a method of adding value for the organisation largely based on the existing, often tangible assets, but growth may not guarantee value added.

■ The resource based view of the firm acknowledges that brands and intellectual property are key exploitable assets, in conjunction with other resources discussed elsewhere in this book.

■ Brands are a major means of differentiation of one product or service from those of the competition. However, it is the customers' perception of the brand that ultimately determines the true brand value. This is the reason why a valuable brand is an important asset of the organisation.

■ Some organisations build the brand through effective brand management and continual investment. However, many brands suffer brand value erosion by poor management and external, often unexpected, factors.

■ In many firms intellectual property has been managed by the legal or technology departments but IP should be associated with marketing. The value of IP is measured in the marketplace through value generation and value extraction, in which marketing plays a major role.

KEYWORDS

brand association	intangible assets
brand piracy	intellectual property
country of origin	network marketing
entrepreneurial marketing	resource based marketing
grey marketing	tangible assets

CASE STUDY — Inner city regeneration – Urban Splash

One of the biggest turnaround challenges is the regeneration of run-down inner city areas. Not least because of the need to persuade customers to live in an area that they probably would have avoided in the past because of fears of security, but also because of the difficulty of bringing together in partnership organisations with quite different responsibilities and objectives, developing a vision for an area that everyone will support, and having the design and delivery skills to make the vision a reality that will excite potential customers.

Urban Splash, led by its charismatic chairman, Tom Bloxham, has been a pioneer for over ten years in giving new life to and finding new uses for factories and other industrial buildings in Manchester and Liverpool, with highly creative designs to create a mix of living areas, work space, retail outlets, open space and leisure facilities. New health, education and transport facilities are provided as part of the developments.

Urban Splash is the lead developer in a government backed initiative to create New Islington, the third millennium community, by transforming an area close to Manchester city centre, the Cardroom Estate at Ancoats. The area was at the centre of the industrial revolution but in the last few decades the industrial base and the employment it supported were decimated by recessions and intensive global competition. Now the area has streets of boarded up houses, derelict factories and a lack of facilities, such as schools, a health centre and shops.

Along with Urban Splash the partnership includes the existing residents, English Partnerships, New East Manchester, Manchester City Council and the Manchester Methodist Housing Association. Alsop Architects are the creators of the strategic framework for the project.

The area is bordered by two canals that will provide the focal point. The partnership is seeking to question, challenge and re-examine current practices too. For example, they aim to make the development energy efficient and environmentally responsible. Urban Splash explains that the ambitious plans aim to make the developer part of the energy supply chain with proposals for fixed cost energy bills, with the intention that the energy suppliers should make more money from selling less in order to incentivise the development of more energy efficient buildings.

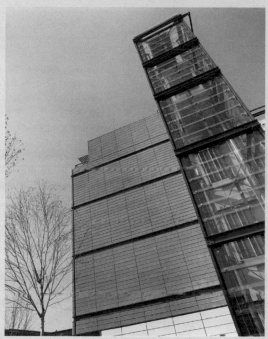

Source: Urban Splash

Questions

1 Fully evaluate the problems and potential benefits of innovation and marketing of major projects at the interface between the private and public sector and explain how this affects marketing strategy decision making.

2 What should the role of the entrepreneur, for example Tom Bloxham, be in such public–private ventures?

Sources: adapted from various public sources; www.Urbansplash.com

DISCUSSION QUESTIONS

1 Most organisations set growth targets and focus on increasing revenue from their existing portfolio. Under what circumstances would you consider this to be an appropriate strategy and what alternative strategies are available?

2 Using examples to illustrate your case explain the critical success factors in building a global brand.

3 Select a brand of your choice and explain in detail how it adds value to customers and the organisation that owns it.

4 In what circumstances does intellectual property contribute to the assets of an organisation. Explain why in some science or technology based organisations IP protection is a high priority, whereas in others it is not.

5 Do you agree with the proposition that: 'building the competitive advantage of an organisation around the creation and extraction of value from intangible rather than tangible assets results in a much more difficult organisation to manage'. Fully justify your views.

REFERENCES

Davis, J.L. and Harrison, S.S. (2001) *Edison in the Boardroom – How Leading Companies Realize Value from their Intellectual Assets*, Chicester: Wiley.

de Chernatony, L. (2001) *From Brand Vision to Brand Evaluation*, Oxford: Butterworth-Heinemann.

Doole, I. and Lowe, R., (2004). *International Marketing Strategy: Analysis, Development and Implementation*, 4th edn, London: Thomson Learning.

Doyle, P. (2000) *Value-based Marketing: Marketing Strategies for Corporate Growth and Shareholder Value*, Chicester: John Wiley.

Ho, S. (1997) 'The emergence of consumer power in China', *Business Horizons*, September–October.

Hooley, G.J., Saunders, J.A. and Piercy, N.F. (1998) *Marketing Strategy and Competitive Positioning*, 2nd edn, Harlow: Prentice Hall.

Kaitiki, S. (1981) 'How multinationals cope with international trade mark forgery', *Journal of International Marketing*, 1(2).

Kapferer, J-N. (1997) *Strategic Brand Management. Creating and Sustaining Brand Equity Long Term*, London, Kogan Page.

Khashani, K. (1995) 'A new future for brands', *Financial Times*. 10 November.

P'eterlaf, M.A. (1993) 'The cornerstones of competitive advantage: a resource-based view', *Strategic Management Journal*, 14.

Prahalad, C.K. and Hamel, G. (1990) 'The core competence of the corporation', *Harvard Business Review* 68(3).

Shrimp, T. (2003) 'Integrated marketing communications', in Hoffman, D. *et al.*, *Marketing Best Practice*, Mason, OH: Thomson South-Western.

Sullivan, P.H. (2000) *Value-driven Intellectual Capital; How to Convert Intangible Corporate Assets into Market Value*, Chicester: Wiley.

CHAPTER

9

REFOCUSING THE PORTFOLIO TO EXPLOIT NEW MARKET OPPORTUNITIES

Introduction

Products and services, which satisfy customers, generate the revenue that is essential for the organisation's survival and growth. Clearly the organisation must efficiently and effectively manage many other supporting activities if it is to be successful, but the management of the portfolio and the associated pricing of the products and services is at the heart of the organisation's activities.

The portfolio must be coherent, deliverable by the functions and departments of the organisation and integrated with the other elements of the marketing mix in the form of an attractive, acceptable, understandable and ultimately satisfying offer to customers. The aim might be to achieve product and service leadership or a sustainable position in relation to other competitive products. In this chapter we focus on the creation and maintenance of a portfolio of products and services that offer value for money for customers. This includes product and service enhancement, new introductions and deletions.

A key task in a highly competitive market is to resist the forces of commoditisation by finding ways to further differentiate the organisation's offering from those of competitors, and add perceived value for customers. For international marketers the additional challenge is in deciding upon the balance to be struck between standardising some aspects of the portfolio across regions of the world and adapting others to local needs.

Maintaining and building the profitability of the products and services is a key challenge in portfolio management and so strategic pricing decisions coupled with cost reduction, where appropriate, are critical to the success of the portfolio. Again we emphasise that the decisions should be taken not in isolation but in conjunction with other factors. Because of their nature and complexity, global markets create other problems in the pricing and financial management of products and services, and this is dealt with in later sections of the chapter.

Learning objectives

By the end of this chapter the reader should be able to:

- Select appropriate product and service strategies to build a sustainable portfolio

- Define the role of new product development in competitive strategies
- Apply appropriate pricing policies and strategies that will enhance the value added from the portfolio
- Determine the relationship between costing, pricing and the marketing mix factors
- Set prices with a full undertanding of the factors that affect the decision

PORTFOLIO DECISIONS

Earlier chapters have discussed the need for reorientation of the marketing strategy, and this will inevitably lead to some major decisions about the necessary changes to the **portfolio of products and services**. The decisions about what specific products and services to delete, retain or develop need to be taken within a framework of six drivers:

- Product and service decisions: the overall value contribution to the organisation's strategy of the existing portfolio.
- Customer segment decisions: standardisation and adaptation of products and services for different customer segments.
- New product development decisions to refresh or refocus the portfolio.
- Service development and enhancement.
- Pricing decisions: the inter-relationship between the pricing strategy and the portfolio of products and services to deliver stakeholder value.
- Integration decisions: the integration of the portfolio with other aspects of the marketing mix.

PRODUCT AND SERVICE DECISIONS

The first driver is the value of the contribution to the organisation's marketing strategy of the products and services within the existing portfolio, but this requires evaluation and a full understanding of the current and likely future situations.

Product and service analysis

Evaluation of the current range is essential, therefore, and there are many concepts and techniques that might be used to analyse the product and service portfolio including the product life cycle and a range of portfolio analysis methods, discussed by Wilson and Gilligan (2004).

As a result of analysis using these techniques a number of questions can be answered, including:

- Which products and services perform well or badly, in terms of volume and value contribution to overheads and profitability?
- Which phase of the life cycle and cell of the portfolio matrices is each product and service in, and in which direction are they moving?
- Which market segments, including geographic segments, best generate sales of existing and newly introduced products?

- Which customers and distribution channels are generating the greatest volume, value and profitability?
- How successful is the introduction of new products and services measured by the diffusion rates?
- Where do the opportunities exist for the development of new products, services and processes?

From this it will be possible to make decisions about the strategies that should be adopted for individual products and services and categories of products and services, both globally and in specific market segments. This has implications for product elimination, product re-invigoration and new product development.

It is important to emphasise that many of the analytical methods should be regarded as concepts that will help inform the strategic decision making process. They are not quantitative tools for forecasting and making detailed product planning decisions, such as predicting likely future demand. For detailed forecasting sophisticated software is required.

Product and service strategy considerations

The analysis might lead to suggestions about which products should be supported, discontinued or replaced by new products; in practice strategic marketing decisions about individual products and services are rarely easy. Decisions are affected by environmental factors, including legal and technology changes, green environment and ethical issues, as well as the competitor factors leading to the shortening of product life cycles and changes in customer expectations, purchasing and usage behaviour and a greater awareness of fashion.

Such analysis leads to decisions being required around portfolio management.

Building on success

A common criticism of product and service management is that managers spend too much time on turning around under-performing products and services rather than on proactively building successes. A major reason for Coca-Cola's success has been based simply on making the product available in every possible location. The least risk option in Ansoff's growth matrix (Figure 9.1) is increasing market penetration followed by new market development.

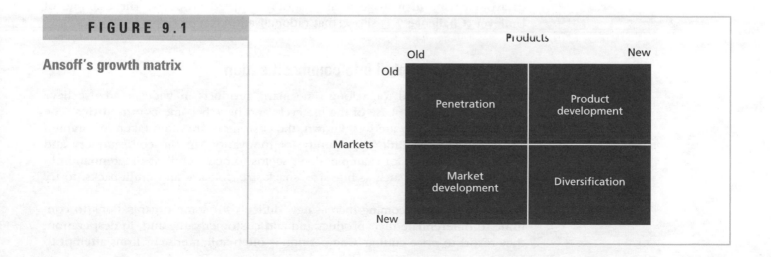

FIGURE 9.1

Ansoff's growth matrix

Integrating product and service offers

The value contribution might come from the contribution of the individual product or service 'standing alone' or through the combined value generated by integrating the product and services. For example, a company selling computing hardware, software and services may create more customer value and contribution to the company by offering an integrated package rather than selling the individual components, each of which may be in a highly competitive market.

Retaining poorly performing products

Portfolio analysis might suggest certain products should be removed from the range offered. However, there are reasons why poorly performing or **unprofitable products** should be retained. A product with low volume sales might be an essential part of a range. It might be a loss leader and leverage sales of complementary, higher volume or value products. The product might be what everyone remembers the brand for, and may still have an important role in communication. Discontinuing it could lead to brand damage. Retaining the product might be important in retaining some residual customer loyalty until a replacement is developed and introduced. However, keeping a poorly performing product might simply confirm an old fashioned product range in consumers' minds and reduce the brand value in the longer term.

In sectors such as shipbuilding, aircraft manufacture or defence equipment manufacture it is often necessary to ensure that the production line, skills and knowledge are retained until the next big order materialises. Decisions need to be taken about whether contributing to overheads is a sufficient reason to retain a product. It is worthwhile remembering that discontinuing a product that contributes to overheads will result in other products having to share an additional overhead burden that could lead to them becoming loss making as a result.

Rationalisation

There will always be those that argue to retain weaker products and, because of this, many organisations carry too large a product range. **Rationalisation** is necessary periodically in order to reduce inventory, reduce production line changeover time and increase the focus on managing and marketing better performing products rather than trying to revive under-performing products. In international markets many firms seek to standardise products as far as possible to avoid having to manage weaker, locally adapted products. The example of Unilever (Challenge 9.1) shows that rationalisation can be risky.

The downward spiral into commoditisation

Having been around for a long time many products in widespread use have reached the mature phase of the life cycle and have become **commodities**. The product and services are well known, the customers are often taken for granted and there appears little opportunity for innovation. In the confectionery and snack food markets, for example, there seems to be an endless differentiation in size and packaging, such as bite-size, snack-size, fun-size and multi-packs, to try to avoid this.

However, it is becoming increasingly difficult for some organisations to continue to differentiate their product and add customer value and, in desperation, they resort to price cutting. Competition is often still intense as firms attempt to hold on to sales volume. Moreover, e-commerce has resulted in increased price transparency, allowing customers to compare prices and buy from the lowest priced supplier, forcing the suppliers of higher priced alternatives to lower their prices or risk going out of business. As supermarkets become more powerful they are able to apply pressure to suppliers to force them into offering volume discounts. To put further pressure on suppliers their own label is applied to an ever broader range of products with consistently low prices. Supermarkets routinely take branded new developments, put their own brand onto the products, copy rather than differentiate and accelerate the commoditisation process.

As a result branded commodities often offer no differentiation and no better quality than the unbranded or own-label alternatives, and certainly there is less scope for charging a premium for many branded goods.

Becoming the lowest cost supplier of commodities

Firms that supply commodities have no alternative but to aggressively and continuously reduce costs throughout their supply chain, be prepared to source components and services from quality suppliers from the lowest cost locations and outsource finished products, where appropriate, rather than make their own products. For many years the textile and garment making industry has been driven by cost advantage to source from emerging countries. Banks and insurance companies are lowering their costs by making staff redundant in high cost locations and relocating their service operations to low cost countries. They encourage customers to use lower cost distribution channels, such as telephone and internet banking. As we have seen in Chapter 7, electronic hubs will further increase the pressure towards commoditisation in the B2B sector.

CHALLENGE 9.1   **Unilever's faltering steps on the path to growth**

In 1999 Unilever launched its five year 'path to growth' strategy, after deciding to cull many of its 1500 brands and concentrate on just the 400 brands they believed had the best growth prospects in global markets. The annual targets that were set were 5–6 per cent growth per annum. In October 2003 the company reported profits on target but reported that its 400 leading brands would show only 3 per cent growth. One response to this on a local level was for the Slim-Fast brand in the UK to launch a new range of products under the slogan: 'Stop dieting, start losing weight'.

Frozen foods, home care and fragrances, such as Calvin Klein, also performed poorly. Although contributing only 10 per cent of overall sales, they were expected to contribute a further 0.9 per cent of leading brand sales growth.

Question What are the arguments for and against brand culling and focusing on global brands?

Unilever
Source: Grey Worldwide Montreal

Source: P. Aldrick, Unilever brands stall on 'path to growth', *Daily Telegraph*, 30 October 2003

Differentiation by adding value

It is easy for firms to be drawn into believing that they are in the business of selling a specific product or service made to a specific design with the inevitable consequence of trying to achieve ever lower prices. But some of the most successful firms have been able to create customer perception of lower prices on commodity products, whilst differentiating their services and adding value.

For example, Tesco has grown from being the 'pile it high, sell it cheap' food retailer of the late 1960s to become the leading UK food retailer. It has achieved this through continually differentiating the relatively mundane activity of food shopping by adding customer value through a whole range of successful, often small initiatives. Many of these are service based – offering greater convenience for families, avoiding delays at checkout and providing loyalty bonuses.

Innovators appear in all sectors and always seem to find a way to differentiate products. With the benefit of hindsight it often seems obvious to the rest that there were opportunities for differentiating the products but it was, perhaps, not obvious to the major players at the time or they were unwilling to take the risk of introducing a new product or service. Most breakthrough innovations come from new competitors. The challenge for firms is to continually reinvigorate their commodity products by a series of relatively small incremental improvements in the design, functionality and usability that will maintain customer interest and loyalty.

Focusing on solutions rather than specific products

The biggest change that suppliers can make in a commodity market is changing from supplying products to offering solutions, ideally on a bespoke basis to individual customers. So a company manufacturing oil becomes a fluids management company, ensuring that the lubricants are available and accessible just-in-time where they are needed.

Stock broking at its most basic is a relatively simple task undertaken by experts who have created a mystique around the task in order to justify quite high commissions. The very low cost, on-line brokers, such as Schwab, have made stock broking more transparent. Rather than compete with ever lower costs the brokers have turned to providing complete solutions for their customers, such as wealth management, with a range of additional services added. One of the dangers of moving from products to solutions is that a completely different approach to costing and pricing and, indeed, the whole delivery system is needed, and this may require a complete change of mindset in the organisation.

Without this change it is easy to fall into the trap of giving away services for free in an attempt to sell a product. In fact the provision of additional services can be very expensive.

PORTFOLIO DECISIONS FOR NEW CUSTOMER SEGMENTS

In the previous section we discussed the decisions that are needed to maintain or improve the organisation's portfolio performance in its existing markets. Many of the decision options that we discussed for portfolio development, such as the rationalisation of the portfolio, becoming the lowest cost supplier, adding value through differentiation or focusing on providing solutions, will have the effect of repositioning the product and service for existing segments but could also lead to targeting an additional or different segment. Although other elements of the marketing mix, such as communications, will contribute to the firm's overall success, with new customer segments it is the product and service decisions that are at the heart of the changes. It is necessary to decide on the nature and level of changes that need to be made to the existing product or service and then make decisions on some or all of the elements of the total product offer shown in Figure 9.2.

Standardisation and adaptation of products and services

The advantages of standardisation are economies of scale, benefits from the experience curve effect and increased customer awareness and familiarity. However, the purchasing and usage processes of different segments are affected by many factors including different legal requirements, usage conditions and levels of cultural acceptability.

If the new segments to be targeted are geographically based – a new country market or a new region of the world – then a more fundamental rethink of the product and service portfolio offering is required. Mesdag (1985) proposed the idea that a company has three basic choices: to sell what the organisation already has; to sell what people actually buy; or to sell the same thing globally disregarding national frontiers. Keegan (1989) took this further by suggesting that the main variables in doing business across borders are product and promotion, in which case the options are: one product, one message worldwide; product extension, promotion adaptation; product adaptation, promotion extension; dual adaptation and product invention.

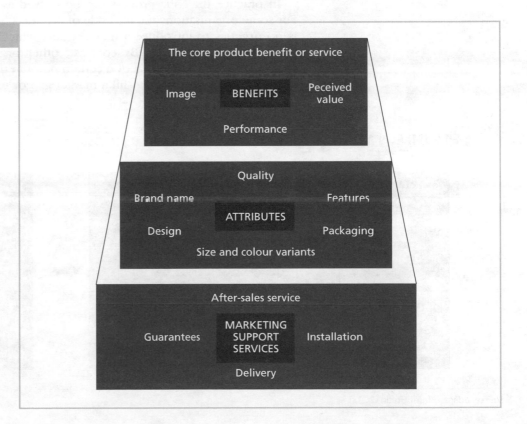

FIGURE 9.2

The total product offer
Source: adapted from Kotler (2002)

NEW PRODUCTS AND SERVICE DEVELOPMENT DECISIONS

New product development covers a variety of intellectual and functional areas, according to Tzokas *et al.* (2003), including marketing, technology management, R&D strategy, business policy, production and operations management, engineering, design and innovation management. This means that NPD embraces a huge range of topics not traditionally considered to be part of marketing and yet for NPD to be successful a new product must satisfy customer needs and wants, add customer perceived value and be distinguishable from and better than competing offerings. This is where marketing should make a major contribution to NPD.

In Chapter 7 we dealt with the broader perspectives of innovation but here we focus specifically on product and service developments and particularly the process of NPD. The NPD process is usually described by writers, such as Griffin (2003), as a linear 'single gate' decision making process involving essentially the same stages suggested by Kotler. These are shown in Figure 9.3. The role of marketing in the NPD process in many organisations is often to provide information on and link with the market and provide co-ordination between the functional areas, by integration of the contributions of both internal and external organisations.

The linear decision making process reflects, perhaps, a rather traditional approach to NPD decision making with the main emphasis being placed on delaying major investment and resource utilisation as long as possible until the risks of failure of the project have been significantly reduced. It also emphasises the importance of integration of the contributions of the functional areas around the NPD stages, including marketing research, R&D, operations, finance, marketing and sales, to enable 'kill or proceed' decisions to be made as quickly and thoroughly as possible. The NPD process also emphasises an effective management approach and discipline demonstrated by Saurabh Srivastava in Bollywood as shown in Spotlight 9.1.

In practice the NPD process can be viewed as either linear or simultaneous. For some organisations the life cycle of products is quite long and therefore there is no urgency to introduce a new product which might cannibalise sales of the product it is to replace. By contrast, other organisations, particularly in fast changing sectors, know that by a certain point in time a competitor will introduce a new product or service to fill a market gap or exploit new technology that has

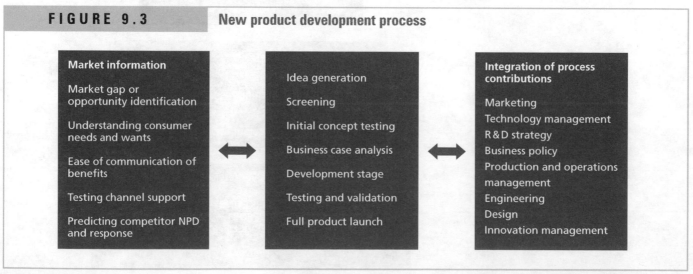

FIGURE 9.3 **New product development process**

Market information	Idea generation	Integration of process contributions
Market gap or opportunity identification	Screening	Marketing
Understanding consumer needs and wants	Initial concept testing	Technology management
	Business case analysis	R&D strategy
Ease of communication of benefits	Development stage	Business policy
Testing channel support	Testing and validation	Production and operations management
Predicting competitor NPD and response	Full product launch	Engineering
		Design
		Innovation management

Source: adapted from Griffin (2003)

already been developed and announced. In these situations, time to market is critical and so the stages in the NPD process must proceed simultaneously. For example, testing the concept on consumers, carrying out the analysis necessary for preparing the business and investment case, and designing packaging might be proceeding at the same time that the product is being specified and developed.

In managing NPD the major challenge is to achieve a balance between the inevitable cost and risks associated with NPD. Trying to develop and commercialise genuinely innovative new products requires many ideas to be pursued simultaneously, before the best is chosen for commercial development. The cost of pursuing ideas that will not be taken to market can be high. For example, in the pharmaceutical industry the ratio between compounds being investigated and commercialised is extremely low as the case study of AstraZeneca at the end of the chapter shows.

However, the cost and risk of minimising NPD activity and instead marketing old or 'me too' products and services can be equally high in lost potential revenues and margins. The balance that needs to be struck in the level of R&D investment and risk tolerated will vary between sectors and also between organisations, according to their current market position and growth aspirations. Some organisations, such as 3M and AstraZeneca, have targets for the

---

SPOTLIGHT 9.1   Bollywood does management

Bollywood has been highly successful in making movies. So successful perhaps that it has not been necessary to try too hard. The recipe for decades has been to put together a script that is similar to old Hollywood blockbusters, assemble a cast of stars, find a 'lucky' director, anyone who is prepared to invest money and a little good fortune. This is how Bobby Bedi, movie maker and managing director of Kaleidoscope Entertainment had done it too until 2000.

As a new investor in Kaleidoscope Saurabh Srivastava founder/chairman of Infinity Technology Investments, observed that Bollywood had 'brilliant movie makers but no movie managers'. Most studios seemed to produce only one film per year. The risks in movie making, he realised, were not so great once the film was released, provided the film generated reasonable box office revenues, TV rights and overseas sales. The real risks were pre-release. Many movies were started but not completed, many overshot their budget and others were stopped because they failed to find a distributor. He believed that good management could improve this.

The solution has been to treat movies like fmcg products and use the NPD process of market research, tight scheduling and budgetary controls. Directors and distributors are used to select ideas and scripts. Throughout the production budgets and time schedules are prepared by production managers and producers, monitored daily and variances investigated.

Marketing starts by getting distributor buy-in ahead of production. Films for the urban young are promoted to the target audience in coffee bars and contests are held to win tickets. Scenes of the film might be shot in high profile locations.

Kaleidoscope further reduces risk by following a diversification strategy, with each film having a different budget, theme, creative team and even a different audience. Big budget movies are usually co-productions and the capital to finance the film comes from financial institutions and investors, who buy shares in the company, rather than through *ad hoc* financing.

The results speak for themselves. By the end of 2003 the fifth film was in preparation with one of the earlier ones, Saathiya, released in December 2002, receiving rave reviews from the critics and generating Rs 18 crore in India, the US and the UK. Srivastava is projecting spectacular growth in profits from Rs 1 crore in 2002 to Rs 200 crore by 2007/8.

Question Has Saurabh Srivastava found the solution – can creative businesses be improved through a managed process?

Sources: adapted from FT Information; Global News Wire; Asia Africa Intelligence Wire; Syndications Today; Business Today (India), 23 November 2003

percentage of total company sales or profits that will come from new product introductions.

No matter what balance is reached, the pressure is increasing to become more cost effective in NPD, whether a firm is seeking a breakthrough 'new to the world' product or service or simply refreshing the product portfolio with brand and line extensions.

Success and failure in NPD

The problem with NPD is the high risk of failure. Griffin (1997) found that although failure rates had been reduced in the decade previous to 1995, only one in five ideas made it through to success. In different industries, the conversion rates from idea to commercial success vary considerably and, of course, the cost and profit impact of new products is different also. However, from the research of many writers, including Griffin (1997; 2003) and Cooper (1994), it is possible to make some generalisations about what leads to new product success and failure.

It is suggested that products and services are often abandoned during the NPD process because of:

- a lack of available technology
- a change in the firm's strategy
- a competitor's pre-emptive new product launch
- market information which suggests that the new product or service will not meet customer needs or expectations

Griffin found that 55 per cent of products and services that are launched also fail.

Achieving success in NPD

The key to success is an effective NPD strategy which includes the development of the central and supporting processes, in order to generate a flow of new products that might vary in market impact but will include some high revenue or high margin generators. This approach is preferable to trying to spot one blockbuster new product some time in the future.

In order to do this Griffin suggests there are three fundamental requirements of the process:

- uncover unmet needs and problems
- develop a product with competitive advantage
- shepherd the products through the firm.

Tzokas *et al.* (2003) suggest that market information is central to achieving success in NPD and summarise the research studies that have highlighted its role within the following strategic success factors:

- Ensuring product performance improvements over what is already available.
- Achieving synergy with existing firm technologies and manufacturing capability and learning new capabilities quickly.
- Achieving marketing synergies, such as channels and promotion, often because of the need to target a new segment.
- Integrating the contributions of marketing and R&D.
- Identifying attractive markets with growth potential.

- Effectively carrying out the NPD process, including pre-development activities such as idea generation, screening, concept and business case investigation.

- Obtaining support from top management.

- Speed in development.

So far in this section we have focused on the critical success factors in fulfilling the NPD task, but we emphasise again that equally important is building the organisational structure, culture, skills and supporting processes, discussed in Chapter 7, that create the environment in which the individual with ideas can be effective. At the centre of this must be creative individuals who drive the developments.

Shanteau (1992) has identified the importance of individuals having:

- **Domain knowledge**: not only textbook knowledge but also knowledge from experience, and being able to contextualise the information.

- **Psychological traits**: including self-confidence, excellent communication skills, ability to adapt to new situations and a clear sense of responsibility.

- **Cognitive skills**: highly developed attention abilities, a sense of what is relevant, ability to identify exceptions and work under stress.

- **Decision strategies**: whilst decision strategies are context specific, others are more widely applicable, including using dynamic feedback, relying on decision aids, disaggregating complex decision problems and pre-thinking solutions to tough problems.

- **Task characteristics**: whether experts can behave competently in carrying out the NPD tasks.

SERVICE DEVELOPMENT AND ENHANCEMENT

In discussing the development of services Hollensen (2003) explains three categories of service that involve people processing (e.g. education and travel), possession processing (e.g. car repair and laundry service) and information based services (e.g. banking and telecommunications). Within portfolio management it is useful then to distinguish between the new services that are introduced, particularly e-business services, the development and improvement of existing ser-vices and the enhancement of products by adding service improvements. Rationalisation is, perhaps, a less important issue for service companies, although services are regularly withdrawn as strategies wear out and demand for them reduces.

In seeking to develop new services and enhance existing ones, the differences between 'pure' products and 'pure' services, and the extra three service Ps provide the drivers for development. In thinking through these characteristics of services it is possible to identify where service gaps appear and, as a result, where customers fail to get an acceptable level of satisfaction from the service.

Intangibility

The key here is to 'tangibilise' the service in customers' minds and this has become a feature of services marketing, by emphasising the tangible elements, for example, the use of promotional gifts. In e-commerce services it is interactivity that is used to overcome the lack of customer involvement in the service.

Perishability

The challenge of matching service supply and demand is at the heart of marketing services and yield management (see Spotlight 9.2) supported by IT is being used to achieve a better match and so improve the value for money.

Heterogeneity

Service organisations have made great efforts in training staff to provide a standard service and routine responses. However, this is no longer enough. The move to mass customisation and one to one marketing has meant that as well as delivering the core services routinely, companies are differentiating between customers and customising the services they receive, as Challenge 9.2 shows.

Inseparability

Being unable to separate the service producer from delivery presents considerable problems for the market diffusion of services based on high level skills, such as hospital or business consultants. Again advances in communications are enabling knowledge and skills to be more efficiently transferred and applied over greater distances.

People

Providing consistent service and customer 'delight' continues to challenge service providers and we turn to this later. However, it is important to remember that it is customers that decide the success of a service based upon their experiences compared to their original expectations. By contrast, a product is judged a success in the factory if it complies with the specification after manufacture. With this in mind it is essential for most service providers to set, manage and, ideally, just exceed customer expectations.

CHALLENGE 9.2 — Selecting customers for relationship building

Sophisticated technology is being used in the call centre operations of banks, telecoms firms, tour operators and utilities to identify the consumers with the highest potential purchasing power, so that they will receive different service levels according to their potential value to the company. In some companies, customers are classified according to their 'lifetime value', which for a bank could be as high as £250 000.

A computer identifies where the customer is calling from or the customer is asked to provide postcode details and this is then mapped according to categories assigned to postcodes. Information company Experian has 52 lifestyle rankings, including 'rising materialists', 'clever capitalists', 'rootless renters' and 'smoke stack shift workers'.

The callers are then routed to different operatives, who might use different scripts to answer their queries. Research found that the wealthiest customers were routed to the most articulate staff, engaged in small talk in an effort to build relationships and offered the best deals, whereas poorer customers were given less time and offered the standard service. Holiday companies might even offer different prices for the same holiday for customers they perceive to be wealthy as against poorer customers.

Question Will this strategy improve customer service and add stakeholder value?

Source: adapted from Winnett, R. and Thomas, Z., 'Are you a second class customer', *Sunday Times*, 19 October 2003

Physical evidence

The corporate identity design, symbols, logo, atmosphere and artefacts communicate strongly to customers alongside the products and services. Businesses are now much more aware of how powerful an effect this can be in service differentiation but as a result it is essential to have consistency across global markets.

Process

Organisations must make it easy, pleasant and a personalised experience for customers to deal with them. Many firms, however, still organise the customer management process for their own convenience rather than what is best for customers.

Customer satisfaction

Research in the early 1990s identified the gaps in service delivery between what organisations offer in the form of technical features and customer perceptions, and these gaps are shown in Figure 9.4.

In thinking about customer perceptions Hoffmann (2003) notes that what irritates customers most about service providers is apathy, brush-off, coldness, condescension, robotism, the rulebook and being given the runaround.

Research by Parasuraman *et al.* (1988), identified the essential **SERVQUAL** dimensions as follows:

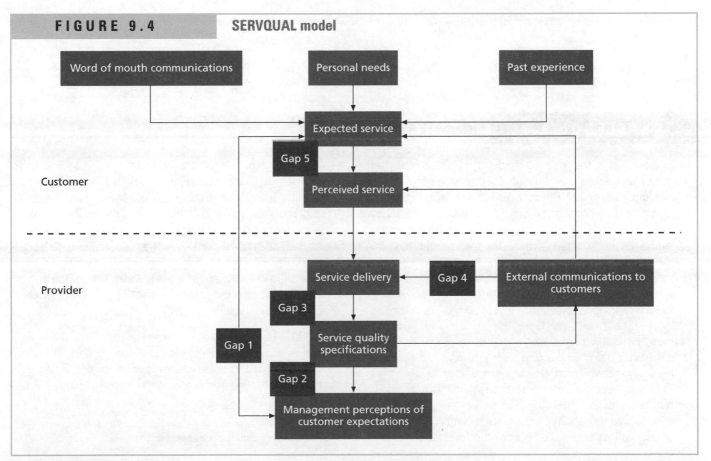

FIGURE 9.4   SERVQUAL model

Source: Parasuraman *et al.* (1988)

- **Tangibles**: physical facilities, equipment, personnel and communications materials.
- **Reliability**: accurate and dependable delivery of the promised service.
- **Responsiveness**: willingness to help customers and provide prompt service.
- **Assurance**: knowledge and courtesy of employees and their ability to convey trust and confidence.
- **Empathy**: caring individualised attention to customers.

What follows from this is the implication that whilst service providers should focus on the introduction of technical development and service enhancement to add customer value and reduce costs, what is equally important is ensuring that the customer perception of the services is improved. This is particularly problematic when it is necessary to satisfy a number of stakeholders with slightly different expectations, as shown in Challenge 9.3.

PORTFOLIO PRICING DECISIONS

Many organisations believe that pricing is the most flexible and controllable element of the marketing mix. They often consider it to be largely independent of the rest of the portfolio and marketing mix. In this section we review the nature and role of pricing, pricing objectives and management and consider its relationship with the other elements of the marketing mix.

CHALLENGE 9.3   Network Rail

Network Rail is the 'not for dividend' operator of Britain's rail network and is charged with the provision of a safe, reliable and efficient rail infrastructure. It was set up by the UK Department of Transport to buy Railtrack out of administration in October 2002. Its customers are the train operating companies who pay a levy to use the tracks, but it has other important stakeholders including travellers, the government treasury and health and safety departments.

It owns and maintains tracks, signals, tunnels, bridges, viaducts and level crossings. It also owns the network's 2500 stations, and manages the largest and busiest of them, providing access to the tracks for every passenger and freight train, timetabling their journeys and operating the signalling which controls their movements.

A draft report from the National Audit Office claimed that Network Rail had failed to deliver value for money, while its strategy and progress were 'falling short of expectations' with spending rising from the forecast £4 billion a

year to £6 billion. The NAO added that 'having aspired to change the Railtrack culture, Network Rail is not doing enough to drive forward that change'. Staff surveys reveal 'considerable resistance to change within the organisation'.

In the face of criticism that contracting out maintenance work had been inefficient and was jeopardising safety, Network Rail decided to stop using private contractors to maintain Britain's railways. The work was taken in-house, a decision which affected seven contracting firms and more than 18 000 workers.

Question How can Network Rail chairman, Ian McAllister, balance the differing stakeholder expectations and increase customer orientation and service enhancement?

Source: Sue Marriott from various public sources

The nature and role of pricing

Pricing does play a pivotal role in strategic marketing decisions. This is largely based on the fact that pricing changes appear to prompt an immediate response in the market. For example, discounting a price might achieve an immediate sale, whereas spending the same money on advertising might possibly lead to increased future sales, but might not. However, despite the apparent simplicity of using pricing as a major marketing tool, many managers find pricing decisions difficult to make. This is in part due to the fact that whilst most firms recognise the importance of pricing at a tactical level in stimulating short term demand, far fewer recognise the importance of the strategic role of pricing.

To make good **pricing strategy decisions** it is necessary to have a clear understanding of both the uncontrollable factors in the market environment, such as customer expectations and competitor pressures, and the factors that the organisation can control, such as the other marketing mix factors. Some organisations see their relatively fixed and controllable cost base as the only significant factor in determining prices, and use cost based pricing as a simple strategy to apply. However, Table 9.1 shows a number of other factors that should be taken into account when making pricing decisions using a customer- or competitor-oriented pricing strategy. A number of these relate specifically to international pricing.

Cost management

With increasing pressure on prices and margins cost management is as important as value adding. For firms that use a cost plus pricing strategy there is a direct relationship between costs and prices. Many retailers and distributors have a formula for setting prices. The formula might be different for different product categories within the firm and it might also be adapted for price sensitive products, including those with **every day low prices** (EDLP) and loss leaders intended to entice customers into the store to buy other, more expensive items. These are the products for which the customers are likely to know the price. The formula is used to allocate fixed costs and overheads, and set anticipated profit margins. The formula might be based on such factors as sales volume, revenue, warehouse and transport costs, shelf space required, stock turnover, and so on. Firms that use customer or competitor based pricing also tend to apply a formula to allocate variable and fixed costs, but allow some scope for adjusting the final price. Consequently margins will differ between product categories or individual products. Special order or low volume items will typically carry higher gross margins whilst volume items will carry lower gross margins.

The annual budget will specify volumes, prices and margins for individual products, product categories and customers. Variances will be reported regularly on volumes and average price against the budget so that corrective action can be taken by managers. In many firms an approximation of the Pareto rule works with 20 per cent of the customers contributing 80 per cent of the sales, but the problem is that the largest volume customers get the largest discounts and often do not generate the greatest net profit. Table 9.2 shows the effects of discounting prices. It is easy for managers to cut prices under pressure. The impact is immediate if a new order depends upon it. Unfortunately later it becomes much more difficult to raise prices, especially when competitors believe that they must resort to low prices too.

Activity based costing is used to measure and cost the resources used for every activity of the organisation. The costs are then attributed to both product and customer categories. The allocation of fixed costs and overheads to product categories and customer categories becomes critical in assessing product and customer category profitability, but in many organisations the decisions are still often based on quite subjective judgements.

There are substantial differences in the cost profiles of different products and services. For example, a high proportion of the costs for cosmetics will be marketing promotion costs, for pharmaceuticals it will be research, development and testing although marketing costs are now similar, for steel making it will be energy and raw materials, and for paper making it will be raw material, energy

TABLE 9.1	Factors affecting pricing decisions
	Factors
Environmental	• Government influences and constraints • Currency fluctuations • Business and economic cycle stage, level of inflation • Use of non-money payment (barter) or leasing
Company	• Need for cash, revenue, margin, profits • Cover for investment, fixed and semi-fixed costs, where there are medium term commitments • Corporate and marketing objectives: volume, growth, share • Firm positioning and image • Legacy from previous strategies • Comparative cost structures, manufacturing, experience effect and economies of scale • Available resources • Nature and size of inventory • Logistics and operational infrastructure
Product	• Product positioning • Product range, portfolio relationships • Life cycle, substitutes • Product differentiation and unique selling propositions • Nature and role of product development
Market	• Market growth, demand elasticities • Consumers' perceptions, expectations and ability to pay • Need for product adaptation and better market servicing • Market structure, distribution channels, discounting pressures • Customers' need for credit
Customers	• Acceptable price range • Customer perceptions of the products, service and image of the organisation • Segment differences (including channel differences) • Need for deals and built in discounts
Competition	• Nature, power and structure of competition • Industry structure and the nature of channel competition • Share/position • Competitive strength • Reinforcement of positioning

and environment management costs. Much of the electronic components production capability is located in low labour cost countries but today labour costs account for a very low proportion of overall costs. It is vital, therefore, to understand the dynamics of the cost–price relationships and sensitivities.

The challenge for firms delivering services is to balance supply and demand for products and services in order to obtain the maximum output from expensive assets. For example, in practice there can be marginal difference in the cost of services offered on each journey by airlines and trains, but firms substantially alter the price according to the time of travel. The commuter segment is large and needs to travel at certain times. Others travelling for different reasons have more flexibility and will be prepared to travel at different times. Spotlight 9.2 shows how Stelios Haji-Ioannou is attempting to apply the yield management concept used in the airline business to other businesses.

The difficulty of establishing the elasticity of demand

The importance of these factors varies according to the context in which the pricing decision is going to be made. With so many factors it is difficult to build up a pattern of inter-dependencies between the factors. Whilst textbooks discuss the **elasticity of demand**, in practice extraneous variables can make it extremely difficult to establish even a simple relationship. Tactical pricing changes offer little towards understanding relationships. For example a manager might try to work out the increase in volume that occurs when the price to consumers of a food product is decreased on the supermarket shelf by '20p off'. The extraneous variables could be a competitor running a '3 for the price of 2' sales promotion in another supermarket, the introduction of a competitive product, a health scare mentioned in the newspaper or the current customers for the product buying substantial extra stock at the lower price to meet their requirements for a number of weeks. In practice the existing customers might consume no more product over the longer term and no new customers are won over. The manager might offer other justification for the price discounting sales promotion, such as to keep the product in the customers' eye or to prevent losing customers, but it may take some time, if not forever, to determine the relationship and also whether the sales promotion was worthwhile.

In seeking to establish such relationships between variables, the other mix factors have a significant effect. For example, customers expect fashion brands to be expensive and so low prices in exclusive outlets will be treated with

| TABLE 9.2 | The effects of discounting: the increase in turnover (%) needed to offset a price reduction |

Price reduction	Gross margin				
	10%	15%	20%	30%	40%
2%	25	15	11	7	5
4%	67	36	25	15	11
6%	150	67	43	25	18
8%	400	114	67	36	25
10%		200	100	50	33

SPOTLIGHT 9.2   EasyEverything

EasyJet is a low fare airline that operates a number of routes within the Europe market. Stelios Haji-Ioannou set up the airline backed by £500 million from his father. EasyJet grew rapidly during the late 1990s by undercutting the flight operators that offered a full customer service package. An easyJet flight from Luton to Amsterdam cost between £70 and £130 against the full service flights which cost from £315. EasyJet's main base is Luton, which is 30 miles from London. Flights are available to European destinations, such as Geneva, Amsterdam, Nice, Palma and Amsterdam, and to UK destinations, such as Edinburgh, Belfast and Liverpool. As easyJet grows it has set up new centres of operation in the UK and Europe.

EasyJet is able to offer low prices by operating out of modest headquarters in Luton and avoids the cost of dealing with intermediaries, such as travel agents. The majority of customers buy tickets over the internet and the remainder by phone, paying by credit or debit card.

Catering consists of a trolley service of snacks and drinks that have to be paid for by customers. There is one class of passenger, thus avoiding the need to provide different seating and additional crew, each taking up extra space. By doing this easyJet's Boeing 737-300s are able to carry 148 passengers compared to 109 on the full service airlines. The company's promotion, which consists of simple press and magazine advertising, largely focuses on the destinations and low prices.

The key to the easyJet strategy is maximising the income generated from each flight by carrying as many passengers as possible on each journey. They achieve this by offering very low prices to the first passengers to book a particular flight. The price for seats on the flight is then increased for passengers booking closer to the departure date. Yield management software is used to manage the complex calculations that ensure the revenue for each flight is maximised by balancing the price and number of passengers that are likely to travel on that particular flight. By contrast the full service airlines have always sought to hold prices artificially high irrespective of demand. They offload low price seats close to departure date.

Stelios relinquished his role as CEO in 2002, but still retains his involvement with easyJet (as the largest single shareholder in the airline he is both interested and implicated in its performance). Still only 35, he was looking to transfer his price and cost cutting yield management business model to other sectors and create an easyEverything group of companies. The car rental service was already established. An early and loss making attempt to create easyInternetcafés was revived. Stelios rented some of McDonald's unused floor space in Swiss Cottage, London and set up a pilot with Burger King in Piccadilly Circus to try to get more traffic through the café. The 'chips and fries' concept, McInternet, is already used by McDonald's in Brazil.

Stelios is also trying to establish other businesses, using a similar low cost model with ocean cruises and cinemas. The cinema concept, for example, is based on the fact that the films have to be shown, the staff employed and the cinema heated on a Tuesday afternoon when, perhaps, only one or two customers would choose to go and pay the full price. Stelios believes, however, that many more would go if they only had to pay 20p. They should see this as good value and get into the habit of seeing films more regularly. Maybe they will come back at busier times of the day and pay the full price.

Question Can yield management, the concept that Stelios has made so successful in easyJet be applied to other business sectors?

Source: Robin Lowe from various public sources

Stelios Haji-Ioannou
Source: easyGroup

Stelios Haji-Ioannou
Source: easyGroup

suspicion and might lead to low sales. Customers might also be suspicious if a consultancy firm suddenly reduces its daily rates. They may prefer the consultancy to be 'reassuringly expensive' because of the high demand created by their expertise rather than low prices being charged because they are desperate for business.

Many organisations take a much simpler approach, usually based on cost plus a margin. They set a price largely independent of customer, competitor and environmental factors. The problem with this approach is that, when used in the wrong context, it usually fails to maximise the possible returns and this drains value from the organisation. Many organisations charge well below the optimum price because they wrongly believe that volume always increases with low prices. There may be breaks in the elasticity of the demand curve and so even substantial price reductions may have little effect on volume. Although pricing and costing decisions have the potential to be precisely calculated, in practice the decisions are often made for subjective reasons without taking into account the full long term implications of both the financial and the non-financial factors.

In practice low price may prompt customers to purchase only if the rest of the offer is acceptable. For a B2B customer there is little point in paying low prices if the delivery is unreliable, the lead times are too long, the customer service is unhelpful and the ordering process is unnecessarily cumbersome. Suppliers in this situation would be more successful if they addressed these service quality issues before further reducing prices.

Faced by the sheer complexity of considering so many variables many organisations resort to instinctive decisions. Quite often the organisation's choice of approach to pricing is a consequence of who drives the decisions, whether it is the finance or marketing department and even which manager has the strongest personality.

Consumers do not always behave rationally and apply logic. Banks and building societies offer incentives to customers in the form of interest rate discounts to persuade them to remortgage their house and switch providers. The firms use a model to manage the complexity of the factors involved and predict consumer demand, expected revenue generated and levels of risk if demand exceeds or fails to meet the optimum level. The models can operate at the level of individual consumer decisions and the company experts can identify the 'right' moment for the consumer to make the best remortgaging decision.

However, consumers do not make decisions based on a mathematical model, an appreciation of interest rate trends and the financial markets nor with the benefit of hindsight. For example, some consumers might remortgage their property just two or three years before the end of the term and so fail to recover the high costs of surveys and administration. Because of these factors product and service development decisions can only partially be made on the basis of quantitative forecasting.

Price making and price taking

Organisations tend to be either **price takers** or **price makers**. Price takers have only limited ability or willingness to control prices and so follow the market leader's pricing strategy and respond reactively to changes in price. Because of their power, size, market leadership or competitive advantage, price makers are able to set prices. For example, powerful organisations are able to temporarily set prices so low that they force a competitor out of business. Over the years, too, there have been many examples of oligopolies illegally running a cartel to fix prices artificially high in order to maximise their profits.

A price maker tends to think of the relationship between profit, price and cost as follows:

Price makers can add value and, within reason, recover the costs through higher prices. By contrast a market taker tends to think of making a product that will undercut the market leader's price by an amount that is attractive to potential purchasers. In order to make the required profit there will be a limit on the costs allowed in the supply chain.

For example, Ford might compare the price of a specific version of a product such as the Galaxy with the closest equivalent version of what it might consider to be its main competitor in the segment, say a Toyota Previa, and price the same or slightly undercut it. After subtracting the profit required to satisfy shareholders the allowed costs for building the car can be set. Ford would then cut its own costs and also pass on the necessary cost reductions needed from its suppliers who would be expected to find a way of delivering the required product or service within these limits.

Pricing objectives

Because of their different current market positions and future business development aspirations, organisations adopt **pricing objectives** that drive their strategic marketing decisions. The options are detailed in Table 9.3.

Pricing strategies

In delivering these objectives the fundamental decision for the firm is which of the pricing strategies should be used:

- cost plus – with standard percentage mark up on costs
- customer orientation
  - price based on perceived value
  - pricing based on segment analysis
- competitor orientation
  - price based on going rate
- market oriented pricing
  - to achieve volume and cost leadership
  - for quality or value leadership

Price management

If the segmentation process has been carried out sufficiently well to identify different segments and managers fully understand the different customer requirements, it should be possible to differentiate the products and services for the different segments and so justify different prices. This should lead to revenues being maximised.

Segment pricing decisions

It is worth remembering that pricing is the only mix element that generates revenue – everything else adds cost. As we have highlighted on a number of occasions in this book, however, prices are under continual pressure due to more intense competition, similarity of product offers due to the increased speed of copying, increasing price transparency because of the internet search engines, and harmonisation of prices within common markets. Customers are more knowledgeable, more sceptical about added value and less loyal to brands. B2B customers have worldwide purchasing networks to compare prices, purchase and obtain delivery. The question in this section, therefore, is whether the organisation can charge customers for the added value elements of the offer, or must other costs be reduced?

TABLE 9.3	Pricing objectives and purpose	
	Pricing objectives	*Purpose*
	Survival	To generate cash flows simply to stay in business
	Return on investment	Achieve a level of return that will be comparable with other forms of investment
	Market stabilisation	Price wars can be damaging to all participants, whereas stability enables product and service developments to be made
	Maintenance and improvement of position	Prices are set in relation to competition: same, higher or lower, depending on the total 'offer' in order to manage relative market positions
	Reflecting product differentiation	Superior products, as perceived by customers, should command premium pricing
	Market skimming	Some firms prefer to charge higher prices and maximise the profitability of new products. They leave the market when lower priced competitors enter the market
	Market penetration	Many firms price to build market share. The speed of penetration will determine pricing levels
	Early cash recovery	Firms may need to recover investments in R&D and marketing quickly if cash flow is a problem
	Preventing new entry	Charging low prices in a market can deter new competitors from entering.

Price reductions and mistakes in pricing

Competitive actions, often unexpected, can threaten short term revenue and performance and managers are often under great pressure to make an instant response. It is too tempting, quick and easy to cut prices in order to deal with an immediate shortfall in sales volume. This action often prompts a price war. However, it is much more difficult and takes much more time and effort to secure price increases to restore profit margins. Quite often the task proves impossible, and so price cutting, intended to be a short term tactic, ends up either as a routine feature of the sector or establishes a long term lower pricing point.

The problem is that price reductions are usually made in response to a new situation such as a competitor announcing lower prices or a sudden decrease in sales due to an apparent change in fashion. Decisions are often made very quickly with no time to assess or test the implications, but they usually have a major impact on profits. Quite often the organisation fails to understand the impact of extraneous variables and so nothing is learned from the price change, and the organisation is no better informed when a similar situation occurs later.

Mistakes also occur because prices are too often based on costs, not market conditions, set independently of the mix and so do not reflect superior quality and brand value, and make no attempt to reflect the product and service differentiation. Pricing often fails to recover the additional cost of differentiation and service enhancement.

Consumer prices are inflated by extended distribution channels, where mark ups and margins are applied even when the intermediaries are adding little value. In this situation managers find it difficult to decide whether to remove intermediaries or maintain the status quo and not upset intermediaries with whom they have had a long term relationship, even though the organisation and its distributors might both be being priced out of the market by more aggressive competitors with shorter routes to market.

The ability to deal with competition

A key aspect of price management is the ability of the company to deal with competitors and a number of factors might affect this, including:

- relative competitive positions: leader, follower or me too
- cost levels and scope for price cutting
- level of resources to fight a war
- dependence on the product or service and willingness to withdraw from the market
- commitment to market sector
- potential returns from price cutting
- past price history
- distinctiveness and brand loyalty

Opportunity to increase price

We have emphasised the need for a strategy that focuses on adding value, but usually non-price factors that might help to differentiate a product from its competitors and persuade customers to buy, add cost. Therefore, it is essential to fully appreciate the situations where considerable scope exists for price flexibility. If, for example:

- the offer has unique value
- the customers' awareness of substitutes is low
- it is difficult to make comparisons
- the product cost is insignificant within the total outlay (for example of a project)
- the customer benefit is substantial compared to the cost
- the product is used in conjuction with a major investment that has already been made
- there is a shared cost and the specific price of the product is not separated.

Pricing problems are often the result of past laziness in failing to analyse the current situation, a lack of appreciation of the changes taking place, expediency in taking short term decisions, and complacency in not realising the increasing capability of competitors. Many organisations do not vary pricing between segments as much as they could and often the pricing is defensive. Knowing the price dynamics of the segment can be significant in achieving profitability. This includes frequency of purchase, degree of necessity, unit price, degree of comparability and degree of fashion or status.

International pricing problems and decisions

Organisations tend to adopt one of three pricing strategies in international markets:

- **Ethnocentric pricing**: charging the same price 'at the factory gate', so prices in different markets reflect the additional cost of getting the products there.
- **Polycentric pricing**: prices are adapted for each market according to the local situation.
- **Geocentric pricing**: fixing a single price across markets, especially where there is price transparency, for example, within a region.

In international marketing there are a number of additional factors that should be taken into account in price decision making:

- The greater scope of the international organisation should allow it to benefit from economies of scale and the experience effect, provided that it is committed to achieving these gains through standardisation of some of the marketing programmes or management processes.
- Different market segments that are based on different cultures or countries are likely to require adaptations to the marketing mix in a similar way to different segments in a domestic market, but on a much larger scale. The cost of adaptation can be very significant if not managed carefully.
- Many domestic organisations have some experience of costs varying because of fluctuating exchange rates as a result of buying components and services from different countries. For international organisations fluctuating exchange rates can become a major problem because of the scale and scope of both purchasing and selling products in foreign markets.
- When competing globally there is a continuous need to source products, components and services at ever lower costs from anywhere in the world.

■ When compared to domestic marketing, however, the key difference is that international marketers not only set and agree prices with foreign customers but in emerging countries quite frequently they must also arrange the financing for the deal.

In international marketing firms must deal with a number of problems as shown in Figure 9.5, and Doole and Lowe (2004) present a fuller explanation.

Whilst barter is used extensively in international markets, Challenge 9.4 shows how it is used in domestic markets too.

INTEGRATION DECISIONS

An important theme for decision making is integration, and to maximise shareholder value it is essential to consider porfolio and pricing management together.

Table 9.4 shows the relationship between some elements of the marketing mix and cost and pricing issues. It provides the drivers for making decisions that lead to additional value generation and cost reduction.

Effective integration of the portfolio, costing and pricing management is achieved through an in-depth understanding of the dynamics of the market including customer sensitivity to price and perceptions of quality and value; competitor commitment to markets and products and the resources they have available; the distinctiveness of the product, the effectiveness of the distribution chain and the internal cost structures.

FIGURE 9.5

International pricing problems

Source: Doole and Lowe (2004)

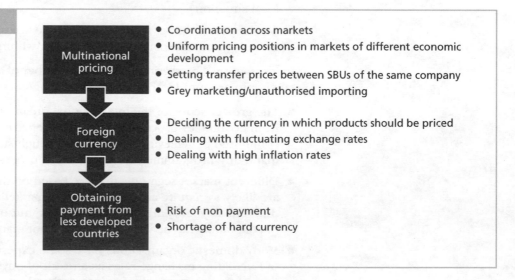

Multinational pricing
- Co-ordination across markets
- Uniform pricing positions in markets of different economic development
- Setting transfer prices between SBUs of the same company
- Grey marketing/unauthorised importing

Foreign currency
- Deciding the currency in which products should be priced
- Dealing with fluctuating exchange rates
- Dealing with high inflation rates

Obtaining payment from less developed countries
- Risk of non payment
- Shortage of hard currency

CHALLENGE 9.4   Barter more flexible than money?

There are three basic forms of barter. In a simple retail barter deal individuals or small businesses can barter individual items on a relatively small scale. The Artist Formerly Known as Prince persuaded Sheryl Crow, Ani DiFranco and Gwen Stefani to appear on his album 'Rave Un2 the Joy Fantastic' in exchange for him contributing to their albums. In this way, managers and record companies were taken out of the deal. A fledgling Uruguayan film company competing for the best foreign film at the 2002 Oscars used barter to make up more than 50 per cent of the film costs needed to pay for materials, artists' lodgings and food when it needed to film in Spain. In corporate barter, firms have exchanged large amounts of surplus stock for products or services that they want. There is a strong barter trade in television programmes that are exchanged between television companies in order to fill up schedules. A complicated system is used to measure and assess audience appeal, in order to work out the barter value of the programmes.

Countertrade typically involves complex, international mega-deals, often involving major projects, such as the purchase of aeroplanes or defence equipment. However it is often used to pay for goods when the supplier will not take a weak local currency in return for the goods supplied. Some years ago ABBA, the Swedish pop group performed in Poland and preferred to be paid in potatoes rather than the local currency which, at that time was weak.

Barter is used in many industries and is facilitated by barter agents such as the ITEX Corporation in New York. At an individual level Swapshop.com provides the service on-line in the UK. Travel barter is particularly significant and involves companies, such as Woolworths, receiving hotel rooms in exchange for surplus stock that a barter agent can turn into cash. So long after the invention of money why should barter still be an attractive option for firms and individuals?

Question What do you consider to be the advantages and disadvantages of barter in this form?

Source: various on-line sources

TABLE 9.4   The relationship between the marketing mix, costs and pricing

	Providing opportunity to increase prices	*Providing cost reductions*
Product portfolio	• Better sourcing • Better plant utilisation • Better use of raw materials and labour • Design or specification changes	
Service enhancement	• Better use of labour and processes • Better use of assets (yield management)	
Promotion	• Better choice of communication methods from mix elements • More targeted, less mass communications	
Channel	• More value through better channel management • Re-intermediation	• Disintermediation
Relationship	• Cost effective 1:1 marketing • Value chain contribution	• Supply chain efficiency

SUMMARY

- Product portfolio decisions are needed to enhance customer and company value through achieving greater focus on successful products and services, coping with increasing commoditisation and integrating products and services to provide solutions.

- Product portfolio decisions involve targeting new segments (domestic or international) through achieving an appropriate balance between standardisation and adaptation, customer benefits and the relative cost of each approach.

- The portfolio needs to be refreshed regularly through new product developments that include new breakthrough products and continuous incremental improvements.

- New product development success rates can be increased by developing appropriate support structures and processes.

- Pricing strategy decisions can add stakeholder value if they are built on a better understanding of the market dynamics, the environment and the scope that is available to increase margins by better price management.

- Integration of the marketing mix activities leads to better decisions that prioritise the activities that will secure higher margins.

KEYWORDS

commodities	price takers
elasticity of demand	pricing objectives
every day low prices	pricing strategy decisions
new product development	rationalisation
portfolio of products and services	SERVQUAL
price makers	unprofitable products

CASE STUDY   AstraZeneca

AstraZeneca (AZ) is the world's third largest pharmaceutical company. It was formed from Astra of Sweden and Zeneca, which was originally part of ICI (UK). AZ also has a strong presence in the USA. It has research installations in Sweden, the UK and the USA. Most countries in which it operates have some AstraZeneca facilities. The operations are located to take advantage of the local cost base, where the expertise is and where competition is likely to come from in the future. For example, generic drugs, which provide the low cost competition once the patents have run out, tend to originate from firms in China, India and Italy. These could be the countries where expertise is developed further so these firms could become the major players in global pharmaceutical R&D too.

Eighty per cent of the world's population cannot afford the drugs, but gradually the emerging markets are developing a middle class that can afford drugs. For example it is estimated that the middle class in India is now twice the size of the UK market. The priority disease treatment targets are often different in emerging countries and so, for example, AZ has recently set up research facilities in Bangalore in India where treatments for tuberculosis are being developed.

Seventy per cent of its research is conducted in house. The remainder of the research is carried out by specialist research companies, universities and other partners.

Customers

The customers of AZ include the patient, doctor, healthcare provider and pharmacist, and these often have differing requirements and expectations of treatments. For example, the hospital pharmacist may prefer drugs that can be stored at room temperature, rather than those that have to be stored under special conditions, and may want dosage preparation to be easy too.

The healthcare provider in the UK will usually be the NHS, but in the USA might more frequently be the patients themselves or an insurance company. Depending upon their own cost drivers, some healthcare providers might prefer to supply expensive drugs if this can be offset by reducing the patient's stay in hospital by a day. Differences exist around the world with the average length of hospital stay in Japan being 27 days, compared to four days in the UK.

The process of new drug development

The process of developing new drugs can take up to 15–20 years from initial target identification through to launch. Clearly there is a high risk of failure and much of the huge amount of research taking place will not lead to a commercial product. Many top scientists will spend their lives working in pharmaceutical research without ever having worked on a commercially successful drug.

Typically, pharmaceutical firms have a library of 1 million compounds to screen for possible suitability. Perhaps only one in fifty of the targets identified will reach the stage of producing a compound. Between one in ten and one in twenty will reach the stage of trial in humans. Only one in twenty of these will then generate revenues in excess of US$0.5 billion. For products that are launched commercially the cost will be between $200–750 million. The highest cost is in stage three clinical trials where the product may need to be tested on tens of thousands of patients.

Therefore there are some major challenges for NPD. The efficacy of a drug is only known after it has been tested on patients. For example, a drug that is found to be suitable for treating cancer might need to be tested on patients suffering from 15 different types of cancer in order to find out which one it will be effective against. For disease prevention drugs it may be necessary to track patients for 20 years before a drug is really known to be effective. As is well known it is becoming increasingly difficult to find drugs to combat infection. Not all the same diagnoses are the same disease and patients from different genetic backgrounds (ethnic origin) often have different responses to drugs.

As with NPD in other industry sectors it is vital, therefore, to spot potential failures very early in the process and run different stages of the NPD process in parallel. For example, at the same time that the compound is being developed studies will be established to identify the reasons for failure in order to try to reduce the risk of failure at a very late stage. There is considerable growth in modelling the science of setting dosages and creating biomarkers that are indicators of the biological activity associated with the disease.

Criteria for success

Clearly the most important issue is that the safety barriers for the drug must be high so that the consequences of misdiagnosis, dosage errors, incompatibility with other treatments and the incidence of adverse patient reactions are minimised. However, whilst the safety barrier needs to be high for drugs used over long periods, they can be lower for life or death situations.

Risk

A major issue is commercial risk. Low risk drug development is achieved by creating the best in the class. One way of trying to do this is by life cycle extensions, by generating new formulations from well established products and concentrating on producing and marketing generic drugs.

High risk development is achieved by being the first in the class, but because there is nothing to compare with, it may be difficult to set and meet realistic expectations. The ideal is to generate therapies for chronic illnesses that will be used over the long term. Of course in satisfying an unmet need there is likely to be a greater risk of side effects.

The risk is high if there is difficulty in proving the benefits of the new therapy or there are only marginal benefits over existing therapies, as it is not possible to launch drugs that have no demonstrable advantages over drugs already on the market. There can also be risks if the complexity of manufacture and distribution leads to high costs that cannot adequately be recovered in the price.

It is essential to carefully define the patient group and develop attributes that are better than existing treatments or that will treat a new therapeutic target. The key criteria for NPD are improved potency, safety and improved dosing intervals (preferably no more than two doses per day). The trials must then show the drug to be better in some criteria and at least equal to the competitor drugs in other criteria.

Questions

1 What are the future challenges facing pharmaceutical companies?

2 What are the key drivers of the strategy for managing the portfolio?

Source: Robin Lowe from various public sources

DISCUSSION QUESTIONS

1 As an independent on-line food retailer offering home delivery, your competition includes the home delivery service of the major supermarkets. Analyse the factors that you should take into account when setting the level of prices.

2 Evaluate the costing and pricing problems that might be faced in expanding a specialist engineering business into four neighbouring European countries. What steps would you take to reduce risk?

3 Identify the factors that you would take into account and the process that you would adopt to rationalise a range of furniture manufactured and stocked for the retail trade. What might be the arguments for retaining some unprofitable products in the range?

4 Explain the concept of yield management and how it can be applied to services, using appropriate examples to illustrate your answer.

5 Increasing transparency of pricing is reducing many products to the status of commodities. Explain some reasons for this and what strategies might be employed in response to this threat.

REFERENCES

Cooper, R.G. (1994) 'New products: the factors that drive success', *International Marketing Review*, 11(1): 60–76.

Doole, I. and Lowe, R. (2004). *International Marketing Strategy: Analysis, Development and Implementation*, 4th edn, London: Thomson Learning.

Griffin, A. (1997) 'PDMA research in new product development practices: updating trends and benchmarking best practices', *Journal of Innovation Management*, 14(6): 428–58.

Griffin, A. (2003) 'Marketing's role in new product development and product decisions', in Hoffman, D. *et al.*, *Marketing Best Practice*, Mason, OH: Thomson South-Western.

Hoffmann, K.D. (2003) 'Services marketing', in Hoffman, D. *et al.*, *Marketing Best Practice*, Mason, OH: Thomson South-Western.

Hollensen, S. (2003) *Marketing Management: A Relationship Approach*, Harlow: FT Prentice Hall.

Keegan, W.J. (1989) *Multinational Marketing Management*, New York: Prentice Hall.

Kotler, P. (2002) *Marketing Management, Analysis, Planning, Implementation and Control*, Harlow: Prentice Hall.

Mesdag, M. van (1985) 'The frontiers of choice', *Marketing*, 10 October.

Parasuraman, A., Zeithaml, V. A. and Berry. L.L. (1988), 'SERVQUAL: a multiple item scale for measuring customer perceptions of service quality', *Journal of Retailing*, 64(1): 12–40.

Shanteau, J. (1992) 'Competence in experts: the role of task characteristics', *Organisational Behaviour and Human Decision Processes*, 53.

Tzokas, N., Hart, S. and Saren, M. (2003) 'New product development, a marketing agenda for change', in Hart, S. (ed.) *Marketing Changes*, London: Thomson Learning.

Wilson, R.M.S. and Gilligan, C. (2004) *Strategic Marketing Management*, 3rd edn, Oxford: Butterworth-Heinemann.

INTEGRATING COMMUNICATIONS TO BUILD RELATIONSHIPS

Introduction

Average organisations sell products and services that meet customer requirements. The more successful organisations are able to rise above the rest because they understand what goes on in customers' heads, what prompts them to behave as they do towards the organisation's products and services and what encourages them to stay loyal. The largest organisations are able to use that knowledge to communicate effectively and, as far as possible, personally with their customers to explain that their mission is to mobilise their own and distribution partners' resources to satisfy their needs. Through relationship management they work hard to develop meaningful relationships with their most profitable customers that will encourage them to stay loyal, and through the distribution channels they ensure that customers can obtain the products and services when and where they want them. The largest organisations recognise too that in carrying out this mission they will use communications to convert their internal and other key external stakeholders from merely interested parties to strong advocates of the business.

The importance of communications is recognised by the fact that most organisations regard it as not only highly influential in helping them to meet their performance targets but also as being their single biggest management problem. Indeed the problem is exacerbated as organisations become more geographically spread, rely more on partners in the extended organisation, aim to satisfy a broader range of stakeholders from different cultures, with different expectations, use a wider variety of communications media and offer more complex value propositions rather than a simple physical product.

Against the background of the organisation's need to cost effectively add value, communications is an aspect of the business that is often difficult to justify objectively because its impact on performance is rarely immediate, is difficult to measure and, when used in isolation from other marketing activity, has little effect. The key to success in marketing communications and customer relationship building is to integrate the disparate communications into a cohesive strategy and take strategic decisions that fit with the other complementary marketing mix activities.

In this chapter we focus upon the nature and role of marketing communications inside the organisation and the need to integrate all aspects of marketing communications. In planning marketing communications it is essential that decision making takes account of the various tools and their suitability for different marketing contexts and stages of the customer purchasing process. Finally we discuss the importance of developing customer relationships that will increase stability and improve performance.

Learning objectives

By the end of this chapter the reader should be able to:

- Evaluate the role of integrated marketing communications in a competitive global strategy
- Understand the concept of relationship marketing and the role of long term customer relationships in creating and delivering value
- Determine the importance of managing marketing relationships in generating customer commitment

THE NATURE AND ROLE OF COMMUNICATIONS

The starting point in a discussion of integrated communications and customer relationship building is to re-emphasise our earlier comments about the importance of understanding the tangible and intangible requirements of the customers, their beliefs and attitudes, and how their purchasing behaviour is affected. It is also vital to understand the expectations of the broader range of stakeholders and be able to communicate how far the organisation can go in satisfying their requirements too. This might go beyond mere product functionality decisions and involve the organisation in making decisions in highly sensitive, often political areas. For example, supermarkets are required to take a stance on their approach to the inclusion of GM foods in their range, and fashion and sports goods manufacturers must adopt a stance on the ethical working practices of their contractors. Communications decisions that are made without a deep understanding of customers, competition and other market dynamics will be destined for failure.

The role of marketing communications in the organisation needs to be periodically reviewed to ensure that it is contributing as much as possible by adding value both to the organisation and the customers. If there is no requirement within the organisation to justify communications expenditure using a rigorous quantitative and qualitative evaluation, it is only too easy for lazy managers to simply provide more of the same, rather than to continually provide fresh, interesting, attention seeking and persuasive communications for customers. Assailed constantly by a vast number of marketing communications, customers become bored. They may continue to buy the same product and services because of routine and inertia rather than because of a real desire for the product. Eventually their boredom may turn to resentment if their loyalty is not rewarded. If a new competitor emerges with a better **value proposition**, communicated in an interesting way, they will be willing to make the switch.

The contribution of marketing communications

Marketing communications and customer relationship building are concerned with presenting and exchanging information with various individuals and organisations to meet defined objectives and deliver specific results. This means not only that the information conveyed must be understood accurately by recipients but also that elements of persuasion are also required. This aspect of communications is the traditional **promotion** P (promoting to external stakeholders) of the marketing mix and includes advertising, personal selling, PR and sales promotion.

Communications should go further, however. Embracing as it does the ideas of conveying information it is the most helpful term in implying the need for a two way process in marketing. Most organisations recognise the need for two way dialogue with customers and this has led to the concept of relationship marketing with the objective of building interactive relationships with the most profitable and valuable customers. In practice communication has a critical role to play throughout the organisation. Internal communications between the organisation's staff and also communicating and building relationships with its alliance and supply chain partners are essential as organisations become larger, more diverse, complex and with fewer clear boundaries. It is vital in explaining the organisation's plans and actions to a wide range of stakeholders, such as shareholders, government departments, pressure groups and the community that might be affected by its actions.

Davidson (2002) explains that an organisation communicates in eight ways:

- Actions: what it does.
- Behaviour: how things are done.
- Face-to-face by management: through talks, visits and meetings this shows what the management thinks is important.
- Signals: from the organisation's actions, facilities and objects, including executive bonuses, dress, buildings.
- Product and services, and particularly their quality.
- Intended communications: such as advertising, which is not always received as the organisation expects.
- Word of mouth and word of web (including e-mail).
- Comment by other organisations: such as pressure groups, competitors and the media.

In a domestic environment the process of communicating is difficult enough, but achieving success in international marketing communications is made particularly challenging by a number of additional factors including the complexity of different market conditions, differences in media availability, languages, cultural sensitivities, regulations controlling advertising and sales promotions, and the challenge of providing adequate resources to achieve the desired effect.

Internal, interactive and external marketing

Figure 10.1 shows the external and internal marketing communication flows and emphasises the need to consider three dimensions: external, internal and interactive or relationship marketing.

Internal marketing

For a large diverse firm a key task is to ensure that all staff employed in its business units are aware of the strategies, tactics, priorities and procedures that are needed to achieve the firm's mission and objectives. As partnerships between supply chain members move closer it becomes necessary to include external firms within the **internal communications network** and the use of intranets has facilitated this over the last few years.

The communications needs of staff in remote locations are often overlooked as they receive messages that become unclear as they cross cultural and language boundaries in the same way that external audiences may misunderstand the firm's external communications. In these circumstances staff in remote locations can become closer to the staff of local customers and even competitors than head office, making it vital that they regularly receive information about the strategy as well as being reminded of the standards and values of the organisation.

Interactive marketing

Customers judge the performance of an organisation through every contact they have, so in a complex organisation it is essential for each member of staff to deliver consistent service to customers. This includes the call centre operator, service engineer and salesperson in each location. To support interactive marketing, staff are trained in how to serve the external stakeholders, take appropriate decisions that fit with the strategy and contribute to the processes that co-ordinate the firm's activities. As an example of this the consequences of poor co-ordination of marketing communications are discussed later in this chapter.

External marketing

The traditional role of marketing communications is largely concerned with providing a mechanism by which the features and benefits of the product or service can be promoted as inexpensively as possible to existing and potential customers using the promotion mix (personal selling, advertising, sales promotion and public relations) with the ultimate purpose of persuading customers to buy specific

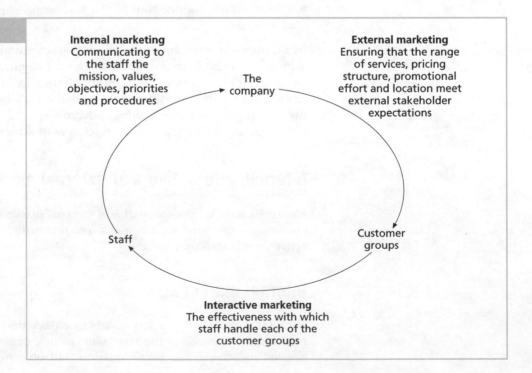

FIGURE 10.1

Three types of marketing

Internal marketing
Communicating to the staff the mission, values, objectives, priorities and procedures

The company

External marketing
Ensuring that the range of services, pricing structure, promotional effort and location meet external stakeholder expectations

Staff

Customer groups

Interactive marketing
The effectiveness with which staff handle each of the customer groups

products and services. Communications, however, have now become much more important within the marketing mix, and the purposes for which marketing communications might be used externally are now more diverse. They include the need to communicate with a more diverse range of stakeholders and deliver higher levels of customer service through interactive, network or relationship marketing. Fill (1999) identifies the DRIP factors to explain that marketing communications can be used to:

- Differentiate products and services
- Remind and reassure customers and potential customers
- Inform
- Persuade targets to think or act in a certain way.

Four levels of communications and relationship building

The communications and relationship building activities in the organisation embrace four distinct strategic elements and these are shown in Figure 10.2.

Communicating the corporate identity

As stakeholders in general have become more aware of the good and bad practices of organisations, companies increasingly use **corporate identity** to constantly and more widely communicate their core values and standards to their internal and external audience, in order to demonstrate their responsibility to shareholders, trustworthiness to customers and care and concern for the local community, environment and local employees.

The corporate image or logo is the most visible part of the identity and, in some firms, is the only element of the marketing activity that is consistent around the world. However, the corporate identity of the firm should be more meaningful, pervasive and memorable, and should be reflected in clear and distinctive communications with simple accompanying messages. Organisations often support their corporate identity and associated beliefs and values through the use of

FIGURE 10.2

The dimensions of external marketing communications

External stakeholders			
Communicating the corporate identity	Communicating the product service differentiation	Delivering the product, service and support	Using communications to build relationships
Communication to all stakeholders of a clear and distinctive corporate identity for the firm supported by sponsorship and public relations	Communication of a distinctive brand image, unique positioning of the product and reasons to buy, supported by advertising, personal selling and sales promotion	Communication and delivery of the product and support services through intermediaries in the distribution channel	Communication with existing and potential customers regularly and systematically to build close relationships, supported by database management and IT

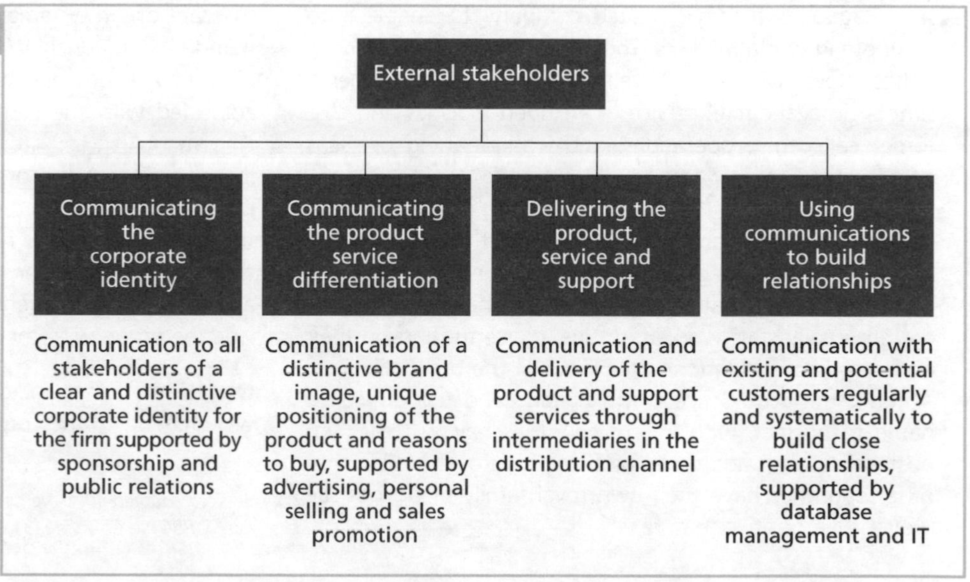

appropriate associations, celebrity endorsement, sponsorship and proactive public relations activity to demonstrate that they are 'good citizens'. Corporate identity can be a sensitive issue as changing it can send out strong messages to its internal and external stakeholders. British Airways earned the wrath of the (then) prime minister of the UK, Margaret Thatcher, when it decided to remove the Union Jack flag from its planes' tail fins. The Royal Mail group introduced a new corporate identity, as Spotlight 10.1 shows, but is planning to withdraw that too.

Communicating product and service differentiation

As we have discussed, increased competition and the maturation of markets have led to many firms offering largely similar core product and service specifications with the result that, in addition to its traditional role of promoting products and services, marketing communications is increasingly used to provide the firm with an important source of **differentiation**, for example, by providing customers with an easily recognisable and distinctive brand image, and by explaining the unique positioning of the product. Challenge 10.1 explains how it was largely advertising imagery that was used to establish the original best selling lager brands in the UK.

However, with the vast increase in the range and volume of communications that consumers are exposed to as they go about their normal work and leisure, making one product or service distinctive becomes an increasing challenge. There are a wide variety of promotional tools that might be used to persuade customers to buy the firm's products and services and the information and communications technologies are increasing this choice all the time. The challenge for the firm is to use these tools as cost effectively as possible to reach out to consumers wherever they are in the world.

SPOTLIGHT 10.1   Consignia – a new corporate identity for the Post Office

The challenge for Keith Wells, who led consultancy Dragon Brands was to create a new identity for the 100 per cent UK government owned Post Office Group, which was being repackaged as a public limited company to enable it to compete in world markets. The group consisted of the Post Office, Royal Mail and Parcelforce, and was no longer a simple domestic mail service. It included logistics and customer call centre operations, and was planning overseas acquisitions.

Wells found that the public had strong images of trust, honour and valour, and postmen battling through blizzards to deliver the mail to grateful, smiling children, but was also confused about what the three arms of the group actually did. Internally staff worked in silos, concentrating on their own activities and ignoring the work of the other divisions. Abroad, the Post Office is too generic and too difficult a name to protect, with lots of countries having their own post offices. An additional problem for Royal Mail is that other countries have their own royal family or do not see 'Royal' as a positive feature.

Wells came up with the made up word Consignia, which has 'consign' in it, is similar to 'insignia', and sounded vaguely royal. The dictionary definition was 'to entrust in the care of'. The name was approved by the government minister and launched. Unfortunately the name was boycotted by unions and hated by customers, and its launch coincided with the start of poor corporate performance. Chairman Alan Leighton has produced a major restructuring plan to turn the group around and has expressed the intention of replacing the name in 2004. It is rumoured that the group will use the name Royal Mail. Perhaps the intention is to associate Consignia with the previous loss making and job cutting imagery and removing the name will provide the group with the opportunity for a fresh start.

Question   What factors should be taken into account when changing the corporate identity?

Source: adapted from Verdin, M., Consignia: Nine letters that spelled fiasco, *BBC News Online*, 31 May 2002

CHALLENGE 10.1   Lager – marketing dream?

Along with a number of other low strength lager brands, such as Kestrel and McEwans, Scottish and Newcastle (S&N) have axed Hofmeister. To understand the reason for this decision it is necessary to understand the role of marketing in the development of lager in the UK since its first introduction.

Hofmeister was a 3.2 per cent alcohol 'standard' lager in the UK created originally as a result of economic and cultural factors. It was a British adaptation.

Millions of Britons package-holidaying abroad in the 1960s and early 1970s got the taste for lager, but lager was sold there in smaller measures than the traditional UK pint pot and at 5 per cent alcohol level. The breweries in the UK liked to sell lager, especially in bottles, which were easier to serve, but they were concerned that British drinkers would not be able to consume the 5 per cent lager in the volumes they were used to. So the 3.2 per cent standard was produced by brewing it for a shorter period.

This, however, also created a marketing challenge, albeit one backed by huge budgets – how to sell lagers, such as Hofmeister, Harp, Carling and Skol that had less flavour and few points of tangible differentiation – and resulted in many highly creative advertising campaigns to emphasise the intangible differentiation. Heineken hit on the idea of emphasising 'refreshment' and Carling gained first place for its brand using the long running 'I bet he drinks' campaign.

Stella Artois, 'Reassuringly Expensive'
Source: Lowe Worldwide

UK lager is usually marketed by emphasising the brand heritage despite the fact that it is usually brewed in the UK. The only British lager, GB, based on Stella Artois, started well in test areas but was eventually replaced with Australian brand Castlemaine XXXX by its new owners Interbrew, who believed it was better to build up an existing brand. Stella Artois, a Belgian beer brewed in Wales and sold on its French heritage, was one of the biggest marketing triumphs. It was launched in the UK in the 1980s and, fitting well with the aspirations of its customers at the time to prefer the finer things in life, marketed using advertisements that emphasised continental sophistication with the tag line 'reassuringly expensive'. In practice it is discounted almost everywhere.

Over time British drinkers have moved towards premium, higher strength lager of 5 per cent. The market leader, Carling, emphasises that its beer is brewed to 4.2 per cent for a fuller flavour. However, to believe that it was its 3.2 per cent alcohol content alone that killed off Hofmeister overlooks other factors. In the 1980s, the Hofmeister advertisements featured a bear wearing a pork-pie hat in a shiny velour jacket, playing snooker, surrounded by cockney lads. They were a product of that age 20 years ago. The male dominated public house advertising is no longer appropriate. More women are now drinking pints, more trendy drinks have been introduced and more people simply prefer to stay at home and drink wine.

Question   To what extent should marketing promotion reflect the differences in product offerings or be the source of that difference through creating appealing images?

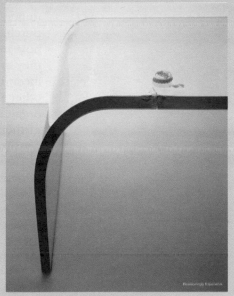

Stella Artois, 'Reassuringly Expensive'
Source: Lowe Worldwide

Source: Wheeler, B., The death of cheap lager, *BBC News Online*, 16 October 2003

Communicating and building relationships through channel development

In this discussion of the integration of marketing communications we have included distribution, although it will be discussed in more detail in Chapter 11. Clearly distribution has two dimensions, the physical transfer of goods (logistics management) and distribution channels. Whilst logistics management plays a key role in the organisation's operations and the timely and efficient delivery of goods to the customer, it also has a very important effect in communicating the right message. In this book we focus on the distribution channels and the development and management of alternative routes to market that play a key role in building the relationship between customers and the organisation, not least because an intermediary, such as a dealer, distributor, retailer or partner, may provide the only personal interaction that takes place. As we shall see later in Challenge 10.4 on-line intermediaries and partners increase the speed and accessibility for on-line customers of less highly visible firms, and the association with better known websites and brands can increase the impact, too.

Using communications to build long term relationships

More intense global competition has provided consumers with a greater choice of products and services that they perceive to be capable of satisfying their needs and providing new experiences. Customers increasingly feel that there is less risk of dissatisfaction in switching to alternative branded products and services, evidenced, for example, by the degree of switching to own label products from supermarkets. Customers are now less likely to stay loyal to one supplier or brand.

With the increasing cost of marketing communications and the need to find potential customers from the ever wider international audience, organisations are becoming much more aware of the high costs of winning new and 're-winning' old customers and the relatively lower costs of retaining existing customers. Attention has been drawn to how much a single customer might purchase of one product over his or her lifetime. Readers might like to calculate how much they buy from a food retailer, car manufacturer or travel company if they stay loyal to that supplier for 5, 10 or 20 years. Food retailers now offer incentives for customer loyalty, such as reward cards and money off vouchers for other products and services they offer, such as petrol and banking services. The organisations then use the information they have gained through reward cards to further build relationships by routinely communicating with their most profitable consumers to inform them of new products and special offers.

However, it is in the B2B sector where relationship marketing is particularly valuable for organisations in retaining the most profitable customers, and so firms are now much more willing to invest resources in systems and processes such as **customer relationship management** to retain their existing customers. However, it should be recognised that to be effective it is necessary for the benefits of relationship marketing to be two way, and the customer must also find value in having a relationship with a supplier.

The concept of relationship marketing has taken on an increased level of significance as improvements in information and communications technology enable firms to communicate in a much more intelligent way by basing their messages on a better knowledge of the characteristics and responses of their existing and potential customers and a better understanding of what they consider to be beneficial.

SUCCESS AND FAILURE IN MARKETING COMMUNICATIONS

The reasons for marketing communications ineffectiveness

All forms of marketing communication have a fundamental purpose which is to ensure that the intended messages (those which are part of the firm's strategy) are conveyed accurately between the sender and the receiver, and that the impact of unintentional messages (those which are likely to have an adverse effect on the firm's market performance and reputation) are kept to a minimum. Spotlight 10.2 focuses on the fact that even CEOs can unintentionally take for granted or even insult their customers.

However, at each of the steps in the intended communication, shown in Figure 10.3, problems can arise. All the time that messages are being communicated there is **noise** in the background from other communications that interfere with the intended communication. This noise might devalue or discredit the intended message or simply cause it to be lost in the volume of communications as the target audience concentrate on communication that they consider to be more interesting. The question for firms is to decide if they are genuinely creating awareness, attracting customers' attention and persuading them to take action or generally adding to the huge quantity of largely ignored communications.

They must also decide if their communications process is really two way and whether provision in the feedback is made to ensure that the receiver has understood the message as it was intended and has responded positively to it.

International marketing communications is particularly problematic, as can often be seen from the business press, which contains many serious but frequently amusing anecdotes about the failed attempts of major firms to communicate in international markets. Mistakes in the use of language, particularly using

---

SPOTLIGHT 10.2   Doing a Ratner

Perhaps the most dangerous thing a CEO can do is to make an 'off the cuff remark'. In the UK this is called 'doing a Ratner'. This recalls an incident in 1991 when Gerald Ratner, the CEO of the Ratners jewellery chain, joked at a meeting of the Institute of Directors that the company 'sold a pair or earrings for under a pound, which is cheaper than a prawn sandwich from Marks & Spencer but probably wouldn't last as long'. He followed this up by saying a sherry decanter was so cheap because it was 'total crap'. Consumers do not like to be taken for fools and £500 million was wiped off the company value, and in 1994 Ratner and his name were removed from the company.

In 2001 the boss of the Topman clothing brand gave an interview to trade magazine *Menswear* and, asked to clarify the Topman target customer, said 'Hooligans or whatever'. He added 'Very few of our customers have to wear suits to work. They'll be for his first interview or first court case.'

In 2002 Woolworths' Gerald Corbett explained underperformance by saying that some city centre stores are vast open deserts with nobody there', and in 2003, EMI CEO,

Alain Levy, annoyed its Finnish subsidiary after cutting 40 artists from the company's list by saying 'he did not think that there were many people in the country 'who could sing'.

In 2003 the boss of Barclays Bank, the largest credit card company, Mike Barrett, giving evidence to a UK government committee, said that astute customers would do well to steer clear of credit cards; he and his four children avoided them too because they were too expensive. Barrett was being criticised because interest rates on a Barclaycard had fallen by only 3.5 per cent to 17.9 per cent since 1992, despite UK interest rates falling by two thirds.

Question   What is the best way to manage the fall out from these unguarded comments – assuming it is difficult to stop bosses speaking?

Source: adapted from Wilson, B., Barclays chief's gaffe recalls Ratner howler, *BBC News Online*, 17 October 2003

messages which do not translate or are mistranslated, are a particular problem. But more serious is a lack of sensitivity to different cultures amongst international communicators. Besides the often highly visible failures that make firms appear to be incompetent and insensitive and devalue the brand, there are many examples of wasted effort and resources that are not so widely publicised.

The problems that prevent effective communications can be within the organisation's control or outside the organisation's control.

Within the organisation's control:

- Inconsistency in the messages conveyed to customers by staff at different levels, in different locations, on different but related topics.
- Different styles of presentation of corporate identity, brand and product image from different departments and country business units which can leave customers confused.
- A lack of co-ordination of messages, such as press releases, advertising campaigns, and changes in product specification or pricing.
- Failure to appreciate the differences in the fields of perception (the way the message is understood) of the sender and receiver. The field of perception tends to be affected significantly by the self-reference criteria of both parties. This is, perhaps, where the greatest problems arise because, as we have already discussed, avoiding this requires knowledge of different market environments, cultural empathy and the willingness to adapt the communications programmes and processes to local requirements.
- Ignoring the needs of different audiences.
- Achieving little impact from a single message.
- Lack of synergy and reinforcement from multiple communications.
- More than one message communicated simultaneously, so confusing the recipient.
- Setting unclear objectives and undertaking meaningless measuring.
- Trying to achieve too much with one communication to justify the high cost.
- Inconsistency with the distribution channel.
- Agencies focusing on creativity rather than selling the product.

Whilst some of these are caused by insufficient knowledge, inappropriate attitudes and lack of empathy, other areas of potential communications failure are concerned with the ineffectiveness of the firm's strategy, planning and implemen-

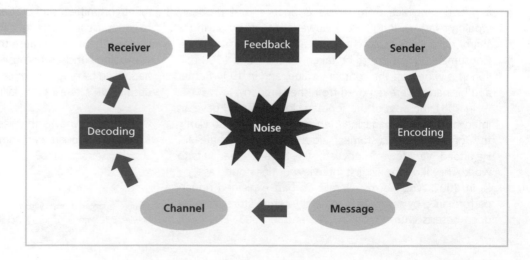

FIGURE 10.3

Model of communication

tation, and the degree to which the staff within the organisation fail to understand and are not fully involved in the communications planning process. It is almost inevitable that some communication failures occur from time to time and it is vital that firms learn from their mistakes. To ensure success in these areas it is important to have in place an effective control process.

Whilst it can be argued that the majority of these failures are ultimately within the control of the company, a number of situations arise where the firm's communications can be affected by factors which are outside the firm's control or extremely difficult to control. Examples of these situations are:

- Counterfeiting or other infringements of patents or copyright. Not only does the firm lose revenue but it may also suffer damage to its image if consumers believe the low quality goods supplied by the counterfeiter are genuine.

- Parallel importing or grey marketing, which is distribution through channels that are not authorised by the organisation, communicates contradictory messages that do not reflect the image of the brand and thus confuse consumers. This can be particularly problematic if the parallel importer seriously undercuts the prices charged by the official channel, in which case customers may believe they are being 'ripped off' by the official channel.

- Competitors, governments or pressure groups attack the standards and values of organisations by alleging, fairly or unfairly, bad business practice. Perhaps surprisingly, despite their huge resources, some of the largest firms are ineffective in responding to allegations from relatively less powerful stakeholders. For example, companies such as Shell, Exxon and McDonald's have suffered following criticism of their lack of concern for the environment. The lack of standards and control of the internet has made the problem worse. For example, anti-Coca-Cola websites can post negative communications without the need to substantiate the messages.

THE INTEGRATION OF COMMUNICATIONS

Stakeholders receive messages, both intended and unintended, from every part of the organisation's activities, from the clothes that customer facing staff wear, the packaging design, the delays in answering the telephone at the call centre to stories in the newspaper about the chief executive's extravagant partying habit. As the number of communications have increased dramatically and customers have become more critical and sceptical, the importance of integrated marketing communications (IMC) has been emphasised in order to avoid conflicting messages and instead communicate consistent and mutually supporting messages. Fill (1999) points out that traditional mass communication strategies have given way to more personalised, customer oriented and technology driven approaches. To be successful requires a completely different approach, focusing on the individual customer and Kotler (2003) says that 'A company needs to orchestrate a consistent set of impressions from its personnel, facilities and actions that deliver the company's brand meaning and promise to its various audiences'.

Shrimp (2003) provides a definition of **integrated marketing communications** which focuses on five features:

- start with the customer or prospect
- use any form of relevant contact
- achieve synergy through consistency across the communication elements
- build relationships
- affect behaviour.

Communications is also one element of the organisation's corporate and marketing activities and the communications decisions should take account of and complement the work of the other functions. The communications strategy should therefore fit within the organisation's hierarchy of strategies and global activities. Customers receive many communications from various sources within the organisation, and these should be integrated too.

The benefits of integration

Given the fact that individual messages have little overall impact on customers on their own, it follows that the effect of communications will be significantly greater if the many messages are consistent, uniform and mutually supporting in the way that they build the image of the brand, product and service and reinforce the standards and values of the organisation.

It is easier to justify the cost and control communications activities if they are integrated and the cumulative effect, rather than the individual effect, is assessed. Measurement of individual actions is difficult, given the extraneous variables that create noise, and so it is more sensible to measure the effects of the combined actions.

Corporate strategy

Although usually considered to be a part of the marketing mix, in many organisations communications takes on a much more important role than this would imply, because of the need to communicate the objectives, strategies and performance to external and internal stakeholders, including shareholders and staff. It is just as important to maintain good practice in message presentation in corporate communication as marketing communications. In the UK, on the same day and to the dismay of its rural customers, Barclays Bank announced both the closure of many branches in rural locations and big pay increases for its main board directors.

Many aspects of the organisation's corporate behaviour can affect and be affected by the communications strategy. For example, the management style, organisation culture, human resources and recruitment policies convey important messages to a variety of stakeholders and, particularly important, to customers. For example, Asda Wal-Mart in the UK routinely scores well in employee satisfaction surveys.

The organisation's overall management style and internal culture can have a significant effect on the levels of trust in relationships with commercial partners, such as suppliers and distributors. This is particularly important in international markets, especially in Asia, where relationships will founder if not underpinned by a strong relationship and personal trust between managers from partner organisations.

Marketing and brand strategies

It is the role of the communications strategy to deliver specific activities and thus follow the direction set by the organisation's marketing or brand strategy. However, it can also play a lead role in defining the direction that the marketing or brand strategy takes. For example, there are many examples of creative and distinctive advertising of fmcg products defining the very essence of the products and services and thus driving forward the whole brand and marketing strategy. There are also many examples of organisations failing to find equally memorable campaigns to maintain the momentum and interest of customers. Despite other elements of the strategy being sound, performance often suffers.

Global integration

As organisations operate more internationally, travel and communications become more global because of the internet and satellite television, so the consistency of communications across borders becomes essential. This means that organisations must decide on the degree of standardisation of their communications programmes and processes. Doole and Lowe (2004) explain the benefits of economies of scale and the experience curve effect that greater standardisation offers but also the many disadvantages and pitfalls associated with over-standardisation across borders of communications. Consequently they argue that adopting the same process for advertising or launching new products across borders rather than having exactly the same campaign is more likely to prove effective for most businesses.

Business unit marketing strategy

At a more local, business unit level it should be possible for managers in charge of communications to work closely with colleagues responsible for development, operations, key account management, sales and customer service centre management to develop a highly integrated approach that offers a seamless service to customers. Even here, however, this will not happen automatically and the strategic marketing decision making processes must be deliberately set up to achieve the required integration.

Marketing mix integration

Customers continually receive communications from the organisation that are the result of marketing mix actions. Every element of the marketing mix communicates with customers, as shown in Figure 10.4. Some are intended and some are unintentional but all must be integrated. Research by a global cosmetics business found that on their multi-lingual packaging British customers strongly objected to the English translation appearing below the French and German translations.

It is important to remember that in many markets non-verbal communications have a greater impact than verbal communications or words, especially given the amount of time that a customer might give to looking at one communication. For example, the colours and styles used in creative work communicate non-verbally with the customers, reinforcing the images and customer perceptions. Organisations, such as Marks & Spencer, have used such consistent packaging design in some of their product ranges that customers could instantly pick out their packs, even if all reference to the company and brand had been removed. Customers can pick up small errors in colour matching and design, so discipline in the use of the corporate identity is essential. In different cultures the significance of colours, symbols and numbers is so great that they alone could deter customers from buying a product.

Decision making in the marketing communications plan

In discussing the implementation of the marketing communications strategy it is useful to reflect on some of the key concepts that underpin the decisions that are needed at each stage. Table 10.1 shows a typical framework, the key components of an integrated **communications plan** and areas for analysis or decision options.

As we have discussed earlier in the book, situation analysis should establish a clear current and desired position for the organisation within its market environment context. The analysis should also confirm the organisation's current business and marketing strategic capability within its business sector. From this it should be possible to establish the organisation's ability to influence and persuade its customers through its integrated communications strategy. It is then vital to decide the size and nature of the gap that must be filled between the organisation's current and desired position, as this will establish the scale of the communications task.

It will also enable decisions to be made about the communications objectives to be set, as these must be different from the overall marketing strategy objectives. It may seem surprising, but many organisations still see advertising and marketing objectives to be one and the same thing and ignore the fact, mentioned earlier, that communications have often substantial but ultimately limited scope to influence overall marketing performance.

In a similar way the communications strategy is a subset of the marketing strategy and should provide a clear explanation of how the objectives will be delivered. The starting point is usually a restatement of the segmentation,

FIGURE 10.4

Messages from the marketing mix

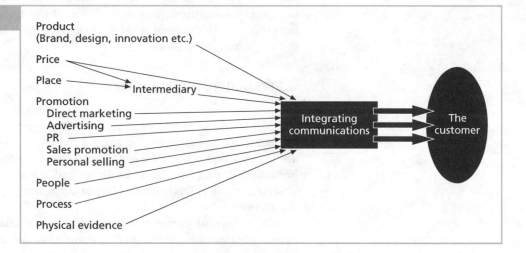

TABLE 10.1

Communications plan framework

Situation analysis	Environment
	Market: stakeholders, competition customers, structure
Objectives	Financial, non-financial
Strategy	Growth (e.g. product, market development)
	Segmentation, targeting and positioning
Tactics	Marketing mix (7Ps)
Actions	Budgets and plans
Control	Measurement, evaluation, correct deviations

targeting and positioning strategy and the role of communications in the tactics and actions, which are now discussed.

In discussing the communications actions we have focused on the key decision making areas of target audiences, tools and media, messages and budgets.

Audiences

A clear understanding of the target buyers, their background, experience and preferred information sources provides the organisation with a profile that will help in the creation of the message and the selection of appropriate marketing tools and media. Different segments and new generations respond differently to marketing communications. For example, in B2B markets, organisational purchasing is a more formal process and involves a buying centre (shown in Table 10.5) comprising a number of staff, each with different responsibilities and motivations for buying from one firm rather than another. Often organisations have a stereotype view of how decisions are made by their customer. IT suppliers will target IT managers and pharmaceutical companies will target those prescribing the drugs in the belief that these are the decision makers. In practice decision making is more diffuse and involves more of the customers' managers. Because of this it may be necessary for the marketer to make specific, targeted, but different appeals to each person in the buying centre.

Communications tools and media

The key decisions in media planning are the choice of media made by customers and their access to it. The key dimensions are:

Reach: the percentage of the target audience exposed to the message at least once during the relevant period.

Coverage: the size of the potential audience that might be exposed to a particular media vehicle.

Frequency: the repetition cycle of the communication.

Gross rating point (GRP): the reach multiplied by the frequency and a measure of the total number of exposures of the communication.

Efficiency: a further key dimension of decision making, given the need to reach as many potential customers as possible, given a constant budget.

TABLE 10.2	Buying roles	
Users	Often initiate the purchase and define the specification
Influencers	Help define the product and evaluate the alternatives
Deciders	Decide product requirements and suppliers
Approvers	Authorise the proposals of deciders and buyers
Buyers	Have the formal authority for selecting suppliers and negotiating terms
Gatekeepers	Can stop the sellers reaching the buyer centre

Decisions on media planning involve a trade off between reach, frequency and the impact on customers that is being sought through the communications. Experience suggests (Shrimp 2003) that different buying situations require different patterns of, for example, advertising schedules.

Recency

A further question is whether purchase decisions are actually the result of advertising. The concept of recency suggests that it is important to plan the communication to catch those that are ready to buy. Some suggest that the main stimulus to purchase is running out of the product, so there may be little point in advertising at other times.

The communication tools

The main communications tools are included in Table 10.3, together with a general comment about their relative effectiveness. In practice the choice of tools will be determined by the following four criteria: cost, communication effectiveness, credibility and control and by the specific context. For example, Wilson and Gilligan (2004) explain that the cost effectiveness of the marketing tools varies at different stages in the product lifecycle.

TABLE 10.3	The main marketing communications tools	
Advertising	• Legitimises the brand	• Shows commitment and confidence
	• Creative expression	• Creative presentation of emotional and functional benefits
	• Image building	• Over long periods builds distinctive personality
	• Economical	• Low cost exposure to large audiences, but low impact
Sales promotion	• Impact	• Strong and quick effect on sales
	• Trial	• Encourages trial in low-involvement markets
	• Expensive	• As they involve price reduction, expensive and can cannibalise full price sales
	• Image erosion	• Frequent promotions can erode quality image
Public relations	• Credibility	• News stories more credible than paid for ads and promotions
	• Imprecise	• Little control over message and audience
	• Low cost	• Can obtain substantial free exposure
	• Difficult	• Depends on perceived importance and interest in message
Personal selling	• Two-way	• More pursuasive and offer can be modified
	• Closure	• Deal can be agreed, and buyer is expected to respond
	• Relationships	• Friendships encourage loyalty and continuing business
	• Expensive	• Costs of a transaction can be in excess of £200
Direct marketing	• Personalised	• Specific and customised for one person
	• Responsive	• Invites immediate response and can rapidly increase sales
	• Interactive	• Fast preparation of messages, and easily changed
	• Targeted	• Precise targeting at specific segments

Source: adapted from Doyle, P. (2000)

B2B

For most B2B communications decisions there is a small target audience and so the mass market tools, such as advertising (apart from trade press advertising) and sales promotions, would not normally be used. Direct marketing, PR and personal selling are likely to be more effective media.

Advertising

The role of advertising is to inform, persuade, remind and reinforce. It has been the mass communication method for B2C for decades but it is a one way communication and is more difficult to target effectively than more interactive communications tools, such as internet marketing. Moreover, TV advertisements are typically becoming shorter, placed together and there are more of them, and it has become easier for viewers to switch between channels, so reducing their impact. Kotler (2003) suggests that few advertisements are likely to cover their costs in increased sales and that they should not be expected to deliver the sales targets of inferior products. Advertising should not be a substitute for proper design and performance of a product or service.

Sales promotion

Kotler maintains that sales promotion is a short term trigger to act and is concerned with transaction marketing, not building relationships, building current sales rather than building the brand. Indeed sales might be increased short term, but in the long run profitability will be hit. Sales promotions are typically used with weaker brands and attract brand switchers. Firms must decide whether frequent sales promotions are either necessary or useful in growing sales, because they will not help to build the brand value.

PR

PR is often underused and undervalued by firms. It is perceived by customers as more authoritative and believable than communications, such as advertising, which obviously come from the firm. The press are always hungry for stories in order to fill their ever-expanding programmes and newspapers, and are grateful for interesting and newsworthy stories that are inexpensive to obtain. Firms are able to negotiate trade press editorial together with advertising in order to gain cost effective exposure for their products. The disadvantage of PR for firms, of course, is that it is difficult to control. For example, a story can be published rather differently from the way it was intended, but this can be overcome by building and managing relationships with the media.

PR covers many activities such as Challenge 10.2 and one of the key roles of PR is managing crises that might adversely affect the company or brand value from time to time.

Sponsorship

Many firms sponsor events or individuals and the key decision is whether it will be regarded as a cost or an investment. Sponsorship (Shrimp 2003) consists of the event exchange, which is the fee paid for being associated with the event and the marketing of the association by the sponsor. To obtain the maximum benefit a sum two or three times the cost of the sponsorship is needed for pre-event and follow up activity. Overall success is likely to be greater if there is a match between the event audience and the firm's target customers.

Sponsorship of individuals, such as sports stars, can be high risk but very beneficial when it works well. However, there are many instances of sponsorship deals that have failed because of unfortunate associations, for example with Michael Jackson and Mike Tyson, but also many successful deals, including (so far) David Beckham, Tiger Woods and Venus Williams.

Personal selling

In the past some organisations managed personal selling ineffectively and confused selling with order taking. Personal selling is becoming ever more expensive and organisations have other ways of communicating with customers to collect orders, such as telephone selling, sales agents and direct and e-marketing. Consequently personal selling is being used more selectively, and is usually managed better, with emphasis given to salesperson motivation, direction and control. It is still necessary where complex negotiation and persuasion are needed, and where there is sufficient margin to cover the four or five visits that might be needed to make the sale.

Direct marketing

Direct marketing traditionally took the form of direct mailing and telephone selling, supported by database management of the information, but the major change has come from e-business development. For many firms their direct marketing strategy means using a combination of direct marketing techniques, striking a balance between the various routes to market, and integrating the initiatives and responses through database management.

Messages

As we have indicated earlier the challenge is to make messages that stand out from the crowd. To do this they must be simple and Kotler (2003) suggests, where possible, should be based on a single benefit or a story or character that the customers know and can associate strongly with the proposition. The message should coincide with and reflect the customers' aspirations and be periodically

---

CHALLENGE 10.2   **Doughnuts – cheaper than advertising**

As an illustration that advertising is not the only way to introduce new products to a market, the Krispy Kreme Doughnut Company (USA) does not have a traditional media/advertising budget. Instead it simply gives away doughnuts. It finds this is a cheaper and more effective way to develop new markets. Before entering a new market it gives away millions of free doughnuts through radio and TV stations and newspapers. It provides discounted products for charitable organisations to sell on for fundraising.

The company does not have as many stores as Dunkin' Donuts, just 292 compared to Dunkin' Donuts' 3600 in the USA but its turnover exceeded US$1 billion in 2003.

Question   Is this merely eccentricity or is it cost effective to adopt more innovative promotions? If so, in which situations?

Source: adapted from Lin Lay Ying, 'The nuts and bolts of successful marketing', *New Straits Times Press* (Malaysia), 20 December 2003

refreshed. However, Ries (2004, www.adage.com) warns against wasting money on bad marketing slogans in Challenge 10.3.

Given the high cost of communications and the pressure to achieve short term results, it can be tempting to try to include everything that the organisation would like to say to a customer in one rather long and complex message to persuade them to buy. In practice customers are reluctant to part with their hard earned cash for a product or service that they have only just heard of. In the B2B market even the most persuasive salesperson may have to make three or four visits before the customer is persuaded to buy.

In practice customers need to be taken through three stages, as shown in Table 10.4. To achieve the best effect, different messages, marketing communications tools and contributions from the whole marketing mix might be required at different times in this process. In a B2B situation, even a different member of the buying centre might need to be targeted at each of these stages. There are a range of communications models (see Fill 1999; Shrimp 2003) that follow approximately the same sequence, and one of these is shown in Figure 10.5.

It is suggested that such models may be appropriate for and illustrate high involvement decisions, such as the purchase of a car, but not low involvement decisions, where impulse buying replaces the measured process.

CHALLENGE 10.3 Wasting money on bad advertising slogans

Huge amounts of money are spent on creating slogans that capture the essence of the brand. However, it is vital that the slogan leaves a strong message in people's minds and not just a vague, warm and fuzzy feeling. Canon's slogan is the meaningless 'Know-how', Delta's is 'On top of the World', Hitachi's is 'Inspire the Next' and Nissan's is 'Enjoy the Ride'. Food company Tyson spent US$40 million on advertising with the slogan 'its what your family deserves', which Ries observes is not how people talk.

It is essential to articulate the concept of the brand. Volvo is a safe car, BMW is fun to drive and Mercedes is about prestige. It is also useful to emphasise the brand being the first: Coca-Cola, the first cola and Red Bull, the

first energy drink; or to emphasise brand leadership: 'The real thing' for Coca Cola, 'Where winners rent' for Hertz, and 'Italy's No. 1 pasta' for Barilla.

Of course, Nike has its 'Just do it' slogan, but to make a meaningless slogan memorable, it spent US$623 million on advertising in 2002, and similar amounts for years, promoting the same message.

Question Which advertising slogans are memorable? Do you remember which products they advertise and do they make you buy?

Source: adapted from Ries, A., www.adage.com, 12 January 2004

TABLE 10.4 Persuasive communication stages

Cognitive	Customers need to be first made aware of the product so that they can understand its benefits
Affective	It is then necessary to create positive attitudes in the customer towards the product, such as desire and preference over competing products
Behavioural	Customers then move to a stage where they will take action and make their first purchase, repurchase or instigate the organisational purchasing process

Budgets

Wilson and Gilligan (2004) identify the various approaches to budgeting:

- what the organisation can afford
- matching competitors' spend or the norms for the industry
- a fixed percentage of past sales
- a fixed percentage of past profit
- a fixed amount to carry out a specific objective or task.

Each has merits and disadvantages, and the decision about which approach to take is determined by the organisational context. In fact the approach to budgeting often indicates the company's view about the marketing communications budget and whether it is regarded as a cost or an investment, and the degree of measurement and analysis they are prepared to undertake to assess the effectiveness.

Given the difficulty of measuring the effectiveness of marketing communications, the budgets of many firms are decided in a rather *ad hoc* way. There can be internal battles regarding each brand's or product's share of the budget and one manager's gain can be another's loss. This can lead to a manager's success being measured in terms of the amount of money secured rather than the impact that has been achieved in the marketplace.

On the other hand, in an environment characterised by 'hard edged marketing' there can be a tendency for firms to over-compensate for the difficulty of measuring the unmeasurable by simply selecting the marketing communications tools that can be measured. This would explain why, for example, sales promotions and direct marketing are probably over-used and PR is under-used and under-valued. The tools that have an obvious impact and can be measured largely deliver short term benefits, whereas the tools, such as advertising or PR, that offer the most valuable long term effects, such as awareness raising and brand reinforcement, are usually more difficult to measure. The values of the majority of today's greatest brands today have been built by a consistent and supportive marketing mix and mass advertising.

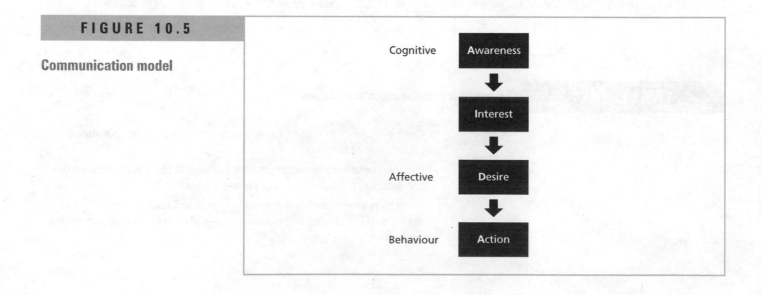

FIGURE 10.5

Communication model

Control

Despite some reservations about their inappropriate use, a variety of measurement methods shown below are used from decision making:

- regular auditing
- pre-activity research and measurement
- ongoing research and measurement
- post-activity research and measurement
- tracking research
- benchmarking.

The measurements can involve contributions from internal staff, customers and other outside agencies and experts. It is worthwhile emphasising a number of points about decisions on marketing communications evaluation.

- There should be a strong link between measurement and the objectives set and this might mean that measurements should relate to the holistic benefit that is gained from integrated communications.

- The main purpose of evaluation might be considered to be control in order to correct short term deviations from the intended performance, but more importantly, it should be to inform strategy development.

- The most beneficial dimension of evaluation should be to learn from mistakes and good practice and this learning should be shared with colleagues through an appropriate database.

Figure 10.6 contains a checklist to consider the effectiveness of particular campaigns and market communications plans.

DEVELOPING PROFITABLE, LONG TERM MARKETING RELATIONSHIPS

So far in this chapter we have focused upon the communications strategies that might be used to ensure that the firm's broad base of stakeholders around the world are aware of the company's standards and values, the distinctiveness and quality of its brands, products and services, and that customers are exposed to the messages that will encourage them to buy the firm's products and services rather than those of competitors and receive delivery of the products and services, where appropriate, through intermediaries and partners. Once customers have been won over, usually at a considerable cost, firms increasingly realise that

---

FIGURE 10.6	
Evaluation: was the programme a success?	**Q** Were the communication objectives delivered?
	Q What was the contribution to marketing strategy (integration)?
	Q Was the programme efficient and value for money?
	Q Was the message effective – how was it received?
	Q Was the programme a success with the target audience?
	Q Did it have impact on other stakeholder audiences?
	Q Was the communication tool and the media effectively used?
	Q Was the overall process and plan effective and efficient?
	Q Could it have been done differently and in a better way?
	Q What was learned?

it is less costly if they can persuade them to stay loyal to the firm rather than lose them to a competitor and so face the cost of winning them over again. The cost of failing to satisfy customers can be high in potential lifetime revenue.

Customer retention is particularly important for B2B marketing, where the number of opportunities to win over new customers may be very limited and the loss of a major customer could have a disastrous effect on the firm. The lifetime value of the customer is considerable, but the cost to the customer of changing to a new supplier can also be considerable. Both supplier and customer have something to gain from the relationship marketing concept, which is based on the ideology of achieving a 'win–win' and mutual benefit, but the practical benefit of customer retention is most significant.

In response to this the importance of relationship marketing (RM) began to be recognised in the 1970s, and relationship marketing was explained as a new theory and practice in the 1990s (Groonroos 1996). Of course marketers have always recognised that building relationships is a key part of the supplier–customer relationship, especially when supply exceeds demand. Relationship marketing is concerned with developing and maintaining mutually advantageous relationships between two firms in a supply chain and using their combined capability and resources to deliver the maximum added value for the ultimate customer. It involves a more holistic approach to understanding the market dynamics and developing implementation strategies to respond to changes in the market needs that have been identified. As with many concepts, organisations attempt to apply relationship marketing universally in often inappropriate situations. It is questionable what benefits fmcg consumers might obtain from RM.

CHALLENGE 10.4   On the right site

Previously, on-line retailers with limited resources have concentrated on making sure that they could beat the algorithms of search engines such as Google, so that their names would come to the top of the list of websites that appear when you type in a particular keyword. However, Google has now changed the way it decides which websites appear first.

What has become important is creating links with firms that are targeting similar types of customers. Fine wine firm Berry Brothers and Rudd advertised special offers on the website of a luxury property rental firm and saw a significant increase in demand. Website www.madeinsheffield.com sells Sheffield made cutlery and pewter and has done deals with retail portals in the UK and USA, such as Catalogue City. It estimates that two thirds of its trade comes via search engines. This is why search engines are crucial to on-line advertising and further developments, such as the new Google project 'Froogle', which will combine free listing of websites and special offers, could be significant as they might stop high spenders always appearing at the top of the list.

Ultimately, however, most on-line retailers recognise that it is reputation and word of mouth recommendation that is still the key marketing tool.

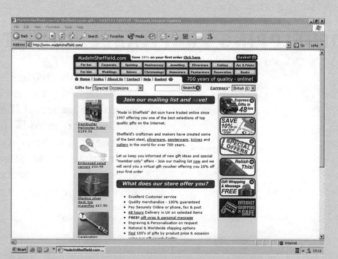

Source: www.madeinsheffield.com

Question   How can relationships with intermediaries and different 'categories' of customers be developed to achieve the maximum effect?

Source: adapted from Webber, M. Clever marketing boosts internet sales, *BBC News Online* 18 December 2003

The concept of relationship marketing

There are significant differences between adopting a traditional marketing approach based on individual transactions, in which the emphasis is placed on the 4Ps of the product marketing mix (particularly the product P), and an approach based upon building relationships by emphasising the three extra Ps of the service mix (particularly the people P). At the core of relationship marketing is the idea that rather than simply trying to add customer service onto a pre-determined product offer, based on a rigid marketing mix, the firm should provide customer satisfaction by offering a flexible marketing mix offer to meet the customer's evolving needs, through putting together cross-functional teams.

Clearly this makes sense for high involvement purchases but less sense for low involvement or near commodity products and services. Horovitz (2000) suggests that in relationship marketing the 4Ps of the traditional marketing mix are changed altogether, and replaced by the 4Cs of relationship marketing: customer needs and wants; costs; convenience; and communication.

There are different levels of customers and intermediaries might increasingly be treated like customers, at least in terms of building relationships, as Challenge 10.4 shows.

There is some discussion about whether the concept of relationship marketing can and should be applied to all marketing contexts. Groonroos (1994) suggested that relationship marketing becomes more relevant when moving to the right of the continuum illustrated in Figure 10.7.

Throughout the firm the objectives of relationship marketing are to:

- Maintain and build existing customers by offering more tailored and cost effective business solutions.

- Use existing relationships to obtain referral to business units and other supply chain members that are, perhaps, in different parts of the world and not currently customers.

- Increase the revenue from customers by offering solutions that are a combination of products and services.

- Reduce the operational and communications cost of servicing the customers, including the work prior to a trading relationship.

The challenges of implementing a relationship marketing strategy

Inevitably relationship marketing requires a different philosophy in the firm and changes in the marketing and communications strategy objectives, budgets and performance measurements. Groonroos (1996) suggests that **relationship marketing** has two distinct dimensions, shown in Figure 10.8: strategic relationship marketing and tactical relationship marketing.

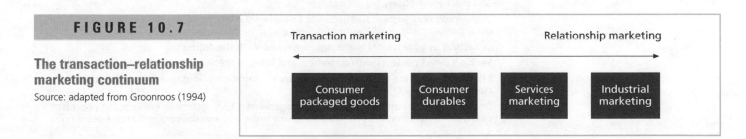

FIGURE 10.7

The transaction–relationship marketing continuum

Source: adapted from Groonroos (1994)

Transaction marketing   Relationship marketing

| Consumer packaged goods | Consumer durables | Services marketing | Industrial marketing |

Seeking direct contacts

A further implication of relationship marketing is that it is necessary to build relationships not only with the final customers but also with those other stakeholders that might influence the final purchase. Payne *et al.* (1995) suggest that this includes internal staff as individuals and groups, professionals and satisfied customers that might help build relationships through word of mouth recommendations, individuals and organizations that influence the marketing environment, employees that are recruited, are retained and help build respect in the wider community, suppliers and customers. All of these must be targeted for relationship marketing to be used effectively, confirming the importance of integrated communications.

However, the power and influence of the organisation in these markets will vary considerably around the world, and the relative importance of them depends upon the specific context of the firm's activity. In the technology sector, for example, key influencers and high profile lead customers may be located in a particular country market, but their decisions might influence purchasing decisions in the whole industry.

Database development

The starting point is to build an information technology system that will integrate the RM activity. Central to the system is a database that will identify those customers with whom it is worthwhile developing a relationship. The database can best be built from the company's records of its interactions with customers and then supplemented with purchased lists of possible customers. Chaffey *et al.* (2003) explain that the details about the customer should include:

- personal and profile data, including contact details
- transaction data including purchase quantities, channels, timing and locations
- communications data, including response to campaigns.

Shrimp (2003) explains how recency, frequency and monetary value of purchases can be used to identify the priority customers, who in relationship marketing terms are likely to be the most valuable to the firm.

Wasserman *et al.* (2000) explain that **data mining** is used to 'discover hidden facts contained in databases'. Identifying relationships between data contained in

FIGURE 10.8	The strategic issues of relationship marketing are identified as:
The dimensions of relationship marketing	Defining the business as a service business
	Recognising that the key competitive elements are concerned with offering a total service rather than simply selling a product
	Managing the firm with a process management perspective and not from a functional perspective (the process of creating value for customers rather than managing operations and marketing purely for efficiency)
	Developing partnerships and networks to handle the whole service process, e.g. by making close contacts with well-known suppliers and intermediaries
	The tactical or operational issues are concerned with the following:
	Seeking direct contacts with customers and other stakeholders
	Building a database covering the necessary information about customers and other stakeholders
	Developing a customer relationship management (CRM) system to manage the processes of customer information, product and service ordering, and delivery and after sales service

databases provides a basis for cost effectively targeting prospective customers, developing co-operative relationships with other companies and better understanding the patterns of customer purchasing behaviour.

Chaffey *et al.* (2003) explain that the key objectives are: customer retention, customer extension (increasing the depth and range of customers) and customer selection (segmenting and targeting). Chaffey and Smith (2001) point out that 'it is necessary to select the best customers and not the bad customers who haggle about prices, pay late, constantly complain, grab all the promotions and leave you as soon as another company comes along'.

Whilst much of the data can be collected by in-house activities it is important to recognise that huge initial investment is needed in setting up databases and also that maintaining them can require a huge financial commitment, given that up to 20 per cent of the data will be out of date by the end of a year. Consultants Peppers and Rogers of 1to1.com conclude, therefore, that it is not for mass marketers or those firms with limited budgets.

Customer relationship management

International consumer markets are characterised by their sheer size and the relative anonymity of their customers. Even small retailers cannot possibly know their customers' individual behaviour, attitudes, intention to purchase, and experiences (good or bad) in dealing with the firm, whereas an industrial marketer with only a few customers possibly can. As we have discussed in the section on databases, technology has been developed to try to integrate RM activity and manage the vast amounts of supporting information. Customer relationship management (CRM) is effectively computer software coupled with defined management processes and procedures to enable staff throughout organisations to capture and use information about their customers to maintain and build relationships. Companies such as Siebel (USA) have built their business around such concepts.

O'Malley (2003) suggests that improving customer relationships requires a systematic approach:

- Evaluate the nature of existing relationships with all stakeholders.
- Consider what level of relationship is necessary and appropriate, given the specific business context, product and service and resources available.
- Develop the strategy, taking into account the need for staff development, the necessary changes to organisation systems, such as customer service and billing, and the impact on marketing strategies, such as advertising or direct marketing.
- Assess the need for additional technology to support CRM.
- Calculate the costs to implement the strategy.

Although CRM should play a decisive role in integrating communications and developing relationships with the customer as the focus, Kotler (2003) points out that in practice many firms have embraced the concept and have spent between US$5 and 10 million on CRM systems, but have been less than satisfied with the results. He quotes the CRM Forum research that suggests less than 30 per cent of companies are satisfied, with the problems not usually software failure (2 per cent) but rather organisational change (29 per cent), company politics/inertia (22 per cent), lack of CRM understanding (20 per cent), poor planning (12 per cent), lack of CRM skills (6 per cent), budget problems (4 per cent), bad advice (1 per cent) and other (4 per cent).

The problems arise when firms see CRM systems as a quick fix to try to manage vast amounts of data. They make broad generalisations about customer segments and are often too insensitive to different consumer cultures and concerns. Indeed, O'Malley (2003) suggests that often the technology is used but not understood for a process of customer management that staff are unfamiliar with. Too often the CRM systems are driven by the IT requirements and therefore technology driven. As a consequence they may track and respond to behaviour but fail to take into account the differing customer attitudes, which are at the heart of international marketing. Too often CRM is not adopted on an organisation wide basis and instead is adopted by individual departments for very specific reasons. It also gets modified because of the need to interface it with existing legacy systems and so it becomes fragmented, and, rather than reducing cost, actually increases it. The introduction of CRM leads to raised expectations of service levels, amongst customers and staff, and if this is not delivered then CRM can have a detrimental effect on the business.

The opportunities for relationship marketing to offer benefits are increasing because of improvements in communications and IT, and increased cross-border purchasing. However, Christy *et al*. (1996) suggest that the successful establishment of relationship marketing depends on the extent to which each player understands the potential rewards and also the reciprocal duties necessary to make it work. Moreover, Fournier *et al*. (1998) emphasise that the consumer is not necessarily a willing participant in the relationship mission, and unless this is recognised, relationship marketing will prove to be of limited value. Indeed the question must be asked whether the majority of consumers will derive any benefit from a relationship with an MNE – the benefits will mainly be with the firm.

For relatively low purchase price items there is a danger that the costs to the firm of building customer loyalty might outweigh the costs of a more traditional approach to marketing products and services. It is difficult to measure the relative merits of short term costs against longer term revenues, and few companies are willing to take a long term view based upon their assumptions of what might happen in the future.

In practice the methods of relationship marketing in consumer markets are diverging from relationship marketing in the business sector. In consumer markets relationship marketing will become more concerned with making one to one connections with customers through interactivity, and promoting and placing products and services in the appropriate media at just the right moment. Business relationship marketing is leading to ever closer relationships and partnerships for essential supply chain supplies, but also more transient purchasing relationships for commodity items as discussed in Chapter 8.

Permission marketing

Godin (2002) has explained that in the past customers were bombarded by up to 500 marketing messages per day from traditional communication sources, but today customers can expect to see up to 3000 messages because of the new communications technology available. This means that the effect of individual messages is diluted amongst this volume of what he refers to as interruption marketing. He has introduced the term **permission marketing** to suggest that the communications will be more effective if customers agree to receive more communications from the firm. This opt-in approach is preferable to an opt-out approach in which the customer would have to take the initiative in asking a firm not to send messages.

Privacy

There is a conflict between the interests of the firm and those of the customer in developing databases. In order to offer more individually targeted, personalised and relevant communications the firm requires ever more detailed and potentially sensitive information from the customer. However, the customer is reluctant to give firms personal information. They appreciate that certain firms, such as insurance companies might need the information in order to process a transaction, can be trusted and will respect local country privacy laws, such as the 1998 Data Protection Act in the UK. However, they have more concern over the possibility of the firms passing on the sensitive information deliberately or accidentally to other firms that will not be so scrupulous in its use. It is very easy to pass information electronically to other companies or countries.

SUMMARY

- Organisations must put customers and other stakeholders at the centre of their decision making, and, by integrating their marketing communications, ensure that, as far as possible, they receive consistent and coherent messages.

- With the increasing proliferation of marketing communications it is essential to assess the relative value of each tool when making marketing communications decisions.

- It is important to recognise that the tools must be carefully matched to the situation in which they are going to be used.

- It is also vital to ensure that internal staff and staff in the extended organisation (distributors, supply chain and partners) also receive effective communications, especially when the organisation is geographically spread.

- Winning new customers is extremely expensive and it is preferable, particularly in the B2B sector, to use communications to build long term relationships with customers.

- Relationship marketing involves integrating all aspects of marketing activity and, as part of this, developing marketing communications that are specific and therefore cost effective.

KEYWORDS

communications plan	internal communications network
corporate identity	noise
customer relationship management	permission marketing
data mining	promotion
differentiation	relationship marketing
integrated marketing communications	value proposition

| CASE STUDY | MyTravel |

UK travellers are becoming increasingly picky about where they go on holiday and how they get there. People are moving away from package holidays in favour of companies who deal in specialist breaks and low cost airlines, and are more willing to go on-line and sort things out for themselves. This is causing trouble for some in the travel industry.

MyTravel reported record losses of £911 million. Peter McHugh, their chief executive, admits that the company lost control of its UK operations. It had too many aeroplanes, cruise ships and beds which made its fixed costs too high. There were also suggestions that failing to get to grips with a new computer system had led to MyTravel mispricing holidays.

The group has made 3000 redundancies, and nine directors have left the company in the last year. McHugh intends to halve the chartered cruise fleet, cut the number of hotel beds, and reduce the number of aircraft it leases. He has made a number of non-core disposals, saying he intends to focus on core business in the UK and look after important markets in Scandinavia, the USA and Canada.

Despite this, McHugh predicts continuing losses next year, but asserts that the group have sufficient cash reserves to ride out the storm and predicts a return to profitability in 2005. Other analysts infer that the reason MyTravel survives is because the banks have lent them so much money that they can't afford to pull the plug.

McHugh believes that there is a lot of life left in the traditional package holiday and says that MyTravel's problems are financial and nothing to do with product quality. He feels the recipe for future success lies in a greater amount of flexibility in the business. However, some industry sources are not so sure.

MyTravel gained valuable breathing space with a £1.3 billion re-financing package in the summer, but a lot will depend on whether the restructuring plans are bold enough and the all important issue of whether customers will still have the confidence to book holidays with MyTravel for next summer, given the fragility of their finances.

Questions

1 What is needed to return MyTravel to profitability?

2 Prepare a list, with justification, of the areas where decisions are required in communications, distribution and relationship management to support this strategy.

3 Develop an innovative approach that might be taken to increase on-line sales revenue for MyTravel.

Source: Sue Marriott, Sheffield Hallam University

DISCUSSION QUESTIONS

1 Low cost airlines primarily use web based communications for promotion and selling tickets. What are the advantages and limitations of their approach and what arguments would you offer in support of using other forms of marketing communications?

2 As the marketing manager of a supplier of CRM systems, prepare an outline presentation for the CEO of a B2B supplier of office equipment, explaining the benefits of a CRM system and the change that the company would have to make in order for it to be successful.

3 Increasingly, the manufacturers of soft drinks and chocolate are using marketing campaigns in schools. This includes supplying equipment for schools in return for vouchers from proof of purchase of the items. What are the arguments for and against such campaigns?

4 As a company supplying complete, leading edge, IT business solutions for the finance sector, including hardware, software and support services in contracts worth up to US$100 million, identify the key communication activity that you might undertake to support the account management and sales teams.

5 As the marketing manager of an international charity, prepare a presentation to a group of fund raisers explaining the charity's decision to adopt a more professional approach to marketing communications, the consequences in terms of costs of the various activities undertaken and some ways in which innovative approaches might be used to increase donations.

REFERENCES

Chaffey, D. and Smith, P.R. (2001) *E-marketing Excellence*, Oxford: Butterworth-Heinemann.

Chaffey, D., Meyer, R., Johnston, K. and Ellis-Chadwick, F. (2003) *Internet Marketing: Strategy, Implementation and Practice*, Harlow: FT Prentice Hall.

Christy, R., Oliver, G. and Penn, J. (1996) 'Relationship marketing in consumer markets', *Journal of Marketing Management*, 12(1–3).

Davidson, H. (2002) *Committed Enterprise: How to Make Values and Visions Work*, Oxford: Butterworth-Heinemann.

Doole, I. and Lowe, R. (2004) *International Marketing Strategy: Analysis, Development and Implementation*. 4th edn, London: Thomson Learning.

Doyle, P. (2000) *Value-based Marketing: Marketing Strategies for Corporate Growth and Shareholder Value*, Chichester: John Wiley.

Fill, C. (1999) *Marketing Communications: Contexts, Contents and Strategies*, London: Prentice Hall.

Forsyth, R. (2001) 'Six major impediments to change and how to overcome them in CRM', *CRM Forum*, 11 June.

Fournier, S., Dobscha, S. and Divid, G.M. (1998) 'Preventing the premature death of relationship marketing', *Harvard Business Review*, January–February: 43–51.

Godin, S. (2002) *Permission Marketing: Turning Strangers into Friends and Friends into Customers*, New York: The Free Press.

Groonroos, C. (1994) 'From marketing mix to relationship marketing: Towards a paradigm shift', in *Marketing Management Decision*, 32(2): 4–20.

Groonroos, C. (1996) 'Relationship marketing strategic and tactical implications', *Marketing Management Decision*, 34(3).

Horovitz, J. (2000) 'Using information to bond customers', in Marchand, D. (ed.) *Competing With Information*, New York: Wiley.

Kotler, P. (2003) *Marketing Insights from A to Z: 80 Concepts Every Manager Needs to Know*, Chicester: Wiley.

O'Malley, L. (2003) 'Relationship marketing', in Hart, S. (ed.) *Marketing Changes*, London: Thomson Learning.

Payne, A., Christopher, M., Clark, M. and Peck, H. (1995) *Relationship Marketing for Competitive Advantage*, Oxford: Butterworth-Heinnemann.

Shrimp, T.A. (2003) *Advertising, Promotion*, 6th edn, Mason, OH: Thomson South-Western.

Wasserman, T., Khermouch, G. and Green, J. (2000) 'Mining everyones' business', *Brandweek*, 28 February: 36.

Wilson, R. and Gilligan, C. (2004) *Strategic Marketing Management*, 3rd edn, Oxford: Butterworth-Heinemann.

CHAPTER

11

ADDING STAKEHOLDER VALUE THROUGH THE EXTENDED ORGANISATION

Introduction

So far, in considering marketing mix decisions we have focused on the organisation's marketing proposition from the internal decision perspective (the product and service offer and price setting) and the external decision perspective (the communications and relationship building activity with customers). In this chapter we consider models for connecting the organisation to its market in order to maximise the impact of its activities. By market connectivity models we mean the various ways in which the organisation can collaborate with others in order to achieve more efficient supply chain contributions, more effective market entry into foreign markets and greater market presence in domestic markets than would be possible if working alone, by using the traditional methods of supplying markets through distributors, dealers and retailers.

Out of necessity, in today's markets organisations cannot be islands. In the previous chapter we emphasised the need to build relationships with customers, especially in B2B markets. However, many organisations need to go further and extend their market reach and presence by making connections, collaborating and working through networks and alliances in order to reduce the potential impact of competitive threats and, by offering comprehensive solutions rather than just individual products, adding value for a wider range of customers and so increasing the size of the overall potential market.

We have therefore set this chapter in the context of making decisions to maximise the marketing value and impact by exploring alternative routes to market and adopting different business models of collaborative working. The rationale is that through an extended organisation the impact and effectiveness can be increased beyond the boundaries of the organisation's directly owned assets and activities.

We first discuss the concept of the value chain and the decisions that are needed for an organisation to be an effective member of a supply chain by being able to contribute value to the chain and building and managing relationships with others that can offer complementary value adding activities.

We then discuss briefly the range of market connectivity models, including those that have a specific application for achieving market entry into international markets. Of particular interest in developing the new routes to market through the extended organisation are the flexible, responsive network marketing and alliances that are made possible by information and communications technology.

The chapter is completed by a discussion of the key decisions that are made by the organisation in formalising alliances, through taking equity stakes to create joint ventures and make acquisitions and mergers.

Learning objectives

By the end of this chapter the reader should be able to:

- Make value chain decisions and understand the key factors that should influence the decisions
- Assess distribution channel performance and evaluate alternative routes to market
- Define the market entry methods and appreciate how to select between the available options
- Examine the role of alliances and the creation of value through supply chain development and marketing partnerships

COMPETING THROUGH THE VALUE CHAIN

For most organisations the key determinant for a sustainable business model is an efficient and effective supply chain that harnesses the contributions from all the participating organisations.

The value chain concept

Porter (1985) proposed the **value chain concept** as a tool for breaking down the organisation's strategically significant activities into a series of elements that incur cost but also add value by contributing to the differentiation of the organisation's proposition. By working through the value chain contributions it is possible to assess the firm's capabilities in each area. It provides a framework, for example, for assessing 'make' or 'buy' decisions. The overall value proposition might be strengthened or weakened by a decision to outsource a component, such as manufacturing or the call service centre operation, to a specialist provider.

If the concept is applied to the complete **supply chain** of a product or service rather than an individual organisation, it is possible to assess the individual value contributions of different firms and decide whether to vertically integrate or dis-aggregate activities according to whether the overall benefits and value can be enhanced by integration or specialisation. As well as making strategic marketing decisions about the individual value contributions, the other important aspect is how effectively the members of the supply chain are able to co-operate to collect-ively remove cost and deliver a stronger value proposition to the final customer than a competing supply chain.

Challenge 11.1 shows a different form of piggybacking by small firms, who obtain value from the distribution networks of larger firms.

As supply chains have become better established, based on inter-dependency and greater trust between the participating organisations, so the supply chain becomes the competitive force rather than competing individual organisations. Even though the part of the supply chain that is most recognisable to the customer is the brand name owned by one lead firm, in practice the future success of that firm becomes increasingly dependent on the success of the other firms in the chain.

Close relationships between organisations are essential and are underpinned by efficient, effective information management and communications. Information technology is essential, therefore, as an enabler in the integrated value chain to remove transaction costs and improve communications.

Outsourcing decisions

Individual members of the supply chain must justify their role by cost effectively undertaking a series of activities that contribute value. Equally the internal functions of the organisation undertake a series of value adding activities that must be justified because they can also be outsourced to third parties or undertake the work themselves. In making **outsourcing** (make or buy) decisions there are some potential advantages and disadvantages to consider. Potential advantages of outsourcing include:

- lower cost
- use of focused, specialist suppliers
- reduced investment in facilities
- leveraging external expertise.

Potential disadvantages of outsourcing include:

- possible loss of control
- could be less responsive
- loss of intellectual property
- could create a competitor.

In international marketing a firm might enter a foreign market relying upon a local contractor to supply products or services, or might set up an assembly plant to assemble a finished product from components made in the domestic country. This may be useful in reducing costs but might also help to avoid tariff and non-tariff barriers.

CHALLENGE 11.1   Clustering for international success

In many countries there is a belief that smaller firms will be more successful if they overcome their resource limitations by forming clusters with industry leaders to compete for business overseas. The idea is for smaller firms to piggyback on the overseas distribution networks and marketing of the larger firms. Taiwanese manufacturers have used this strategy to form integrated supply chains to succeed internationally for some years, and have formed additional clusters in private education, in the automobile sector and the gas industry.

In Singapore a scheme called International Partners or iPartners has targets for the period 2004-2007 of securing

40 iPartner projects involving 160 companies to develop international business using clusters built around some larger firms.

Question Explain in detail how this type of clustering and collaboration might have benefits for the smaller firm. Could there be any benefits for larger firms?

Source: Ministry of Trade and Industry Singapore at http://www.mti.gov.sg/public/NWS/frm_NWS_Default.asp?sid=39&cid=1836 23 October 2003

The impact of technology as a supply chain enabler

Technology enabled supply chain management has helped firms to grow through exploiting market development opportunities, reducing costs by improving the efficiency of outsourcing, and enabling small firms to have similar competitive cost bases to large firms through **e-procurement**. It is vital that each part of the supply chain of the product maximises the added value and this is made possible by integrating the activities. A supply chain for a complex product might typically involve such distinctly different activities as design, manufacture of raw materials, component assembly, advertising, logistics and local servicing, and the most efficient members of the supply chain will increasingly be located around the world.

The internet has facilitated the change from paper- or person-based transactions to digital transactions, increasing the immediacy of communications. It has enabled firms to gain a much better picture worldwide of who supplies goods and services and to what specification. It has provided a better understanding of where costs are incurred in the value chain and therefore where cost savings can be made. Once set up, e-procurement can reduce operating costs and so savings can be made. Initially companies have focused upon the peripheral, non-core parts of the supply chain, such as buying stationery, office equipment and travel, but they are increasingly turning their attention to the core activities of buying raw materials, key components and services.

Whilst our comments so far have been on the enduring supply chain models with a high degree of trust and dependency between members, quite the opposite model can also apply. E-commerce allows procurement partnerships to be set up and dissolved instantly in real time. There is no lasting relationship, only a frequent opportunity to bid according to a particular specification, and win or lose potential orders. Suppliers and buyers need to have flexible, highly responsive systems and processes to manage the rapid changes that are necessary to survive in this type of market. Suppliers are in completely open competition with other firms from around the world and will only survive and grow if they have an appropriate management style and company culture.

Cost savings can be made in all areas of the supply chain, such as inventory reduction and just-in-time sourcing. Using this type of model a step change can be made in the quality of the offer, too. Amazon is able to offer 4.7 million books and music titles by quickly obtaining stocks held anywhere in the world, whereas an average bookstore might physically hold only 170 000 titles. On-line travel agents enable independent travellers to create an itinerary from thousands of travel suppliers and then make all the reservations with one 'click'.

In service call centres the cost of employing a person capable of dealing with service calls in India is about one tenth of the cost of employing a person in the UK for an equivalent level of performance. Very often service centre calls are routine and technology can be used to make further savings by replacing people based transactions with 'intelligent' computer based responses.

A supermarket extranet will allow hundreds of suppliers to have access to its data warehouse, so they will know how their particular product is selling in each individual store, and be able to manage the inventory system to ensure that the supermarket never runs out of stock.

MODELS OF MARKET CONNECTION

In international marketing the term **market entry** is used to explain the alternatives available to a firm first entering the market. In practice most of the methods can be used in domestic marketing and are not solely associated with initial market entry. As the firm develops, the market, technology and competitive conditions change, senior managers become more ambitious and customers want to buy products in different ways and in different locations, so the organisation may well adopt alternative **routes to market**.

For most organisations the conventional method of connecting with the market is through a sales force, supported possibly by dealers, distributors and retailers who stock and supply the consumers, and this is our starting point.

THE EVOLUTION OF DISTRIBUTION CHANNELS

The traditional routes to market, the **distribution channels**, are through the organisation's own sales force and through **intermediaries**, such as distributors, dealers and retailers. A frequent reassessment of the use of these routes is necessary, comparing the relative cost base and effectiveness of these and other methods of connecting with customers.

Sales force

There are certain situations, for example in pharmaceutical selling, where it is essential to have a directly controlled **sales force** that is capable of promoting the organisation's products and services, negotiating and securing business, and engaging in two way communications to keep customers and the organisation informed of developments. However, the cost of a sales force is high compared to telephone selling and direct marketing. Moreover, it is expensive to recruit and train highly effective sales people and demanding of management time to maintain sales force motivation. Consequently, where sales can be achieved by alternative routes to market many organisations have cut their sales force.

However, this is a symptom of a more serious problem. In many organisations there appears to be a lack of understanding of the relative roles of sales and marketing and insufficient co-ordination of the two activities into an integrated sales and marketing strategy.

Distribution through intermediaries

Intermediaries often provide the only point of personal contact for marketers but they can also fulfil many other roles too. However, the nature and value of their contribution varies considerably according to the context in which they are operating. Many organisations have already reviewed or are reviewing the traditional role of intermediaries and the value contributions of the intermediaries that they have, and, supported by advances in technology, they are assessing the potential benefits of new routes to market that are proving to be more appealing to customers. In addressing the decisions that need to be made, therefore, we first consider the traditional roles before highlighting the ways in which they have changed. Rosenbloom (2003) identified a number of key decision areas in channel management and these are shown in Figure 11.1.

The role of intermediaries

Wilson and Gilligan (2004) discuss the development of a suitable channel structure, how it should be designed and the role of intermediaries within it. The role of intermediaries is characterised by their ability to:

- Be part of the organisation's push strategy and make products available to customers when and where they want them.
- Reduce cost by efficiently performing distribution functions.
- Manage discrepancies between the quantities manufacturers want to supply and the quantities customers want to buy (break bulk).
- Offer a greater range from complementary product suppliers.
- Manage smaller transactions and local delivery.
- Provide customer service and build relationships.

Traditionally the view was that the manufacturer was best placed to supply the customer directly in the following situations:

- complex products with continuous development
- made to order products
- where a high level of service and support is required
- where there is a small customer base
- where the transactions are high volume or value
- where it is easy to cover the locations
- where shipments are large scale, planned and just-in-time
- where high level feedback is required.

FIGURE 11.1

Key decision areas in channel management
Source: Rosenbloom (2003)

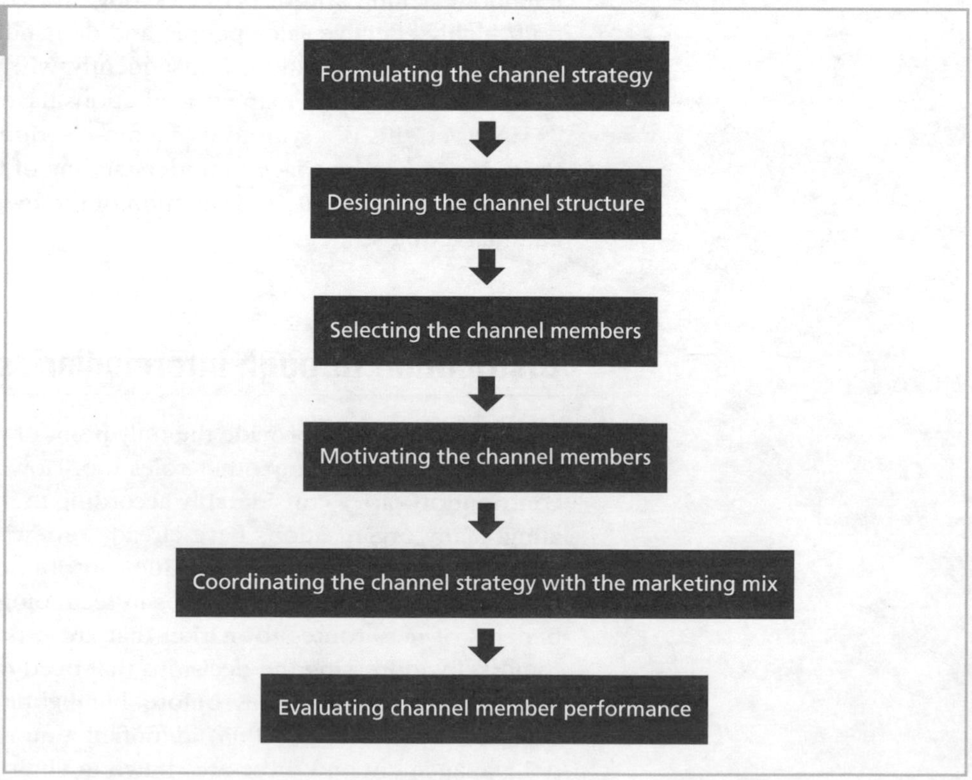

Formulating the channel strategy

Designing the channel structure

Selecting the channel members

Motivating the channel members

Coordinating the channel strategy with the marketing mix

Evaluating channel member performance

Intermediaries are best placed to deal with:

- a simple product with basic service levels
- standard stocked lines
- a large customer base
- smaller customers
- markets that are geographically difficult to cover
- small random deliveries from stock
- low level feedback.

The intermediary role typically involves a number of responsibilities including:

- collection of information
- promotion of the products
- financing of inventories
- delivery and physical transfer
- a degree of risk sharing
- an ordering function.

A major problem for any organisation is motivating and managing the intermediaries, as it makes huge demands on management time. The organisation must provide channel leadership in order to direct and influence the overall channel performance, build the channel as a competing system by encouraging co-operation between intermediaries that in other circumstances might be competing, and manage channel conflicts by identifying and resolving the sources of conflict.

It is necessary to select channel members, evaluate them according to pre-set criteria, such as service levels, company objectives and financial stability, drop them if they under-perform and replace them with others. Where appropriate, areas and product ranges must be allocated and the role of the intermediaries defined in terms of inventory, selling, marketing, invoicing, support services, and so on.

Managing intermediaries in foreign markets is particularly problematic, given the differences in legal frameworks, culture, language, service expectations and communication distances that make motivation, management and development particularly problematic.

In thinking about all these management responsibilities it becomes obvious why organisations might be tempted to remove intermediaries, shorten the distribution channels and, using technology support, carry out the roles themselves. Figure 11.2 poses some of the questions that should be considered when making routes to market decisions.

FIGURE 11.2
 	
Routes to market decisions
	Q How well is the channel performing compared with the competition?
	Q Which channel is likely to be the strongest in the future?
	Q What will be the future key roles of the channel?
	Q How well is the channel currently performing these roles?
	Q What are the development implications of this:
	  – for the organisation
	  – for the channel members

Disintermediation and re-intermediation

The internet offers the possibility for an organisation to efficiently handle many more transactions than was previously possible. An evaluation of the contribution of the channel might lead to a reassessment of the value of the intermediary and a decision to remove the intermediary. The benefits to the organisation are the removal of channel infrastructure costs and intermediary margins and the opportunity to develop a direct relationship with the final customer. 'Cutting out the middleman' is described as **disintermediation**. Chaffey *et al*. (2003) observe that at the start of the e-business boom it was expected that there would be widespread disintermediation. In some sectors there has been disintermediation but in others the results have been disappointing, with the marketing organisation incurring substantial additional IT, order management and logistics costs more than offsetting the forecasted savings. Other sectors have continued without significant restructuring. In practice it seems that in many sectors customers still need additional help in selecting products and services.

The counter-change to disintermediation is **re-intermediation** and the creation of new firms to provide the advice in a different form. Whilst many financial services products lend themselves to on-line selling, it is a laborious task to compare the many offerings from competing companies. Consequently many brokers have set up websites such as www.charcolonline.com, www.trustnet.com and www.moneyextra.com to allow customers to compare many different financial product offerings.

In many sectors there are now intermediary websites that enable potential customers to compare products for the home, holidays and travel. Of course this means that the internet marketer must ensure that they are represented on key sites where there are high volumes of potential customers, and ensure that they are offering competitive prices.

Alternatively the marketer might set up his own intermediary to compete with the existing intermediaries, and this is referred to as **countermediation**. A group of airlines set up www.opodo.com as an alternative to www.expedia.com to offer airline tickets and Thomson Travel Group set up www.latedeals.com to compete with www.lastminute.com for late holiday bookings.

Challenge 11.2 shows an interesting marketing collaboration which appears to have significant potential if it is also linked to new routes to market.

Retailing

Although it is not our intention to discuss retailing in detail it is worthwhile to emphasise that retailing, as a service business, follows many of the trends of other service businesses, discussed in Chapter 9. There is an increasing concentration of retailers, as the most successful, such as Wal-Mart and Tesco, seek to continually add customer value through enhanced services, and to reduce costs through improvements in the supply chain costs and logistics.

Conventional retailing is coming under some pressure from the online e-business retailers and, again, the more successful are responding by improving the performance of their on-line stores. Re-intermediation and disintermediation are features of retailing in many different sectors and this appears to be where the most innovation is occurring.

MARKET ENTRY DECISIONS

The international market entry options are shown in Figure 11.3, and cover a span of market involvement from virtually zero, when the firm merely makes the products available for others to market but effectively does no marketing itself, to businesses that have a huge presence and totally control every aspect of their operation worldwide. These options include those that are particularly relevant to international markets, but most of the methods are also used in domestic markets. Doole and Lowe (2004) provide a fuller account of international market entry.

The market entry decision is taken within the firm and is determined to a large extent by the firm's objectives, attitudes and capabilities. In order to select an appropriate and potentially successful market entry method, it is necessary to consider a number of criteria, including:

CHALLENGE 11.2   **Alliance marketing – cool frozen foods?**

The music industry is always trying to find ways of linking music to brands in order to increase revenues. Warner Music is seeking to take this one stage further by identifying fmcg companies such as Proctor & Gamble, with brands ranging from drinks, personal hygiene, cosmetics to frozen food, that are in need of an injection of 'cool and hip' and suggesting ways in which they could make the brand more fashionable by creating a marketing alliance with certain artists or types of music. This follows on from research that suggests consumers are increasingly making purchasing decisions based on what the products – even grocery items – say about their own lifestyle.

Compilation or single artist CDs, with the brand in the title, might be sold in the normal way through record retailers. The artists would be sponsored and shown publicly using the product. Warner, part of AOL Time Warner, which also owns film companies Warner Brothers and New Line Cinema and other publishing and media interests such as Time Inc., IPC Media and AOL's internet distribution arm, offers seemingly endless possibilities using the full range of promotion tools and routes to market. A further advantage of this link is that the music business is multi-national and for some artists, global, offering the possibility of increasing international market development for the brands.

Question Is this an opportunity to make a fast buck for Warner or do you think this kind of collaboration in distribution is a glimpse into the future?

Source: adapted from Hemsley, S., 'Even cooler frozen food, *Financial Times*, 18 November 2003

FIGURE 11.3

Market entry options
Source: Doole and Lowe (2004)

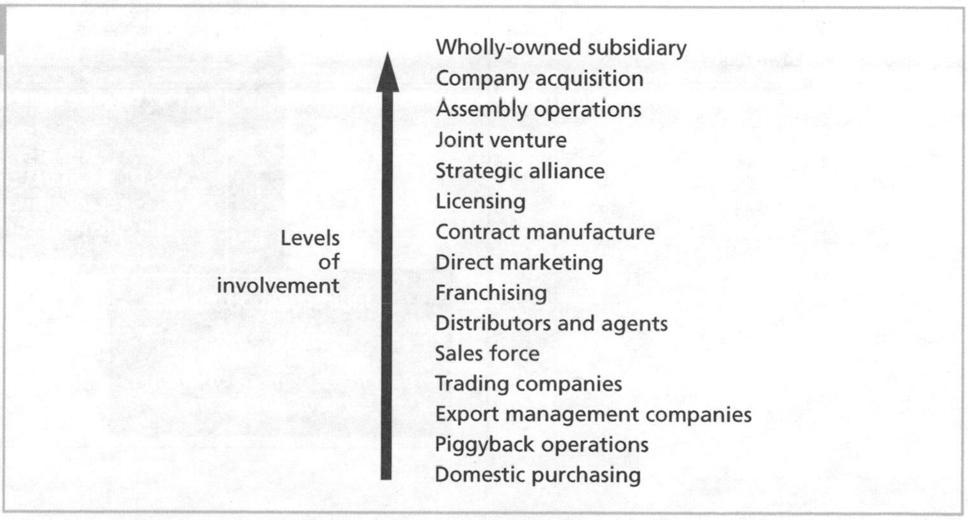

Levels of involvement

Wholly-owned subsidiary
Company acquisition
Assembly operations
Joint venture
Strategic alliance
Licensing
Contract manufacture
Direct marketing
Franchising
Distributors and agents
Sales force
Trading companies
Export management companies
Piggyback operations
Domestic purchasing

- The company objectives and expectations relating to the size and value of anticipated business.
- The size and financial resources of the company.
- The company's existing market involvement.
- The skill and abilities of the company management and their attitude towards the company's market expansion.
- The nature and power of the competition within the market.
- The nature of existing and future barriers to entry for new entrants.
- The nature of the product itself, particularly any areas of competitive advantage, such as intellectual property protection.
- The timing of the move in relation to new markets and new competitive situations.

RISK AND CONTROL IN MARKET ENTRY

We referred earlier to the fact that one of the most important differences between the methods is the firm's level of involvement. This has significant implications for the firm in terms of the levels of control and risk that result, and is shown diagrammatically in Figure 11.4. The range of risks that face firms is most acute in less developed countries where the environment and market are less stable and where conventional business practice is less established. The diagram suggests that associated with higher levels of involvement is not only greater potential for control, but also higher potential risk, usually due to the high cost of investment.

Of course, in an undeveloped market the potential return may be higher too. Partnerships, in the form of **joint ventures** and **strategic alliances**, offer the apparent advantage of entering growth markets more effectively and achieving higher levels of control at lower levels of risk and cost, provided that there is a

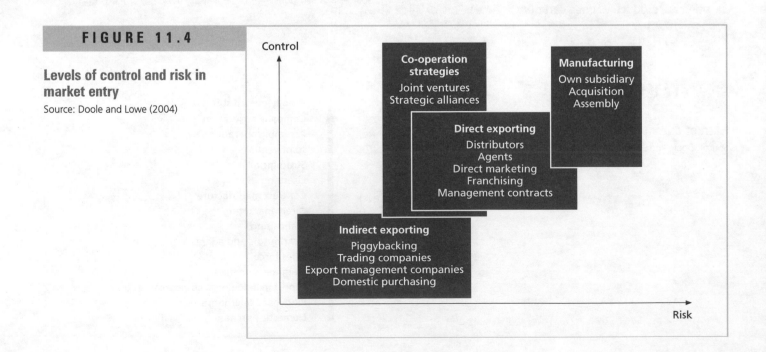

FIGURE 11.4

Levels of control and risk in market entry

Source: Doole and Lowe (2004)

high degree of co-operation between companies and that their individual objectives are not incompatible.

In making a decision on market entry, therefore, the most fundamental questions that the firm must answer are:

- What level of control over our business do we require?
- What level of risk are we willing to take?
- What cost can we afford to bear in making market connections?

In answering these questions it is important to consider not only the level of control, risk and cost, but also the relative importance that the firm might place upon the different elements of its marketing activity. For example, lack of control over certain aspects of the marketing process, such as after sales servicing, may affect the reputation and image of a company or brand because consumers frequently blame the marketer rather than the distributor or retailer for the poor quality of after sales service they have received.

Marketing indirectly to customers

For firms that have little inclination or few resources for marketing, the simplest and lowest cost method of market entry is for them to have their products sold by others. This approach is often adopted by community based enterprises that may be financed from public sector sources or through sponsorship. Firms that are component suppliers or service providers for just one or two major firms might do little marketing even though their products may be used worldwide. The objective of firms that use this method of entry may be to benefit from the opportunities that arise without incurring any expense, simply to sell off excess capacity with the least possible inconvenience, especially into foreign markets. Firms such as these often withdraw from this activity as soon as their sales into the home market improve. Whilst indirect exporting has the advantage of the least cost and risk of any entry method, it allows the firm little control over how, when, where and by whom the products are sold. In some cases, for example, a domestic company may even be unaware that its products are being exported, and equally unaware when demand in foreign markets dries up.

Marketing directly to customers

If a company wishes to have more control over its marketing, or to secure a more permanent long term place in markets, it must become more proactive, through becoming directly involved in the process of marketing and selling. This requires definite commitment from the company and takes the form of investment in the marketing operations through the allocation of time and resources. The traditional direct market connection in domestic markets and in exporting to international markets is through sales agents, distributors, dealers and retailers, as discussed earlier in this chapter.

The benefits over marketing indirectly are that the proactive approach makes it easier to exert more influence over the activities, resulting in a number of specific advantages for marketing firms such as greater control over the selection of market segments, greater control over the elements of the marketing mix, improved feedback about the performance of individual products, changing situations in individual markets and competitor activity, and the opportunity to build up expertise in marketing.

The disadvantages of marketing directly are that the direct investment necessary is considerable because the whole of the marketing, distribution and administration costs will have to be borne by the company. In taking this decision, the company must be quite sure that the costs can be justified in the light of the market opportunities identified.

There are ways of achieving high levels of control of the marketing strategy and still controlling costs. Direct marketing, franchising and licensing can be at 'arm's length' from the market, as market involvement is still limited. More information collection, analysis and evaluation is needed to ensure that marketers understand the subtle changes in local markets and are able to respond. All three market entry strategies require the company to develop empathy with their customers in the local markets and modify their offerings accordingly. In each case, for example, it is essential to be sensitive to the local culture and legislation.

Direct marketing

Direct marketing is being used in many more situations, both domestic and international, mainly because of the opportunities that come from the internet to develop more interesting business models and achieve greater interactivity through websites. This interactivity does allow e-business marketers to be more in tune with the market than they used to be, provided they are able to interpret the information they receive.

Franchising

Franchising is a way of exploiting a successful business formula with considerable benefits to the franchisor and franchisee (a tried and trusted formula). Spotlight 11.1 is an example of how franchising, in this case Subway, works for the franchisee.

Whilst it does appear to be a low risk method of setting up a business for the franchisee and a route to growth for the franchisor it is not without risks for each. Some franchisors have been criticised for being too strict in their interpretation of the business model and locating franchises too close to each other, causing cannibalisation, whilst franchisees need to be controlled if they try to move too far away from the model.

Licensing

Licensing has been used very effectively by a variety of organisations to exploit creative and technological ideas, including media, sports and technology businesses. There are again very obvious advantages of low outlay, but again it is often difficult to control the licensee and financial damage, or damage to the company's reputation or image, can result.

Investment in new ventures for new market segments

Having so far considered market entry strategies that are based on the development, manufacture and supply of product from the firm's existing operations, we now turn our attention to strategies that involve significant investment in new ventures to connect with new market segments.

At some point in its development, a stage is reached when the pressure increases on a firm to make a substantial commitment to exploit the opportunities in a new business sector, country or region in the form of new investment in its route to market. Some of the reasons why a firm might start producing in one or more of its international markets are:

- **To gain new business.** Local production demonstrates strong commitment and is the best way to persuade customers to change suppliers, particularly in industrial markets where service and reliability are often the main factors when making purchasing decisions.

- **To defend existing business.** Imports to a number of countries are still subject to tariff and non-tariff barriers and, as their sales increase, so firms become more vulnerable to locally produced competitive products.

- **To move with an established customer.** Component suppliers often set up their local subsidiaries in order to retain their existing business, compete with local component makers and benefit from increased sales.

- **To save costs.** By locating production facilities overseas, costs can be saved in a variety of areas such as labour, raw materials and transport.

- **To avoid government restrictions** that might be in force to restrict imports of certain goods.

It is possible to avoid the commitment and risk of a fully owned operation abroad by contracting out the manufacturing or service delivery. Even if a manufacturer decides to make the components in the domestic plant, there can be some advantages to having an assembly plant in a host country.

SPOTLIGHT 11.1   Subway franchisee in Australia

Greg Katsap operates one of the 534 Subway stores that have opened in Australia since 1987. Kapsap, 28, resigned as an IT manager and opened his outlet in March 2003. As people are becoming more conscious about what they eat, Subway seemed a good franchise with a ready made market with growth potential, stressing that its food is low in fat, with the menu featuring a choice of breads, hot and cold meats, vegetarian and seafood fillings. His store employs 12 people and serves between 1400 and 2000 customers per week.

Katsap spent some time number crunching before he decided to go ahead, but is happy with his decision despite the long hours and stress of running a business. Katsap believes he can make a lot of money – he is already planning his second store with Subway and is expecting to add more, hoping to be able to semi-retire at an early age.

New ventures are more likely to succeed if they are a franchise, because the brand, business model and plan are established. However, the costs of franchising can be high. Subway franchisees pay a one off US$12 500 and an 8 per cent weekly royalty on turnover, and the cost of designing and equipping a store is US$240 000. Subway provides two weeks training before the store is opened for business and ongoing support. Although Subway would not make promises on turnover, Katsap found them keen to help him succeed, because it would make more money for them. He was also able to talk to existing operators in order to get an idea of what was possible.

There are some bad days. He has noticed that if it is raining it will be a terrible day. Sales improve substantially on fine days!

Question What are the advantages and disadvantages of franchising and being a franchisee?

Source: Subway

Source: adapted from: Black, Anthony, 'Greg takes a subway ride', *Sunday Herald Sun* (Melbourne, Australia) 19 October 2003

For most multi-nationals operating a global or multi-domestic strategy, however, there is a requirement to demonstrate that they have a permanent presence in all their major markets. The actual form of their operations in each market is likely to vary considerably from country to country, with the largest multi-national companies operating many market entry variants depending on the particular situation.

For most companies the cost of setting up an overseas manufacturing operation to exploit international markets is initially much higher than expanding the domestic plant by an equivalent amount. Whilst the equipment costs are likely to be similar, and other costs such as labour, land purchase and building may even be cheaper, it is the cost involved in transferring technology, skills and knowledge which normally proves to be expensive and is often underestimated. Cultural differences, too, can lead to start up and management problems even for very experienced management.

MARKET ENTRY BASED ON PARTNERSHIP

When we look back at this period in history there is a strong possibility that the most significant long term change that will have taken place in marketing decision making will be increased collaboration between organisations in gaining market entry and building the supporting value chain. It is very possible that this will be the most significant consequence of the information technology revolution.

In response to the changing market environment, Miles and Snow (1984) predicted the increasing vertical disaggregation of business functions, with activities such as manufacturing, research and development and distribution being undertaken by separate organisations. Various terms, such as partnerships, alliances and marketing networks, have been applied to describe the resulting strategic collaborations that ensure that these groups of independent organisations add value for all their stakeholders through effective and efficient co-operation.

The move to increased strategic marketing collaboration is being accelerated by the globalisation of world markets that require marketers to make their products and services available globally; the change in the boundaries between markets, with the result that organisations in those markets need to acquire new skills and capabilities; and the desire amongst customers to have solutions rather than individual products and services, which requires offers to be made from new combinations of products and services.

The whole purpose of these collaborative methods of working is to enable the organisations in the form of a supply chain to respond quickly and flexibly to the new opportunities emerging, not only to achieve first mover advantage but also to offer a cost effective solution for the customer.

Whilst we tend to focus on collaborative working to market products and services, place marketing, illustrated in Spotlight 11.2, is even more dependent on collaborative working, vision and clear leadership.

Of course, as we have discussed earlier, it is also important to avoid being involved in products, services and processes that are becoming obsolete and thus draining value from both customers and the organisations. This is particularly important, given that the more complex the industry the more difficult it is for the organisation to be 'leading edge' in each of its activities, given the high investment needed in R&D.

Throughout this chapter we have emphasised the importance of collaboration in the value chain and we now turn to more strategic partnerships in order to leverage value from the extended organisation. These strategies fall into two categories.

- Limited life collaborations, including marketing networks and strategic alliances.
- Equity based collaborations, including joint ventures, mergers and acquisitions and reciprocal share holdings.

SPOTLIGHT 11.2   Ken Livingstone improving the image of London

Along with over 15 million UK tourists, 12.65 million overseas tourists are predicted to visit London in 2004. This compares with 9 million foreign tourists to Paris, 5 million to Amsterdam, 3.9 million to Rome and 3.5 million to Dublin. It represents a 5.9 per cent increase on 2003. In 2003 worldwide international arrivals fell by 1.2 per cent, the biggest ever drop, attributed to a drop in visits to the USA and Asia because of Sars and post-Iraq security fears. However, during this period London's share of overseas visits increased from 1.65 per cent to 1.72 per cent, the first rise in 10 years. Overseas visitors are expected to spend £6.25 billion.

London has benefited from its marketing activity, with Lonely Planet describing it as 'being back in the spotlight and one of the most dynamic hubs on earth'. However, tourists can be fickle. Too many people wanting to go to the same place, congestion and poor travel infrastructure lead to frustration and disappointment, and can deter future visits. Despite the development of new attractions, visitors tend to visit the main sites in the centre; 4.6 million visited the most popular London attractions, the British Museum and Tate Modern, and 4.1 million visited the National Gallery and the British Airways London Eye.

Co-ordination of many people and organisations is vital to tackle the problems that may deter visitors and the mayor might be crucial in this. Rudy Giuliani, the former mayor of New York, was credited with cleaning up crime and making the city a better and safer place for people to live and visit.

The mayor of London, Ken Livingstone, has made considerable efforts to tackle two of the main problems in London – traffic congestion in the centre and the poor state of the Underground trains. Livingstone introduced congestion charges for traffic entering the central zone and this has successfully reduced traffic, but not without criticism, for example, from depart-

Mayor of London
Source: M. and C. Saatchi

ment store owners in Oxford Street, who have complained of reduced sales. He has had a turbulent relationship with the governing UK Labour party, but has the popular support of the London electorate. His bigger challenge throughout his term as mayor has been to persuade the government to accelerate the modernisation of the Underground trains, but this has proved more difficult and tourists will have to wait a long time before this problem is solved.

Question What are the principal ways of making a city more attractive to visitors, how can collaboration between suppliers help and what should the role of the mayor be in achieving success?

Mayor of London
Source: M. and C. Saatchi

Source: adapted from various public sources

LIMITED LIFE COLLABORATIONS

The types of marketing networks

Marketing networks have existed for a long time but, facilitated by advances in technology, many more different types are emerging. Researchers have investigated the various types of marketing networks and have attempted to explain the nature of them. Hooley *et al*. (2004) summarise the alternative approaches including:

- *The hollow network* co-ordinates but is dependent on many other organisations that satisfy customer needs. They are often described as brokers or agencies.

- *The flexible network* tends to be based on inter-organisation links that are long term but flexible. Many pharmaceutical companies have links with entrepreneurial biotechnology firms.

- *The value added network* is based on the core organisation maintaining key functions or operations internally, for example, design, development and marketing but outsourcing many value adding activities.

- *The virtual network* is a more stable network of organisations, such as Hewlett-Packard and Motorola, that use long term partnerships to meet the needs of different markets using changing technology.

When making decisions to collaborate, all the organisations taking part must benefit and see a significant new opportunity as in the case discussed in Challenge 11.3.

The participants must also be satisfied with the balance between potential returns and the risks associated with the collaborative venture, and accept that the reason for its formation is that neither partner has the necessary technology, marketing financial or management capability to run it alone. The advantages of collaboration might include some of the following:

- The reduction or spreading of the market and product risk.

- The potential synergy of the combined skills and capabilities of the partners and the ability to leverage their combined learning.

- Greater ability to deliver the organisation's objectives.

- The ability to fill gaps that either partner might have in resources and skills.

- Protection separately for each partner's corporate identity.

CHALLENGE 11.3   **Publishing alliance to exploit ophthalmology opportunity**

China has almost 20 per cent of the world's blind population and a backlog of cataract cases that exceeds 2 million, and there is a huge demand for high quality, in depth information on the latest global innovations in eye care. It is for this reason that Advanstar Healthcare Communications, part of one of the largest trade magazine publishers in the USA, formed an alliance with eSinoMed Ltd, a leading provider of global medical intelligence to the mainland Chinese market, to publish *Ophthalmology Times China*, specifically for the

Chinese market, where there are 22 000 ophthalmologists. It will be backed up by a dedicated website.

Question How might the two companies secure the maximum benefits from this arrangement?

Source: adapted from Advanstar Healthcare Communications and eSinoMed announce alliance to launch *Ophthalmology Times China*, PR Newswire, 23 January 2002

There are, however, a number of disadvantages too, including:

- The possible decline of interest by one partner.
- A conflict of interests between the activities included in the collaboration and in the separate corporate activities.
- Cultural differences between the two organisations' managements.
- Lack of clear decision making, where ownership is shared.
- Changes in the individual strategic requirements of the partners.
- The difficulties of managing a collaborative venture that might be viewed critically by the 'parents'.
- Giving away intellectual property, commercial secrets and competitive advantage.

Of these considerations, the key variables that need to be taken into account when making marketing decisions about the nature of the strategic collaboration are the purpose of the collaboration, the closeness of the relationship and the nature of the environment (Hooley *et al*., 2004).

The purpose of the collaboration

There are a number of reasons for collaborations that cover all the functions of the business including R&D, manufacturing, operations, finance and marketing. Collaborative arrangements are used as key mechanisms to achieve global presence and reach. Moreover, because of political decisions and legal restrictions, collaborative arrangements may be essential and in some cases the only alternative.

The closeness of the inter-organisation relationship

The closeness and length of the relationship between partners depends on the purpose and situation. An expedient, short period, essentially arm's length collaboration might be used for the purpose of completing a specific marketing transaction, for example, a civil engineering project, or managing periods of market turbulence. The collaboration must be capable of being set up, altered and dissolved quickly.

By contrast, a very close collaboration is possible in a more stable market environment, where customers can benefit from long term relationships.

Strategic alliances

Whilst all market entry methods essentially involve alliances of some kind, during the 1980s the term strategic alliance started to be used, without being precisely defined, to cover a variety of contractual arrangements which are intended to be strategically beneficial to both parties but cannot be defined as clearly as licensing or joint ventures. Alliances usually involve collaboration between certain parts of two or more organisations for a specific and usually limited purpose and thus are usually less risky than collaborations between complete companies.

Bronder and Pritzl (1992) define strategic alliances in terms of at least two companies combining value chain activities for the purpose of competitive advantage, and offer a number of reasons why they might be set up, including:

- technology swaps
- R&D exchanges
- distribution relationships
- marketing relationships
- manufacturer–supplier relationships
- cross-licensing.

Perhaps one of the most significant aspects of strategic alliances has been that they have frequently involved co-operation between partners who might in other circumstances be competitors.

There are a number of driving forces for the formation and operation of strategic alliances.

- *Insufficient resources*: the central argument is that no organisation alone has sufficient resources to realise the full global potential of its existing and, particularly, its new products. Equally, if it fails to satisfy all the markets which demand these products, competitors will exploit the opportunities which arise and become stronger. In order to remain competitive, powerful and independent companies need to co-operate.

- *The pace of innovation and market diffusion*: the rate of change of technology and consequent shorter product life cycles mean that new products must be exploited quickly by effective diffusion out into the market. This requires not only effective promotion and efficient physical distribution, but also good channel management, especially when other members of the channel are powerful.

- *High research and development costs*: as technology becomes more complex and genuinely new products become rarer, so the costs of R&D become higher. There are many examples of alliances in technology areas to generate new technological opportunities but, of course, partner companies in the strategic alliance then need to achieve higher sales levels of the product.

- *Concentration of firms in mature industries*: many industries have used alliances to manage the problem of excess production capacity in mature markets. There have been a number of alliances in the car and airline industries, some of which have lead ultimately to full joint ventures or takeovers.

- *Government co-operation*: as the trend towards regionalisation continues, so governments are more prepared to co-operate on high cost projects rather than try to go it alone. There have been a number of alliances in Europe – for example, the European airbus has been developed to challenge Boeing, and the Eurofighter aircraft project has been developed by Britain, Germany, Italy and Spain.

- *Self-protection*: a number of alliances have been formed in the belief that they might afford protection against competition in the form of individual companies or newly formed alliances. This is particularly the case in the emerging global high technology sectors such as information technology, telecommunications, media and entertainment.

- *Market access*: strategic alliances have been used by companies to gain access to difficult markets, for example, a number of US and European companies have formed alliances with local companies to enter the Japanese market.

A number of research studies (e.g. Bonder and Pritzl, 1992; Devlin and Blackley 1988) have investigated good practice in the formation of alliances, and from these it is possible to conclude that:

- Two thirds of alliances experience severe leadership and financing problems during the first two years.

- There is a need to analyse the situation, identify the opportunities for co-operation and evaluate shareholder contributions.

- There needs to be a clear understanding of whether the alliance has been formed as a short term stop gap or as a long term strategy. It is, therefore, important that each partner understands the other's motivations and objectives, as the alliance might expose a weakness in one partner which the other might later exploit.

- It is apparent that many strategic alliances are a step towards a more permanent relationship, but the consequences of a potential break up must always be borne in mind when setting up the alliance.

EQUITY BASED COLLABORATIONS

We now turn to collaborations in which organisations take an equity stake in another organisation, through joint ventures, mergers, acquisitions and shareholdings. We accept that many acquisitions are by no means collaborative, but it is useful to consider them at this point. Whilst evaluation and planning are critical for the success of collaborations, the form of collaboration may be dictated by the context in which the decisions are made, too often arrangements are made by organisations for expediency, in desperation, to reverse poor performance or out of fear of the unknown.

In practice Doyle (2000) suggests that whilst there have been some successes, many collaborations fail and are dissolved, many more would not stand up to a rigorous post-collaboration evaluation and still more are not perceived by their managers to be delivering the anticipated synergies that were predicted prior to setting up the collaborative arrangement. Bleeke and Ernst (1993) note that:

- Acquisitions and alliances create shareholder value at roughly the same rate.

- Whilst acquisitions are best suited to core businesses and existing geographic areas, alliances are more effective for related business and new international markets.

- Alliances between strong and weak partners rarely work because the dominant partner puts its own interests above those of the alliance.

- Alliances need autonomy to make their own decisions.

Alliances and joint ventures have a limited life, with 75 per cent of the alliances that are terminated acquired by one partner

Given these concerns it is useful to reflect on the potential of these organisational forms to add value for the organisation over and above what it could achieve working independently by collaborating simply at arm's length, and also to assess the risks associated with these forms that might lead to erosion of value for all stakeholders.

Joint ventures

Joint ventures occur when a company decides that shared ownership of a specially set up new company for marketing and/or manufacturing is the most appropriate method of targeting a new customer segment, for example, international market entry. It is usually based on the premise that two or more companies can contribute complementary expertise or resources to the joint company which, as a result, will have a unique competitive advantage to exploit.

Whilst contributing complementary expertise might be a significant feature of other entry methods, such as licensing, the difference with joint ventures is that each company takes an equity stake in the newly formed firm. The stake taken by one company might be as low as 10 per cent, but this still gives them a voice in the management of the joint venture.

There are a number of reasons given for setting up joint ventures. These include:

- Restrictions on foreign ownership in a number of countries.
- Partners in the host country can increase the speed of market entry when good business and government contacts are essential for success.
- Complementary technology or management skills provided by the partners can lead to new opportunities in existing sectors, such as in multimedia.
- Global operations in R&D and production are prohibitively expensive, but necessary to achieve competitive advantage.

The main advantages to companies entering joint ventures are that, first, they have more direct participation in the local market, and thus gain a better understanding of how it works; second, they should be better able to finance and profit from their activities; and third, they are able to exert greater control over the operation of the joint venture.

There are, however, some significant disadvantages of joint ventures as a market entry method. As joint venture companies involve joint ownership, there are often differences in the aims and objectives of the participating companies which can

---

CHALLENGE 11.4   Venture break up – storm in a teacup?

For 40 years BM Khaitan and George Williamson (Assam) have participated in an Indian–British partnership that has given them a powerful position in the industry and helped them to counter competition from cheaper foreign teas. In 2001 the joint venture was disbanded with BM Khaitan buying out the 26.5 per cent stake held by George Williamson in Williamson Magor, the tea planter, while Williamson took full control of its 17 tea gardens in North East India, which yield 20 million kg of quality tea per annum.

There were a number of reasons for the termination of the partnership. Changes in the law allowed foreign firms to take 100 per cent ownership of Indian firms and, seizing the opportunities from low share valuations, a number of foreign companies were taking the opportunity to buy shares of their Indian listed affiliates, in order to gain greater control of brands and products, especially as the economic situation improved.

Williamson was also concerned about BM Khaitan's diversification. In the mid-1990s the firm had paid an inflated price for the Ever Ready battery unit of Union Carbide and the high interest payments it had to make took potential investment from the tea business. The terms of the partnership restricted it to exporting to the UK but, under pressure from the Indian government, BM Khaitan wanted to exploit other markets in Iran, Iraq, Russia and the USA.

BM Khaitan also wanted to grow less Darjeeling, the champagne of tea, and more Assam tea. Assam tea bushes are ready for picking in half the seven years of Darjeeling. The company was also seeking to expand by buying brands in the US market. Its main Indian rival, Tata Tea, had bought the UK's Tetley Tea and Hindustan Lever, the Indian subsidiary of Unilever. By contrast, Williamson intended to acquire more tea gardens in India with the intention of continuing to export primarily to the UK.

Question   Is there a life cycle for joint ventures and alliances and, if so, what do you believe could actually be the cause of the ending of this partnership?

Source: adapted from 'Foreign groups move to assert control over Indian alliances', *Financial Times*, 28 June 2001

cause disagreements over the strategies they adopted. Challenge 11.4 shows the reasons why a joint venture in the tea market ended.

If ownership is evenly divided between the participant firms, these disagreements can often lead to delays and failure to develop clear policies. In other joint ventures the greater motivation of one partner rather than another, particularly if they have a greater equity stake, can lead to them becoming dominant and the other partner becoming resentful.

There are many examples of the local partner turning out to be a liability, either because of incompetent management, corruption or other unethical behaviour, which can reflect on the partner. The other disadvantage of this form of market entry compared to, for example, licensing or the use of agents, is that a substantial commitment of investment of capital and management resources must be made in order to ensure success. Many companies would argue that the demands on management time might be even greater for a joint venture than for a directly owned subsidiary because of the need to educate, negotiate and agree with the partner many of the operational details of the joint venture.

Some experts recommend that a joint venture should be used by companies to extend their capabilities rather than merely exploit existing advantages and is not recommended if there are likely to be conflicts of interest between partners.

Company acquisitions and mergers

Acquisitions and mergers play a key role for many multi-national firms in achieving globalisation because:

■ They are perceived to be a faster way to penetrate a market. Developing new products, IP and brands can take years, and some companies have simply failed to create an innovative, internal culture, which is essential to do this.

■ For many Western companies, particularly those from the UK and USA, the considerable pressure to produce short term profits means that speed of market entry is essential and this can be achieved by acquiring an existing company in the market. By contrast, building an effective distribution channel can take years, whereas acquisition can take months.

■ Acquisition gives immediate access to a trained labour force, existing customer and supplier contacts, recognised brands, an established distribution network and an immediate source of revenue.

■ Often acquisition means removing a major competitor from the market, thus enabling prices to be increased.

In certain situations acquisition is the only route into a market. This is the case with previously state owned utilities. By 2003 nine out of 23 water companies in the UK were foreign owned by RWE (Germany), Suez, Vivendi and Bouygues (France), Union Fenosa (Spain) and YTL (Malaysia).

An acquisition strategy is based upon the assumption that companies for potential acquisition will be available, but if the choice of companies is limited, the decision may be taken on the basis of expediency rather than suitability. The belief that acquisitions will be a time saving alternative to waiting for organic growth to take effect may prove to be untrue in practice. It can take a considerable amount of time to search and evaluate possible acquisition targets, engage in protracted negotiations and then integrate the acquired company into the existing organisation structure.

Another disadvantage of acquisition is that the acquiring company might take over a demotivated labour force, a poor image and reputation, and out of date products and processes. All of these problems can prove costly and time consuming to overcome. However, when done well, acquisition can be an extremely effective method of developing a global business.

Throughout the last few years there has been considerable debate about acquisition and mergers as a method of achieving rapid expansion. The rationale that is used for acquisition is that an ineffective company can be purchased by a more effective company, which will be able, first, to reduce costs; second, to improve performance through applying better management skills and techniques; and third, to build upon the synergy between the two companies and so achieve better results.

In practice Doyle (2000) notes that the failure rate of acquisitions is high, given that usually too much is paid for the company being acquired. Premiums paid by acquiring companies are often 50 per cent above the company's pre-acquisition value, lower for a friendly takeover and higher for a hostile takeover. Often the market and company's growth potential are over-estimated, management fail to realise the possible synergies and promised savings do not materialise. Moreover, morale in the acquired company is often low, with the result that the best staff leave and the merged company under-performs.

Reciprocal share holdings

In this chapter we have considered many different methods of co-operation between partners. Over the years many firms have taken an equity stake in another firm for a variety of reasons. **Reciprocal share holdings** might provide an opportunity to influence the strategy of that firm, create a basis upon which to share expertise between the firms or establish a platform that might lead to a more formal business relationship, such as a merger, as well as generating a return on the investment. The joint working of Renault and Nissan has benefited both companies. Nissan was saved from bankruptcy and the company was turned around by Renault helping to launch a more attractive and competitive range of cars. Renault then became the recipients of Nissan's expertise in quality and production efficiency. Their reciprocal share holding has not led to a merger.

It is quite clear that global firms are adopting a range of partnership arrangements to maximise their global performance and presence. The businesses are becoming increasingly complex as they embark on joint ventures with the associated formal responsibilities, strategic alliances, short term contractual obligations and share holdings that might be the basis for closer future co-operation. The case study about Star Alliance at the end of this chapter illustrates many of the issues raised in this chapter.

Inevitably the challenge for management is to maximise the opportunities that come from synergy and the complementary activity of the partners. To do this it is necessary to select partners that are willing and able to contribute at least some of the following:

- complementary products and services
- knowledge and expertise in building customer relationships
- capability in technology and research
- capacity in manufacturing and logistics
- power in distribution channels
- money and management time.

Management must also deal with the added complexity and potential for conflicts between two quite different partners that arise because of differences in:

- objectives and strategies
- approach to repatriation of profits and investment in the business
- social, business and organisation cultures
- commitment to partnership and understanding of management responsibilities.

SUMMARY

- Analysis of the value contributions of the supply chain should lead to decisions to allocate responsibilities, internally and externally, and acceptance that outsourcing can add value.
- Information and communications technology is used to facilitate developments in supply chain management to improve performance and add customer value.
- Re-evaluation of channel effectiveness and new channel opportunities by many organisations has lead to disintermediation and re-intermediation decisions.
- The choice of route to market for new customer segments, particularly in international markets, is determined by the organisation's desire for market involvement and control set against the perceived risk.
- Organisations can extend their reach and influence in markets by developing market entry strategies based on collaboration and closer partnerships.
- In faster changing markets, different forms of collaboration are being used by organisations, including marketing networks, strategic alliances and joint ventures.
- Whilst these collaborative strategies have attractions, many organisations still prefer total control and grow through mergers and acquisitions, despite the high failure rate.

KEYWORDS

acquisitions and mergers	outsourcing
countermediation	reciprocal share holdings
disintermediation	re-intermediation
distribution channels	routes to market
e-procurement	sales force
intermediaries	strategic alliances
joint ventures	supply chain
market entry	value chain concept
marketing networks	

Star Alliance – ever closer

Responding to the low cost airline challenge, Star Alliance (which is made up of 15 airlines – the largest of the four main airline groupings) is reinventing itself. Formed in 1997 to co-ordinate networks and frequent flier points, in 2002 the Alliance carried 300 million passengers generating revenues of US$75.6 billion. The addition of US Airways increased the daily departures from 11 000 to 14 000 per day to 132 countries. It was this depth of global market penetration that helped Star Alliance avoid the cut backs that many airlines suffered after September 11 2001.

The Alliance is now quickly moving to a strategic partnership, which aims to deliver the efficiency improvements and cost savings that would normally be the result of merger or acquisition. The regulatory frameworks of most countries prevent mergers of airlines from different countries.

The airlines in the Alliance have adopted single policies for customer services, complaints, ground handling contracts, crisis management and communications. Plans for common baggage facilities, operations centres, ticket counters and lounges, and joint promotions, are all part of further establishing the Star Alliance brand.

Star Alliance is now aiming to establish itself as a lower cost but not budget airline, like easyJet and Ryanair in Europe, Southwest and JetBlue in the USA and Virgin Blue in Australia. It is developing a strategy that combines the best of the budget and Star Alliance business models. The benefits of premium product and loyalty schemes of the network airlines can be combined with electronic ticket sales, transparent pricing and better cost structures through yield management techniques.

The airlines will maintain their distinctiveness and cater for global travellers, but will adopt more aggressive integration of business functions to reduce duplication in areas such as purchasing, IT and marketing. Now the Alliance members are taking further steps to closer co-operation. Joint business ventures are about sharing assets. The Star Alliance FuelCo is a jet fuel purchasing company that has been set up in the USA. Air Canada, Austrian Airlines, Lufthansa and SAS are working with manufacturers on a common regional aircraft. The Alliance is supporting 'Yokoso Japan', the Japanese government's marketing programme to double the number of visitors to Japan by 2010. The ultimate integration would be to replace the current nine reservation systems of members with one and to share the alliance's main asset – the aircraft.

Questions

1 The objective of partnerships of this nature is to build competitive advantage through adding value for all stakeholders. What are the arguments for and against?

2 Given the legal restrictions preventing mergers and acquisitions, do you consider an alliance of this type to be as effective as a wholly owned organisation? Support your arguments using other examples.

Source: adapted from *The Dominion Post* (New Zealand), 17 December 2003

DISCUSSION QUESTIONS

1 Do you agree that a multi-national organisation such as Ford or Shell could outsource all its value chain activities and leave the firm to be run successfully by just a few people? Justify your viewpoint saying how it could be organised and why it could or could not be done.

2 What are the arguments for mergers and acquisitions and how can they contribute to delivering global competitive advantage? Research suggests that only about one in three delivers the promised stakeholder benefits. Why do you think this is?

3 Using examples from the travel industry, under what circumstances might organisations remove intermediaries from their supply chains (disintermediation) or add intermediaries (re-intermediation)?

4 Projects which require large amounts of investment and specialised technology are sometimes undertaken on a joint venture basis. Explain

the rationale behind this form of global alliance and outline the major advantages and disadvantages.

5 A small specialist engineering firm with 200 employees, based in Germany, is seeking to develop other international markets in Europe. What market entry and distribution options does it have and what criteria might it use to decide between the options?

REFERENCES

Bleeke, J. and Ernst, D. (1993) *Collaborating to Compete: Using Strategic Alliances and Acquisitions in the Global Marketplace*, New York: Wiley.

Bronder, C. and Pritzl, R. (1992) 'Developing strategic alliances: a conceptual framework for successful co-operation', *European Management Journal*, 10(4).

Chaffey D., Meyer, R., Johnston, K. and Ellis-Chadwick, F. (2003) *Internet Marketing: Strategy, Implementation and Practice*, Harlow: FT Prentice Hall.

Devlin, G. and Blackley, M. (1988) 'Strategic alliances – guidelines for success', *Long Range Planning*, 21(5).

Doole, I. and Lowe, R. (2004) *International Marketing Strategy*, 4th edn, London: Thomson Learning.

Doyle, P. (2000) *Value Based Marketing*, New York: Wiley.

Hooley, G., Saunders, J. and Piercy, N. (2004) *Marketing Strategy and Competitive Positioning*, Harlow: FT Prentice Hall.

Miles, R.E and Snow, C.C. (1984) 'Fit, failure and the hall of fame', *Californian Management Review*, Spring: 10–28.

Porter, M.E. (1985) *Competitive Advantage: Creating and Sustaining Superior Performance*, New York: The Free Press.

Rosenbloom, B. (2003) 'Marketing channels and distribution', in Hoffmann, D. *et al.*, *Marketing Best Practices*, Mason, OH: Thomson South-Western.

(1995) *Companion Encyclopaedia of Marketing*, London: Routledge

Wilson, R.M.S. and Gilligan, C. (2004). *Strategic Marketing Management*, Oxford: Butterworth-Heinemann.

ISSUES IN MEASURING MARKETING PERFORMANCE AND STAKEHOLDER VALUE

Introduction

In the preceding chapters we have examined the capabilities organisations need to build to make effective strategic marketing decisions. We have also investigated the strategic marketing decisions companies need to make throughout the marketing process to build a sustainable competitive advantage. Equally, however, a company has to make decisions as to the approach it should take to ensure the decisions taken are effectively implemented. It therefore has to consider how it is going to evaluate its marketing performance and how it is going to control its marketing programmes.

However, to build a competitive advantage which is sustainable over time, a company cannot simply consider its own internal requirements. It also has to ensure it meets the expectations of all its stakeholders, be they shareholders, customers, employees or the wider community that its strategic marketing decisions may affect.

In this chapter we examine the decisions a company has to make in deciding how to approach its evaluation of marketing performance. We also explore the wider dimensions of strategic marketing decision making and discuss the goals and expectations of stakeholders and the impact they have on strategic marketing decisions and the achievement of a sustainable competitive advantage.

Learning objectives

After reading this chapter you should be able to:

- Understand the implications of strategic marketing decisions for implementation and control
- Critically assess the use of performance measurement systems for the evaluation of the implementation of marketing strategies
- Assess the issues of corporate and social responsibility in achieving and sustaining a competitive advantage
- Appreciate the ethical considerations in strategic marketing decision making
- Apply relevant tools and techniques to the measurement of stakeholder value

CONTROL AND EVALUATION OF STRATEGIC MARKETING DECISIONS

Control and evaluation measures within a company are designed to make sure the marketing decisions and the resultant programme of marketing activities achieve the desired result. Any process of controlling and evaluating the performance of marketing programmes resulting from the strategic marketing decisions made has to be set against a background of clear, concise and understandable objectives, as discussed in Chapter 5 of this book. Companies are continually striving to find relevant and appropriate measures by which to measure and control the complexity of marketing programmes and show how they contribute to the economic value of a company, and in turn, shareholder added value. In Chapter 4 we discussed the financial techniques relevant to the measurement of performance. In this chapter we focus on the management issues in establishing the process for performance evaluation.

Control systems vary enormously across companies and selecting the right approach will very much depend on the market the company is competing in, the goals and objectives it has set, and the structure and culture of the organisation. Control systems have four primary objectives:

■ *To set standards* to which marketing strategies should aspire. These will be set as part of the marketing strategy development process and relate specifically to the goals and objectives set. These goals and objectives need to be translated into specific operational standards which are then driven throughout the organisation and implemented at every level.

■ *To measure performance* in a meaningful way. What metrics constitute meaningful measures is an important decision for companies, as is the method of measurement they decide upon. Both of these decision areas will be examined in the following sections. Such measurements to be meaningful, need to be able to measure quantity (how much was achieved?) and quality (how good was the performance and how much did the achievement of the performance cost the company?).

■ *To assess areas of strengths and weaknesses* in marketing programmes. Measuring performance is of little value in itself if the results are not analysed and the strengths and weaknesses of the programmes being evaluated are not identified. Whilst the identification of any variance from expected performance has to be identified, it is just as important to understand the reasons for the variance. The pursuance of this objective means that in setting up a control and evaluation mechanism, the company also has to be prepared to invest resources into researching the reasons behind the performance outcomes if the control and evaluation strategy is to have the capability to rectify the problems identified. As we discussed in Chapter 2, control and evaluation procedures are an integral part of the signal learning capability of a company. It is the integration of these learning activities and the knowledge management system within a company which will give it the ability to analyse and assess the strengths or weaknesses of the performance and diagnose the specific problem areas.

■ *To establish mechanisms for taking corrective action* when required. Once the results have been analysed and the reasons behind any variance from expected performance results understood, decisions need to be taken as to what action is necessary to rectify the situation. The reasons for the variance in performance may be the result of internal problems for which corrective action can easily be taken. This will involve the company in being responsive to the signals the evaluation procedures have highlighted. Equally, however, the variance from **expected performance** may be due to some extraneous environmental factor over which the company has little control. If these factors are seen as fundamental to the way the firm achieves its competitive advantage, it will involve the company in reflecting on the basis on which it competes in the market and perhaps being prepared to respond by reorienting its entire strategy, thus involving the company in 3R learning. In such cases a completely new set of strategic decisions would be made as the company attempts to reorient its strategy to meet the changing environmental needs.

PERFORMANCE EVALUATION PROCESS

If marketing managers are to influence the strategic direction of their companies, it is imperative that the impact strategic marketing decisions make can be judged against the organisation's key performance indicators. However the **performance metrics** used need to be flexible enough to cope with the changing priorities in the market and the developing strategic priorities of the company. Businesses have traditionally seen the added value of marketing activities as residing primarily in intangible assets such as brands, intellectual property and strategic relationships. However, there has been much criticism that such intangible measures are not transparent, are difficult to quantify and have a tenuous tangible linkage to added shareholder value. The main question that proponents of value based marketing argue a company has to address is, how does a company integrate its marketing activities into the financial reporting of a business and use metrics to quantify marketing's contribution to business?

In establishing performance evaluation process, therefore, there are some basic but fundamental questions which managers need to ask.

- What are they going to measure?
- What are the organisational mechanisms for the measuring activities?
- How is performance to be measured against a balanced range of goals and objectives?

What are they going to measure?

The dilemma many companies face is deciding what performance measures they should use to review the performance of marketing activities. A company needs to identify the key areas for measurement that are critical to the success of their performance in the market and that have a demonstrable and direct impact on the performance of the company and therefore shareholder/owner added value. This involves understanding which measures are the key drivers of added value to the business. Measures should not be used for their own sake, nor is there a need to measure every marketing activity; what is important is that companies identify the few critical success factors which really matter and ensure they have robust metrics in place to measure and control performance in these areas.

In deciding what **key performance indicators** to monitor it is important that a company has a clear understanding of its strategic priorities so that it can ensure the performance metrics used are important from a market perspective, not necessarily simply from an internal perspective.

Wilson and Gilligan (2004) suggest managers have to think carefully and in detail about the market's critical success factors and then review the organisation's performance against each of these. To assess on which areas a firm should place its emphasis in deciding performance metrics, a firm needs to identify:

- what is important in terms of increasing customer value and gaining competitive advantage in the market place
- what performance measures are critical in these areas.

The performance–importance matrix (Figure 12.1) can help in thinking this through.

In choosing the metrics to apply, the CIM (2003) suggest metrics need to be robust and reliable and to have the following characteristics:

- They should be clearly linked to business objectives of **economic value added** and have validity in that the metric should give a clear indication of what it is that is being measured.
- They should be focused on measuring the key indicators in a clear way so they are easily understood. They should not be overly financial or analytical, or so complex that they are not meaningful to interested parties.
- They should encompass broad and balanced factors and incorporate a range of marketing measures.
- They should be able to track performance reliably over time and so visibly signal changes in performance.
- They should be cost effective; the financial and staff time resources required to collect and analyse the data should not outweigh the benefits.

There are several types of controls that a company would choose to implement programmes for:

- Strategic controls: these ascertain how far the planned results have been achieved.
- Efficiency controls: these examine ways of improving the efficiency of marketing and particular aspects of the implementation of marketing programmes.
- Annual planning controls: these assess whether planned results have been achieved against the annual targets set within the planned budgets.
- Profit controls: these investigate whether marketing activities are adding value and assess the profit contribution of the entire portfolio of products and services
- Brand equity controls: these ascertain the equity invested in brands as measured by a variety of techniques such as consumer and end user metrics, innovation metrics and trade/customer metrics.

FIGURE 12.1

The performance–importance matrix

Source: adapted from Wilson and Gilligan (2004)

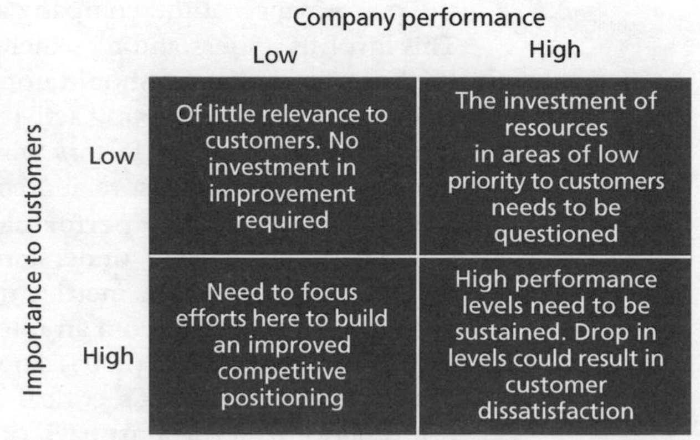

	Company performance Low	Company performance High
Importance to customers Low	Of little relevance to customers. No investment in improvement required	The investment of resources in areas of low priority to customers needs to be questioned
Importance to customers High	Need to focus efforts here to build an improved competitive positioning	High performance levels need to be sustained. Drop in levels could result in customer dissatisfaction

Table 12.1 gives an indication of the type of metrics used by companies. The reader is directed to Chapter 4 of this textbook for a detailed discussion of the techniques involved in assessing a number of the financial metrics.

What are the organisational mechanisms for the measuring activities?

The three main mechanisms through which performance measurement takes place are the annual budgeting procedures, the auditing mechanisms and benchmarking processes.

The annual budgeting procedures are commonly used for evaluation and control purposes and typically are based on the objectives that have been set within the marketing plan for that particular year. At a superficial level these will relate to profit and turnover forecasts. However, in the setting of standards for the performance measurement system, these goals and objectives would have been translated into specific operational objectives throughout the organisation. It is through the annual budgeting procedures that it can be assessed how far these have been implemented at every level.

The problem with using the **budgeting procedures** is that by definition they are short term and most marketing strategies have long term objectives. Thus they are useful for signal learning purposes and for identifying short term deviations from the planned forecasts. This may well mean that corrective actions would be limited to short term tactical changes rather than any rethinking of the strategic direction. However, when the budgeting process is used on a continuous basis and a longer term perspective is taken in measuring performance against budgets, then it has much more relevance for longer term strategic marketing decisions.

It must also be remembered that budgets are based on forecasts and estimates. In analysing any variance from the expected performance levels the manager also has to question the basis on which the forecasts were made. If the assumptions were misguided, it is these assumptions that need to be questioned and not the performance outcome.

The auditing mechanisms: an integral component of the marketing planning process is the conducting of a series of audits in the building of the knowledge

TABLE 12.1	Financial and non-financial metrics
Financial metrics	*Non-financial metrics*
shareholder added value	external rankings
economic value added	market share
return on investment	sales volume/growth
return on net assets	unfulfilled orders
cost/revenue/profit ratios	meeting delivery schedules
profits	market penetration levels
profitability	customer commitment/loyalty
cash flow/liquidity	number of customer complaints
return on sales	market image and awareness levels
production costs	employee motivation
unit costs of marketing activities	employee turnover

capability on which to base strategic marketing decisions. As we emphasised in the early chapters of this book, strategic marketing decision making is a continuous process occurring on a daily basis in any proactive company seeking to achieve a sustainable competitive advantage. Likewise, the auditing procedure is not something that is carried out in the early stages of strategy development and then forgotten once the strategic decisions are made. The auditing process is intertwined with the decision making process, which itself is intertwined with the control and evaluation process. Thus, while the auditing processes established by a company are important for signaling likely changes and problems in the marketplace in the strategy development process, they are equally important in controlling and evaluating marketing programmes and ensuring performance standards are met.

Auditing processes need to be established to monitor the marketing environment, the marketing strategy, the organisation and systems set up to deliver the strategy, as well as the functions and profitability of different aspects of the marketing programme. In setting up control and evaluation procedures, all the above areas will be regularly monitored and performance assessed against the objectives and standards articulated in the marketing strategy.

Benchmarking procedures: A number of companies, in evaluating marketing programmes, measure their performance against known benchmarks. These may be industry based, in which case the company is comparing its performance against the average known performance in the industry, or they may be competitor based. In this case the company is identifying key competitors and their known performance on specific measures and setting the target of either matching or perhaps outperforming them in particular measures. **Benchmarking** against competitors allows a company to measure its own performance as well as that of competitors; it also focuses the control and evaluation procedures on areas of competitive advantage by comparing performance levels on critical success factors to the organisation.

In a large multi-national, benchmarking may be set against best practice exhibited by subsidiaries, and other subsidiaries may be set the target of matching performance. Benchmarking is a method of comparison and assumes the performance of the unit used as the benchmark is a good norm to aim for; it is commonly used by companies to identify key performance measures and design and implement programmes to improve a company's performance on key issues relative to specific competitors, the industry norm or perhaps standards set by strategic business units within an organisation.

How to ensure performance is measured against a balanced range of stakeholder goals and objectives?

In this textbook emphasis has been placed on the concepts of value based marketing and the principle of shareholder/owner added value. In measuring performance, therefore, companies have to ensure that they incorporate these values into their mechanisms and measure performance against a range of shareholder and stakeholder expectations.

Shareholders as well as other stakeholders are increasingly looking for mechanisms by which performance can be assessed against the key drivers of business growth rather than simple financial measures. Kaplan and Norton (1996) argue that some traditional accounting measures, such as return on investment and earning per share, give misleading signals for companies trying to identify areas of innovation and improvement. Equally, however, they argue that it is fallacious to think that performance can be evaluated simply by using non-financial measures in the hope that improved financial performance will follow. In introducing the **balanced scorecard**, they suggest companies should not have to choose but should have a mechanism whereby performance is measured against a balanced range of goals and objectives.

The balanced scorecard (see Figure 12.2) is essentially a management system to measure current performance and to set priorities for future performance. It takes companies beyond the conventional metrics of sales, profit and cash flow, and incorporates many vital goals and measures against which a company can evaluate its performance, rather than simply relying on one measure alone. Four elements are addressed:

■ The financial perspective: what is our added value to shareholders/owners?

■ The customer perspective: what is our added value to customers?

■ The internal business perspective: what must we excel at to create value?

■ The innovation and learning perspective: how can we create and improve added value?

By using such techniques as the balanced scorecard, companies are able to ensure the evaluation and control processes focus performance measures on key growth drivers that help a company build the capability to compete effectively in the market. Such techniques also enable companies to take a much wider perspective and incorporate the measures important to employees, customers and other external stakeholders. For a company to be effective in the long term and

---

FIGURE 12.2

The balanced scorecard

Source: CIM Stage 3 Diploma Tutor Pack; adapted from Kaplan and Norton (1996)

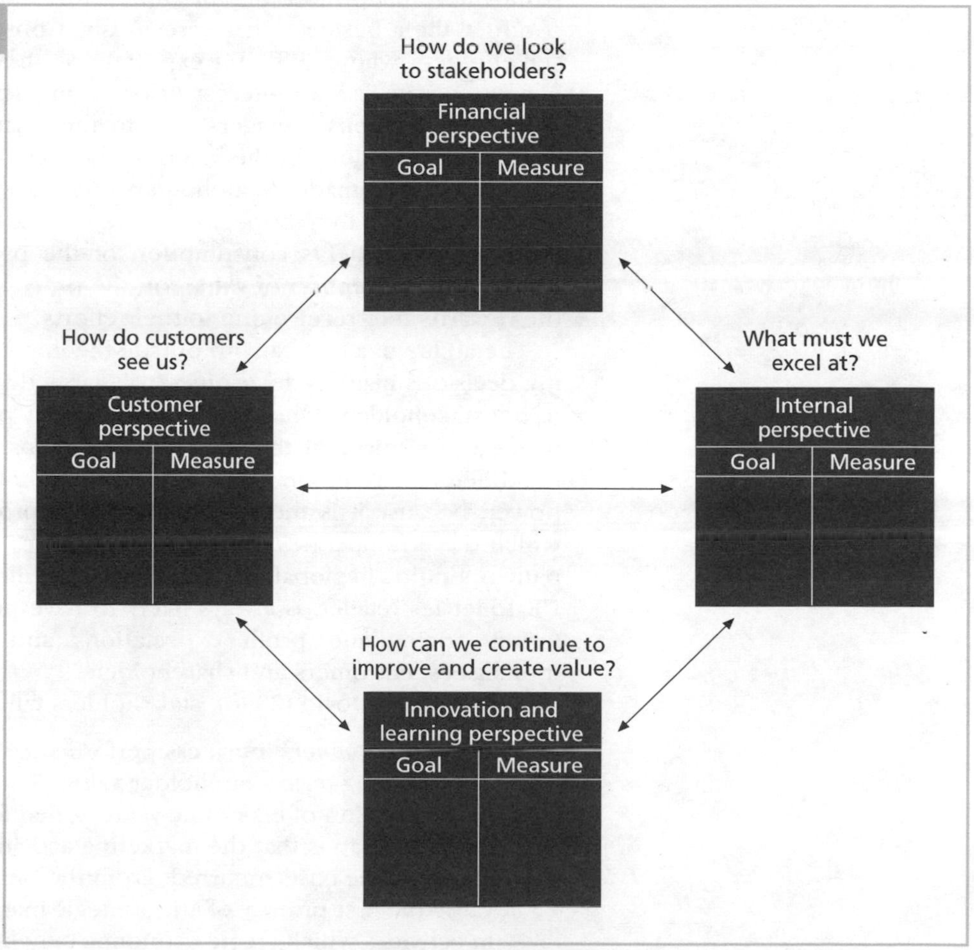

build a sustainable competitive advantage, it of course has to deliver shareholder/owner added value but increasingly it has to ensure it meets the expectations of all its stakeholders. The balanced scorecard can be used by companies to measure **stakeholder value** and so assess company performance against goals and expectations. In the following section we will examine stakeholder expectations and discuss how a company needs to manage these to achieve a sustainable competitive advantage.

According to the CIM (2003), marketing managers should aim to drive and shape the value based marketing agenda. This means that managers need to assess marketing activities on the basis of how they add value to customers, shareholders/owners and stakeholders. By doing this the CIM suggest that marketing managers will:

- make the right decisions faster
- have the ability to identify the best sources of long term value
- be able to create value for both shareholders/owners and customers
- focus creativity and resources on justifiable investments
- drive business decision making and direction.

STAKEHOLDER EXPECTATIONS

The complexities of competing in a global marketing environment mean companies have many more organisations and people who have a stake in how they conduct their business than previously. Consequently, firms have many more stakeholders whose differing expectations they have to manage. A stakeholder is anyone who has an interest in or an impact on the organisation. In making marketing decisions managers need to appreciate that different stakeholders have different perceptions of the value they expect to receive from the strategic marketing decisions made. Shareholders/owners will perceive value in terms of the financial benefit they hope to receive, whilst customers will perceive value in terms of the benefits consumption of the product or service will give them. Employees' perception of value, on the other hand, will be couched in terms of the rewards they receive due to their efforts.

The ability of a company to pursue the implementation of the strategic marketing decisions made is determined to a large degree by the aims and expectations of the stakeholders, who directly or indirectly provide the resources and support needed to implement the strategies and plans. It is important to clearly identify the different stakeholder groups, understand their expectations and evaluate their power, because it is the stakeholders who provide the broad guidelines within which the firm operates. Figure 12.3 identifies the typical stakeholders of a company operating in global markets. The Body Shop, the environmentally conscious UK toiletries retailer, is always likely to have problems balancing the widely differing pricing and profit expectations and environmental concerns of its franchisees, customers and shareholders.

According to Doyle (2000), stakeholders fall into a number of major groups:

Shareholders/owners: business performance is increasingly judged on creating long term shareholder value. Shareholders/owners are interested in the creation of economic value added for a company. Thus the priority for this group is that the marketing activities of a company create a value in excess of the costs incurred. From the perspective of shareholder/owner value the first priority of any strategic marketing decision is that it results in activities which create economic benefits which in turn translate into economic value. The concept of economic value added and the techniques of how this can be measured are fully examined in Chapter 4. A basic fundamental of business survival is that it is only by generating economic profit and added value to shareholders/owners that any company can stay in business.

Employees: the knowledge and skills that employees have are the intangible assets of an organisation that can help a company create and deliver superior value to the customer. If we accept the notion that it is the company that learns the fastest that can sustain its competitive edge, then investment in the capabilities of employees to maximise this capability is vital. However, there may be a conflict with this and the notion of delivering economic value added that has to be resolved in any company. The delivery of economic value added may mean the transfer of business assets to other locations or even the closure of business units. This obviously has implications for the employment security of staff as well as the potential of employees for commitment to the organisation and job satisfaction.

Managers: it is common in companies where there is separation of ownership and management control for managers to be more interested in short term profitability and short term growth as these may be more closely aligned to how they are rewarded. Again, there may be a conflict here to be resolved, as there may be a divergence in thinking between managers who are looking for short term reward and shareholders looking for longer term increase in shareholder value.

Customers: without customers there is no business, without customer value there is no economic value added. The source of a company's long term sustainability is satisfied customers that are loyal to the company. Unfortunately customer satisfaction on its own cannot deliver economic value added, so again we have a potential conflict that has to be resolved. The sustainable competitive advantage that will deliver economic value

FIGURE 12.3

Typical stakeholders of a company

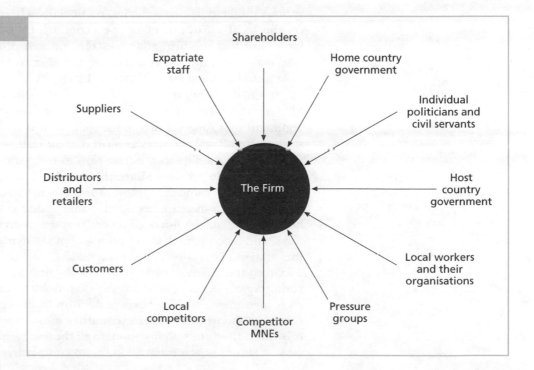

added has to be achieved by maximising customer value at a cost that generates cash for the company.

Suppliers: a totally integrated marketing effort requires the co-operation and commitment of all the partners involved in the route to market of the products and services being offered by the company. However, the turbulent competitive environment in which companies operate means that flexibility in relationships with suppliers is necessary for companies if they are to have the ability to shift resources as required. This may mean there is again a dilemma to be resolved in that partners in the supply chain may be looking for long term security, predictability and satisfactory profit margins. As customer needs change, new technologies make it increasingly easier to find new sources of supply which could bring firms into conflict with the traditional partners in their supply chain.

Community and society: the community of a firm today is both local, national and potentially international. Companies today are seen to have a social responsibility to ensure that their actions are in line with the expectations of the society in which they operate, with regard to their ethical behaviour, their environmental behaviour and the consequences their strategies may have on the communities in which they operate. However, the acceptance of social responsibility may have a significant cost element which in turn could cause a conflict with the goal of maximising economic value added.

Whilst the senior management of the firm usually aim to develop and adopt strategies which do not directly oppose stakeholder expectations, they do, of course, frequently widen or alter the firm's activities due to changes in the market and competition. Moreover, a wide range of stakeholders influence the strategic marketing decisions of an organisation by forcing it to give greater attention to its political, commercial and ethical behaviour, as well as taking more interest in the actual operation of the business and the performance and safety of the products. As a result of this, companies need to explain their strategies and plans to stakeholders through more detailed annual reports, to staff through a variety of briefing methods, and to pressure groups and the community in general through various public relations activities, particularly when their activities have an impact on the local environment or the economy. In global markets it is particularly important that the firm addresses the concern of its host country stakeholders, who may physically and culturally be very distant from the headquarters, as Coca-Cola found in India (see Challenge 12.1).

Particular attention should be paid to the different expectations of the stakeholders and their power to influence the firm's strategic direction. There is an argument that suggests that in the long term shareholder/owner value is the best strategy for all stakeholders as most of their claims on a company will depend on the company's ability to generate cash to meet their demands. However, whilst a company has to produce **shareholder added value** to stay in business, without customers and without employees there is no business. Ultimately the only sustainable way to increase economic value added is by creating value for all stakeholders. The stakeholders of a company are therefore inter-dependent in many ways, and a company has to find a way of satisfying each of their expectations in the strategic marketing decisions it makes.

Given the different expectations of the firm's stakeholders, it is inevitable that conflicts will occur. For example, shareholders usually want a high return on their investment and may expect the firm to find countries with low production costs, but the workers in these countries want an adequate wage on which to live. It is often the firm's ability to manage these potential conflicts that leads to success or failure in achieving a long term competitive advantage.

International pressure groups are another important stakeholder multi-national firms have to manage. Global communications and the ability of the World Wide Web to draw together people with shared interests have led to the growing power of globally based pressure groups. Such has been the success of a number of these, it is now the case that pressure groups are seen by many global operators as one of the key stakeholders to be considered in international strategy decision making. The role of pressure groups in global markets tends to be to raise awareness of issues of concern. Some that have received wide press coverage affecting marketing strategies are:

- Greenpeace's efforts to raise awareness about threats to the environment.
- The anti-globalisation lobby demonstrating against the perceived dark global forces they see manifested in the World Trade Organisation.
- The anti-child labour movement (see Challenge 12.2).

Gap, the clothes manufacturer and retailer, responded to the revelation that companies holding a licence to produce their products were using child labour by applying the employment guidelines and dismissing the 'child'. This only exacerbated the anger of the pressure groups. Levi's, another target of the anti-child labour movement, finding themselves exposed to the same bad publicity, dismissed the 'child' but agreed to fund their education up to the point when they would be eligible to seek employment. This pacified the pressure group in the short term but one is left wondering what Levi's would do if they subsequently discovered that there were another few thousand under-age employees across other factories they use, or, if there was a sudden influx of employees that were recruited and then declared themselves as under-age in order to seek educational support?

CHALLENGE 12.1   Coke is it?

In November 2003, the Coca-Cola Company of America gave evidence to a village council in Southern India in an attempt to keep open a bottling plant threatened with closure. Their appeal failed to convince and the company's case was dismissed as 'incomplete and unsatisfactory'.

The claim was that the bottling plant was draining water from wells, drying up ponds and affecting the lives of over 2000 families dependent upon the underground water for crops. Coca-Cola was under threat of losing its operating licence, against the argument that the bore holes were using 1 million gallons of water a day and forcing villagers to abandon their coconut groves and vegetable crops.

Coca-Cola employs over 250 people on this site and considers opponents to be 'anti-capitalist' activists, not farmers with legitimate grievances. Sunil Gupta, vice-president of Coca-Cola India, claimed that the company has been the target of a handful of extremists and that it is lack of rainfall that has caused water supplies to be exhausted. Available figures suggest that there has been a 60 per cent reduction in rainfall quantities over the last two years.

This has been just one of a number of allegations against the company in the Kerala region, and as a part of their approach to addressing these, the Coca-Cola website carries detailed responses to a number of 'erroneous allegations', covering: the use of bio-solids as a soil amendment; issues of product quality against allegations of contamination; and the complaints around water resources, outlined above.

As a company operating in global markets with one of the most recognised brands in the world, such challenges are, perhaps, to be expected. But coming, as this does, in the continued shadow of September 11, the current occupation of Iraq by US led forces and a general undercurrent of anti-American feelings in certain areas, could this be a signal of more troubles to come?

Question What are the wider implications for Coca-Cola in sustaining their competitive advantage in global markets?

Sources: Andy Cropper, adapted from The *Guardian*, 19 December 2003 and Inter-Press Service, 17 December 2003

One of the main roles of international public relations is to try to manage the expectations and aspirations of pressure groups and all the stakeholders of a company. In making strategic marketing decisions, one of the key responsibilities is to establish good practice to respond to publicity generated by pressure groups on issues where organisations have been seen not to meet **stakeholder expectations**.

ETHICS IN STRATEGIC MARKETING DECISIONS

Meeting stakeholder expectations often involves the company in making decisions with regard to the **ethical considerations** in their proposed marketing strategies.

Cultural sensitivity is often at the heart of the ethical dilemmas that managers face when operating in global markets. There are few, if any, moral absolutes and few actions for which no one can provide reasonable justification. Almost every action can be justified on the basis that it is acceptable in one particular culture. In thinking about ethics managers need to be aware that simply defining what is ethical by the standards, values and actions of their own culture may be insufficient in satisfying all the stakeholders of an organisation that operates globally. What is often seen as an acceptable business practice in one culture can be seen as ethically questionable in another. Managers from different cultures will always be able to challenge, for instance, the US, Indian or Japanese perspective of what is ethical, as can be seen in the comparison between Western and Eastern business practices in Spotlight 12.1.

CHALLENGE 12.2 The football stitching game

A poster in the Chamber of Commerce building in Sialkot, a village in Pakistan, reads 'A child employed is a future destroyed'. Sialkot is a major centre for producing soccer balls, and it received bad publicity when a journalist exposed local manufacturers who were employing child labour to stitch the balls.

The Atlanta Agreement was an international declaration to try and stop child labour. After this was signed 66 local manufacturers volunteered to stop child labour and allow monitors to check on their production. Now Save the Children believe that there is almost zero child labour.

Before the agreement most of the cutting and laminate printing was done in factories, whereas stitching was outsourced to families around the villages. Now stitching is done by full time employed adults in centres. This has had a number of beneficial effects. Saga Sports, which makes 4–5 million balls a year for Nike and other brands, now has better control systems, shorter delivery times and lower inventory.

However, the balls are now costly to make and consumers are not willing to pay extra for adult only certified products. Chinese machine stitched balls are cheaper and their machine stitching is now suitable for more expensive balls. Indeed, Saga are setting up a factory in China. Pakistan's share of the soccer ball market dropped from 65 to 45 per cent. Some smaller producers went out of business and family incomes fell by about 20 per cent.

Save the Children supports the Atlanta Agreement but makes a distinction between child labour and child work, which they believe can give children income, skills and self-confidence without damaging schooling. Before the agreement 80–90 per cent of children who were stitching footballs at home already went to school. Of greater concern are those industries, such as brick and surgical instrument making, which are less well publicised and controlled.

Question Evaluate how far you think such ethical considerations should impact on the strategic marketing decisions of a company.

Source: Doole and Lowe, *International Marketing Strategy*, 2004

The ethical challenges facing marketing managers are many. In recent years such issues as environmental abuse, the use of child labour, poor working conditions and the low levels of pay in third world factories have received particular attention. Western consumers in choosing brands look for reassurance that the product has been produced in what they see as a socially responsible manner (see Challenge 12.2). Anita Roddick built the Body Shop empire on the basis of ensuring her ingredients came from authentic sources of supply that did not lead to the destruction of the environment and that the indigenous producers received a fair price for the products they sold. She has recently launched an ethical fashion chain. Her key selling points for the new range of clothes are that they are not associated with child slavery and that the people that make them are able to earn a proper living wage and enjoy good working conditions.

Consumers globally are becoming better informed through better education and faster and more effective communications. Increasingly, therefore, they are able to question the actions of multi-national enterprises, as we saw in the discussion of the role of pressure groups earlier. For their part, whilst the largest multi-nationals are extending their influence within the global markets, they are becoming more vulnerable to criticism. Over the last few years, quality and service have improved considerably but now firms are increasingly expected to ensure that their behaviour is ethical and in the interests of the global community which makes up their market. A good example of this has been the spate of lawsuits against the tobacco giants and the recent trend to hold the food giants accountable for the unhealthy eating patterns of their consumers, as discussed in Challenge 12.3.

However, marketing executives, when making strategic marketing decisions as to how to operate their businesses across different cultures, will find themselves facing moral and ethical dilemmas on a daily basis on a wide range of issues.

SPOTLIGHT 12.1   Conflicting Asian–Western business practices

Western businesses do not understand the way networking plays such a huge role in Asian business. Asian companies generally believe relationships come first, whereas Western firms prefer to get straight to business and only form relationships when they are needed. The principle of Guanxi and dependence on the networks of family and friends are an integral part of Asian business strategy, and the opportunities that arise from business connections often result in conglomerates of apparently unrelated business. This system of complex conglomerates seems illogical and sometimes unethical to Western management, where building core competencies is common. An integral part of conducting business in Asia is gift giving. However, in many Western countries such practice is seen as bribery/corruption. German and Swiss executives tend to feel uncomfortable accepting gifts, which they view as bribes because they do not want to be seen as being under obligation to the other party. In China it would be virtually impossible to gain any local government approval without offering financial inducements.

As for Asian–Western relationships, many frustrations emerge because of the differences in business practices. For example, the lack of continuity caused by Western managers moving around from job to job makes it difficult for Asian managers to form the connections necessary for doing business. Moreover, since Asian partners are frequently involved with a number of other firms, conflicts of interest arise. Western managers often complain that their Asian counterparts tend to focus on attaining short term profits to invest in new ventures with new partners rather than the preferred Western method of building brands or expanding market share.

Question With more transactions between Asian and Western businesses, how can these differences be resolved?

For further information on the contrasts between Asian and Western business systems see Chen (2004) *Asian Management Systems*, 2nd edn, London: Thomson Learning

Some of these, currently receiving particular attention, are bribery and corruption, counterfeiting and piracy.

Bribery and corruption

An integral part of conducting business internationally is the practice of gift giving. However, in many Western countries such practice is seen as bribery/corruption and is tightly regulated and controlled. Business gift giving (or bribery, depending on your view), if improperly executed, could stop sensitive negotiations and ruin new and potential business relationships. However, business gift giving in many cultures is an important part of persuasion. In cultures where a business gift is expected but not given, it is an insult to the host.

In cultures which view bribery as an **acceptable business practice**, the communication style is more implicit, non-verbal and more reliant on hidden cues in the context of personal relationships. In Japan, for example, a highly developed and affluent society, gift giving practices are widespread in the business culture. Refusing to participate in gift giving in such cultures can cause hard feelings and misunderstandings between business clients. Financial inducements are often seen as important steps in bringing a person into the inner circle of a business relationship or to strengthen the relationship between a buyer and a seller.

By contrast, in Northern Europe and the USA managers rely on explicit contracts, communication is more formal and explicit, and negotiations are based on a more legalistic orientation. Laws applying to bribery tend to be very well laid out. In some cultures, all business gifts will be viewed as illegal bribes; on the other hand, other cultures view gifts, pay offs and even bribes merely as a cost of business. Bribery and corruption are part of the commercial traditions of many parts of Asia, Africa and the Middle East. Transparency International, a global counter-corruption watchdog, ranks Indonesia as the most corrupt country,

---

| CHALLENGE 12.3 | Food giants are weighed up |

Lawyers in the USA who took on the tobacco industry now have the food giants in their sights, claiming that consumers have been duped into eating large quantities of unhealthy food. The result is that obesity is on the increase and that American children may be the first generation to live shorter lives than their parents because of it.

Kraft Foods is the number one manufacturer of processed foods in America, with brands such as Ritz Crackers, Kool-Aid, Jell-O and Oreo. Perhaps concerned about the potential lawsuits that could be filed against them, Kraft have recently announced they have stopped marketing direct to schools and that they are taking measures to reduce portion sizes as well as reduce the fat content of their products.

However, John Banzhof, the professor of legal activism at George Washington University, the man who has led many of the campaigns against the tobacco companies, believes too little is being done by the company and is concerned that Kraft still actively markets to children. He says food companies have to do a much better job of labelling their food products if they want to avoid lawsuits, and prioritises three areas:

- information on the fat content at the point of sale
- appropriate warnings as to the possible consequences of over indulging in the food
- providing healthy alternative foods.

Question Do the food companies have a corporate social responsibility to help consumers avoid obesity, or should consumers take personal responsibility for their own eating habits?

Source: adapted from Seaton, J. (2004) 'Weighty problem', *Marketing Business*, December 2003/January 2004

followed closely by Vietnam. They estimate that in Vietnam 20 per cent of infrastructure spending finds its way into the pockets of corrupt officials.

Piracy

Piracy has been a particular problem for the global music and software industry. The advent of digital technology and the ability to download from the internet have made the copying of such things as CDs much easier. Ninety-eight per cent of software in China is estimated to be pirated software. The music industry, too, has financially suffered from such practices. It is estimated that 27 per cent of Americans and 13 per cent of Europeans download music, which the music industry sees as a major cause for the decline in sales worldwide.

However, whether piracy is the cause is questioned by some commentators; they argue that while some consumers are buying less CDs it has actually led others to buy more. The decline in sales, it is suggested, is more likely to be due to fiercer competition and the market maturing rather than simply a result of piracy.

Even on piracy, different cultures have varying perspectives. The US courts take a very stringent view and prosecute offenders that are caught. In China and India, views on intellectual property rights are much more difficult to define. The International Intellectual Property Alliance claims that 90 per cent of musical recordings sold in China are pirated. Since China joined the World Trade Organisation, regulations have been put in place to ban such practices. However, piracy is still problematic. Even amongst professionals there are differing views. Robbie Williams, a UK superstar, recently stated publicly that he thought there was nothing wrong with piracy and that there was very little anyone could do about it.

Counterfeiting

A counterfeit is something that is forged, copied or imitated without the perpetrator having the right to do so, and with the purpose of deceiving or defrauding (whereas piracy does not attempt to defraud but openly sells pirated copies). In China at least US$16 billion worth of goods sold each year inside the country are counterfeited. Procter & Gamble estimates that 10–15 per cent of its revenues in China are lost each year to counterfeit products. The Ukraine now exports counterfeit optical discs, Russia markets counterfeit software, while Paraguay markets imitation cigarettes. Counterfeit pharmaceuticals are routinely marketed to countries unable to afford the expensive products of the authentic drug companies, often these are sub-standard, or have fake labels. It is estimated by the World Health Organisation that between 5–7 per cent of drugs sold are counterfeits with potentially fatal consequences.

American industries lose US$200–250 billion a year to counterfeiting. The fact that many global manufacturers have moved their production to third world countries is seen by some to have opened the floodgates to counterfeiting. The global brands have been able to take advantage of low labour costs, but have given insufficient attention to securing intellectual property rights in such countries. In today's markets, where so much of the added value of a product is in its brand identity, counterfeiters have been able to exploit consumers' expectations of quality and service with counterfeit products. The internet has also helped build the market for counterfeit products, it is estimated that approximately US$25 billion worth of counterfeit goods are traded each year over the internet.

Much of the problem stems from **cultural attitudes** to the rights of anyone to own intellectual property. The Chinese have argued that if all ideas can be copyrighted, they should be able to patent the compass, ice cream, noodles and many other products they have given to the world. Such attitudes have led to inadequate laws on intellectual property rights (IPR) in many countries. By 2006, all members of the World Trade Organisation, however, should have started the process of implementing TRIPS, an international treaty on IPR that lays down basic rules for protection and enforcement. Some countries, notably China, since joining the WTO, have introduced laws so that companies can protect their intellectual property assets. How those rights will be enforced in practice, however, remains to be seen. In Europe, the European Commission has proposed new rules to harmonise member states' legislation on IPR enforcement. This is particularly important as the EU has embraced new members, such as Poland, where counterfeiting is a serious problem.

Although nations and organisations often provide ethical guidelines on bribery, counterfeiting, etc., ultimately marketing managers have to make decisions based on their own personal views of what is and is not ethical. Managers need to form a view as to what constitutes ethical decision making within an organisation. In taking such a view managers need to reflect on how their views on what constitutes ethical behaviour reflect changing societal views of acceptable behaviour, how decisions will be viewed by stakeholders, and the perceived and real impact upon the organisation of making those decisions. Central to their concerns is the importance the company places on the need for an ethically responsible approach to its operations on the global markets. However, interwoven within this are the commercial concerns of the business and how it meets the expectations of its stakeholders with regard to its ethical behaviour, whilst delivering added value to its shareholders.

Companies are increasingly of the view that organisational behaviour considered to be unethical can decrease a firm's shareholder value, whilst behaviour considered by stakeholders to be ethical can enhance a company's competitive advantage on global markets and so increase shareholder value. Attempting to take an ethically responsible decision, however, could mean the loss of, perhaps, an efficient and cheap source of supply, or in some cases the loss of a potential deal. It also presumes that in making purchasing decisions consumers do make ethical choices. Some companies argue that whilst consumers are aware of ethical issues, this awareness does not necessarily translate into purchasing action. This issue is discussed in Challenge 12.4.

The consequence of an ethically responsible approach would involve increased resources and attention being applied to a number of areas, such as:

■ An increased need for accurate and timely information.

■ Increased attention to press, public reaction and global pressure groups.

■ Closer relationships with stakeholders and members of the supply chain to ensure all interests are taken into consideration.

■ Being prepared, when serious risks are identified, to take positive and constructive action.

CORPORATE SOCIAL RESPONSIBILITY

The discussions in the previous sections all point to the importance of the modern organisation taking a **collaborative stakeholder approach** if it is to achieve a sustainable long term competitive advantage. The central concern of the company should be to understand its stakeholders and create the right conditions to satisfy stakeholder expectations on a continuous basis. This means strategic marketing decisions at a corporate level have to show that they embody an ethical, social and ecological responsibility if the long term interests of all stakeholders, including shareholders, are to be met; in other words they have to clearly evidence a strong corporate social responsibility.

In Chapter 1 we discussed the importance of companies having strong core values which were shared throughout the company. Pivotal to a company achieving a **corporate social responsibility** are the shared values between the company and its stakeholders. Society increasingly expects companies to show an ethical responsibility in the decisions they take and share their social responsibility with their stakeholders. Thus it is becoming increasingly apparent that, to sustain a long term competitive advantage, companies need to show at a corporate level that they have a strong awareness of their social responsibility and that it is a key component of the values on which they build their marketing strategies and an integral consideration in the decisions they make. This means that companies have to consciously engender a culture of shared responsibility amongst all their stakeholders: shareholders, employees, customers and suppliers, as well as the wider community. This involves developing in the strategic marketing decision process an ethic of collective good, which is marked by a voluntarily accepted solidarity amongst stakeholders that the company, along with themselves, holds a common interest in achieving a sustainable future.

The Corporate Social Responsibility Index published by Business in the Community (www.bitc.org.uk) assesses the extent to which the strategies of companies are translated into responsible practice throughout the organisation. Companies are evaluated in four key areas: community, environment, marketplace and workplace. 3M, AstraZeneca, BT, mmO2, Sainsbury's, Marks & Spencer, Shell International and Tesco all scored maximum points in these areas, and were placed in the top quintile of the index.

CHALLENGE 12.4   How the ethical consumer makes decisions

Ethical consumerism is, of course, nothing new, the campaign against Nestlé's sale of baby milk into Africa and boycotts of South African products during the days of apartheid have attracted widespread support.

Ethical consumers have helped to raise awareness of Third World debt and, as a result, prompted government action. And, clearly, they tap into a latent anti-Americanism; people love eating McDonald's, but are happy to protest against them for a variety of reasons – protection of the rainforest and anti-globalisation, to name but two.

Most consumers are moderate, but the issues these campaigners raise are steadily changing their expectations of corporate social responsibility and this, in turn, is influencing their purchasing behaviour.

For example, concerns about animal welfare have fuelled demand for Freedom Food, organic meat and dolphin friendly tuna, while growing environmental awareness has prompted a massive growth in organic/quasi-organic and bio-dynamic products. Greater social awareness has led to the development of Fair Trade products and anti-child labour campaigns.

However, some moderate ethical consumers are highly selective about what they will boycott. Many vegetarians eat non-vegetarian cheese or wear leather shoes. People who openly claim to be concerned with the environment use their cars instead of public transport. Fashion conscious youngsters buy Nike trainers if that's what the fashion pack dictates and people resist paying a couple of pence extra for Fair Trade coffee even though they claim to be concerned about Third World labour exploitation.

Question How far should marketing managers incorporate consideration of the ethical consumer into the strategic marketing decision process?

Source: adapted from Seligman, P., Financial Times Information, 11 July 2002

Companies therefore need to develop a deliberate strategy to build a culture of social responsibility within the company and amongst its stakeholders. According to the Gale Group (Keijzers, 2003) a corporate social responsibility (CSR) strategy, will encompass a number of principles:

The formulation of a set of business principles expressing CSR values. Companies will then include these principles in all operational documents laying down guidelines for management and employees. The company will also publish detailed reports on their CSR policy for their stakeholders. For managers making marketing decisions, CSR issues impact on the dilemmas they have to resolve every day. Such CSR dilemmas require explicit acknowledgement from senior management, and in laying down the principles they are laying the foundation on which managers are able to resolve such dilemmas. Within a global organisation, setting down such principles may of course be problematic if its business units across its global markets have a high degree of autonomy and so a different perception of the CSR priorities.

A *programme of open public debates* with stakeholders regarding options and choices involved in the issues of the sustainability of CSR. Through these the company tries to ensure that it is informed about what the outside world is thinking and gains an understanding of what is expected from it at the same time as ensuring stakeholders are made aware of the dilemmas it faces. Thus the dialogue establishes a sense of understanding and can result in a change of attitude not only within the company but also amongst stakeholders.

The publication of external reports on priority CSR topics which will include an assessment of the company's performance in priority areas. The prioritisation of such topics for investigation and publication will require the engagement of external and internal stakeholders. Most companies would only publish such reports on a narrow field of topics perceived as being of the highest priority to their stakeholders.

Explicit procedures for the auditing and monitoring of the CSR principles laid down. Information on the CSR dilemmas faced by managers will be collected through questionnaires, focus groups or an internal consultation process. However, for this process to have value and be credible, the process of analysis will be initiated and monitored by the senior management and the auditing and reporting carried out by external agencies.

An external change process to jointly craft and implement new policies to progress the development of CSR for the sustainable development of the company. It is not enough to understand the stakeholder demands with regard to CSR issues, the company also has to show it is willing to overcome the obstacles identified and be open to changing and developing solutions as a result of the joint learning process with its stakeholders. In order to create long term success and continuity, a company must not only improve its level of knowledge of the CSR concerns of its stakeholders but must also build strategies to change as a result of the outcomes of the processes it has put in place.

Thus in order to sustain a competitive advantage over the longer term, strategic marketing decision makers have to ensure they manage the expectations and aspirations of their stakeholders, and demonstrate that they have a strong sense of corporate social responsibility. In achieving this the ethical dimensions of decision making will need to be considered throughout the marketing process.

SUMMARY

- A company needs to identify the key areas for measurement that are critical to the success of their performance in the market and that have a demonstrable and direct impact on the performance of the company and therefore shareholder added value.

- The three main mechanisms though which performance measurement takes place are the annual budgeting procedures, the auditing mechanisms and benchmarking processes.

- The balanced scorecard is a management system to measure current performance and to set priorities for future performance. It is through such mechanisms that the value added to all stakeholders can be measured.

- The central concern of the company should be to understand its stakeholders and create the right conditions to satisfy stakeholder expectations on a continuous basis.

- Society increasingly expects companies to show an ethical responsibility in the decisions they take and share their social responsibility with their stakeholders.

KEYWORDS

acceptable business practice	ethical considerations
auditing processes	expected performance
balanced scorecard	international pressure groups
benchmarking	key performance indicators
budgeting procedures	performance metrics
collaborative stakeholder approach	piracy
control systems	shareholder value added
corporate social responsibility	stakeholder expectations
cultural attitudes	stakeholder value
economic value added	

CASE STUDY — The right direction for Qibla Cola?

Qibla Cola is marketed as an alternative to the established cola brands which provides consumers with the 'ethical' choice' of supporting charitable causes whilst at the same time quenching their thirst. It is also true to say that the development of the new brand has been motivated out of a desire to offer the public a non-American alternative.

The Qibla Cola Company (www.qibla-cola.com) have used their strong ethical beliefs to influence a range of soft drinks they are hoping to distribute around the globe. Ten per cent of any profits will be invested into charitable trusts managing health, water and poverty relief schemes. The idea is that the profits arising from individual countries will finance the poverty relief schemes in those same countries. This is not such a new idea – Zamzam, from Iran, was launched way back in 1954, and has long been offered as an ethical *alternative* (in their view) to established cola products. Mecca Cola, which originated in France, is another example. Mecca uses 20 per cent of any net profit for charitable causes.

All these colas have links to particular causes but are not meant for the sole consumption of the supporters of that cause. Qibla, Mecca and Zamzam have links to the Islamic religion but are marketed widely and not meant to be consumed only by those of the Muslim faith. Qibla is a generic term in Arabic meaning 'direction', Mecca is the holy city and Zamzam is holy spring water.

The company philosophy of Qibla is to develop a global brand that reflects an ethical underpinning both to the products that are offered and to how the company integrates and benefits the communities in which it has operations. Consumers, they suggest, are increasingly concerned about the low level of social responsibility shown by larger multi-nationals and the influence and adverse impact such corporations have on the cultural heritage of many countries. To a certain extent their beliefs reflect a latent anti-Americanism and a concern that, increasingly, consumers' choice of products is limited to US offerings.

They are also tapping into the growing ethical awareness amongst consumers. Consumers are taking into account ethical considerations in deciding between brands. This can have an adverse effect on companies if consumers for whatever reason decide to boycott products from certain suppliers.

In the UK, Mintel ('Attitudes towards ethical foods', February 2001) suggests companies perceived as 'unethical' are losing up to £2.6 billion per year! Some consumers will choose not to return to a brand once the unethical finger has been pointed at them – it would appear that consumer behaviour is increasingly influenced by this issue particularly in the music and fashion markets, markets of interest to young consumers.

Qibla is sold through internet sites as well as from over 2000 independent retailers in the UK. Qibla Cola is promoted and sold through Islamic sites that allow consumers to make choices in the knowledge that all the goods are acceptable to their faith. The retailers offer a local presence and the opportunity for Qibla to build brand awareness at the point of sale.

Distribution is limited, as many of the retailers selling Qibla do not have sufficient shelf space, and most offer competitive alternatives such as Pepsi and Coca-Cola. This is important for small independent retailers who do not wish to be seen as taking a political stand and do not wish to cause friction between Muslim and non-Muslim communities. The company is in discussions with cash-and-carry and supermarket chains to try to gain an agreement to give brands such as Qibla Cola more prominence at the point of sale.

Pricing is set similar to the other premium brands. The challenge for Qibla then is to get the consumer to try and return – for both flavour and ethics.

Qibla have expanded internationally by forming marketing partnerships with like minded distributors in a number of countries. These relationships are formed on the basis that the partners share the same views and provide the opportunity for investment into local charitable causes dealing with problems encountered in that specific area. Qibla Cola is sold in the UK, Canada, the Netherlands and Norway. They have recently expanded into the USA, India, Pakistan, the United Arab Emirates and Malaysia.

Questions

1 How far can the ethical philosophy of the Qibla Cola Company be advantageous in building a sustainable competitive advantage?

2 What would you suggest are the advantages and disadvantages of this type of product in terms of global branding, distribution and perception?

3 How might Qibla Cola increase its global distribution activity?

Source: Qibla-Cola Ltd.

Source: Jeanette Baker, Sheffield Hallam University; adapted from www.qibla-cola.com; Carter, M. (2004) 'New colas wage battle for hearts and minds', *Financial Times*, 8 January; Day, J. (2003) '"Protest" drinks range targets Muslims', The *Guardian*, 23 April; Jeffery, S. (2003) 'Is it the real thing?', The *Guardian*, 5 February.

DISCUSSION QUESTIONS

1 Identify the barriers to measuring and evaluating performance that marketing managers may encounter. Suggest how these barriers might be reduced.

2 Critically evaluate the role of control and performance evaluation in the strategic marketing decision process.

3 Identify the major stakeholder groups for an organisation known to you. How far are the expectations of the different groups met by the organisation? How can the organisation measure its added value to its stakeholders?

4 'To sustain a competitive advantage all companies have to show a strong sense of corporate social responsibility.' Using examples, discuss how far you agree with this statement.

5 Wearwell plc has a chain of competitively priced garment retail outlets across Europe. A recent survey has uncovered a serious problem of abusive and restrictive working practices in some of the textile factories in Asia, from where Wearwell's suppliers source many of the garments. However, to change suppliers would greatly increase the cost of the garments. What are the implications to Wearwell on the sustainability of their competitive advantage? What would you recommend them to do?

REFERENCES

CIM (2003) 'Shape the agenda: hard edged marketing', Chartered Institute of Marketing, www.shapetheagenda.com, September.

Doyle, P. (2000) *Value Based Marketing: Marketing Strategies for Corporate Growth and Shareholder Value*: Chichester: Wiley.

Kaplan, R.S. and Norton, D.P. (1996) 'The balanced scorecard: measures that drive performance', *Harvard Business Review*, January–February.

Keijzers, G. (2003) 'Creating sustainable directions: evolving stakeholder approach in seven multinationals', *Journal of Corporate Citizenship*, 10. 79–91.

Wilson, R.M.S. and Gilligan, C.T. (2004) *Strategic Marketing Management: Planning, Implementation and Control*, 3rd edn, Oxford: Butterworth-Heinemann.

INTEGRATIVE LEARNING ACTIVITY

The management challenge of strategic decision making in global markets

Introduction

In this book we have discussed the significance and role of strategic decision making in global markets and emphasised the fact that individual decisions at any point in the marketing process (analysis, strategy development, implementation and control) could become the drivers of a significant reformulation of an organisation's marketing strategy and even lead to a complete reinvention of the business. In recent years too much emphasis has been placed on managers going through marketing planning processes with the expectation that a new strategy will somehow emerge. Whilst it is acknowledged that business processes are essential for strategy development and implementation, they do not act as a substitute for quality decision making.

The best organisations make a small number of very significant decisions that set a new direction for the future and provide new levels of stakeholder value. Managers can then deliver a manageable number of objectives through day to day business process implementation decisions.

In practice, it is individual managers who make the decisions. Their decisions are influenced by their own skills, capabilities, attitudes and experience. In an increasingly competitive market they are expected to make quality decisions that are bold and innovative, wrong-foot the competition and lead to offers that appeal to customers. To do this managers must build their experience by learning through reflection on events that have occurred, experimentation (trial and error) and studying best practice from others.

In this final integrated learning activity we provide the framework for identifying where the few high quality decisions are needed in your own organisation or one of your choice. In doing this we emphasise the need to distinguish between the step changes that are determined by market focused strategic decision making and the supporting incremental changes that are routine, process driven.

Learning objectives

On completing this activity the reader should be able to:

- Distinguish between 'life changing' decisions and important, but consequential, incremental decisions made through the business processes
- Identify where in an organisation bold, imaginative step change decisions can change the organisation's fortunes
- Identify what makes a quality decision by adding value for all stakeholders

The tasks

1 Choose an organisation (or preferably a strategic business unit within an organisation) that you consider to be under-performing its market potential. The organisation might be your own or one of your choice, selected through researching the business press. The organisation or business unit might:

 - be experiencing a general downturn in performance (sales, profits, return on investment, market share, etc.)

 - have performed badly in one particular geography (area, country or region)

 - be growing but have the potential to grow even faster

 - be a newly established organisation.

2 In Part 1 of the text we discussed the key determinants of quality strategic decision making and the criteria upon which decisions should be based. You need first of all to decide which of these key determinants should be the organisation's primary focus.

3 In Part 2 of the text we discussed the areas of marketing where innovative decisions lead to a step

change in performance and value added to stakeholders. You should identify the four or five areas where bold and innovative decisions will steer the organisation through into an increasingly profitable future.

4 Having identified the areas you should then decide what would (at the same time) differentiate your organisation's offering from that of competitors, provide a leap in value for stakeholders and deliver superior performance.

Getting started

Choosing an organisation

A number of the organisations highlighted in this book could provide the subject for the exercise as an alternative to your own organisation. Whether or not you choose your own organisation, you should aim to learn about strategic marketing decision making good (and bad) practice from other organisations from your own and other sectors.

Throughout this book we have highlighted organisations and managers that have faced or are facing critical decisions. You should not simply regard these as situations to be studied as a snapshot, but rather learn from the consequences as the story unfolds, by researching the business press.

Part 1: the key determinants of strategic decision making in global markets

Below we have identified four key questions that set the scene for identifying the key decision areas. In answering the questions you need to look for evidence from past performance as well as clear indications of the commitment from senior managers to achieve the necessary change

How does the organisation response to market ambiguity?

The global marketing environment is often dynamic, unstable and competitive. For the average organisation the response to this is to take risk averse decisions that aim merely to ensure survival. But it is these very market environment ambiguities that provide the opportunity for the pioneering organisations to strike out in a new direction by developing a clear vision, a strong core purpose and distinctive competitive advantage. The key is to offer a unique customer value proposition supported by the delivery of a totally integrated marketing effort.

Is the organisation a learning organisation?

For under-performing organisations, learning is often interpreted as the acquisition of information. It is *ad hoc*, anecdotal and often seen as a power source for individual managers. The superior performance of the market leaders is linked to consistent, high quality decision making that is the consequence of a highly developed learning capability, learning processes and effective knowledge management. Knowledge of markets, building organisational capability and developing the right ambition and attitude are key factors in exploiting the emerging and continually changing developed markets.

How does performance measurement affect the organisation's strategic decisions?

Whilst the key objective of an organisation is to maximise the shareholders' or owners' wealth, the way that the management chooses to do this has an important impact on other stakeholder interests. Performance measurement has a key role but must be set alongside other factors. Managers can experience problems in measuring performance and using financial tools in decision making to support and justify their major decisions, but better managed organisations use this constructively.

What is the scope of the organisation's ambitions?

Average organisations go through the process of annual planning with the objective of developing an effective strategy based on distinctive competitive advantage. Often, however, this is hope rather than belief and planning essentially becomes a substitute for decision making. However, there is little point in planning if the organisation is not committed to making a change.

High performing organisations have an ambitious vision and a clear idea of the role they intend to play within their industry, supply chain and defined geography. They move relentlessly, year by year towards their objectives. They are constantly learning and recognise when their strategy is in danger of wearing out. They are prepared to respond with the major pre-emptive changes that are needed to deliver global efficiency, effectiveness and competitiveness.

Their performance is based upon superior insights into customer attitudes and buying and usage behaviour that enables them to accurately segment the market and target the segments they are best able to serve, by positioning their total offer in an appealing and distinctive way.

Part 2: where innovative decisions are needed to deliver a step change in performance and stakeholder value

The objective of this part of the Integrative Learning Activity is to identify areas of strategic marketing decision making that will deliver a step change in sustainable competitive advantage for the organisation by providing superior customer value. Throughout this book we have emphasised that this might come at any point in the marketing strategy process, and in this section we focus upon strategy development and implementation decisions. To assist in identifying the key areas we have posed four questions below.

How does the organisation respond to market opportunities and threats?

Pioneering companies create or proactively respond to industry breakpoints by exploiting the opportunities and managing the threats that arise as a result. They create a culture that supports step change and incremental innovation to achieve fast growth. Underperformers tend to focus on the opportunities that are built largely by using their existing resources and assets.

Is the organisation building value through an appropriate mix of tangible and intangible assets?

Growth achieved by relying on the exploitation of tangible assets no longer guarantees increased stakeholder value for the best performing organisations. Brand, intellectual property and knowledge management are key exploitable intangible assets, and are becoming an increasing source of differentiation between competitive offers.

Does the organisation effectively integrate the marketing mix?

The best performing organisations fight the increasing commoditisation of products and the downward pricing spiral by adopting an integrated approach to marketing mix management, including service and brand enhancement.

Customers receive an increasing number of fragmented and confusing communications. The best organisations ensure the consistency and integration of all the messages that customers receive from them, but also work hard at managing their relationships, primarily with customers but also with other stakeholders.

They use collaborations with suitable partners to add customer value by outsourcing and effective supply chain management. They take new market entry and distribution channel decisions that achieve an appropriate balance between their involvement and risk in a market, the control they can exert over their marketing activity and how their presence is perceived by customers.

How does the organisation ensure the quality of its decisions?

The best performing organisations use a range of evaluation and measurement techniques to control and identify the management decisions that have a demonstrable and direct impact on market performance. However, the best organisations use the available techniques to improve the quality of strategic decision making by aiming to meet the expectations of a variety of stakeholders. This includes making decisions that demonstrate their willingness to share social responsibility by behaving ethically.

The critical success factors in strategic marketing decision

Market leaders are able to identify and explain what really differentiates their products and services from those of a competitor, and they recognise that the differentiators can come from any part of the marketing process. In doing this they are able to distinguish between customer satisfiers and dissatisfiers.

Dissatisfiers are those factors, the 'hygiene' factors, which when absent in the organisation's offer will lead to customer dissatisfaction. They require constant managerial attention. Dissatisfiers, however, do not persuade customers to buy.

The satisfiers are the true differentiators between competitive offerings and should provide exceptional customer satisfaction.

In strategic marketing decision making, however, it is important to recognise that, over time, satisfiers become dissatisfiers as they are increasingly taken for granted by customers. Now, customers believe it is their right to expect reputable organisations to routinely offer quality products and reliable service. Consequently, to win customers, organisations must offer more than routine quality and service. Customers increasingly differentiate between very similar competitive offerings by buying the brand that has unique positioning and emphasises the intangible benefits with which they most closely associate.

Technology – differentiator or dissatisfier?

Many organisations believe that superior capability in either product or information technology is a differentiator and the source of competitive advantage, and in some industries it may be. Indeed, as we saw in Chapter 7, when applied, technology both drives and provides a response to change. However, with their greater familiarity with technological advances, the fascination of technology has worn off for many customers, and so technology has become a dissatisfier. Customers expect efficient IT management and are irritated by unco-ordinated customer services and websites that are unreliable and difficult to navigate, and increasingly frustrated with organisations that fail to prevent spam, on-line fraud and disruption by hackers.

There has also been a change of mindset in many organisations. As a dissatisfier, they see IT and computing capability as the next utility, just like electricity, and so seek to outsource their IT systems, so they can concentrate on their core activities: the outputs of the IT systems and ensuring the IT systems support their desire for increased customer orientation.

In completing the tasks outlined you need to consider the following key factors:

Some concepts and issues to be addressed

Strategic development decisions	■ Commitment to acquiring knowledge assets and capabilities that will maintain and build competitive advantage
	■ Consistent investment in intangible assets, especially branding and new expertise
	■ Recognise industry breakpoints (and the threats and opportunities created) that require a new strategic response
	■ Flexible exploitation of market gaps and opportunities rather than new product development alone
	■ Achieve fast growth by offering customers a quantum leap in value (as perceived by them) but also maintain the lead by continual incremental innovation
	■ Keep ahead of the customer by anticipating future requirements, rather than simply trying to meet their current needs and incremental expectations
	■ The development of a trans-national approach to segmentation, with its implications for global marketing management
Strategy implementation decsions	■ An integrated approach to portfolio management, communication and customer value enhancement
	■ Management of the customer interface with the organisation so that the customer's experience is exceptional
	■ Build customer loyalty and retention by relationship marketing and management
	■ Reassessment of supply chain value by outsourcing non-core activities, where appropriate
	■ Partnership building, even with the competition, when appropriate
	■ Increase value added by leveraging the contributions of the extended organisation and so secure new routes to market
	■ Performance measurement to support decision making and also to set the aspirations, standards and values of the organisation, especially in the area of ethical behaviour
	■ Application of best practice lessons from other organisations or industries adapted to the new context

The way forward and the strategic decision making manager's role

In identifying the key strategy development and implementation decision areas it is essential, therefore, for managers to make time to focus primarily on the satisfiers, the key strategic marketing decisions that through effective implementation will achieve a step change in stakeholder value and organisational performance.

Whilst it is essential to deal with the dissatisfiers and so avoid customer dissatisfaction, such elements of marketing as quality, service and IT systems should be managed as a routine, albeit supported by continual incremental improvements.

The major contribution that managers can make, therefore, in strategic marketing decision making is to take time to:

■ Reflect on the current situation and the lessons from the past.

- Use the learning from this to re-evaluate the organisation's distinctive competencies, competitive advantage and operational efficiency.
- Take the decisions that will redirect the organisation to provide superior stakeholder value and so achieve exceptional customer satisfaction and organisational performance.

Some useful websites:

www.economist.com
www.ft.com
www.cim.co.uk
www.bbc.co.uk

Index